REGULATING ASSISTED REPRODUCTIVE TECHNOLOGIES

Reproductive science continues to revolutionise reproduction and propel us further into uncharted territories. The revolution signalled by the birth of Louise Brown after IVF in 1978 prompted governments across Europe and beyond into regulatory action. Forty years on, there are now dramatic and controversial developments in new reproductive technologies. Technologies such as uterus transplantation, that may enable unisex gestation and babies gestated by dad, or artificial wombs that will completely divorce reproduction from the human body and allow babies to be gestated by machines, usher in a different set of legal, ethical and social questions to those that arose from IVF. This book revisits the regulation of assisted reproduction and advances the debate on from the now much-discussed issues that arose from IVF, offering a critical analysis of the regulatory challenges raised by new reproductive technologies on the horizon.

AMEL ALGHRANI is a senior lecturer in law and Associate Dean (Education) in the School of Law & Social Justice at the University of Liverpool.

CAMBRIDGE BIOETHICS AND LAW

This series of books was founded by Cambridge University Press with Alexander McCall Smith as its first editor in 2003. It focuses on the law's complex and troubled relationship with medicine across both the developed and the developing world. Since the early 1990s, we have seen, in many countries, increasing resort to the courts by dissatisfied patients and a growing use of the courts to attempt to resolve intractable ethical dilemmas. At the same time, legislatures across the world have struggled to address the questions posed by both the successes and the failures of modern medicine, while international organisations such as the WHO and UNESCO now regularly address issues of medical law.

It follows that we would expect ethical and policy questions to be integral to the analysis of the legal issues discussed in this series. The series responds to the high profile of medical law in universities and in legal and medical practice, as well as in public and political affairs. We seek to reflect the evidence that many major health-related policy debates in the UK, Europe and the international community involve a strong medical law dimension. With that in mind, we seek to address how legal analysis might have a trans-jurisdictional and international relevance. Organ retention, embryonic stem cell research, physician assisted suicide and the allocation of resources to fund health care are but a few examples among many. The emphasis of this series is thus on matters of public concern and/or practical significance. We look for books that could make a difference to the development of medical law and enhance the role of medico-legal debate in policy circles. That is not to say that we lack interest in the important theoretical dimensions of the subject, but we aim to ensure that theoretical debate is grounded in the realities of how the law does and should interact with medicine and healthcare.

Series Editors
Professor Graeme Laurie, *University of Edinburgh*
Professor Richard Ashcroft, *Queen Mary University of London*

REGULATING ASSISTED REPRODUCTIVE TECHNOLOGIES

New Horizons

AMEL ALGHRANI

University of Liverpool

CAMBRIDGE
UNIVERSITY PRESS

University Printing House, Cambridge CB2 8BS, United Kingdom

One Liberty Plaza, 20th Floor, New York, NY 10006, USA

477 Williamstown Road, Port Melbourne, VIC 3207, Australia

314–321, 3rd Floor, Plot 3, Splendor Forum, Jasola District Centre,
New Delhi – 110025, India

79 Anson Road, #06–04/06, Singapore 079906

Cambridge University Press is part of the University of Cambridge.

It furthers the University's mission by disseminating knowledge in the pursuit of
education, learning, and research at the highest international levels of excellence.

www.cambridge.org
Information on this title: www.cambridge.org/9781107160569
DOI: 10.1017/9781316675823

© Amel Alghrani 2018

First published 2018

Printed and bound in Great Britain by Clays Ltd, Elcograf S.p.A.

A catalogue record for this publication is available from the British Library.

Library of Congress Cataloging-in-Publication Data
Names: Alghrani, Amel, author.
Title: Regulating assisted reproductive technologies : new horizons / Amel Alghrani.
Other titles: Cambridge bioethics and law.
Description: Cambridge, United Kingdom ; New York, NY : Cambridge University Press,
2018. | Series: Cambridge bioethics and law | Includes bibliographical references and index.
Identifiers: LCCN 2018022365 | ISBN 9781107160569 (hardback)
Subjects: | MESH: Reproductive Techniques, Assisted – legislation & jurisprudence |
Ectogenesis – ethics | Uterus – transplantation | United Kingdom
Classification: LCC RG133.5 | NLM WQ 33 FA1 | DDC 176/.2–dc23
LC record available at https://lccn.loc.gov/2018022365

ISBN 978-1-107-16056-9 Hardback

For Habeeb

CONTENTS

FOREWORD

On 25 July 1978, a much-wanted little girl was born in the small Lancashire town of Oldham. As she lay in her cradle, Louise Brown would have been blissfully unaware that her birth signalled a revolution not just in reproductive medicine but in society as a whole. Louise was of course the first baby to be born as a result of *In Vitro Fertilisation* (IVF); or, as the media preferred to say, she was the first test-tube baby. Since that day a whole generation (including the author of this book, Amel Alghrani) has grown up taking IVF for granted. Infertility is no longer something that must simply be accepted as a vicissitude of life. An embryo could now be created outside the body of a woman and then implanted in the mother to be gestated as normal. Louise's mother, who could not conceive naturally because of an obstruction in her Fallopian tubes, was able to give birth to Louise, and later to a second daughter.

Looking back forty years and knowing what we know now about the subsequent developments in the reproductive technologies, Louise's birth after IVF using her married parents' gametes does not seem so earth shattering. Other more dramatic and controversial developments were to follow. To give but a few examples: Dolly, the most famous sheep in the world, offered the prospect of cloning human beings; Pre-Implantation Genetic Diagnosis (PGD) enabled doctors to screen embryos for serious genetic disease and paved the way for 'saviour siblings'. In 1978, the news of the birth was amazing, prompting great celebration and heart-warming media coverage rejoicing for the Browns and other couples unable to have a child. But at the same time the birth gave rise to prophecies of doom and condemnation of unnatural practices. In particular, the ability to create a child outside the womb and the potential for research on in-vitro embryos led to attempts to ban embryo research and effectively stop IVF in its tracks. Enoch Powell's Unborn Child Protection Bill came very close to becoming law.

Governments across Europe and beyond were slow to respond, fearful of the moral debates that raged around IVF and the opposition of the Catholic Church and other religions. In the United Kingdom, a Committee of Inquiry chaired by Dame Mary Warnock reported in 1984 and the Human Fertilisation and Embryology Act was enacted in 1990, by which time Louise Brown was 12 years old. Nonetheless, the United Kingdom legislated much more swiftly than many other states and, as Dr Alghrani explains, the Human Fertilisation Act 1990 came to be seen as a model for regulation abroad, albeit often denigrated in the United Kingdom itself. The central problem with the 1990 Act was that no sooner than Royal Assent had been granted, the Act became outdated. Research and developments in the reproductive technologies gave rise to ethical dilemmas and legal questions that the lawmakers had never envisaged. The law could only play 'catch up', aided by judges ready to give imaginative interpretations of the Act, leaning towards the spirit of the Act rather than the letter of the law.

At the heart of this book is a plea that the law relating to the reproductive technologies should, as far as possible, be proactive rather than constantly reactive. Amel Alghrani seeks to look to the new horizons in relation to how we should regulate assisted reproductive technologies on and beyond the horizon today. Thus, in Chapters 3 and 4 of Part II, she explores the questions that will be posed by ectogenesis (artificial wombs), venturing into a field that until very recently was much more the concern of literary scholars and science fiction. Few of us will not have read Aldous Huxley's *Brave New World*. In the final two chapters of the present book, the focus is on uterus transplantation and the prospect that a uterus could be transplanted into a man. Uterus transplantation illustrates vividly just how formidable a task Dr Alghrani faced in writing this book. When she began her work, the possibility of a successful uterus transplant seemed some years away. Then, in September 2014, a Swedish team announced the first live birth to a woman who had received a donated womb from a living donor. In a sense, the Swedish success demonstrates the importance of the message at the heart of this book – legislators and regulators cannot afford to sit on their hands and say to themselves, 'don't bother about ectogenesis or male pregnancy yet: it won't happen till tomorrow'. Unlike the promise of jam in *Alice through the Looking Glass*, in the field of the reproductive technologies 'tomorrow' becomes today at a frightening speed.

The reader fascinated by how the frontiers of research to develop the reproductive technologies are changing society may be tempted to rush straight to Part II and the exciting, brave new world of babies gestated by 'dad', or by machines. They should avoid that temptation. Understanding the context within which radical developments in science, law and ethics may come about is crucial to an informed assessment of regulating new reproductive technologies. Part I sets the scene, giving a critique of the principles of regulation and addressing the fundamental problems arising when gamete donors disagree. The clash of claims by A to a right to reproduce and B to a right not to reproduce is poignantly demonstrated in the sad case of Natalie Evans. On her recovery from cancer, Ms Evans sought to have embryos implanted: embryos that had been created with her eggs and fertilised with sperm from her then partner before Ms Evans underwent chemotherapy. The couple's relationship had broken down and her ex-partner successfully blocked her access to what she saw as 'her' embryos.[1] Ectogenesis will exacerbate the questions around who is entitled to decide about the fate of embryos and fetuses. Imagine that an embryo is created with gametes from A and B, and the couple celebrate the placement of their 'child to be' in the ectogenic chamber. Some weeks later A and B fall out, and B asks for the chamber to be switched off. A objects and wants the fetus to be allowed to develop and be 'born' at the due time. Does it matter if A is the 'mother' or 'father'? Do words such as mother and father continue to have any meaning? Is it relevant how many weeks the fetus has been gestated? If a uterus is successfully transplanted into a man, and he changes his mind against the wishes of his partner, do laws designed to address termination of pregnancy in a woman apply?

By beginning the book with a strong account of the framework of regulation of the more established reproductive technologies, Amel Alghrani ensures that, in moving on to the more dramatic possibilities on the horizon, her argument is well grounded. She considers ethical and social perspectives, as any work on this subject must. The principal focus of this book, however, is the law. All too often in debates about the regulation of healthcare and biomedical science, law is depicted as rather boring and simplistic. Other 'experts' are prominent in the arguments about what society should do; the lawyers are just there to work out how to enforce the outcome. Dr Alghrani demolishes such an attitude. She shows that law is far from dull or simple. And necessarily she contends with the reality that the 'experts' vary rarely, if ever, agree. Lawmakers, legislators and judges confront the dilemma of how to develop laws

---

[1] *Evans* v. *United Kingdom* (Application no 6339/05); [2007] 22 BHRC 190 [54] (ECtHR).

within a society that includes divergent views on, for example, matters of the status of the fetus, payments for gametes or surrogacy and gendered roles in parenting.

Exploring new horizons in the reproductive technologies is exciting. The future of human reproduction is of interest to most if not all humans. This is a book that will make the reader think; it challenges prejudices and at some points prompts concern about where the journey to the future is taking us. Readers will disagree about the solutions to the dilemmas that Dr Alghrani presents. Some readers will challenge her conclusions. No one will be bored by this book, and very many of us will be much better informed.

Professor Margaret Brazier

ACKNOWLEDGEMENTS

I would like to thank my son and family for their patience and support while I wrote this manuscript. I love you, and perhaps now this is complete we can enjoy spending more time together!

I wish to record my thanks to my two former PhD supervisors, who later became my mentors and friends, who have shaped my ideas and have been a constant example to me of how academia should be done: with humour, humility and hard work. I remain inspired by their sheer intellectual brilliance; they are Professors Margaret Brazier and John Harris.

Thank you to my colleagues at the University of Liverpool for generously covering my period of research leave to write this book and for the continued intellectual and emotional support. I would like to thank those colleagues and friends who read parts of the manuscript and made many invaluable suggestions: a big thank you to Professor Marie Fox, Hannah Quirk, Craig Purshouse, Johanna Byrant and Padraig McAuliffe.

To my friends, Danielle, Deena, Dana, Taibah and Eva, who over the years have provided me with much encouragement and welcome distractions during the writing of this book.

Lastly, thanks are owed to the two anonymous reviewers of the proposal for this manuscript, who provided very useful feedback that I have endeavoured to incorporate.

TABLE OF CASES

TABLE OF STATUTES AND STATUTORY INSTRUMENTS

ABBREVIATIONS

ARTs	Assisted Reproductive Technologies
CCG	Clinical Commissioning Groups
CoP	Code of Practice (HFEA)
CQC	Care Quality Commission
DoH	Department of Health
ECtHR	European Court of Human Rights
HCSTC	House of Commons Science and Technology Committee
HFE Act 1990	Human Fertilisation and Embryology Act 1990
HFE Act 2008	Human Fertilisation and Embryology Act 2008
HFE Act	Human Fertilisation and Embryology Act 1990 (as amended)
HFEA	Human Fertilisation and Embryology Authority
HTA	Human Tissue Authority
IVF	In Vitro Fertilisation
MRC	Medical Research Council
NICE	National Institute for Health and Care Excellence
PGD	Preimplantation Genetic Diagnosis
PND	Prenatal Diagnosis
RCOG	Royal College of Obstetricians and Gynaecologists
VLA	Voluntary Licensing Authority

~

Introduction

Good afternoon ladies and gentlemen. This is your pilot speaking. We are flying at an altitude of 35,000 feet and a speed of 700 miles an hour. I have two pieces of news to report, one good and one bad. The bad news is that we are lost. The good news is that we are making very good time.[1]

As Leon Kass's quote suggests, in the arena of assisted reproductive technologies we are making rapid progress and reproductive science continues to propel us further into uncharted territories. In the last four decades we have witnessed a 'reproductive revolution':[2] great strides have been made to alleviate the effects of infertility. Advances such as *in vitro fertilisation* (IVF),[3] sex selection,[4] reproductive cloning,[5] embryo selection for the purpose of creating 'saviour

---

[1] L. Kass and J. Wilson, *The Ethics of Human Cloning* (Washington, DC: AEI Press, 1998).

[2] A phrase used in the title of a book by R. Lee and D. Morgan, *Human Fertilisation and Embryology: Regulating the Reproductive Revolution* (London: Blackstone Press, 2001).

[3] IVF refers to *In Vitro Fertilisation*, whereby a woman's ovaries are stimulated (usually as a consequence of fertility drugs). Several eggs are then retrieved and fertilised in the laboratory. One or two fertilised eggs are then transferred to a receptive uterus and, if all goes well, a normal pregnancy follows. See R. Edwards, P. Steptoe and J. Purdy, 'Establishing Full Term Human Pregnancies Using Cleaving Embryos Grown in Vitro' (1980) 87 *BJOG: An International Journal of Obstetrics & Gynaecology* 737–756. A. Steptoe, 'Biology: Changing the World – A Tribute to Patrick Steptoe, Robert Edwards and Jean Purdy' (2015) 18(4) *Human Fertility* 232–233. J. Wang, 'In Vitro Fertilization (IVF): A Review of 3 Decades of Clinical Innovation and Technological Advancement' (2006) 2(4) *Therapeutics and Clinical Risk Management* 355–364.

[4] See M. Meseguer, et al., 'Gender Selection: Ethical, Scientific, Legal, and Practical Issues' (2002) 19(9) *Journal of Assisted Reproduction and Genetics* 443. R. Klitzman, 'Struggles in Defining and Addressing Requests for "Family Balancing": Ethical Issues Faced by Providers and Patients' (2016) 44(4) *Journal of Law, Medicine and Ethics* 616–629.

[5] See M. L. Lee, 'The Inadequacies of Absolute Prohibition of Reproductive Cloning' (2004) 11(3) *Journal of Law and Medicine* 351–372. S. Frankin, *Dolly Mixtures: The Remaking of Genealogy* (Durham: Duke University Press, 2007). B. Steinbock, 'Reproductive Cloning: Another Look?' (2015) 2006(1) *University of Chicago Legal Forum* 87–111. A. Langlois, 'The Global Governance of Human Cloning: The Case of UNESCO' (2017) 21(3) *Palgrave Communitcations* 21.

siblings',[6] uterus transplantation[7] and mitochondria (that allows a child to be genetically related to two mothers)[8] have all emerged as part of a rapidly changing branch of medicine, each promising to upset the status quo and to transform human reproduction.

As new technologies continue to revolutionise reproduction, they challenge our legal and ethical assumptions surrounding parenting, family formation, gender roles, obstetrics and neonatology. In the United Kingdom, it was the IVF revolution in the late 1970s and the surrounding debates that provided the impetus for regulation of assisted reproduction. This scientific breakthrough of the world's first 'test tube baby' – so called because she was conceived outside a female host – gave rise to a wave of public concern surrounding the possible harms, risks and ethical dilemmas associated with the use of new artificial reproductive technologies to create children. In order to allay such fears, the UK became one of the first countries in the world to regulate fertility treatment. In 1982 the Government commissioned the Warnock Committee of Inquiry to examine scientific developments in the fertilisation and embryology field.[9] Following publication of the Committee's Report[10] and a protracted process of public consultation through Green and White Papers, Parliament eventually passed the Human Fertilisation and Embryology Act 1990 (HFE Act 1990)[11] as the principal means of regulating assisted reproductive technologies. Reproductive science is a moving target, however, and not long after enactment of the HFE Act 1990, increasing legal challenges highlighted the vulnerabilities of the statute. Cases on issues ranging from disputes between gamete

---

[6] S. McLean and S. Elliston (eds.) (2013) *Regulating Pre-Implantation Genetic Diagnosis: A Comparative and Theoretical Analysis* (London: Routledge, 2013). R. Scott, 'Choosing between Possible Lives: Legal and Ethical Issues in Preimplantation Genetic Diagnosis' (2006) 26(1) *Oxford Journal of Legal Studies* 153–178. C. Hsin-Fu et al. 'Preimplantation Genetic Diagnosis and Screening: Current Status and Future Challenges' (2017) *Journal of the Formosan Medical Association* (in press).

[7] See M. Brännström, 'Uterus Transplantation and Beyond' (2017) 28(5) *Journal of Materials Science: Materials in Medicine* 7.

[8] See D. Griffiths, 'The (Re) Production of the Genetically Related Body in Law, Technology and Culture: Mitochondria Replacement Therapy' (2016) 24(3) *Healthcare Analysis* 196–209. R. Scott and S. Wilkinson, 'Germline Genetic Modification and Identity: The Mitochondrial and Nuclear Genomes' (2017) *Oxford Journal of Legal Studies* 1–30.

[9] Report of the Committee of Inquiry into Human Fertilisation and Embryology, 1984, Cm 9314 (The 'Warnock Report').

[10] See previous note.   [11] Hereafter referred to as the HFE Act 1990.

progenitors over the fate of their frozen embryos,[12] the creation of saviour siblings[13] and controversy surrounding reproductive cloning[14] all exposed the weaknesses of the HFE Act 1990. As Margaret Brazier pointed out as far back as 1999:

> Warnock deliberated at a very early stage of the 'reproductive revolution'. Neither the science nor the infrastructure which now underpins the 'reproductive business' was well developed.[15]

Over the next fifteen years, the legal landscape within which the HFE Act 1990 was operating in had altered greatly; the Human Rights Act 1998, Gender Recognition Act 2004, Human Tissue Act 2004 and the Civil Partnerships Act 2004 had all come into force. Numerous legislative initiatives and amendments had been introduced to consolidate the HFE Act 1990, often on an ad hoc basis. Such amendments included allowing embryo research to be licensed for therapeutic stem cell research[16] and human reproductive cloning. In 2004, the law was amended so as to permit donor-conceived children to know information regarding the genetic lineage and access the identity of their gamete donor on reaching the age of 18.[17] As these initiatives demonstrated, the law enshrined in the HFE Act 1990 had quickly become outdated. As the government conceded, 'time, particularly in this field, does not stand still'.[18] The Human Fertilisation and Embryology Authority (HFEA), the independent statutory authority responsible for licensing fertility treatments and research conducted using human embryos, acknowledged:

> the regulatory landscape has changed considerably over the last decade and human reproductive technologies have developed into both a mainstream and a complex, cutting-edge area of healthcare.

---

[12] *Natalie Evans* v. *Amicus Healthcare Ltd and Others; Lorraine Hadley* v. *Midland Fertility Services Ltd and Others* [2003] EWCH 2161, [2004] 1 F.L.R 67 (Fam); *Natalie Evans* v. *Amicus Healthcare Ltd and Others* [2004] EWCA (Civ) 72, [2004] 2 F.L.R 766, CA; *Case of Evans* v. *The United Kingdom* (Application 6339/2005), [2006] 1 FCR 585 (ECtHR); *Evans* v. *United Kingdom* (Application no 6339/05); [2007] 22 BHRC 190 [54] (ECtHR).

[13] *R (on the application of Quintavalle)* v. *HFEA* [2003] 3 ALL E.R 257 [2005] 2 ALL ER 555.

[14] *R* v. *Secretary of State for Health, Ex P Quintavalle* [2003] 2 W.L.R 692.

[15] M. Brazier, 'Regulating the Reproduction Business' (1999) *Medical Law Review* 166, at p. 173.

[16] The Human Fertilisation and Embryology (Research Purposes) Regulations 2001.

[17] Human Fertilisation and Embryology Authority (Disclosure of Donor Information) Regulations 2004.

[18] Human Tissue and Embryos (Draft) Bill, (Cm 7087) foreword by Caroline Flint, Minister of State for Public Health, May 2007.

Regulation of this field should adapt to these changes by trying to avoid
overlap and by becoming more proportionate, efficient, targeted, flexible
and able to accommodate new developments.[19]

Unlike unassisted reproduction, which is largely regarded as a private
choice,[20] assisted reproduction and the use of ARTs have been singled
out by the UK as warranting specialist regulation and being a branch of
medicine of such particular concern and significance that the state should
have a direct stake in its evolution.[21] The UK's comprehensive regulatory
regime in this area has been described as the first of its type and one that
has been widely copied throughout the world.[22] The UK is not alone in
deeming reproductive medicine to be of especial regulatory concern, but
for those governments committed to specialist regulation, governing this
ethically charged domain is no easy feat. Jackson framed the challenge
this poses well when she stated:

> The relationship between law and human reproduction is a complex and
> fascinating one ... Creating a regulatory framework capable of accom-
> modating all of the ethical dilemmas thrown up by this rapidly shifting
> terrain undoubtedly represents one of the most important and difficult
> tasks for law in the twenty-first century.[23]

Facilitating the march of science and keeping abreast of new developments presents constant challenges. Prior to the enactment of the Human
Fertilisation and Embryology Act 2008 (HFE Act 2008), it was a fair
assertion to describe the UK law in this area as 'marching with medicine,
but in the rear and limping a little'.[24] It was against this background that
the government belatedly accepted that if the legislative framework was
not to be superseded by technology; it was time to redraft the legislation:

---

[19] Human Fertilisation & Embryology Authority, *Response by the Human Fertilisation &*
Embryology Authority to the Department of Health's Consultation on the Review of the
Human Fertilisation and Embryology Act (24 November 2005), p. 2. www.hfea.gov.uk
/docs/ReviewoftheActResponse.pdf.

[20] Although note restrictions to abortion in the UK may rightly be regarded as an interference with one's private choices in the context of unassisted reproduction – see S. Mc
Guinness, 'A Guerilla Strategy for a Pro-Life England' (2015) *Journal of Information Law*
and Technology 238–314.

[21] Brazier, 'Regulating the Reproduction Business'.

[22] E. Jackson, 'The Human Fertilisation and Embryology Bill 2007' (2008) 3(4) *Expert*
Review of Obstetrics & Gynecology 429–431, at p. 431.

[23] E. Jackson, *Regulating Reproduction, Law Technology and Autonomy* (Hart Publishing:
Oxford, 2001), p. 1.

[24] *Mount Isa Mines* v. *Pusey* (1970) 125 CLR 383.

The Government thought a review into existing legislation was timely and desirable in light of the development of new procedures and technologies in assisted reproduction, possible changes in public perceptions and attitudes on complex ethical issues, and the continuing need to ensure effective regulation in this area to reduce uncertainty and the scope for legal challenge.[25]

Following much activity in this area[26] the lengthy process of updating the legislation culminated in the HFE Act 2008.[27] Welcoming Royal Assent, Lisa Jardine, Chair of the Human Fertilisation and Embryology Authority at the time, stated:

> This is a momentous day for the HFEA and for those with fertility problems. The regulatory system that has served us so well has been renewed. Parliament has provided a clear framework for the future and a solid base on which to regulate 21st century practice within 21st century law.[28]

Closer examination of the regulatory framework and a look forward at new horizons in the context of reproductive technologies, suggests Jardine was perhaps overly optimistic about the achievements of the new legislation. The HFE Act 2008 is an amending statute, and as Jackson observed much of the regulatory architecture in the 1990 legislation 'remains intact'.[29] In retaining the architecture of the 1990 legislation and merely amending or adding certain provisions, the government missed an ideal opportunity to consider how to equip the regulatory

---

[25] Impact Assessment on the Human Fertilisation and Embryology Bill (2008), Evidence Base, Background, para 3.

[26] The government announced a review of the HFE Act 1990 in January 2004, citing developments in reproductive medicine since the enactment of the 1990 legislation, and conducted a public consultation in 2005. In December 2006 the government published the policy proposals in the White Paper: *Review of the Human Fertilisation and Embryology Act: Proposals for Revised Legislation (including establishment of the Regulatory Authority for Tissue and Embryos)* (Cm 6989). The Human Tissue and Embryos (Draft) Bill (Cm 7087) followed in May 2007. This was scrutinised by the Joint Committee of both Houses; see the House of Lords and the House of Commons, *Joint Committee on the Human Tissue and Embryos (Draft) Bill*, July 2007 (HL Paper 169-I, HC Paper 630-I). Policy proposals from the White Paper and pre-legislative scrutiny were then incorporated into the Human Fertilisation and Embryology Bill, which was introduced into Parliament on 8 November 2007.

[27] The HFE Act 2008 received Royal Assent on the 13 November 2008 and the majority of the HFE Act 2008's amendments came into force in October 2009 (with the exception of the provisions pertaining to parenthood, which commenced in April 2009).

[28] Human Fertilisation and Embryology Authority, Press Release, 'HFEA Chair Welcomes Royal Assent for HFE Act', 13 November 2008, www.hfea.gov.uk/en/1746.html.

[29] E. Jackson, 'Human Fertilisation and Embryology Bill 2007' 429.

framework for what has been described by Welin as the third era of human reproduction.[30] Welin aptly compartmentalised human reproduction into three distinct eras:

> Historically, the first is normal conception inside the woman, the growth of the foetus inside the womb and then, after nine months, birth and the appearance of a new individual. The second era is *In Vitro* Fertilisation (IVF). The foetus starts outside the woman as a fertilised egg, moves to the body of the woman and the foetus travel together in space-time to separate at birth. In the third era of reproductive ectogenesis, the two never travel together. The foetus spends its gestational time outside the woman's body. We have two entities separated in space-time the whole time. The intimate connection consisting in the foetus being part of the woman's body is gone.[31]

Much of the debate and regulation in the UK and other jurisdictions centres on what Wellin labelled the first and second 'eras' of reproduction. The legal and ethical issues raised by IVF, dubbed the second wave of reproduction have been much debated, but as Deech and Smajdor noted, 'IVF was just the start of a long procession of technological developments' and 'public concern over IVF has waned'.[32]

Almost a decade on from the HFE Act 2008, legal challenges levied against the statute have once more exposed vulnerabilities in the regulatory framework.[33] Science has moved on and IVF is now

---

[30] A. Alghrani, 'The Human Fertilisation and Embryology Act 2008: A Missed Opportunity?' (2009) 35 *Journal of Medical Ethics* 718–719. M. Fox, 'The Human Fertilisation and Embryology Act 2008: Tinkering at the Margins' (2009) 17 (3) *Feminist Legal Studies* 333–334.

[31] S. Welin, 'Reproductive Ectogenesis: The Third Era of Human Reproduction and Some Moral Consequences' (2004) 10 *Science and Engineering Ethics* 615–626, at p. 617.

[32] R. Deech and A. Smajdor, *From IVF to Immortality; Controversy in the Era of Reproductive Technology* (Oxford: Oxford University Press, 2007) at p. 10. For a review of the book see A. Alghrani and M. Brazier, 'Book Review: R. Deech and A. Smajdor, From IVF to Immortality: Controversy in the Era of Reproductive Technology' (2008) *Medical Law Review* 469–474.

[33] For instance, there have been challenges mounted against surrogacy provisions, *Re Z (A Child)* [2016] EWFC 34 *Re Z (A Child) (No.2)* [2016] EWHC 1191 (Fam) in which the court made a declaration of incompatibility in respect of s54 (1) and (2) of the HFE Act 2008, which precludes a single person from applying for a parental order for children born via surrogacy. See also *M v. F & SM (Human Fertilisation and Embryology Act 2008)* [2017] EWHC 2176 (Fam). For more on this legal provisions of the HFE Act on surrogacy see A. Alghrani and D. Griffiths, 'The Regulation of Surrogacy in the United Kingdom: The Case for Reform' (2017) 29 (2) *Child and Family Law Quarterly* 165–186. There have been many challenges mounted against HFEA for administrative errors regarding

routine.[34] The reproductive industry is now well established and is thriving globally: in 2017, in the UK alone the value of the sector to UK GDP was estimated to be in the region of £600 million a year.[35] The majority of services (some 60 per cent) are provided by the private sector, with the NHS providing the remaining 40 per cent.[36] Reproductive tourism, whereby people travel from abroad to access fertility services, has increased dramatically in the last 20 years.[37]

parenthood provisions: *Re Human Fertilisation and Embryology Act 2008 (Cases A, B, C, D, E, F, G and H)* [2015] EWHC 2602 (Fam), [2015] All ER (D) 57 (Sep) and *Re Human Fertilisation and Embryology Act 2008 (Cases AD, AE, AF, AG and AH)* [2017] EWHC 1026 (Fam). Lack of adherence with consent provisions was recently challenged in *ARB v. Hammersmith* Ltd [2017] EWCH 2438 (HC), discussed in Chapter 3. In *R (on the application of M) v. Human Fertilisation and Embryology Authority* [2016] EWCA Civ 611 – the HFEA's decision not to allow a couple to export their late daughters egg's to the United States was successfully challenged. They wished a centre in the United States to use the eggs to create an embryo with anonymous donor sperm, which would be implanted into the deceased's mother, so that she could raise any child who may be born as her grandchild in accordance with their late daughter's wishes. In another challenge in *Yearworth* v. *North Bristol NHS Trust* [2010] QB 1 the Court held that the claimants had ownership of, and therefore property rights in, their sperm and that there had been negligent infringement of those rights by the Trust when the storage system failed, causing the samples to thaw and be irreversibly damaged).

[34] The Department of Health, Triennial Review of the Human Fertilisation and Embryology Authority Review Report published in March 2017 noted that worldwide an estimated 5 million babies have now been born following IVF treatment, with more than 225,000 born in the UK and thus 'it could be argued that IVF has become a standard medical procedure that is much less at the cutting edge of medical science than many unregulated treatments' – para 2.4.

[35] HFEA Innovation in Regulation, February 2017, at p. 4.

[36] Ibid. Note that NHS funding comes through Clinical Commissioning Groups (CCGs). NHS England provides commissioning guidance to CCGs. Although The National Institute for Health Care and Excellence (NICE) provides best practice guidance, and recommends in the context of access to IVF that 'In women aged under 40 years who have not conceived after 2 years of regular unprotected intercourse or 12 cycles of artificial insemination (where 6 or more are by intrauterine insemination), offer 3 full cycles of IVF, with or without ICSI. If the woman reaches the age of 40 during treatment, complete the current full cycle but do not offer further full cycles.' However, NICE guidance is not mandatory and is not necessarily followed by clinics. Fertility Network UK, which monitors provision, reported in 2017 that many areas in England are cutting back on provision of IVF on the NHS to save money – see BBC News, 'NHS Access to IVF Being Cut in England' 7 August 2017.

[37] For an interesting paper on reproductive tourism and the large-scale bypassing of domestic fertility services, which is a relatively new phenomenon, see E. Jackson, 'Learning from Cross Border Travel' (2017) 25(1) *Medical Law Review* 23. L. Culley, N. Hudson, F. Rapport et al., 'Crossing Borders for Fertility Treatment: Motivations, Destinations and Outcomes of UK Fertility Travellers' (2011) 26(2373) *Human Reproduction* 2379–80. R. Fletcher, 'Reproductive Consumption' (2006) 7 (1) *Feminist Theory* 27–47.

Reproductive science continues to seek out alternate ways to enable alternative methods of procreation. New reproductive technologies such as uterus transplantation,[38] the creation of bioengineered uteri[39] and artificial gametes[40] now loom on the horizon.[41] I refer to these new technologies, as 'new horizon' technologies. They usher in a different set of legal, ethical and social questions to those that arose from IVF and the 'second era' of reproduction. I suggest the third era of reproduction that Wellin referred to, should also encompass these new technologies in addition to artificial wombs (ectogenesis). The central purpose of this book is to advance debate on from the now much-debated issues that arise from the second wave of reproduction and to begin to offer a critical and legal analysis of the regulatory challenges raised by new reproductive technologies in the 'third era'.

The milestone of a decade on from the government's decision in 2008 to update the principal legislation governing assisted reproductive technologies renders it timely and appropriate to review the regulation in place alongside the latest developments in this area. Throughout, the overarching endeavour will be to examine two possible future advances on the horizon and whether the present regulatory architecture has the mechanisms in place to respond to the legal and ethical challenges they will encompass. The well-established HFEA 'horizon scanning' programme, involves a body of experts who meet regularly to discuss what is likely to be around the corner, scientifically, so that the HFEA can equip itself to respond. In this book, I seek to engage in a 'horizon scanning' of two future reproductive technologies (ectogenesis and uterus transplantation) from an explicitly legal-ethical, as opposed to scientific, perspective.

---

[38] M. Brännström, 'Uterus Transplantation and Beyond'. For media articles on prospect of uterus transplantation into men see M. Bilger, 'Scientists Are Now Attempting to Figure Out How to Get Men Pregnant' *LifeNews.com*, 20 June 2016.

[39] For instance, see the success of uterus transplantation and research currently being undertaken on the creation of bioengineered uterus: M. Brännström, 'Uterus Transplantation and Beyond'.

[40] See A. Smajdor and D. Cutas, 'Artificial Gametes' Nuffield Council on Bioethics Background Paper (2015).

[41] C. Limon, 'From Surrogacy to Ectogenesis: Reproductive Justice and Equal Opportunity in Neoliberal Times' (2016) 31(88) *Australian Feminist Studies* 203–219.

Writing on the regulation of reproductive technologies is difficult, given that it is a fast-paced area of innovation. At the outset it should be noted that I am not a moral philosopher, but rather a medical lawyer dealing with a subject that invokes ethical issues. As such, the principal objective of this book is to critically examine the regulation of assisted reproductive technologies and address whether the present legislative framework can accommodate the challenges raised by the new horizon reproductive technologies. While a growing wealth of literature has emerged on the ethical issues raised by the progress of reproductive science, relatively few commentators address the legal issues or how they may be regulated in practice. This book seeks to fill this lacuna and addresses exactly how, if these technologies come to pass, they can be regulated in practice and what legal challenges they raise. The UK regulatory framework was chosen as a regulatory model, since it was the first of its kind in the world and has provided a global example of a model of regulation of this controversial branch of medicine.

This book is split into two parts:

Part I: Regulating Reproductive Technologies: Challenges Old and New

Before looking to how we should regulate assisted reproductive technologies beyond the horizon today, it is necessary to first address those possible today. This book commences in Chapter 1 with an examination of the complex relationship between law and human reproduction and the regulatory challenges therein. I examine the justification for subjecting those who require assistance or the use of ARTs to procreate to far stricter controls than those who reproduce without assistance, and Parliament's justification for singling out this branch of medicine as an area meriting specialist regulation. The chapter provides a detailed account of the regulatory framework in the UK from a past, present and future lens. Despite the aims of the reforms in 2008 to make sure the regulation of assisted reproductive technologies was fit for purpose in the twenty-first century, the HFE Act 2008 represented a missed opportunity to substantively review and reflect on the regulation and thwarted achievement of this goal.

Chapter 2 examines an aspect from the 'second wave' of human reproduction that continues to generate controversy: disputes between gamete progenitors over the fate of frozen IVF embryos. Whilst IVF is now a well-established technology and one that is widely used globally,[42] it still raises challenges which will grow in complexity as we charge towards the third era of reproduction; namely, how do we resolve disputes between progenitors over their gametes when fertilisation takes place outside a female host and in a 'neutral' environment? In unassisted reproduction, women hold the paramount say, primarily because the embryo/fetus is located within a woman's body and thus her bodily autonomy is engaged.[43] Once fertilisation/gestation can take place in vitro, in a neutral environment, arguably both gamete progenitors are equally situated with regards to the embryo/fetus. How then should disputes that arise as to the fate of those gametes be resolved? Exploring the theme of how ARTs are equalising mens' and womens' reproductive roles, I explore why, if at all, women should retain the decisive say over their embryos/fetuses, irrespective of whether they are in vivo or in vitro. The dispositional authority of gamete progenitors over their embryos becomes more complex when we consider not just embryos growing in vitro, but fetuses which can be gestated and maintained in an artificial womb (ectogenesis) or possibly implanted into a male host (via a uterus transplant). Using two examples of English legal disputes between gamete progenitors, *Evans* v. *Amicus* [2004][44] and *ARB* v. *Hammersmith Ltd* [2017],[45] in this chapter it is argued that the UK framework is not equipped to fairly deal with such disputes. Alternative models, which could be used to regulate such disputes in a more equitable manner, are examined.

Part II: Regulating New Reproductive Technologies

The book then moves on to consider new horizon reproductive technologies.

Chapter 3 is the first of two chapters on ectogenesis: an artificial or mechanical uterus or chamber that can mimic the functions of the maternal uterus. Complete ectogenesis, the gestation of a human being entirely

---

[42] It is estimated that around five million children have been born through IVF and related assisted reproductive technologies (ARTs) ESHRE. (2013).

[43] See *Paton* v. *British Pregnancy Advisory Service* [1979] QB 276 and *Paton* v. *UK* (1981) 3 E.H.R.R 408.

[44] *Evans* v. *Amicus Health Care Ltd and Others* [2004] 2 WLR 713 (Fam.); [2004] WLR 681 (CA); *Evans* v. *United Kingdom* [2006] 1 FCR 585 (ECtHR); [2007] BHRC 190 (ECtHR).

[45] *ARB* v. *Hammersmith Ltd* [2017] EWCH 2438 (HC).

outside the body of a human female,[46] represents 'the final severing of reproduction from the human body'[47] and will eliminate the need for a human host to gestate; consequently it will have repercussions far greater than other advances in the arena of assisted reproductive technologies. Any discussion on the implications of a scientific advance first necessitates a discussion and analysis on where the research is currently up to, how far away this advance is and what research is currently underway into making the advance possible. Thus far, whilst ectogenesis has attracted much curiosity, little attention has been given to the practical realities of conducting such research and how this new reproductive technology may come about. The present chapter addresses this lacuna and examines what may be entailed in the road to ectogenesis and how the regulatory framework in the UK would apply to such research. This chapter commences with a brief discussion on ectogenesis alongside the potential benefits and objections that have been advanced towards the technology and is then split into two parts. Part I examines animal research into ectogenesis that has been conducted internationally before examining how such research would be governed in the UK. Part II examines research into ectogenesis that has been conducted using human embryos and fetuses internationally, before again considering how such research would be governed in the UK. Throughout this chapter, the concern is primarily with ectogenesis as a future development and how research into making this advance a safe method of gestation could be safely performed in this jurisdiction. Examining the research underway into this advance allows for reflection on whether the view taken by the Warnock Committee in 1984[48] that ectogenesis was far off on the horizon remains a valid statement.

Discussion of some of the many regulatory questions that will arise should ectogenesis become a safe method of gestation was deserving of its own chapter and is explored in Chapter 4. Ectogenesis will present similarly complex questions as IVF concerning embryo and fetus status; however, it also renders these issues more complex as 'the theatre of gestation becomes seeable and its players accessible'.[49] This chapter

---

[46] L. Cannold, 'Women, Ectogenesis and Ethical Theory' in S. Gelfand (eds.), *Ectogenesis: Artificial Womb Technology and the Future of Human Reproduction* (Amsterdam and New York, NY: Rodopi, 2006) p. 47.

[47] C. Rosen, 'Why Not Artificial Wombs?' (2003) 3 *The New Atlantis* 67–76.

[48] Warnock Report.

[49] J. Raskin and N. Mazor, 'The Artificial Womb and Human Subject Research' in S. Gelfand, *Ectogenesis: Artificial Womb Technology and the Future of Human Subject Research* (Amsterdam and New York, NY: Rodopi, 2006) p. 159.

considers a number of regulatory questions that will arise once complete ectogenesis becomes possible. The status of the in vitro fetus will become much more pertinent. Many of the cases that have generated legal rules on the status of the fetus have originated in the context of women who seek to terminate a pregnancy against the wishes of the fetuses putative father,[50] or women who refuse to consent to a caesarean section judged by doctors to be in the fetus's interests[51] and other instances concerning fetuses gestated in their mother's womb.[52] This is significantly different from the situation of the in vitro embryo/fetus that will have an independent physical existence and can be gestated in an ectogenic incubator. In view of this, regulators will have to re-examine the legal status of the human fetus.

This advance also necessitates revisiting abortion legislation since legal definitions of the terms 'viability', 'birth' and 'abortion' all struggle to fit into the intricacies of artificial womb technology. Viability, which currently influences the present legislation, will become irrelevant since, once complete ectogenesis is possible, viability (the ability to sustain the life of a fetus outside the maternal womb) will be from conception. In light of this, Parliament may have to reconsider whether the 24 weeks (deemed to be a point of viability, or when a fetus is 'capable of being born alive'), as found in section 1 of the Abortion Act 1967 (as amended by the Human Fertilisation and Embryology Act 1990) should be retained as the cut-off point in the legislation for when a woman can abort in order to prevent risk to her health or that of her children. I consider the claims made by some that ectogenesis could signal an end to abortion, in that the state could mandate ectogenesis in lieu of abortion, so that women who wish to end their pregnancies could only opt for fetal transfer or evacuation into an ectogenic chamber, which would allow her to end her pregnancy without ending the life of the fetus. This speculative potential advance reignites the debate on whether abortion is a right to fetal evacuation or fetal extinction. This chapter addresses but a few of the many regulatory questions that will surface if ectogenesis becomes a safe method of gestation. Given that we arguably already have partial ectogenesis in the neo-natal intensive care units

---

[50] *Paton v. BPAS* [1979] 1 QB 276, *C v S* [1988] 1 QB 135.

[51] *S v. McC; W v. W* [1972] AC 24, *Re T (Adult: Refusal of Medical Treatment)* [1992] 4 All ER 649, CA, *Re MB (An Adult: Medical Treatment)* [1997] 2 FCR 541, St *George's Healthcare NHS Trust* v. *S* [1999] Fam 26, CA.

[52] *Attorney-General's Reference (No 3 of 1994)* [1997] 3 WLR 421. *Re F (In Utero)* [1988] 2 ALL ER 193. *D* v. *Berkshire County Council* [1987] 1 All ER 20.

which help mimic the functions of the maternal environment for those babies born on the cusps of viability, and in light of the therapeutic benefits this technology will offer individuals unable to gestate, there is a strong imperative for carefully considering this technology. It is conceded that at present the science is yet to be developed into this advance and it may even be the case that scientists will not discover how to achieve complete ectogenesis in our lifetime. However, given the rate of scientific advance in this domain and in a bid to be more proactive as opposed to reactive, I argue it is prudent to consider the plethora of legal and ethical questions to which this technology will give rise. In both chapters on ectogenesis, I argue that, despite endeavours in 2008 to update the legislation governing ARTs so that it was fit for purpose in the twenty-first century, existing legislation fails to provide an adequate framework in which to regulate this revolutionary technology or research into making this advance a possibility.

Chapter 5 then moves on to consider another reproductive advance on the horizon, namely uterus transplantation in women. The world's first live birth following uterus transplantation in 2014 represented a huge step forward in reproductive technology. The success of Brännström and his team in Sweden received worldwide media coverage and has given hope to thousands of women around the globe.[53] There have now been eight live births from the Swedish trials. In December 2017, the first birth following uterus transplant in the United States of America was reported.[54] Uterus transplantation is the only known treatment for women suffering from uterus factor infertility and thus the immediate purpose of the procedure would be to restore fertility to patients with an abnormal, damaged or absent uterus. In the UK alone, it is estimated that approximately 15,000 women per year who seek the help of fertility specialists are found to be incapable of becoming pregnant because of uterine factor infertility. Even though these women may have functioning ovaries, the lack of a functioning womb means they have no chance of gestating their own child to term. The possibility of uterus transplantation would provide a means by which these women could experience gestational motherhood.

There are now other teams working towards uterus transplants in the UK, China, France, Belgium, Lebanon and Spain. As the recent successes in

---

[53] M. Brännström, L. Johannesson, H. Bokstrom et al., 'Livebirth after Uterus Transplantation' (2015) (14)385 (9968) *The Lancet* 607–616.

[54] D. Grady, 'Woman with Transplanted Uterus Gives Birth, the First in the U.S.' *The New York Times*, 2 December 2017.

Sweden and the USA have shown, the surgical technique is now possible. Foley has argued the next step should be analysis and exploration into the ethical issues that surround uterus transplantation rather than the continued previous focus on 'Is It Possible?'[55] I concur, and argue that we also need to also explore the legal and regulatory issues to which this advance gives rise. In the absence of strong justifications against this advance, it seems inevitable that this technology will soon move from the research trial phase to clinical treatment. I argue this is precisely *why* if women are to benefit from this novel procedure, it is important to go beyond abstract discussions regarding the possibility of uterus transplantation as a future advance. Instead discussion must now turn to pragmatic considerations about how such an advance would be governed under the present legislative and regulatory framework and whether it can accommodate this novel advance. This chapter examines the difficult regulatory issues this advance raises in the UK, which like many other jurisdictions has separate regulatory regimes for human tissue and organ transplantation and assisted reproduction.

Chapter 6 moves on to consider the more controversial prospect that scientists may soon be able to transplant a uterus not only into cisgender women, but also transgender and gender variant individuals and cisgender men, enabling trans and male pregnancy. For trans individuals wishing to undergo gender reassignment and have their (new) gender legally recognised there are many countries that mandate they must be unable to procreate in their former gender.[56] Permissive countries such as the UK have never imposed such a mandate. The Gender Recognition Act 2004 provides that once an individual has undergone the process outlined in the statute, they are to all intents and purposes, to be identified and treated in their (new) legally acquired gender. Thus, if uterus transplantation is permitted in cisgender women, a trans woman who has gender reassigned, may also claim a right to access such technology and be treated equal to her female counterparts. Trans women could regard pregnancy as the final step in realigning their life in accordance with the gender they psychologically identify with, as opposed to the biological sex assigned at birth. I examine whether, under the present permissive regulatory framework found in the UK, trans women could in theory access a uterus transplant and IVF services so as to experience gestation. Following on from this, I address the prospect that science may soon also discover how to achieve pregnancy in cisgender men. There are crucial

---

[55] J. Folly, 'Uterus Transplantation – A Step Too Far' (2012) 7(4) *Clinical Ethics* 193–198.
[56] In 2017, across the Council of Europe, 20 countries continue to enforce a sterilisation requirement. P. Dunne, 'Transgender Sterilisation Requirements in Europe' (2017) *Medical Law Review* – Advance Access 1–28. Issue 25(4) pages 554–581.

distinctions between transgender women and cisgender men gestating via UTx to be factored in: for instance, the former will most likely be in receipt of estrogen and other 'female' hormones and thus their testosterone may be significantly lowered. Professor Brännström who led the world's first successful UTx procedure in Sweden has asserted that it could one day be technically possible to transplant a uterus into a cisgender man, combined with the use of hormone therapy to enable a pregnancy to succeed. The baby would be delivered via cesarean section and the uterus removed shortly after successful delivery. This chapter explores the legal and ethical implications this gives rise to, and explores the possibility of uterus transplantation and IVF to achieve pregnancy in both trans women and cisgender men. The UK regulatory model is explored and in particular how the legal provisions would apply if either of these possibilities comes to pass.

Whether or not third wave reproductive technologies represent 'The End of Sex and the Future of Human Reproduction';[57] one thing is clear, these new horizons in the domain of reproduction are set to usher in exciting scientific advances. If the benefits of these advances are to be maximised and the regulator adequately equipped to respond to the challenges raised by them, consideration needs to be given to the many ethical, legal and regulatory issues they will generate. The rapid rate at which reproductive technologies unfolds mean they often leave in their trail a complex web of legal, ethical, social and regulatory questions which the government has no option but to address, often in haste and trying to catch up with a fait accompli. It is inevitable that there is going to be some lack of synchronicity between the development of technology and the law's ability to address it, because of science's emphasis upon progress and the law's emphasis on process. Yet, if the law is to maintain (and at times restrain) the march of science, it needs to, as Sublett argues, go 'beyond the mere problems faced today and decide fundamental issues which will provide the basis to solve tomorrow's problems. By doing this a more stable and predictable body of law will develop, enabling the legal profession to meet the dilemmas new technology proposes.'[58] In this final chapter, I sum up whether the current UK regulatory

---

[57]   The title of H. T. Greely's excellent book: see H. T. Greely, *The End of Sex and the Future of Human Reproduction* (Harvard University Press: 2016). For a review of the book, see S. M. Suter, 'The End of Sex and the Future of Human Reproduction by H. T. Greely: Book Review' (2016) 3 *Journal of Law and the Biosciences* 436–444.

[58]   M. Sublett, 'Frozen Embryos: What Are They and How Should We Treat Them?' (1990) 38(4) *Cleveland State Law Review* 585–616, at p. 616.

framework has been reconnected with modern science and whether it is capable of regulating ARTs on the horizon today and tomorrow. Throughout the book is a plea, that the law relating to the reproductive technologies should, as far as possible, be proactive rather than constantly reactive.

This book is up to date as of 1 January 2018.

PART I

Regulating Reproductive Technologies

Challenges Old and New

1

Regulation of Assisted Reproduction

Past, Present and Future

A decade after the UK Government's decision to update the principal legislation governing assisted reproductive technologies, to ensure it was 'fit for purpose in the 21st century',[1] seems an appropriate time to review the regulatory framework in this controversial area. As Brownsword rightly observes, the regulation of new technologies is 'an open agenda that invites on-going reflection'.[2] This chapter commences with an examination of the complex relationship between law and human reproduction and the challenges raised by regulation. Unlike those who can reproduce without assistance, those who require procreative assistance or use of assisted reproductive technologies (ARTs) are subject to far stricter controls.[3] This chapter outlines why this branch of medicine was deemed to necessitate specific statutory regulation and analyses the operation of the regulatory framework in place. The Human Fertilisation and Embryology Act 1990 (HFE Act 1990),[4] as amended by the Human Fertilisation and Embryology Act 2008,[5] will be examined. The HFE Act 2008 retained the Human Fertilisation and Embryology Authority (HFEA) as the independent statutory authority, which oversees regulation of this controversial area and thus the effectiveness of the HFEA in regulating this contentious area is considered. Outlining how assisted reproduction is regulated through a past, present and future lens will enable subsequent chapters of this book to examine critically whether the regulatory framework is equipped to accommodate the challenges that the third wave of human reproduction will usher in.

---

[1] Department of Health (DoH), *Review of the Human Fertilisation and Embryology Act: Proposals for Revised Legislation (Including Establishment of the Regulatory Authority for Tissue and Embryos)*, Cm 6989 (London: DoH, 14 December 2006).

[2] R. Brownsword, *Rights, Regulation and the Technological Revolution* (Oxford: Oxford University Press, 2009), at p. 28.

[3] See A. Alghrani and J. Harris, 'Should the Foundation of Families Be Regulated?' (2006) 18(2) *Child and Family Law Quarterly* 191–210.

[4] Hereafter the 'HFE Act 1990'.

[5] Hereafter the 'HFE Act 2008'.

1.1   The Regulation of Assisted Reproduction: The Past

Advances in reproductive technologies have revolutionised reproduction and continue to diversify and enhance the varied and many ways in which one can now exercise choices about procreation. Such choices are often discussed in terms of 'reproductive liberty' or 'procreative autonomy';[6] ethical principles which have a number of different sources and justifications.[7] Harris, drawing on the writings of Dworkin (who argued that procreative autonomy should be regarded as a democratic liberty just as freedom of speech and racial equality are[8]), claims that according to the principle of procreative autonomy, competent members of society should be left to make their own decisions about how, when and where to reproduce.[9] Only when there is a compelling reason – such as evidence of significant harm to the child – should the state be allowed to intervene in such decision-making. Harris plausibly argues it is clear that procreative autonomy must apply to more than conventional sexual reproduction and also extends to procreation via alternate means, such as via the use of assisted reproductive technologies.[10] I concur with this, and in this book I include within the notion of procreative autonomy the right or entitlement to found a family and acquire children by means other than sexual reproduction. I am interested in how the law regulates those other means by which one can found a family, in particular the regulation of new reproductive technologies that could facilitate individuals' procreative endeavours. While procreation through sexual reproduction is the most common means of founding a family, some individuals may have to – or choose to – explore alternative methods of doing so.[11]

---

[6] For an interesting definition of procreative autonomy as 'the ability to decide whether to have a child without being subject to the government's power to compel the individual to act in alignment with the government desires' – see K. M. Bridges, *The Poverty of Privacy Rights* (California: Stanford University Press, 2017).

[7] Robertson, *Children of Choice* (Princeton, NJ: Princeton University Press, 1994). R. Dworkin, *Life's Dominion* (London: Harper Collins Publishers, 1993). J. Savulescu, 'Deaf Lesbians, "Designer Disability" and the Future of Medicine' (2002) 325 *British Medical Journal* 771. J. Harris, 'Rights and Reproductive Choice' in J. Harris and S. Holm (eds.), *The Future of Human Reproduction: Choice and Regulation* (Oxford: Oxford University Press, 1998).

[8] R. Dworkin, *Freedom's Law* (Oxford: Oxford University Press, 1996).

[9] Harris, 'Rights and Reproductive Choice', 5–37.

[10] Ibid.

[11] For instance, those who suffer from infertility, which is defined by the World Health Organization as a disease of the reproductive system defined by the failure to achieve a clinical pregnancy after 12 months or more of regular unprotected sexual intercourse.

In addition to ethical support for procreative autonomy, an individual's procreative decisions are legally also regarded as a fundamental human right.[12] It is not an unqualified legal right[13] and does not entitle one to positive assistance in founding a family,[14] but what it does mean is that certain sorts of impediments to founding a family are unlawful.[15] Whilst advances have enhanced the ways in which individuals can now exercise their procreative autonomy, reproductive scientific advances and individual rights in this domain have had to be tempered by the public interest in protecting those who engage with emerging reproductive technologies and the children created via such alternative methods,

---

[12] Article 16(1) of the United Nations Universal Declaration of Human Rights 1948 (the UN Declaration) provides that 'Men and women of full age, without any limitation due to race, nationality or religion, have the right to marry and to found a family'. The European Convention for the Protection of Human Rights and Fundamental Freedoms 1950 (the European Convention) declares in Article 12 that 'men and women of marriageable age have the right to marry and to found a family'. Article 8 provides that 'Everyone has the right to respect for his private and family life, his home and his correspondence' and this has been interpreted as protecting the right to have genetically related children. In *Dickson* v. *UK* [2007] 3 F.C.R. 877, Article 8 was successfully relied upon to challenge the prison authority's refusal to allow Kirk Dickson (a prisoner serving a minimum sentence of 15 years for murder) and his partner (who was at liberty) artificial insemination facilities, which they had offered to pay for themselves. The Grand Chamber held that Article 8 was applicable in that 'the refusal of artificial insemination facilities concerned their private and family lives which notions incorporated the right to respect for their decision to become genetic parents'. The court held that no separate issue arose under Article 12 of the Convention and therefore it was not necessary to examine the applicants' complaint under this provision. For more on use of Article 8 to protect procreative rights see M. Eijkholt, 'The Right to Procreate Is Not Aborted' (2008) 12(2) *Med L Rev* 284–293.

[13] See Article 8(2) which provides 'There shall be no interference by a public authority with the exercise of this right except such as is in accordance with the law and is necessary in a democratic society in the interests of national security, public safety or the economic well-being of the country, for the prevention of disorder or crime, for the protection of health or morals, or for the protection of the rights and freedoms of others'.

[14] In *Evans* v. *Amicus Healthcare Ltd; Hadley* v. *Midland Fertility Services Ltd* [2003] EWHC 2161 (Fam), [2004] 1 FLR 67, at paragraph [264], Wall LJ described any right to found a family in the following terms: 'The right to found a family though IVF can only, put at its highest, amount to the right to have access to IVF treatment. Self-evidently, it cannot be a right to be treated successfully. Furthermore, it is a right which is qualified by availability, suitability for treatment and cost.' See also *Briody* v. *St Helen's and Knowsley Area Health Authority* (2001) EWCA Civ 1010, [2001] 2 FLR 1094, per Hale LJ at paragraph [26]: 'While everyone has the right to try to have their own children by natural means, no one has the right to be provided with a child'; and the earlier decision of *R* v. *Secretary of State for the Home Department ex parte Mellor* (2001) EWCA Civ 472 [2001] 2 FLR 1158.

[15] For an example of restrictions that were deemed to be a breach of Article 8 see *Dickson* v. *UK* [2007] 3 F.C.R. 877.

alongside concern surrounding the unknown risks they may carry. Consequently the regulation of assisted reproduction has proved no easy feat.

1.2   The Case for Specialist Regulation of Assisted Reproduction

First, it is important to recall why the UK government regarded ARTs as a branch of medicine that merited specialist regulation. The birth of Louise Brown in Oldham in 1978, the first child in the world conceived through in vitro fertilisation (IVF), was a significant advance for medical science and offered hope for many couples who wished to have children, but struggled with infertility.[16] It also marked the first time that the public had been made aware that IVF and the conception outside a female host was possible. This scientific breakthrough pioneered by Steptoe, Edwards and Purdy[17] gave rise to a wave of public concern surrounding the possible harms, risks and ethical dilemmas associated with the use of new artificial reproductive technologies to create children.[18] There was public 'unease at the apparently uncontrolled advance of science, bringing with it new possibilities for manipulating the early stages of human development'.[19] This unease was clear in the House of Lords Debates in 1984 and reflected in Lord Denning's comment:

> There is at the moment no law and no restriction whatever. Medical scientists and medical men can do as they like ... without any control. These are dangers to our society.[20]

Meacher also noted how fertility treatment and embryo research was publicly perceived as:

---

[16] For more on the pioneering work behind the first IVF baby see: R. G. Edwards, *Life before Birth: Reflections on the Embryo Debate* (London: Hutchinson, 1989). P. R. Brinsden, 'Thirty Years of IVF: The Legacy Patrick Steptoe and Robert Edwards' (2009) 12(3) *Human Fertility* 137–143. For Louise Brown's autobiography see L. Brown, *Louise Brown: My Life as the World's First Test-Tube Baby* (Bristol: Bristol Books, 2015).

[17] See also R. Gosden, 'Jean Marian Purdy – The Hidden Life of an IVF Pioneer' (2017) *Human Fertility* (commentary) – for an excellent paper on Jean Purdy, who is almost forgotten as one of the IVF trio that introduced clinical IVF to the world.

[18] Official Report, House of Lords, 31 October 1984; Vol. 456, c. 541.

[19] Report of the Committee of Inquiry into Human Fertilisation and Embryology July 1984, Cmnd 9314 (1984) p. 4. Hereafter the 'Warnock Report'.

[20] Official Report, House of Lords, 31 October 1984; Vol. 456, c. 541.

a subject that is fraught with fantasies of futuristic horror. Lurid associa-
tions with 'Brave New World' embryology, Nazi medicine or
Frankenstein experimentation, make debate between irreconcilable
moral positions very difficult.[21]

In order to address such public fears, the government in 1982 commissioned an independent inquiry under Baroness Warnock to examine
scientific developments in fertilisation and embryology.[22] The terms of
reference were:

> To consider recent and potential developments in medicine and science
> related to human fertilisation and embryology to consider what policies and
> safeguards should be applied, including consideration of the social, ethical and
> legal implications of their developments and to make recommendations.[23]

The Committee invited evidence and submissions were received from over
3000 organisations, 24 Community Health Councils, 11 Regional Health
Authorities, 22 Universities and 695 individuals.[24] The Committee was
given the task of examining not only existing technologies, but also
potential developments. In undertaking this dual task, Hoppe and Miola
suggest the Warnock Committee would face difficulty from the outset:

> First it had to establish a clear and coherent ethical position surrounding not
> just the moral status of embryos and gametes but also the type of families
> that they were content to facilitate. In this respect the Committee also had to
> ensure that there was some form of enforcement mechanism that would
> ensure that this ethical position was adopted and maintained by clinics
> offering services. Secondly, the Committee had to create a structure that was
> flexible and able to respond to change, so that any future technological
> developments could be brought within the ambit of the Act if necessary.[25]

The Warnock Committee reported in 1984 with 63 specific recommendations, all of which supported specialist regulation of fertility treatment
and embryo research. The recommendations formed the basis of the
subsequent HFE Act 1990. A key conclusion was that the human embryo

---

[21] Hansard, HC, vol 68, col 534, [1984].
[22] Warnock Report.
[23] Ibid.
[24] P. O. Mahony, *Question of Life: Its Beginning and Transmission* (London: Sheed and
Ward, 1990), p. 80. For an article which examines the evidence submitted to the Warnock
Committee, upon which its members ultimately reached their conclusions see
N. Hammond-Browning, 'Ethics, Embryos and Evidence: A Look Back at Warnock'
(2015) 23 (4) *Medical Law Review* 588–619.
[25] N. Hoppe and J. Miola, *Medical Law and Medical Ethics* (Cambridge: Cambridge
University Press, 2014), 161–162.

has a 'special status' and 'that the embryo of the human species should be afforded some protection in law'.[26] Consequently, research on the human embryo beyond appearance of the primitive streak (fourteen days) should be prohibited.[27] Another key recommendation was that there should be a statutory body to oversee the licensing and inspection of all infertility services where the new techniques are used; oversee any use of human embryos in research; provide advice to Government about future developments in this field; and to ensure compliance with good practice across fertility services. These recommendations were accepted and it was decided that regulation of fertility treatment and embryological research was to be via a specialist statute with oversight by a statutory authority.

Publication of the Warnock Report was followed by public consultation through the Green and White Papers[28] which led the government to conclude that both 'assisted reproduction and research involving the embryo of the human species' to be 'legitimate interests of the state' and that 'reproductive and research freedoms must be balanced against the interests of society'.[29] As those public consultations took time, in the period between the Warnock Committee publishing its report and the enactment of legislation (1985–1991), ARTs were self-regulated, in the same manner as most other fields of medicine.[30] This was undertaken by

---

[26] Warnock Report, paragraph 11.17.

[27] Much criticism was levied against the 14-day rule – see M. Mulkay, *The Embryo Research Debate: Science and the Politics of Reproduction* (Cambridge: Cambridge University Press; 1997). D. Jones, 'The "Special Status" of the Human Embryo in the United Kingdom: An Exploration of the Use of Language in Public Policy' (2011) 17(66) *Human Reproduction and Genetic Ethics* 66–83. For a recent paper on this see G. Cavaliere, 'A 14-day Limit for Bioethics: The Debate over Human Embryo Research' (2017) 18(38) *BMC Medical Ethics* 1–12.

[28] See the Legislation of Human Infertility Services and Embryo Research (1986) (Cm 46) and the White Paper, Human Fertilisation and Embryology: A Framework for Legislation (1987) (Cm 259) respectively.

[29] HCSTC Human Technologies and the Law (HC-7) 2004–5, paragraphs 46–47.

[30] The General Medical Council (GMC), whose powers and procedures are set out in the Medical Act 1983, currently undertakes regulation of the medical profession in the UK. The regulation of human tissue and organ transplantation is also subject to statutory regulation (The Human Tissue Act 2004) and oversight by a statutory body (The Human Tissue Authority). On regulation of the medical profession see R. C. Derbyshire, 'How Effective Is Medical Self-Regulation?' (1983) 7(2–3) *Law and Human Behavior* 193–202. B. Hutter and S. Lloyd Bostock, 'Reforming Regulation of the Medical Profession: The Risks of Risk-Based Approaches' (2008) 10(1) *Health, Risk and Society* 69–83. M. Davies, *Medical Self-Regulation: Crisis and Change* (Oxford: Routledge, 2007). J. M. Chamberlain, 'Malpractice, Criminality, and Medical Regulation: Reforming the Role of the GMC in Fitness to Practise Panels' (2017) 25(1) *Medical Law Review* 1.

the Voluntary Licensing Authority (VLA), which was comprised of four representatives of the Medical Research Council (MRC) and the Royal College of Obstetricians and Gynaecologists (RCOG) and five laypersons. This was to be a temporary measure; in 1987 the government published a White Paper,[31] in which a commitment to legislation was made. In April 1989, the VLA emphasised the temporary nature of its existence by changing its name to the 'Interim Licensing Authority for Human In Vitro Fertilisation and Embryology'.

Parliament later enacted the Human Fertilisation and Embryology Act 1990[32] as the principal means of regulating assisted reproductive technologies. The Human Fertilisation and Embryology Authority was established in 1991 as the statutory authority to oversee the regulation and replaced the VLA. Specialist regulation was said to offer certainty and protection to professionals, who would be provided with clear legal and professional guidelines, whilst simultaneously protecting patients, since doctors and scientists would be deterred from irresponsible behaviour. As Deech noted:

> Regulation initially arose from the widespread fears expressed by politicians, the media, the public and the professions about embryo research, its morality and its direction. Subsequently the spread of IVF treatment and clinics came to drive regulation and only then because the National Health Service has declined to fund the generality of such treatment, giving it the potential to become big business with all the dependent drawbacks thereof.[33]

Support for specialist regulation of this controversial branch of medicine continues today. In a book entitled *Test Tube Babies: Why the Fertility Market Needs Legal Regulation*, Cahn surmises her support for regulation as follows:

> So long as we have families, we will want to determine who the parents are. So long as children have questions about their origin, issues surrounding the identity of their biological progenitors will arise. And whenever we deal with technology, we will have concerns about the safety and regulation of that technology, and the protection of those individuals who engage with it. This triptych of legal issues – defining families, forming identities and regulating markets – provides the framework for this book.[34]

---

[31] Human Fertilisation and Embryology: A Framework for Legislation, Cm 259 (1987).
[32] Hereafter referred to as the HFE Act 1990.
[33] R. Deech, 'The HFEA – 10 Years On' in J. Gunning and H. Szoke (eds.), *The Regulation of Assisted Reproductive Technology* (United Kingdom: Ashgate Publishing, 2003) at p. 21.
[34] N. Cahn, *Test Tube Babies: Why the Fertility Market Needs Legal Regulation* (New York, NY: New York University Press, 2009), p. vii.

With enactment of the statute, the UK became one of the first countries in the world to comprehensively regulate assisted reproduction.[35] Jackson noted:

> The UK regulatory regime in this area – the first of its type – has been widely copied throughout the world. It has enabled clear statutory prohibitions to co-exist with a degree of flexibility, which is generally believed to have worked well[36]

In Europe, many other countries have followed suit: all countries in Europe now have some form of ART regulation and Europe is currently the largest market for ART.[37] However Prag and Mills note Europe is the only continent where the legal regulation of ART is widespread, observing that in other major countries where ART is used, such as India, Japan and the USA, largely rely on voluntary guidelines.[38] Countries such as the USA, which govern this controversial branch of medicine via voluntary guidelines, instead of legal regulation, have also been criticised for being outpaced by science and being in 'catch up mode' rather than in 'shaping mode'.[39] Despite arguments that have since been made for lighter regulation,[40] it seems when the Warnock Committee was commissioned it was never a question of *whether* to regulate ART – the real question was *how* to regulate ART and who would do the regulating.

---

[35] Note that following the birth of Louise Brown in 1978, live births after IVF occurred in Australia in 1980, in the USA in 1981 and in Sweden and France in 1982. Following the first IVF birth in Australia, the Government of Victoria established a review of IVF research and practice which led to the proclamation of the Infertility (Medical Procedures) Act 1984, the first legislation to regulate IVF and its associated human embryo research. See J. Cohen et al., 'The Early Days of IVF Outside the UK" (2005) 11 *Human Reproduction Update* 439–459.

[36] E. Jackson, 'The Human Fertilisation and Embryology Bill 2007' (2008) 3(4) *Expert Review of Obstetrics & Gynecology* 429–431, at p. 431.

[37] P. Prag, M. C. Mills, 'Assisted Reproductive Technology in Europe: Usage and Regulation in the Context of Cross-Border Reproductive Care' in M. Kreyenfeld, D. Konietzka (eds.), *Childlessness in Europe: Contexts, Causes, and Consequences. Demographic Research Monographs* (A series of the Max Planck Institute for Demographic Research (Cham: Springer, 2017).

[38] Prag and Mills, 'Assisted Reproductive Technology in Europe' 14(3).

[39] Cahn, *Test Tube Babies.*

[40] See M. H. Johnson and K. Petersen, 'Public Interest or Public Meddling? Towards an Objective Framework for the Regulation of Assisted Reproduction Technologies' (2008) 23(3) *Human Reproduction* 716–728. The authors argue there is no strong or unique claim of actual or imminent potential harm to the public health interest arising from use of ART sufficient to warrant the restrictions on autonomy imposed by such bodies as the HFEA and that consequently, less intrusive lighter touch regulatory mechanisms would suffice.

The UK government was clear that this area was to be regulated via statute with oversight by a statutory body, justified by the fact the state has some interests in assisted reproduction, ensuring high standards of treatment and in restricting reproductive freedom if there are demonstrable harms or negative impacts on society.[41]

However, the UK regulatory framework has also received much criticism; Brazier argued 'there is little conceptual depth underpinning British law. The result is that, again and again, as new medical technologies emerge, we debate the same issues in different guises'.[42] Whilst IVF became commonplace, the rapid pace of medical and scientific advances meant that numerous subsequent challenges were mounted before the courts.[43] Drafted at a time of rapid technological development, the pace of scientific advance meant that the HFE Act 1990 quickly became outdated not long after receiving royal assent. Embryological development subsequently enabled the creation of human embryo by cell nuclear replacement (CNR) – so-called 'cloned embryos'. The creation of embryos by cloning was unknown at the time the HFE Act 1990 was drafted and the definition of an embryo in the statute assumed embryos would be created by fertilisation. As Lord Millett noted in *R (Quintavalle)* v. *Secretary of State for Health* [2003],[44] CNR 'was a later development in embryology which was not foreseen by the Warnock Committee whose Report led to the passing of the Act or by Parliament when the Act was passed'.[45] In that case, the (then) House of Lords in determining whether the HFEA had the power to license therapeutic cloning research and whether an embryo created via cell nuclear replacement was a process covered by the HFE Act 1990, the court adopted a purposive approach. Such an approach was set out in a dissenting judgment in *Royal College of Nursing of the United Kingdom* v. *Department of Health and Social Security* [1981] AC 800,[46] where Lord Wilberforce observed:

> In interpreting an Act of Parliament it is proper, and indeed necessary, to have regard to the state of affairs existing, and known by Parliament to be existing, at the time. It is a fair presumption that Parliament's policy or

---

[41] Select Committee on Science and Technology Fifth Report, paragraph 317.

[42] M. Brazier, 'Regulating the Reproduction Business' (1999) *Medical Law Review* 166–193.

[43] *R* v. *HFEA ex p Blood* [1999] Fam 151. *Evans* v. *Amicus Health Care Ltd and Others* [2004] 2 WLR 713 (Fam.); [2004] WLR 681 (CA).

[44] *R (Quintavalle)* v. *Secretary of State for Health* [2003] UKHL 13, [2003] 2 AC 687.

[45] Lord Millett, paragraph 37.

[46] Although a dissenting opinion in this case, in *Fitzpatrick* v. *Sterling Housing Association Ltd* [2001] 1 AC 27 Lord Wilberforce's analysis was approved.

intention is directed to that state of affairs. Leaving aside cases of omission by inadvertence, this being not such a case, when a new state of affairs, or a fresh set of facts bearing on policy, comes into existence, the courts have to consider whether they fall within the Parliamentary intention. They may be held to do so, if they fall within the same genus of facts as those to which the expressed policy has been formulated. They may also be held to do so if there can be detected a clear purpose in the legislation which can only be fulfilled if the extension is made. How liberally these principles may be applied must depend upon the nature of the enactment, and the strictness or otherwise of the words in which it has been expressed. The courts should be less willing to extend expressed meanings if it is clear that the Act in question was designed to be restrictive or circum-scribed in its operation rather than liberal or permissive. They will be much less willing to do so where the subject matter is different in kind or dimension from that for which the legislation was passed. In any event there is one course which the courts cannot take, under the law of this country; they cannot fill gaps; they cannot be asking the question 'What would Parliament have done in this current case – not being one in contemplation – if the facts had been before it?' attempt themselves to supply the answer, if the answer is not be found in the terms of the Act itself.[47]

Subsequently, there was a fear that this 'purposive interpretation' would be used too widely.[48] This elicited academic criticism that the 'tacit claim that the RCN criteria delineate an objective and value-free mode of purposive interpretation criticism is unconvincing'.[49] It was acknowl-edged that resorting to regulating scientific advancements by the judiciary second-guessing parliamentary intent and innovative statutory interpretation was an inadequate way of regulating this controversial branch of medicine. Unsurprisingly it quickly became apparent statutory reform was needed. A mere year later Collier noted:

The HFEA 1990 was passed at a time when we had only a limited under-standing of where the medical and scientific technology might be able to take us. Over the past 15 years there have been enormous strides in our appreciation of human genetics – and the pace of scientific development is accelerating. What the courts are being increasingly forced to do is to apply 1980s scientific and medical solutions, as contained in HFEA 1990, to 21st century ethical and scientific issues and opportunities. The system

[47] *Royal College of Nursing of the United Kingdom* v. *Department of Health and Social Security* [1981] AC 800, p 822 B-E.
[48] S. Collier, 'Assisted Reproduction – Statutory Overhaul Due' [2004] 154 *New Law Journal* 1201.
[49] K. Liddell, 'Purposive Interpretation and the March of Genetic Technology' (2003) 62 *Cambridge Law Journal* 563, at p. 565.

is cracking as a result . . . stretching the wording of the Act is becoming the norm to a point where it is becoming increasingly difficult to determine where the statutory limits are.[50]

In 2005, the House of Commons Science and Technology Committee's review of human reproductive technologies and the law[51] was published, concluding that Parliament's ability to revisit contentious issues relating to the creation of life and permissible use of human embryos was imperative – thus it was recommended that new legislation be more explicit and provided Parliament with greater powers to debate and amend legislation.[52] The Department of Health subsequently announced a review of the HFE Act 1990[53] and sought views on whether and how the law could be updated in light of new technologies, changes in societal attitudes, international developments and the need to ensure effective regulation. It was made clear, however, that the review process was not intended to consider fundamental or underlying aspects of the legislation.[54] A draft bill of new legislation titled 'The Human Tissue and Embryos Draft Bill' was produced in 2007, which was then scrutinised by a Joint Committee.[55] In November 2007, the House of Lords commenced debate on the newly proposed statute, whose title had changed to the Human Fertilisation and Embryology Bill, aptly reflecting that this was an amending statute to the HFE Act 1990. After much consultation and debate, the passing of the HFE Act 2008 finally completed the protracted process of updating the legislation.

The 2008 statute, like its predecessor, was heavily influenced by the recommendations of the Warnock Report, notwithstanding the fact that science had since then progressed. The statutory amendments introduced by the HFE Act 2008 did not significantly alter the regulatory

---

[50] Collier, 'Assisted Reproduction' 1201.

[51] House of Commons Science and Technology Committee, Human Reproductive Technologies and the Law (London: Stationery Office, 2005).

[52] Ibid., paragraph 82.

[53] Department of Health, 'Review of the Human Fertilisation and Embryology Act: Proposals for Revised Legislation'.

[54] Press Release No 45, Session 2002–2003; Department of Health. Review of the Human Fertilisation and Embryology Act: A Public Consultation. London: Department of Health, 2005.

[55] The Joint Committee also published a report addressing the proposed changes to the legislation (Joint Committee on the Human Tissue and Embryos (Draft) Bill 2007 Joint Committee on the Human Tissue and Embryos (Draft) Bill. 2007. Human Tissue and Embryos (Draft) Bill. Volume I: Report. London: Stationery Office. For Government response to this see the 'Government Response to the Report from the Joint Committee on the Human Tissue and Embryos (Draft) Bill, Norwich: Stationery Office, 2007).

framework.[56] The key changes the HFE Act 2008 introduced pertained to provisions on pre-implantation genetic diagnosis (PGD),[57] the removal of reference to the need 'for a father' from the welfare clause in section 13(5),[58] the prohibition on sex selection for social reasons,[59] a widening of the provisions for embryo research and human admixed embryos,[60] changes to consent provisions,[61] and lastly the 2008 Act inserted new parenthood provisions[62] (allowing for the recognition of both partners in a same-sex relationship as legal parents of children conceived through the use of donated sperm, eggs or embryos and enabling people in same-sex relationships and unmarried couples to apply for a parental order, allowing for them to be treated as the parents of a child born using a surrogate). The parenthood provisions, whilst welcomed, remain unjustly restrictive (for instance, they do not allow single individuals to apply for a parental order for a child born via surrogacy[63]) and have been aptly described by Lady Hale as 'a complicated set of rules, which began in the 1990 Act but have been replaced by the 2008 Act'.[64] Despite

---

[56] Jackson, 'The Human Fertilisation and Embryology Bill 2007' 429.

[57] HFE Act 2008, schedule 2, paragraph 1ZA. See also S. Waxman, 'Applying the Pre-Conception Welfare Principle and the Harm Threshold: Doing More Harm than Good?' (2017) 17(3) *Medical Law International*, 134–157.

[58] Ibid., s14(2)(b). On the reform to the welfare provision see J. McCandless, 'Cinderella and Her Cruel Sisters: Parenthood, Welfare and Gender in the Human Fertilisation and Embryology Act 2008' (2013) 32(2) *New Genetics and Society* 135–153. E. Lee, J Macvarish and S. Sheldon, 'Assessing Child Welfare under the Human Fertilisation and Embryology Act 2008: A Case Study in Medicalization?' (2014) 36 *Sociology of Health & Illness* 500–515. E. Lee, J. Macvarish and S. Sheldon, 'After the "Need for . . . .a Father": "The Welfare of the Child" and "Supportive Parenting" in UK Assisted Conception Clinics' (2017) (6) *Families, Relationships and Societies* 71–87. S. Sheldon, E. Lee and J. Macvarish, '"Supportive Parenting", Responsibility and Regulation: The Welfare Assessment under the Reformed Human Fertilisation and Embryology Act (1990)' (2015) (78) *The Modern Law Review* 461–492.

[59] The HFE Act 2008, schedule 2, paragraph 1ZB.

[60] Ibid., s1, s4A, and schedule 2.

[61] HFE Act 2008, schedule 3, paragraph 7, inserted new paragraph 4A to schedule 3 into the 1990 Act. Although note one instance in which these provisions were not complied with and were subject to legal challenge arose in the case of *ARB* v. *Hammersmith Ltd* [2017] EWCH 2438 (HC).

[62] HFE Act 2008, ss42–47.

[63] HFE Act 2008, s54. For more critical discussion on how the law regulates surrogacy see A. Alghrani and D. Griffiths, 'Surrogacy Regulation in the UK: The Case for Reform' (2017) 29(2) *Child and Family Law Quarterly* 165–186. M. Brazier and S. Waxman, 'Reforming the Law Regulating Surrogacy: Extending the Family' (2016) *Journal of Medical Law and Ethics* 4, 159–180.

[64] B. Hale, 'New Families and The Welfare of the Children' (2014) 36(1) *Journal of Social Welfare and Family Law* 26–35, at p. 27.

attempts to amend the legislation in 2008 so that it was 'fit for purpose' in the twenty-first century, the reforms have been condemned as:

> A piecemeal updating of the previous regulatory regime devoid of any coherent philosophical framework. Thus, criticisms of the 1990 Act's lack of conceptual depth remain valid. To this extent it may have been a missed opportunity.[65]

The 2008 Act was to suffer the same limitations as its forebear in 1990. Eijkholt argues that preference for pragmatism during the reform process meant the present regulatory framework continues to lacks any sound ethical philosophical underpinning and does not offer the quality of regulation that the UK might have hoped for.[66] It is regrettable that a more comprehensive review of the legislation was not undertaken but from the outset, it was clear that the review process was not intended to consider fundamental or underlying aspects of the legislation. It is thus not surprising that HFE Act 2008 suffers in some respects from the same weaknesses of its predecessor. This is also echoed by McCandless and Sheldon who observed: '[n]owhere was a blank piece of paper offered for reform, in a way that allowed for a thorough and fundamental rethinking of the kind of regulation which might best suit this area'.[67] This was not an accidental omission, but rather deliberately done and, as Fox notes, the reforms contained in the HFE Act 2008 were driven largely by the government's desire to avoid reigniting controversies over the legal status of the embryo and abortion and to maintain Britain's position at the forefront of embryo research and related biotechnologies – consequently they represent a missed opportunity to re-think the appropriate model of regulation to govern fertility treatment and embryology research in the UK.[68] It is regrettable that the legislation was updated by the mere amending or adding to the provisions of the 1990 statute, instead of a more comprehensive review, for it meant that in the context of rapidly

---

[65] R. Fenton, S. Heenan and J. Rees, 'Finally Fit for Purpose? The Human Fertilization and Embryology Act 2008' (2010) 32(3) *Journal of Social Welfare and Family Law* 275–286, at p. 285.

[66] M. Eijkholt, 'Procreative Autonomy and the Human Fertilization and Embryology Act 2008: Does a Coherent Conception Underpin UK Law?' (2011) 11 *Medical Law International* 93–126.

[67] J. McCandless and S. Sheldon, 'The Human Fertilisation and Embryology Act (2008) and the Tenacity of the Sexual Family Form' (2010) 83(2) *Modern Law Review* 175–207, at p. 180.

[68] M. Fox, 'The Human Fertilisation and Embryology Act 2008: Tinkering at the Margins' (2009) 17(3) *Feminist Legal Studies* 333–334.

changing reproductive science, regulation is still based on now out dated Warnock recommendations which so heavily influenced the HFE Act 1990.

Despite such criticisms, it was clear in retaining the regulatory architecture and updating the law by amending and inserting provisions, the government favoured retention of specialist regulation of fertility treatment via statute with oversight by the HFEA. The government justified its preference for specialist regulation as follows:

> The HFE Act [1990] was drawn up on the basis that certain activities involving human embryos outside the body, or the use of stored or donated gametes, demanded active regulation and definite legal limits. Ultimately, the Government believes that the force of law remains justified in the distribution of permissions, rights, responsibilities and prohibitions for the development and use of human reproductive technologies. Law and active regulation are necessary to set out and monitor a system of public oversight and accountability, taking account of the principles of good regulation.[69]

The government did not did not believe that a deregulated framework could achieve these objectives and rejected a framework of self- or permissive regulation, with the Government stating; 'Such a framework would introduce a lack of accountability'.[70] ARTs were to remain subject to specialist statutory regulation. The UK is not alone in imposing specialist regulation of this area,[71] as Lee and Morgan noted:

> Most states have on examination, concluded that some form of regulatory control (usually through specially framed and implemented legislation) is preferable to no regulation, although the nature of that regulation and review differs markedly.[72]

However, regulation in this contentious area is fraught with difficulty and the task of negotiating the boundaries between science and society is a precarious balancing act. On the one hand, there is the natural desire to encourage innovative research, which may relieve infertility, whilst on the other, the need to regulate science so as to minimise harms and ensure accountability so as to allay public fears. In regulating this

---

[69] DoH, Impact Assessment on the Human Fertilisation and Embryology Bill (2008) paragraph 7.

[70] Government Response to the Report from the Joint Committee on the Human Tissue and Embryos (Draft) Bill, (Cm 7209) paragraph 8.

[71] Praig and Mills, 'Assisted Reproductive Technology in Europe'.

[72] R. Lee and D. Morgan, *Human Fertilisation and Embryology: Regulating the Reproductive Revolution* (London: Blackstone Press, 2001) at p. 12.

contentious area, the government has had to grapple with these opposing considerations:

> [The] law must adequately reflect two competing (and often conflicting) public policy considerations: on the one hand it must facilitate research in view of the gains in knowledge that may be made in the fields of medical/ biological science and the improvements this may promise for human health; whilst on the other it must repress such research as is regarded as unacceptable, primarily due to doubts about its ethical justifiability.[73]

Maintaining this balance is imperative if the UK is to continue in the tradition of innovation in the field of assisted reproduction and research involving human embryos. The regulatory framework may be perceived to have struck an appropriate balance, since 'the UK has an unrivalled position in the world for scientific research and innovation'.[74] Scientists in the UK continue to lead the way internationally on many developments: the UK was the first country to license groundbreaking mitochondrial donation techniques allowing women who carry the risk of serious mitochondrial disease to avoid passing it onto their children. Mitochondrial diseases are often fatal or life limiting, and until recently there were no treatment options available that allowed such women to have a genetically related child free from the risk of transmission.[75] Research has also been undertaken in genome editing to study gene function in human embryos for the first time.[76] The HFEA claims these groundbreaking developments have happened because of regulation, not in spite of it:

> The Human Fertilisation and Embryology Acts 1990 and 2008 and the HFEA have provided a stable, yet flexible, framework in which UK bioscience and clinical expertise have been able to flourish. Scientists and clinicians have been able to go about their work free of the 'culture wars'

[73] R. Brownsword, 'Regulating Human Genetics: New Dilemmas for a New Millennium' (2004) 12(1) *Medical Law Review* 14–39.

[74] Better Regulation Commission, News, 'Scientific Research: Innovation with Controls' 15 January 2003.

[75] On mitochondrial donation note The Human Fertilisation and Embryology (Mitochondrial Donation) Regulations 2015 came into force on 29 October 2015. For articles on mitochondria see also R. J. Castro, 'Mitochondrial Replacement Therapy: The UK and US regulatory landscapes' (2016) 3(3) *Journal of Law and Biosciences* 726–735 and D. Griffiths, 'The (Re) Production of the Genetically Related Body in Law, Technology and Culture: Mitochondria Replacement Therapy' (2016) 3 *Healthcare Analysis* 196–209.

[76] Johnston, '"Gene-Editing Breakthrough Could Transform Understanding of Human Biology" says scientists', *The Independent*, 20 September 2017.

that have hampered such activity in the USA or the regulatory free-for-all of much of the Far East.[77]

Thus, the justification for regulation of fertility treatment and embryological concern was to allay public concern and to provide a comprehensive regulatory framework, which would ensure accountability and compliance with standards from those working in the field. It is clear that as we enter into 'the third era'[78] of human reproduction, ARTs will continue to be subject to statutory regulation. So long as the framework remains connected to modern science, statutory regulation can be regarded as a good thing: clear advantages of such a framework include the reassurance to the public offered by comprehensive statutory regulation, which has played a role in allaying public concerns surrounding uncertainty around new treatments. Scientific progress has flourished within certain constraints, clinicians working within the controversial realm are protected against claims of unethical behaviour and patients may be regarded as better protected than they would without such regulation.[79]

1.3   Regulation of Assisted Reproduction: The Present

The present regulatory framework is thus made up by legislation found in the HFE Act 1990 (as amended by the HFE Act 2008). It is important to now examine the operation of the regulatory framework in more detail, in order to ascertain in later chapters whether the framework in place is equipped to accommodate the challenges that third wave reproductive technologies, such as uterus transplantation and ectogenesis, will raise.

The Human Fertilisation and Embryology Authority (HFEA)

As noted above, the HFE Act 1990 established the HFEA in 1991, as an executive, non-departmental public body, to oversee regulation in the area of reproductive technologies.[80] Described as representing 'a milestone in biomedical regulation',[81] the HFEA is responsible for licensing and monitoring centres carrying out IVF, donor insemination and

---

[77] HFEA 'Innovation in Regulation' 2017, p. 2.

[78] S. Welin, 'Reproductive Ectogenesis: The Third Era of Human Reproduction and Some Moral Consequences' (2004) 10 *Science and Engineering Ethics* 615–626.

[79] See V. English, 'Autonomy versus Protection – Who Benefits from the Regulation of IVF?' (2006) 21 (12) *Human Reproduction* 3044–3049.

[80] HFE Act 1990, s5.

[81] J. Montgomery, 'Rights, Restraints and Pragmatism: The Human Fertilisation and Embryology Act 1990' (1991) 54 *Modern Law Review* 524–534, at p. 524.

human embryo research and providing a range of detailed information for patients, professionals and government.[82] The HFEA website describes itself as 'a world-class expert organisation in the fertility sector, we were the first statutory body of our type in the world'.[83] The HFEA's responsibilities can be divided into two categories: the 'narrow' regulatory role, namely licensing and inspection of clinics offering fertility treatment and embryonic research: and the 'broader regulatory role' which involves the formation of policy in this area though its involvement in consultation exercises and policy statements.[84] This dual role has led some to criticise HFEA as having a rather 'confused brief'.[85] An examination into how effectively HFEA has discharged these duties necessitates a detailed examination of these roles and also a brief description of the composition of HFEA.

The HFEA is made up of members 'with a range of professional, scientific and clinical expertise together with a lay chair and an overall lay majority membership'.[86] HFEA Members are appointed by NHS Appointments Commission and membership of the HFEA is set out in Schedule 1 of the HFE Act 1990. The HFE Act 2008 maintained the general structure of HFEA but clarifies the rules on the criteria that will disqualify a person from becoming a HFEA member and tenure of office.[87] To ensure that the HFEA has an objective and independent view, the HFE Act 1990 requires that the Chair, Deputy Chair and at least half of the HFEA members are neither doctors nor scientists involved in human embryonic research or the provision of fertility treatment.[88] The Warnock Committee recognised that the regulatory body would need access to scientific and medical expertise and that there should be 'significant' representation from these areas; but it was made clear that:

---

[82] DoH, Impact Assessment on the Human Fertilisation and Embryology Bill (2008), paragraphs 14 and 15.

[83] www.hfea.gov.uk/about-us

[84] Ibid.

[85] A. Dawson, 'The Human Fertilisation and Embryology Authority: Evidence Based Policy Formation in a Contested Context' (2004) 1(1) Health Care Analysis 1–6, at p. 2.

[86] DoH, Human Reproductive Technologies and the Law: Government Response to the Report from the House of Commons Science and Technology Committee, 2005, (Cm 6641), paragraph 72.

[87] HFE Act 2008 s5 and schedule 1.

[88] The number of HFEA members is not specified in the statute, but in practice there have been around twenty and at present there are nineteen. www.hfea.gov.uk.

it is not exclusively, or even primarily, a medical or scientific body. It is concerned essentially with broader matters and the protection of the public interest.[89]

Consequently, the Warnock Report recommended that there should be 'substantial' lay membership and that the chair be a lay member.[90] Whilst the 2004 Select Committee on Science and Technology Committee expressed widespread concerns about the extent of the scientific and clinical expertise of HFEA members, it recognised that the principle of the lay majority is important and should not easily be discarded stating:

We believe that ultimate authority on issues of public concern should lie outside of the scientific and medical communities. At the same time, it is important that any decisions are informed by the science and medicine.[91]

It was believed this would ensure sufficient neutrality in discharging the HFEA's regulatory functions. How effectively HFEA has discharged its regulatory role now merits consideration. The 2008 Act retained HFEA as the statutory authority with oversight of licensing and regulation, but made the following changes to aid the Authority in its ability to discharge its functions effectively, efficiently and economically:[92] it gave due regard to principles of best regulatory practice, including principles of transparency, accountability, proportionality and consistency;[93] it provided for the creation of agency arrangements;[94] the contracting out of some Authority functions;[95] and the power to delegate functions to committees, members or staff.[96] Fenton et al. suggest that 'the new requirements and powers of delegation are a response to the Authority's past failure to manage its significant work-load and an attempt to address some of the underlying problems within the HFEA'.[97]

[89] The Warnock Report, paragraph 248.
[90] Ibid.
[91] HCSTC, Human Reproductive Technologies and the Law, Fifth Report of Session 2004–5, Volume I (HC 7-I), paragraph 198.
[92] HFE Act 2008, section 8ZA (1).
[93] HFE Act 2008, section 8ZA (2).
[94] HFE Act, 2008, section 8B.
[95] HFE Act 2008, section 8C.
[96] HFE Act 2008, section 9A.
[97] Fenton, Heenan and Rees, 'Finally Fit for Purpose? The Human Fertilization and Embryology Act 2008', at p. 276.

1.3.1   The HFEA's Narrow Regulatory Role: Licensing and Inspection

The 'narrow' regulatory role of HFEA, namely the licensing and inspection of clinics, has been deemed to be one of the HFEA's 'most important purposes'.[98] It was thought that patient safety in this contentious area would be best achieved through the licensing and corresponding inspection of clinics. The HFEA has described the licensing process as one of its 'regulatory priorities' in 'ensuring patient safety and promoting the highest standards of clinical care and effectiveness by making sure clinics comply with the HFE Act'.[99] Licences can be granted for the purpose of fertility treatment, for storage and for research.[100] Licence Committees of the HFEA are dubbed 'the gatekeepers for all licensed activities in this field'.[101]

In assessing whether the regulatory framework could effectively regulate the 'third frontier' reproductive technologies, such as ectogenesis and uterus transplantation, it is important to consider how the HFEA discharges this narrow regulatory role. If a fertility clinic wished to research a new reproductive technology, the first step would be to obtain a licence from the HFEA. The clinic would apply for a licence, which will be considered by the HFEA Licence Committee.[102] Whilst the HFE Act 1990 provided that only HFEA members can sit on Licence Committees, the HFE Act 2008 amended this and now provides the HFEA with the power to 'delegate a function to a committee, to a member of the HFEA, or to staff' and to 'establish such committees or sub-committees as it thinks fit'.[103] The benefits of this amendment were stated as follows:

> these new provisions will enable the HFEA to delegate any function, apart from those which can only be exercised by members, to its staff or to a committee. These functions can include licence decisions and development of the Code of Practice. This gives the HFEA the ability to streamline licensing, benefiting licence applicants.[104]

---

[98]   E. Jackson, *Medical Law* (Oxford: Oxford University Press, 2016), Fourth Edition.

[99]   www.hfea.gov.uk/en/1181.html#1.

[100]   Note that following amendments made to the 1990 Act by the Human Fertilisation and Embryology (Quality and Safety) Regulations (SI 2007/1522) implementing the European Union Tissue and Cells Directive, a licence is now also required under the 1990 Act in respect of non-medical fertility services. Non-medical fertility services are defined as any services that are provided, in the course of a business, for the purpose of assisting women to carry children, but which are not medical, surgical or obstetric services. For example internet-based businesses that arrange for donated sperm to be delivered to women at home for self-insemination.

[101]   Human Fertilisation and Embryology Authority website www.hfea.gov.uk.

[102]   See previous note.

[103]   HFE Act 2008, s10.

[104]   Department of Health, Impact Assessment on the Human Fertilisation and Embryology Bill (2008), paragraph 70.

Irrespective of whether the Licence Committee's functions were delegated to a sub-committee made up of non-HFEA members, a decision about licensing particular treatments or research would still have to be made within the framework set out in the legislation. Thus, if an application were made to permit research into complete ectogenesis, for instance, whereby an embryo is taken from fertilisation and placed in an ectogenic incubator to see how long it can artificially gestate, no Licence Committee (irrespective of whether it is composed of HFEA or non HFEA members) could grant this licence, since it would contravene the provisions of both the HFE Act 1990 and HFE Act 2008, both of which provide embryonic research beyond the development of the primitive streak is prohibited.[105]

Providing an application falls within the parameters permitted by legislation, the conditions on which licences are awarded and the inspection process can be found in sections 11–21 of the HFE Act 1990 (as amended). Activities governed and limited by licences are outlined in depth in Schedule 2. Failure to obtain a licence before carrying out any of these activities is a criminal offence, punishable by up to ten years imprisonment or a fine or both.[106]

In addition to controlling the activities of licensed clinics, as part of its narrow regulatory role, the HFEA collects and maintains a formal register of information about research projects, donors, treatments and children born as a result of treatment. Information about the progress of research projects and about the incidence and outcomes of fertility must be published by the HFEA in its Annual Reports. At the time of writing there are 132 active clinics and research establishments and this includes both public sector and private sector work.[107]

How Well Has HFEA Discharged Its Functions?

Serious and systemic failings in ensuring compliance with licensing requirements both pre and post the HFE Act 2008 have resulted in much criticism being levied against the HFEA. Prior to the 2008 amendments, vulnerabilities within the HFEAs inspection processes were

---

[105] HFE Act 1990, s3(3): A licence cannot authorise – (a) keeping or using an embryo after the appearance of the primitive streak. S3(4) provides: For the purposes of subsection (3)(a) above, the primitive streak is to be taken to have appeared in an embryo not later than the end of the period of 14 days beginning with the day when the gametes are mixed, not counting any time during which the embryo is stored. The Human Fertilisation and Embryology Act 2008, s3(2) prohibits the placing in any woman of any embryo other than a permitted embryo or any gametes other than permitted eggs or permitted sperm and s4A applies this 14-day rule to human admixed embryos.

[106] HFE Act 1990, s41.

[107] HFEA Code of Practice Update, April 2017.

revealed in 2002 when the Toft Report was commissioned to investigate the circumstances surrounding four adverse events that had occurred in the Reproductive Medicine Units at the Leeds Teaching Hospitals NHS Trust, West Yorkshire.[108] This involved reports of an IVF mix-up that led to mixed-race twins being born to a white couple;[109] the wrong sperm being injected into eggs, the destruction of six embryos against a patient's wishes and the failure of a freezer in which seven embryos were being cryopreserved.[110] The Toft Report concluded that these adverse events were caused by a mixture of human error, systems failure and several problems with the inspection process, in particular the role of the HFEA executive and the training of inspectors.[111] When the Toft Report was published in June 2004 with a series of recommendations to improve the licensing procedure, the HFEA declared that it was already complying with 85 per cent of the Toft Report recommendations.[112] Despite the recommendation that 'an external body should look at the recommendations of any inquiry and make sure they are implemented in full or at least an explanation is given as to why they have not been implemented in full', the Department of Health decided that it alone would monitor progress. The House of Commons Select Committee criticised this 'casual approach' to ensuring that 'vulnerabilities' in the inspection process are eliminated.[113] In 2005, the British Fertility Society criticised the licensing and inspection process as being an overly bureaucratic, top heavy and a time-consuming process.[114]

It was hoped that amendments made by section 10 of the HFE Act 2008 which provide the HFEA with the power to delegate some of it licensing responsibilities might address some of these criticisms. In July 2014, the HFEA published its first report into adverse incidents

---

[108] Professor Brian Toft, 'Independent review of the circumstances surrounding four adverse events that occurred in the Reproductive Medicine Units at The Leeds Teaching Hospitals NHS Trust, West Yorkshire' (hereafter referred to as the 'Toft Report').

[109] See *Leeds Teaching Hospital NHS Trust* v. *A and others* [2003] EWHC 259. See also J. Miola 'Mix-Ups, Mistake and Moral Judgment' (2004) 12(1) *Feminist Legal Studies* 67–77.

[110] DoH, Independent review of the circumstances surrounding four adverse events that occurred in the Reproductive Medicine Units at The Leeds Teaching Hospitals NHS Trust, (West Yorkshire, 2004) paragraph 1.

[111] Toft Report.

[112] House of Commons Science and Technology Committee Human Reproductive Technologies and the Law, Fifth Report of Session 2004–05, Volume I (HC 7-I), paragraph 232.

[113] Ibid.

[114] Ibid., paragraph 233.

at fertility clinics. The HFEA stated the report (which covered the 2010–12 period) 'was intended to encourage a culture of openness and information sharing where clinic staff are empowered to report mistakes and learn from each other'.[115] The HFEA estimated that 1 per cent of the 60,000 cycles of IVF treatment that are carried out in the UK each year are affected by some sort of adverse incident.[116] Of the 465 reported incidents in the two-year period under review, the three categories with the most incidents were clinical (212), errors in the laboratory (114) and administration errors. There were a further 37 incidents falling into none of those categories.[117]

An example of the aforementioned administration errors and the gravity of the repercussions are illustrated in the case of *Re Human Fertilisation and Embryology Act 2008 (Cases A, B, C, D, E, F, G and H)* [2015],[118] described by the President of the Family Division, Munby J as a judgment 'that relates to a number of cases where much joy but also, sadly, much misery has been caused by the medical brilliance, unhappily allied with the administrative incompetence, of various fertility clinics'.[119] In order for the partner of a woman receiving treatment to acquire legal parenthood, both the woman and her partner must give consent in writing before the treatment and both must be given adequate information and offered counselling.[120] The applicants in the case were parents of children conceived following fertility treatment at various clinics. Each applicant had, at the time of the birth of their child, understood that they were the legal parent of their child, having complied with the legal requirements to acquire parenthood. Following a requirement from HFEA licensed fertility clinics to carry out an audit of their records of patients who were not married/in a civil partnership and who had received treatment, it became apparent that, due to the administrative incompetence of the clinics, the applicants did not have legal parenthood. Munby P. remedied the position by granting declarations of parentage in accordance with s55A of the Family Law Act 1996. The errors had become apparent after the HFEA had requested the audit following the case of *Re E & F (children) (assisted reproduction: parent)* [2013][121] which

---

[115] The Human Fertilisation & Embryology Authority "Adverse incidents in fertility clinics: lessons to learn January–December 2014" http://ifqtesting.blob.core.windows.net /umbraco-website/1146/incidents_report_2014_designed_-_web_final.pdf

[116] Ibid., p. 4.

[117] Ibid., p. 6.

[118] Re Human Fertilisation and Embryology Act 2008 (Cases A, B, C, D, E, F, G and H) [2015] EWHC 2602 (Fam) [2015] All ER (D) 57 (Sep).

[119] Ibid., paragraph 1.

[120] HFE Act 2008, sections 33–58.

[121] Re E & F (children) (assisted reproduction: parent) [2013] EWHC 1418 (Fam) [2013] All ER (D) 279 (Jun).

highlighted administrative shortcomings in fertility clinics, when it transpired in the case that the female partner of the mother, who had conceived as a result of treatment at a fertility clinic, was not the second legal parent, because the requisite consents had not been in place before the gamete transfer. The outcome of the HFEA audit was the finding that 51 of the 109 clinics had 'anomalies' in their records. The President of the Family Division, Munby J stated in *Re Human Fertilisation and Embryology Act 2008 (Cases A, B, C, D, E, F, G and H)* [2015],[122] that he feared the cases before him were 'only the small tip of a much larger problem'.[123]

There have since been a further 13 judgments concerning 34 cases. In *Human Fertilisation and Embryology Act (Cases AD, AE, AF, AG and AH – No 2)* [2017] EWHC 1782 (Fam),[124] Munby J provided guidance in cases involving applications for declarations of parentage in accordance with section 55A of the Family Law Act 1986, where children had been born following donor insemination, but statutory requirements had not been complied with. It was specifically considered whether the process for such applications could be streamlined and simplified in undisputed cases.[125] As Munby J noted, these errors were serious, since they impacted on the fundamental issue of legal parenthood:

> The question of who, in law, is or are the parent(s) of a child born as a result of treatment carried out under this legislation [Human Fertilisation and Embryology Act] ... is, as a moment's reflection will make obvious, a question of the most fundamental gravity and importance. What, after all, to any child, to any parent, never mind to future generations and indeed to society at large, can be more important, emotionally, psychologically, socially and legally, than the answer to the question: Who is my parent? Is this my child?[126]

---

[122] Re Human Fertilisation and Embryology Act 2008 (Cases A, B, C, D, E, F, G and H) [2015] EWHC 2602 (Fam), [2015] All ER (D) 57 (Sep)

[123] Ibid., paragraph 1.

[124] Human Fertilisation and Embryology Act (Cases AD, AE, AF, AG and AH – No 2) [2017] EWHC 1782 (Fam).

[125] Sir James Munby held that (i) however straightforward the case may be, either the applicant or the respondent must be entitled to an oral final hearing if requested; (ii) if it is desired to persuade the court to dispense with an oral final hearing, that must be clearly stated, with the reasons set out, in the evidence or submissions filed; (iii) the evidence or submissions must identify the relevant documents on which it is said the case turns, specify precisely the problem(s) which arise on the documents and identify precisely, with specific references, the authorities relied on in support of the contention that, despite the identified problem(s), the applicant is entitled to the declaration sought.

[126] Re Human Fertilisation and Embryology Act 2008 (Cases A, B, C, D, E, F, G and H) [2015], paragraph 3.

Munby J stated that these cases and the errors therein raised questions 'as to the extent of the regulatory powers of the HFEA in allowing such administrative incompetence to exist'.[127] In light of the aforementioned cases, Munby J has spoken of 'widespread incompetence' in the fertility sector and has questioned the adequacy of the regulatory framework:

> The picture revealed one of what I do not shrink from describing as widespread incompetence across the sector on a scale which must raise questions as to the adequacy if not of the HFEA's regulation then of the extent of its regulatory power. That the incompetence to which I refer is, as I have already indicated, administrative rather than medical is only slight consolation, given the profound implications of the parenthood which in far too many cases has been thrown into doubt.[128]

It is likely there are more couples whose parental legal status may now be in doubt because of such administrative errors. Unsurprisingly, it has been suggested that reform is needed to avoid a repeat of such errors and more effective linking of the registration systems of the HFEA and the three UK General Register Offices.[129]

1.3.2 The HFEA's Broad Regulatory Role: Formulation of Policy

In addition to the HFEA's statutory role in acting as a licensing authority for clinics, the regulatory body is also charged with the 'broader regulatory role' of policy formation and what Pattison has described as the 'the unenviable task of regulating some of the most ethically controversial technologies of the present age'.[130] As Jackson cogently notes:

> Whilst the narrow function might be relatively straightforward, policing the ethical acceptability of reproductive technologies has proven to be a far more divisive and difficult task.[131]

Jackson goes on to state that the reason the government invests HFEA with such discretion in formulating policy is because:

---

[127] K. Gibson, 'Fertile Ground' (2015) 165(7676) *New Law Journal* 9.

[128] Re Human Fertilisation and Embryology Act 2008 (Cases A, B, C, D, E, F, G and H) [2015], paragraph 8.

[129] M. Crawshaw, E. Blyth and J. Feast, 'Can the UK's Birth Registration System Better Serve the Interests of Those Born Following Collaborative Assisted Reproduction?' (2017) 4 *Reproductive BioMedicine and Society Online* 1–4.

[130] S. Pattison, 'Some Problems Challenging the UK's Human Fertilisation and Embryology Authority' (2005) 24(2) *Medicine & Law* 391–401, at p. 399.

[131] E. Jackson, *Regulating Reproduction: Law, Technology and Autonomy* (Oxford: Hart Publishing, 2001), p. 184.

the pace of change is so rapid in this area of medicine that the alternative of requiring the production of new legislation in light of each development would be inefficient, to say the least. Another reason of course is so the government can keep its hands clean of these ethical issues.[132]

The policy formation role is not defined, but stems from section 8 of the HFE Act 1990 which mandates the HFEA to:

> keep under review information about embryos and any subsequent development of embryos and about the provision of treatment services and activities governed by this Act, and advise the Secretary of State, if he asks it to do so, about those matters.[133]

An Annual Report must be produced to the Secretary of State for Health, describing the activities it has undertaken in the past twelve months, and its work programme for the following year.[134] A Minister then puts these Reports before Parliament. Policy decisions are communicated through a Code of Practice, which the HFEA must maintain.[135] The Code of Practice is reviewed twice a year to ensure it is still relevant to the fertility sector. The legal status of the Code of Practice, as Jackson notes is 'a little unclear';[136] while in theory it is not legally binding, a Licence Committee may take into account when deciding whether to vary or revoke a licence if there has been a failure to observe its provisions. At the time of writing the Code of Practice is in its eighth edition.[137] The Code of Practice allows for a degree of flexibility, and, as noted by Jackson, 'there are obvious advantages in using a regulatory updated Code of Practice, rather than primary legislation, to regulate such a fast moving area of clinical practice and research'.[138]

The HFEA has acknowledged 'the area of science and medicine regulated by the HFEA is fast-paced and can be controversial'[139] and that because of its involvement in licensing and policy development, HFEA needs to be aware of new developments.[140] In theory, the HFEA has the mechanisms in place to assist it keep abreast of developments so as not to be caught 'off guard' and to enable it to meet the challenges raised by

---

[132] Ibid., p. 3.
[133] HFE Act 1990, s8.
[134] HFE Act 1990, s7.
[135] HFE Act 1990, s25(1).
[136] Jackson, Medical Law.
[137] First published October 2009 and last revised in 2017. Accessible via www.hfea.gov.uk.
[138] Jackson, Medical Law.
[139] Human Fertilisation & Embryology Authority, Scientific The HSP Scanning at the HFEA, Annual Report 2006, paragraph 2.2.
[140] S. Leather, Minutes of the second meeting of the HFEA Horizon Scanning Expert Panel held on 19 June 2005 in Copenhagen, paragraph 1.2.

novel reproductive technologies. The HFEA set up an Ethics and Law Advisory Group (ELAG), which meets four times a year to review social, ethical and legal issues arising from, or affecting, activities in which the HFEA has an interest.

HFEA also set up a Horizon Scanning Panel (HSP), first introduced in 2004 to act as an early warning system, identifying new scientific and clinical developments that may have an impact on the field of assisted reproduction or embryo research. This allows the HFEA to consider the legal, ethical and scientific implications of any new technique that scientists or clinicians may wish to use in HFEA-licensed research or treatment. Issues that may affect assisted reproduction or embryo research are identified throughout the year by both the HSP members (made up of an international panel of experts)[141] and by the HFEA's policy team, gathering information, by the policy team attending conferences and monitoring journals. The issues are then discussed at the Horizon Scanning Panel's annual meeting. Issues are prioritised by examining whether: the technique is transferrable to humans for research or treatment; the diffusion of the technique is likely to be rapid; there will be public interest or concern; there will be ethical or legal considerations and whether the technique is within the remit of the HFEA. The HFEA's Scientific and Clinical Advances Advisory Committee (SCAAC) and other appropriate HFEA committees then consider these prioritised issues in depth. This may lead to the issue being referred to the HFEA to decide on a policy review, on a new position, or new guidance for clinics and researchers. The HSP published an annual report of its horizon scanning activities up until 2009–10 but then stopped to reduce costs. Interestingly, one of the recommendations of the 2017 triennial report of HFEA[142] was that the HFEA publishes on its website an update on horizon scanning issues, noting, 'it would be valuable and transparent'.[143]

The Government and the Select Committee on Science and Technology in 2004[144] welcomed the creation of the HSP, stating that the HSP would allow HFEA to 'make use of the best available data to

---

[141] The current memberships can be found on the HFEA website.

[142] The Department of Health reviews its arm's length bodies once every three years. The 2017 triennial review looked at the form, functions, governance and performance of the HFEA.

[143] Department of Health, Triennial Review of the Human Fertilisation and Embryology Authority Review Report published March 2017, Recommendation 9, paragraph 4.42.

[144] HCSTC, Human Reproductive Technologies and the Law, Fifth Report of Session 2004–05, Volume I (HC 7-I) paragraph 277.

support its decision-making'.[145] The importance of being equipped to deal with those reproductive advances looming ahead was explicitly recognised by the HFEA, who commented that whilst the majority of the techniques discussed by the HSP:

> are a long way off from being offered to clinics . . . it is useful for the HFEA to be aware of them so that, as far as possible, we have time to consider the legal, ethical and scientific implications of the use of these techniques, prior to an application being received by a licence committee for their use in research or treatment. In addition, when/if the techniques ever become available this process will allow us to ensure that patients are suitably informed and that we have guidance in place so that new treatments are carried out in a safe and appropriate way.[146]

In the previous HSP meetings, topics discussed have ranged from in vitro-derived gametes, human admixed (hybrid) embryos, testicular stem cells, and oocyte and tissue freezing. How effective the HSP is in practice depends on its ability and willingness to deal with controversial advances looming on the horizon, despite the public unease they may generate. As highlighted in the 2017 triennial review of the HFEA, the importance of horizon scanning function of HFEA is clear:

> Some of the activity regulated by the HFEA is at the cutting edge of medical science. If the regulatory framework is to remain relevant, carefully balancing wider ethical and moral views with appropriate support for new innovations, then the HFEA must remain on top of new developments.[147]

Public Opinion

When formulating policy the HFEA has often consulted the public in its 'requirement to balance wider public ethical and moral concerns with the ever-changing scientific landscape of what is possible to achieve'.[148] Novel reproductive advances often bring about public unease, especially if society regards reproductive technologies to be ahead of public debate of the legal, ethical and social issues involved. Part of the HFEA's role is to both reassure the public in its concern that science is not outpacing ethics

---

[145] DoH, Human Reproductive Technologies and the Law: Government Response to the Report from the House of Commons Science and Technology Committee, 2005, (Cm 6641), paragraph 88.

[146] HFEA website: www.hfea.gov.uk/en/1632.html.

[147] DoH, Triennial Review of the Human Fertilisation and Embryology Authority Review Report published March 2017, paragraph 4.40.

[148] Ibid., paragraph 4.45.

but also to ensure that scientific advances are not unduly impeded by ill-informed or speculative fears or religious doctrine.[149] This is further compounded by the fact that beginning of life issues, from the earliest stages of embryonic development and conception through to birth, often elicit strong sentiments, upon which there is much disagreement about what should and should not be done. Drafting law and policy on such controversial matters such as embryonic research, fertility treatment and abortion – topics on which there is no moral consensus – presents one of the most difficult challenges for the government; and yet govern they must. The Joint Scrutiny Committee conceded: 'legislation in an area such as this needs a sufficient level of support from the public and this requires a corresponding understanding of public attitudes'.[150] Effective regulation in this domain needs to be responsive and to consider how it can engage informed public opinion.

In formulating policy, many attempts have been made to engage and measure public opinion. For instance, the HFEA undertook a public consultation in 2002 on sex selection.[151] Until the HFE Act 1990 was amended in 2008, non-medical sex selection of an embryo was not statutorily regulated, but the policy of the HFEA was that such selection should not occur. However, one of the amendments made by the HFE Act 2008 was to render it a criminal offence to select an embryo on the basis of its sex for non-medical reasons. On using public opinion as the foundation of regulation, Harris expressed scepticism, stating that that we have:

> Some reason to be cautious about claims to the effect that forms of public consultation have revealed the moral attitudes or values of the public, and that these must both be respected and inform public decision-making. If what is informing public decision-making is a collection of recorded prejudices or evidence of slavish and uncritical adherence to a sectarian normative system, then perhaps the respectability, if not the authenticity,

---

[149] Deech, 'The HFEA – 10 Years On', p. 21.

[150] Joint Committee on the Human Tissue and Embryos (Draft) Bill, chapter 3.

[151] Human Fertilisation and Embryology Authority (2003) Sex Selection: Options for Regulation. A Report on the HFEA's 2002–2003 Review of Sex Selection Including Discussion of Legislative and Regulatory Options. HFEA, London. For criticism on the report see J. Harris, 'Sex Selection: Options for Regulation – A Critique' (2003) Journal of Medical Ethics, Current Controversies, 3 December 2003. J. Harris, 'No Sex Selection Please, We're British!' (2004) 31 *Journal of Medical Ethics* 286. S. Holm, 'Like a Frog in Boiling Water: The Public, the HFEA and Sex Selection' 12(1) (2004) *Health Care Analysis* 27–39.

of the voice of the people requires challenge rather than faithful reporting and incorporation into the decision-making process.[152]

Exploring the role that public consultations have and should play in ethico-legal decision-making, Fovargue and Bennett similarly note:

> If we rely on public opinion in policy making then we must accept that many of those who respond to public consultations are likely to provide an intuitive 'gut' reaction to the issue. Such reactions may be based on false information, prejudice and/or fear. They may also be inconsistent with some of their other views and, therefore, difficult to defend or justify.[153]

Similarly, the 2017 HFEA triennial review acknowledged that, whilst HFEA has a vital role in supporting informed debate and ensuring that the regulatory framework is informed by all relevant factors, the danger with the public consultation processes and placing too much reliance on the outcome is 'that the respondents are usually those who have a particular interest in the topic. The vast majority of the public do not engage in such consultations.'[154] Whilst this is true of all issues, this is particularly so on an emotive topic such as ARTs. Allowing public opinion to influence subsequent HFEA policy presumes public opinion is informed, reliable and representative. If it is not, it is questionable whether it should be shaping policy. Regulation of ARTs operates in a social context where regulation is shaped by institutions, organisations and individuals in ways not envisaged when the 1990 legislation was initially drafted. Yet the extent to which these diverse bodies influence policy formation has been relatively neglected in legal and ethical discourse.[155] It is crucial that this is addressed if the HFEA is to

---

[152] J. Harris, 'Introduction: The Importance of Bioethics' in J. Harris (ed.), *Bioethics* (Oxford: Oxford University Press, 2001) 12.

[153] Although note the following paper: S. Fovargue and R. Bennett, 'What Role Should Public Opinion Play in Ethico-Legal Decision Making? The Example of Selecting Sex for Non-Medical Reasons Using Preimplantation Genetic Diagnosis' (2016) 24(1) *Medical Law Review 34*, at p. 55.

[154] DoH, Triennial Review of the Human Fertilisation and Embryology Authority Review Report (2017), paragraph 4.45.

[155] For instance key public interest groups, such as Comment on Reproductive Ethics (CORE) have influenced and shaped policy in the context of ARTs. CORE was founded in 1994 by Josephine Quintavalle and Margaret Nolan and is a Catholic pro-life public interest group that focuses on ethical dilemmas surrounding human reproduction, particularly the new technologies of assisted conception. CORE has brought numerous legal challenges and shaped the law regarding fertility treatment and embryo research – see for instance *R (Quintavalle)* v. *Secretary of State for Health* [2001] EWHC 918 (Admin), [2001] 4 All ER 1013. *R (Quintavalle)* v. *Human Fertilisation and*

adequately use public opinion when formulating policy. Attention must be paid to how the HFEA can enhance informed public debate, so that institutions, organisations and individuals can be engaged or consulted in a more informed manner. This is a vital step towards attaining effective, responsive and representative legislation in this contentious area.

How Has the HFEA Discharged This 'Broad Function'?

A Policy Debacle   The HFEA was set up to 'try and resolve moral and scientific problems within a principled framework'.[156] With regard to IVF, the way that the HFEA has discharged this function prior to the 2008 amendments, attracted much criticism and resulted in some commentators questioning whether the HFEA is the correct body to be making policy decisions on controversial ethical matters.[157] The manner in which HFEA has formulated policy has, in some instances, left much to be desired. For example, consider the use of artificial reproductive technologies to help couples procreate without the risk of transmitting a genetic disease to their children. IVF and Pre-Implantation Genetic Diagnosis (PGD) allow couples to create embryos and then screen out the ones affected by the relevant genetic disease, so only the healthy ones can be selected for implantation. The use of pre-implantation genetic diagnosis (PGD) in conjunction with Human Leukocyte Antigen (HLA tissue typing)[158] enables parents who already have a child affected by a fatally genetic disorder to have another baby whose stem cells, taken from the umbilical cord, can 'cure' the existing child, a so called 'saviour sibling'. PGD combined with HLA tissue typing for this purpose was 'very far from the artificial reproductive technology interventions which Parliament had in mind when it passed the

Embryology Authority [2002] EWCH 2785 (Admin), [2003] 2 All ER 105. *R (Quintavalle)* v. *Human Fertilisation and Embryology Authority (Secretary of State for Health Intervening)* [2003] EWCA Civ 667, [2003] 2 FLR 335. *Quintavalle* v. *Human Fertilisation and Embryology Authority* [2005] UKHL 28, [2005] 2 FLR 349. *R (Quintavalle)* v. *Human Fertilisation and Embryology Authority* [2008] EWHC 3395 Admin.

[156] J. Montgomery, 'The Legitimacy of Medical Law' in S. McLean (ed.), *First Do No Harm* (Aldershot: Ashgate, 2006) 1–16, at p. 13.

[157] From the corethics.org website: http://corethics.tiscali-business.it/document.asp?id=CPR.201202.htm&se=4&st=5.

[158] PGD screening embryos to detect for genetic defects and hereditary diseases, while HLA tissue typing would indicate which of the embryos would be a tissue match with a sibling.

legislation in 1990'.[159] As the legislative framework did not address this specific use of IVF it fell to the HFEA to develop policy on its permissibility and the HFEA struggled to deal adequately with the dilemma of saviour siblings. The objections raised against the use of this technology centred around three main arguments: (a) the claim that saviour siblings would be treated as commodities as simply a means to save the life of his or her sibling; (b) a slippery slope argument, which suggests that this practice will lead to the creation of so-called 'designer babies'; and (c) a child welfare argument, according to which saviour siblings will be physically and/or psychologically harmed.[160]

These arguments were unconvincing and initially the HFEA rightly granted a licence to allow embryos to be screened for this purpose under strict guidelines; in order to assist the Hashmi family select an embryo that would be a tissue match for their six-year-old son.[161] Their son Zain, was afflicted with the blood disorder, beta thalassaemia major. As his bone marrow did not produce enough red blood cells, he was often very ill and required daily drugs and regular blood transfusions to keep him alive. Their search for a suitable bone marrow donor had proved unsuccessful and none of Zain's three elder siblings had matching tissue. The Hashmis embarked on having a fifth child, but having later discovered from pre-natal testing that that child too would be afflicted with beta thalassaemia major, Mrs Hashmi terminated the pregnancy. Mrs Hashmi conceived again, and a healthy son was born, but his tissue also failed to match that of Zain. It was at this point, having exhausted all other options to find a cure for their son, that the Hashmis sought PGD and HLA tissue-typing. The initial licence granted to treat the Hashmis was made subject to conditions. Included among the conditions were the stipulations that the sick sibling's condition should be severe or life threatening, of a sufficient seriousness to justify the use of PGD; that the embryos should themselves be at risk of that condition; that all other possibilities of treatment and sources of tissue for the sick sibling should have been

---

[159] S. Leather, '"Saviour siblings transcripts" Progress Educational Trust Debate "Is It Right To Create a Tissue-donor Baby?"' Held on 16 October 2003. For more on PGD see R. Scott, 'Choosing between Possible Lives: Legal and Ethical Issues in PGD' (2006) 26 *Oxford Journal of Legal Studies* 153.

[160] S. Sheldon and S. Wilkinson, 'Should Selecting Saviour Siblings Be Banned?' (2004) 30 *Journal of Medical Ethics* 533–537.

[161] *Quintavalle* v. *Human Fertilisation and Embryology Authority* [2005] UKHL 28. For a commentary on the case see A. Alghrani, 'Case Commentary; "Suitable" to be a "Savior": *Quintavalle* v. *Human Fertilisation and Embryology Authority* [2005] UKHL 28' (2006) 18(2) Child and Family Law Quarterly 407–423.

explored; that the technique should not be available where the intended recipient is a parent; and that the intention should be to take only cord blood for the purposes of the treatment.[162]

While the conditions of the licence permitted the Hashmis to use tissue typing, the HFEA refused to allow tissue typing to another couple, Michelle and Jason Whitaker, who had hoped to undergo fertility treatment to try for a tissue-matched sibling for their son Charlie, who suffered from Diamond Blackfan Anaemia (DBA). Since neither parent appeared to be a carrier of the genetic mutation, it was thought that Charlie's condition was likely to be a sporadic case and thus it could not be argued that PGD was necessary to select embryos free from the condition.[163] The difference between the two cases was that, in the Whitakers' case, the DBA from which their child suffered was 'sporadic' rather than hereditary, which meant that the chances of them having another baby with the disease were no greater than those present in the general population. HLA tissue typing procedure would be performed solely to find a tissue match for their child and not in order to help the couple procreate with a child free from a genetic disorder. Therefore, the HFEA deemed that the Whitakers' case was relevantly different from the Hashmis' since, for the Hashmis, the procedure was in the interests of the new child as well as the interests of Zain.

This distinction was attacked as 'unjustifiable and misguided'[164] and the HFEA formulation of policy attracted much criticism for its inconsistency.[165] The initial policy, permitting tissue typing only where the embryo was also at risk of a genetic disease, lacked logic. Having the responsibility to regulate and monitor such developments, the HFEA may have been justified in formulating policy that permitted or denied the use of PGD and HLA tissue typing on safety grounds.[166] Yet this is

---

[162] As summed up by Lord Brown of Eaton-Under-Heywood, Quintavalle (HL), paragraph 45.

[163] The couple successfully obtained such treatment in Chicago and, in July 2003, Jamie Whitaker was born, a perfect tissue match for his sick brother Charlie and a successful cord cell transplant was subsequently carried out.

[164] S. Sheldon and S. Wilkinson, 'Hashmi and Whitaker: An Unjustifiable and Misguided Distinction?' (2004) 12 *Med L Rev* 137; C. Gavaghan, 'Designer Donors? Tissue Typing and the Regulation of Pre-implantation Genetic Diagnosis' [2004] 3 *Web Journal of Current Legal Issues*.

[165] S. Sheldon, 'Saviour Siblings and the Discretionary Power of the HFEA' (2005) 13 (3) *Medical Law Review* 403–411. S. Sheldon and S. Wilkinson, 'Hashmi and Whitaker: An Unjustifiable and Misguided Distinction?' (2004) 12 *Medical Law Review* 137; C. Gavaghan, 'Designer Donors? Tissue Typing and the Regulation of Pre-implantation Genetic Diagnosis' [2004] 3 *Web Journal of Current Legal Issues*.

not what occurred; instead, the HFEA stated that PGD was permissible dependent on the particular use of the procedure as opposed to the safety of it.[167] After a period of reflection, the HFEA modified its policy and, in June 2004, published new guidance that permitted PGD tissue typing solely to produce a tissue-matched baby. The reason given for this revision was that the HFEA had:

> now carefully reviewed the medical, psychological and emotional impli-
> cations for children and families as well as the safety of the technique.
> There have been three further years during which successful embryo
> biopsies have been carried out, both in the UK and abroad and we are
> not aware of any increased risk.[168]

Following the HFEA's change of policy, Joe and Julie Fletcher obtained permission to have tissue typing to conceive a child who would be able to provide their son, Joshua, who has DBA, with umbilical cord blood cells.[169] The HFEA also altered its position on the use of bone marrow rather than umbilical cord blood as a source of stem cells. The policy formulated by the HFEA in 2001 required a condition that 'the intention' should be only to take cord blood. After a review in 2004, the HFEA decided to delete this condition. Commenting on this policy change, pro-life campaigner, Josephine Quintavalle stated that HFEA had moved ethical goal posts without consulting or even informing the public, she stated:

> Bone marrow donation is invasive and can be painful and never more so
> than for a tiny baby, who derives no benefit from the procedure and is
> unable to give consent. The concept that a baby should be created with
> this specific purpose in mind goes beyond the comprehension of com-
> passionate and civilized citizens.[170]

The HFEA stated that the change in policy stemmed from an acknowledgment that the previous policy was in practice unenforceable, because once the embryo had been implanted and the child conceived, the case passed out of the jurisdiction of the HFEA. The HFEA further noted that,

---

[166] J. Tizzard, 'Saviour Siblings: A Child to Save a Child' (2004) Cardiff Centre for Ethics, Law and Society, www.ccels.cf.ac.uk/archives/issues/2004/tizzard.pdf.

[167] As above. This point has also been made by S. Sheldon and S. Wilkinson, 'Hashmi and Whitaker: An Unjustifiable and Misguided Distinction?' (2004) 12 *Medical Law Review* 137.

[168] See HFEA Press Release, 'HFEA Agrees to Extend Policy on Tissue Typing', 21 July 2004.

[169] Mrs Fletcher gave birth to a daughter, the first potential 'saviour sibling' conceived in the UK, on 14 July 2005.

[170] M. Henderson, 'Secret Ruling on "Designer Babies"' *The Times*, 7 March 2005.

under common law, the 'best interests' test applied by the courts when considering the type of medical procedures that may be performed on a child is much higher when such treatment gives no health benefit to the child concerned and, as such, solid organ donation is extremely unlikely to be held to be in a child's best interest. Arguably, the HFEA should have realised that donation of bone marrow from a baby would fall outside its remit in the first place.

Despite the manner in which the policy on PGD was developed, when the HFEA was challenged in *R (Quintavalle)* v. *Human Fertilisation and Embryology Authority*[171] as having strayed outside of its remit in licensing this procedure, the (then) House of Lords ruled that HFEA had not acted *ultra vires* and that it was the legislative intent that the HFEA would 'regulate and monitor practice in relation to those sensitive areas which raise fundamental ethical questions'.[172] The House of Lords ruled that HLA tissue typing was licensable under the HFE Act 1990 having regard to the background which preceded the statute, the legislative intent behind that Act and upon a construction of the statutory provisions contained therein. The HFEA had thus acted within its remit in licensing HLA tissue typing. The subsequent HFE Act 2008 amendments clarified the circumstances in which PGD and HLA tissue typing are legitimate, and provides that embryo testing is lawful:

> In a case where a person ('the sibling') who is the child of the persons whose gametes are used to bring about the creation of the embryo (or of either of those persons) suffers from a serious medical condition which could be treated by umbilical cord blood stem cells, bone marrow or other tissue of any resulting child, establishing whether the tissue of any resulting child would be compatible with that of the sibling.[173]

Whilst their Lordships in *Quintavalle* declined to criticise the way the HFEA had exercised its jurisdiction in forming policy, the House of Commons Science and Technology Committee,[174] regarded the

---

[171] *R (Quintavalle)* v. *Human Fertilisation and Embryology Authority* [2005] UKHL 28 (HL).

[172] Ibid., at paragraph 17 (quoting the Warnock Report, paragraph 13.3).

[173] HFE Act 2008, Schedule 2, 1ZA(1)(d). Paragraph 1ZA(4) provides that the reference to 'other tissue' in paragraph 1ZA(1)(d) does not include a whole organ. This provision ensures that tissue typing cannot be licensed if the match was to be carried out because the older sibling required a whole organ. For more on the changes see M. K. Smith, 'The Human Fertilisation and Embryology Act 2008: restrictions on the creation of "saviour siblings" and the relevance of the harm principle' (2013) 32(2) *New Genetics and Society* 154–170.

[174] HCSTC, Human Reproductive Technologies and the Law, Fifth Report of Session 2004–05, Vol I (HC 7-I) paragraph 251.

HFEA's development of policy as 'highly unsatisfactory'. The development of the policy also attracted academic criticism,[175] some noting that that the HFEA's 'conditions were arbitrary and ethically muddled'.[176] Notwithstanding these criticisms, without the ability to formulate policy, it is difficult to see how the HFEA could discharge its responsibilities adequately. As noted by the House of Commons Committee:

> The removal of the HFEA's policy function would mean that licence committees would be operating in a vacuum, forced to make decisions from first principles. This would be a lengthy process liable to result in different conclusions for similar cases. The HFE Act [1990] also demands that the HFEA provide advice to the Secretary of State on request. Once again it is difficult to see how this duty could be discharged without a reasoned discussion by the Authority based on a strong body of evidence leading to an agreed view, a process otherwise known as policy-making.[177]

The HFE Act 2008 provisions maintained HFEA's narrow and broad regulatory roles and the government has commended HFEA for their work in regulating this contentious area:

> The HFEA operates in a complex and contentious area, where it will often be criticised or challenged whatever decision or statement it makes. The Government's view is that the HFEA does a good job in these difficult circumstances.[178]

Post 2008, it may be considered that the HFEA has developed policy better: the policy on regulation of emerging novel mitochondrial replacement techniques (MRTs) to reduce the risk of transmitting mitochondrial disease to future children did not develop in the haphazard fashion that PGD and HLA tissue typing did. The use of MRTs in reproductive medicine had not been carried out anywhere in the world and in the UK was banned under the HFE Act 1990, which prohibited the modification

---

[175] See S. Sheldon and S. Wilkinson, 'Hashmi and Whitaker: An Unjustifiable and Misguided Distinction?' (2004) 12 *Medical Law Review* 137; C. Gavaghan, 'Designer Donors? Tissue Typing and the Regulation of Pre-implantation Genetic Diagnosis' [2004] 3 *Web Journal of Current Legal Issues*; J. Tizzard, 'Saviour Siblings: A Child to Save a Child' (2004) Cardiff Centre for Ethics, Law and Society.

[176] C. Gavaghan, 'Designer Donors? Tissue Typing and the Regulation of Pre-implantation Genetic Diagnosis' (2004) 3 *Web Journal of Current Legal Issues*, p. 28.

[177] HCSTC, Human Reproductive Technologies and the Law, Fifth Report of Session 2004–05, Vol I (HC 7-I).

[178] DoH, Human Reproductive Technologies and the Law: Government Response to the Report from the House of Commons Science and Technology Committee, 2005 (Cm 6641), paragraph 80.

of embryos (in the course of IVF treatment) with recognised germline effects. Mitochondria DNA (mtDNA) are present in almost all human cells providing the power that cells need to function. They contain a small amount of mtDNA that is inherited exclusively from the mother through the mitochondria present in her eggs. Unhealthy mitochondria can cause several disorders; the disease affects each sufferer differently and has a wide range of potential symptoms at varying levels of severity, including poor growth, loss of muscle co-ordination, muscle weakness, visual and hearing problems, learning disabilities, heart, liver and kidney disease. The disease can result in painful, debilitating and disabling suffering, long-term ill health and a consequent low quality of life. In its most severe form, a child born with the condition is likely to die at an early age. The UK Department of Health asserted that around 1 in 6500 children is thought to be born with a serious mitochondrial disorder due to faults in mitochondrial DNA.[179] Whilst there is no cure for mitochondrial disease and children affected often die in an agony that cannot be alleviated, advances in reproductive technology meant that there were several novel treatment methods with the potential to reduce the transmission of abnormal mtDNA from a mother to her child and thus avoid mitochondrial disease in the child and subsequent generations.[180]

There were ethical concerns surrounding the perceived tampering with human embryos and around germ line modification:[181] the ethics on first application in human use;[182] replacing unhealthy mtDNA with healthy

[179] A. M. Schaefer et al., 'Prevalence of Mitochondrial DNA Disease in Adults' (2008) 63 *Ann. Neurol* 35–39; C. Palacios-González and M. Medina-Arellano, 'Mitochondrial Replacement Techniques and Mexico's Rule of Law: On the Legality of the First Maternal Spindle Transfer Case' (2017) *Journal of Law and the Biosciences* 1–20. Castro, 'Mitochondrial Replacement Therapy: The UK and US Regulatory Landscapes'.

[180] H. J. Smeets et al., 'Preventing the Transmission of Mitochondrial DNA Disorders Using Prenatal or Preimplantation Genetic Diagnosis' (2015) 1350 *Annals of the New York Academy of Sciences* 29–36. A. Wrigley, S. Wilkinson and J. B. Appleby, 'Mitochondrial Replacement: Ethics and Identity' (2015) 29 *Bioethics* 631–638. M. Alikani, B. C. J. Fauser, J. A. Garcia-Valesco et al., 'First Birth Following Spindle Transfer for Mitochondrial Replacement Therapy: Hope and Trepidation' (2017) 34(4) *Reproductive BioMedicine Online* 333–336. C. Palacios-González and M. Medina-Arellano, 'Mitochondrial Replacement Techniques and Mexico's Rule of Law: On the Legality of the First Maternal Spindle Transfer Case' (2017) *Journal of Law and the Biosciences* 1–20.

[181] A. Newson and A. Wrigley, 'Is Mitochondrial Donation Germ-Line Gene Therapy? Classifications and Ethical Implications' (2016) 31(1) *Bioethics* 55–67. R. Scott and S. Wilkinson, 'Germline Genetic Modification and Identity: The Mitochondrial and Nuclear Genomes' (2017) *Oxford Journal of Legal Studies* (forthcoming).

[182] Nuffield Council on Bioethics, *Novel Techniques for the Prevention of Mitochondrial DNA Disorders: An Ethical Review* (London, 2012).

mtDNA from another donor meant the a child could be genetically related to three parents and consequently have a confused identity;[183] on trans-generational health risks – in that the knowledge regarding the safety of the treatment is uncertain and will remain so until several generations of people have been born from the procedure;[184] and lastly, concerns regarding the anonymity of the donor or 'third genetic parent'.[185]

The HFE Act 2008 amended the 1990 legislation to allow researchers to develop techniques to prevent transmission of maternally inherited mitochondrial disease; however, this was for research purposes only.[186] Following the development of mitochondrial donation techniques to prevent diseased mitochondria being passed on from mother to child by researchers in Newcastle in 2010, the HFEA convened an Expert Scientific Review panel to assess the effectiveness and safety of mitochondrial donation. The Expert Panel comprised of experts with broad ranging scientific and clinical expertise, which reviewed the science in April 2011, March 2013 and June 2014.[187] In its final report the Chair of the Expert Panel, Dr Andy Greenfield, stated: 'in three years study the expert panel has seen no evidence which suggests that these new mitochondrial replacement therapies are unsafe'.[188]

---

[183] A. Wrigley, S. Wilkinson and J. B. Appleby, 'Mitochondrial Replacement: Ethics and Identity' (2015) 29 *Bioethics* 631–638; S. Matthew Liao, 'Do Mitochondrial Replacement Techniques Affect Qualitative or Numerical Identity?' (2017) 31 *Bioethics* 20–26. Although note on this point that mitochondrial DNA accounts for a mere 0.054% of our overall DNA and it does not have any impact on the physical characteristics and personality traits of any resulting child, which come solely from nuclear DNA.

[184] M. Tachibana, M. Sparman, H. Sritanaudomchai et al., 'Mitochondrial Gene Replacement in Primate Offspring and Embryonic Stem Cells' (2009) 461 *Nature* 367–372. J. B. Appleby, 'The Ethical Challenges of the Clinical Introduction of Mitochondrial Replacement Techniques' (2015) 18 *Med. Health Care Philos* 501–514.

[185] J. B. Appleby, 'Should Mitochondrial Donation Be Anonymous?' (2017) Journal of Medicine and Philosophy Advance Access from 28 December 2017. C. Palacios-González, 'Does Egg Donation for Mitochondrial Replacement Techniques Generate Parental Responsibilities?' (2017) *Journal of Medical Ethics* 1–6.

[186] HFE Act 2008, section 3ZA.

[187] Human Fertilisation and Embryology Authority (2012) Review of Scientific Methods to avoid mitochondrial disease 2011. Human Fertilisation and Embryology Authority 'HFEA Launches Public Consultation, Medical Frontiers: Debating Mitochondria Replacement', 2012. Human Fertilisation and Embryology Authority (2013) *Mitochondria Replacement Consultation: Advice to Government*. London, UK: HFEA.

[188] Department of Health, *Mitochondrial Donation: A Consultation on Draft Regulations to Permit the Use of New Treatment Techniques to Prevent the Transmission of a Serious Mitochondrial Disease from Mother to Child* (February, 2014). https://assets.publishing .service.gov.uk/government/uploads/system/uploads/attachment_data/file/285251/ mitochondrial_donation_consultation_document_24_02_14_Accessible_V0.4.pdf.

In February 2014, the Government launched a consultation on draft regulations for the use of MR techniques – Maternal Spindle Transfer (MST) and Pronuclear Transfer (PNT) – to prevent mothers passing on serious mitochondrial diseases. Following a public consultation[189] and extensive Parliamentary debate, new regulations governing MRTs were passed in 2015.[190] The Human Fertilisation and Embryology (Mitochondrial Donation) Regulations 2015 allow for mitochondrial donation techniques to be used as part of IVF treatment to prevent the transmission of serious mitochondrial disease from a mother to her child. The HFEA subsequently granted the first UK licence to conduct MRT (PNT).[191] I would argue that that the law and policy on the MRTs as a development in reproductive medicine, was formulated in a far more acceptable fashion than previous policy and law in this controversial domain.

The Paradox of Legislation   Faced with the prospect of embryo manipulation and unchartered advances in the reproductive arena, regulation in this area was born amidst fears of IVF and the public response urging the governments to regulate this area and prevent unknown human experiments. As noted by Healy in her review of a book by Hayes, aptly named *The Paradox of Legislation*[192]:

> Even champions of de-regulation admit a role for governments in devising regulatory strategies for preventing or controlling catastrophic risks to people, property, and the environment. But, in the lull between crises, demands to avert risk are succeeded by demands to lighten the regulatory burden.[193]

This is certainly true in the context of assisted reproduction, despite the government in 2008 firmly being in favour of specialist regulation in this area, twice the statutory authority HFEA has been met with calls for its abolition.

---

[189] Ibid.

[190] The Human Fertilisation and Embryology (Mitochondrial Donation) Regulations 2015 came into force on 29 October 2015.

[191] HFEA, 'Licence Committee – Minutes: Centre 0017 (Newcastle Fertility at Life), Variation of Licensed Activities to include Mitochondria Pronuclear Transfer (PNT)', 9 March 2017.

[192] J. Healy, 'Book Review, "The Paradox of Regulation: What Regulation Can Achieve and What It Cannot"'(2013) 21 *Medical Law Review* 161–170.

[193] Ibid., p. 169.

Amidst calls in 2008 to update the legislation, there were proposals to abolish the HFEA and instead merge its functions with that of the Human Tissue Authority (HTA) and some functions of the Medicines and Healthcare Products Regulatory Agency (MHRA)[194] to create a new statutory body: the Regulatory Authority for Tissue and Embryos (RATE). RATE was first proposed by the Department of Health's review of arm's length bodies in 2004, and also as part of the earlier Human Tissue and Embryos Bill.[195] RATE was met with considerable opposition and there were concerns that RATE would bring together the regulation of two quite different things; that the HFEA's professional reputation may be lost in any merger;[196] that there would be a loss of specialist expertise, particularly because RATE would have such a wide remit;[197] that it would result in an increase in bureaucracy, cost and effectiveness;[198] and that overall 'any potential gains were at best neutralised, or at worst heavily outweighed, by the potential drawbacks'.[199] A joint committee of both Houses of Parliament, appointed to undertake pre-legislative scrutiny of the draft Bill 'found the evidence against establishing RATE overwhelming and convincing'.[200] The government

---

[194] House of Lords and House of Commons Joint Committee on the Human Tissue and Embryos (Draft) Bill, Session 2006–07, HL Paper 169-I and HC Paper 630-I, paragraph 57.

[195] Draft Human Tissue and Embryo Bill (Cm 7087).

[196] House of Lords and House of Commons Joint Committee on the Human Tissue and Embryos (Draft) Bill, Session 2006–07, HL Paper 169-I and HC Paper 630-I, paragraph 73. Dr Stephen Minger, commented that 'by merging the two entities together you lose that special status of the HFEA, it becomes a watered-down, less tightly regulated and less respectable organisation. It is fair to say that the HFEA is very highly regarded in this country by the general public and certainly by the scientific community, maybe less so by the reproductive medical community'.

[197] Above, paragraph 76.

[198] Above, paragraph 63. Charles Kingsland stated: 'all I can see is added expense, added bureaucracy, with no benefit to my patients'. Dr Tony Calland commented, 'We do not necessarily feel that if these two bodies were to work effectively RATE would be either cheaper, or, in fact, more effective or less bureaucratic'.

[199] Above, paragraph 81.

[200] House of Lords and House of Commons Joint Committee on the Human Tissue and Embryos (Draft) Bill, Session 2006–07, HL Paper 169-I and HC Paper 630-I, paragraph 92. Also at paragraph 66 it is reported that The Royal College of Obstetricians and Gynaecologists, The British Medical Association (BMA), The Royal Society, The Association of Medical Research Charities, The Academy of Medical Sciences, Cancer Research UK, Infertility Network UK, The Royal College of Nursing, The British Fertility Society, The Welcome Trust, Medical Research Council, and the Royal College of Pathologists all expressed profound reservations about RATE.

accepted the recommendation that proposals for RATE be abandoned, stating that:

> Having taken due account of the evidence presented to the Committee, the Government accepts the recommendation to reconsider the proposal to establish RATE. The Government will therefore amend the Bill to drop the proposal for RATE.[201]

The government retained the HFEA as the statutory authority overseeing regulation in this field, opining that maintaining the HFEA would have 'the benefit of maintaining the professional reputation it has earned since 1990, and the respect it has as a model regulatory environment for embryonic stem cell research'.[202]

A mere three years later, during the passage of The Public Bodies Act 2011, the HFEA was once more facing calls for its abolition. This statute created legislative powers for ministers to abolish or merge public bodies listed in Schedule 1 to the Act and to transfer their functions to another body.[203] Section 5 allows ministers to modify the functions of the bodies listed in Schedule 5, or to transfer those functions, or some of them, to another body. The HFEA and the HTA were both listed in Schedule 5 to the Act, so that a minister could modify or transfer its functions, but could not abolish them. Baroness Ruth Deech, herself a former Chair of the HFEA, argued against an amendment that would have allowed minsters to abolish the HFEA, arguing that splitting away the research functions of the HFEA as the Government proposed, risked creating additional bureaucracy and increasing, rather than diminishing, the burden of regulation.[204] She stated:

> The HFEA is like no other quango. Its work touches deeply on the intimate lives of the one in six couples who cannot conceive naturally, the health of babies, scientific research, cures for diseases now and in the future, the profits of scientific companies, and public morality. It is unique, has an international reputation and was a British first. I am seeking to preserve it from being shattered and to prevent lasting damage being caused to that area.[205]

In 2012, noting that that there was considerable overlap between the functions of both bodies and the Care Quality Commission (CQC) the Department of Health consulted on three options: (i) abolish both

---

[201] Government Response to the Report from the Joint Committee on the Human Tissue and Embryos (Draft) Bill, (Cm 7209) paragraph 16.

[202] Ibid.

[203] Public Bodies Act 2011, s1.

[204] House of Lords Debates, 9 May 2011: Column 681–684.

[205] Ibid.

the HTA and the HFEA and transfer their functions to the CQC, with the exception of the HFEA research functions which would be transferred to the HRA; (ii) abolish both bodies but with different provisions for the transfer of their functions; and (iii) allow both bodies to retain their functions but to deliver further efficiencies.[206] Of the 109 responses received, the overwhelming majority favoured the third option. Early 2013, the Department of Health published their response to the consultation, stating: 'We have decided, on balance, that we will not pursue a transfer of functions at the present time.'[207] However, in retaining the HFEA and the HTA it was acknowledged that further efficiencies were needed in the way the HFEA undertook its functions. The Government accepted the recommendations of the independent review by Justin McCracken, to improve the efficiency, transparency and accountability of the work carried out by the HFEA and HTA.[208] In 2017, the Department of Health published its triennial review of the HFEA and the extent that the recommendations made by Mr McCracken had been implemented. The review also considered whether the functions undertaken by the HFEA remain necessary and assessed the HFEA's performance, efficiency and governance.[209] The review noted some operational concerns that were being addressed[210] but concluded that:

> HFEA is a well run organisation, performing necessary functions effectively . . . There was a clear belief from stakeholders, with which the review team concurs, that there remains a need for a regulatory body with substantial expertise of operating in a specialised area of medical science that also raises complex moral and ethical issues.[211]

Thus, the main conclusion of the review was that the HFEA performs necessary functions effectively and should continue to operate as an

---

[206] See DoH, Consultation on proposals to transfer functions from the Human Fertilisation and Embryology Authority and the Human Tissue Authority (2012).

[207] DoH, Government Response to the Consultation on proposals to transfer functions from the Human Fertilisation & Embryology Authority and the Human Tissue Authority (2013), paragraph 18.

[208] DoH, Review of Human Fertilisation & Embryology Authority and the Human Tissue Authority (2013).

[209] DoH, Triennial Review of the Human Fertilisation and Embryology Authority Review Report (2017).

[210] In particular, the serious failings regarding the processes needed to ensure that where donated gametes are used in fertility treatment all parties of fertility treatment have given informed consent and that legal parenthood is firmly established.

[211] DoH, Triennial Review of the Human Fertilisation and Embryology Authority Review Report (2017) p. 5.

executive non-departmental public body. If the HFEA is to continue to hold confidence in its ability to effectively discharge its functions, it is imperative that the recommendations to improve performance, governance and efficiency are acted upon and that the HSP boldly examines future reproductive advances looming on the horizon.

1.4   The Future

As we move towards the third era of human reproduction, the government has made it clear that assisted reproductive technologies will continue to be regulated. Trying to maintain the pace of reproductive science is inherently difficult and yet the law must maintain a regulatory connection to scientific advances so as to avoid becoming obsolete – or imposing an unnecessary brake on innovation. The crucial issue is how the law provides sufficient regulation in a context where the object of that regulation is a 'moving target'. Any attempt to completely 'future proof' the law is not possible, but that does not mean that the government or regulatory authority should not monitor advances looming on the horizon, or be equipped to respond adequately to the challenges that new developments may raise.

A strong case can be made for retaining the present system whereby the HFEA maintains its discretionary power to formulate policy in this area and decide on what treatments to licence, within the parameters set by Parliament. In theory at least, the HSP has the potential to ensure that the HFEA is not caught 'off guard' by new developments and that the law is not lagging behind science, by scanning those reproductive advances that may be possible in the foreseeable future. However, if HFEA is to be adequately informed and equipped (in the sense it has had the time to consider the legal, ethical and scientific implications of the use of novel reproductive techniques, prior to an application being received by a licence committee) then arguably it needs to be bolder and braver when deciding what needs to be prioritised for consideration.

Thus far, this has not always been the case. Consider for instance uterus transplantation to restore fertility to patients with an abnormal, damaged, or absent uterus: this was identified in the 2007/8 Annual Report, but accorded 'low priority' status and dismissed without further consideration. The first human attempt at a womb transplant occurred in 2014 – a mere six years later,[212] demonstrating that it was imprudent to

---

[212] M. Brännström, L. Johannesson, H. Bokstrom et al., 'Livebirth after Uterus Transplantation' (2015) 14(385) (9968) The Lancet 607–616.

dismiss this advance from further consideration in light of scientific interest and the notoriously fast rate of scientific advance.

Artificial gametes were also considered by the HSP. Artificial gametes, as Jackson notes, raise 'one of the most dramatic possibilities that two men (and maybe also two women) could create a baby that is genetically related both of them, in the same way as man and women'.[213] Artificial gametes widen procreative possibilities for those unable to reproduce via traditional methods of sexual reproduction – Testa and Harris described this advance as 'democratising reproduction' because of the potential to enable anyone to create gametes irrespective of their age, sex, relationship status or sexuality.[214] In 2009, the HFEA's Scientific and Clinical Advances Advisory Committee (SCAAC) estimated that while research teams could produce sperm from stem cells in the next few years, the production of eggs from stem cells could take longer. The group thought that it would be at least 5–10 years before eggs or sperm could be produced that could potentially be used in treatment. The SCAG said there were still very significant safety concerns about using in vitro-derived gametes in treatment. However, scientists Tsai et al. claim 'alternate sources of gametes are not merely science fiction but already are a concrete fact'.[215] Yet the current blanket ban in the legislation to permit the use of artificial gametes to achieve a human pregnancy creates little incentive for scientists to continue with their endeavours in this field. MP Evan Harris cited this as an example of where the former HFE Bill fell short, stating: 'This is a good Bill, but the government needs to recognise a few improvements are still needed – such as allowing the use of artificial gametes – before we can say the UK has rational and progressive

---

[213] E. Jackson, 'Degendering Reproduction' (2014) *Medical Law Review* 346–368, at p. 353. On artificial gametes see also A. Smajdor and D. Cutas, 'Will Artificial Gametes End Infertility?' (2015) 23(2) *Healthcare Analysis* 134–147. A. Bredenoord and I. Hyun, 'Ethics of Stem Cell-Derived Gametes Made in a Dish: Fertility for Everyone?' (2017) 9(4) *EMBO Molecular Medicine* 396–398. O. Hikabe, N. Hamazaki, G. Nagamatsu et al., 'Reconstitution in Vitro of the Entire Cycle of the Mouse Female Germ line' (2016) 539 *Nature* 299–303. S. Hendriks, W. Dondorp, G. deWert et al., 'Potential Consequences of Clinical Application of Artificial Gametes: A Systematic Review of Stakeholder Views' (2015) 21(3) *Human Reproduction Update* 297–309. A. Newson and A. Smajdor 'Artificial Gametes: New Paths to Parenthood?' (2005) 31 *Journal of Medical Ethics* 184–186. D. Cutas, W. Dondorp, T. Swierstra et al., 'Artificial Gametes: Perspectives of Geneticists, Ethicists and Representatives of Potential Users' (2013) 17(13) *Medicine, Health Care and Philosophy* 339–345.

[214] G. Testa and J. Harris, 'Ethics and Synthetic Gametes' (2005) 19(2) *Bioethics* 146–166.

[215] M.C. Tsai et al. "Alternative Sources of Gametes: Reality or Science Fiction?" (2000) 15 (5) Human Reproduction 988–998 at p. 995.

regulation'.[216] This is but one example of the new possibilities that the next phase of human reproduction will raise, that I suggest are not adequately dealt with in the current regulatory framework.

It is apparent that if the government is to maintain the pace of reproductive science it needs to be prepared to countenance the regulatory challenges looming on the foreseeable horizon. The UK government has thus far displayed a mainly reactive approach when it comes to regulating reproduction. It is only when new technology is upon us that the government is jolted into legislative action. Consider the issue of reproductive cloning. The government was aware that scientists were researching the technology needed for this advance, but it was only when Dolly the Sheep attracted mass media attention,[217] and a subsequent legal challenge was brought as to the legality of reproductive cloning, that the government reacted by rushing the Human Reproductive Cloning Act 2001 through Parliament.[218] Regulating on an ad hoc basis is not the most effective form of regulation. It is argued that the only way that legislation in this field will be reconnected with modern science in accordance with recommendations of the Science and Technology Committee, is if the government is prepared for those future technologies looming on the foreseeable horizon. Regrettably, without the HSP, there is little planning done for these future possibilities.

If the old problems of the law's misunderstanding of science and the difficulty of maintaining the pace of reproductive science are to be overcome, the law needs to account for these new and novel developments before they are possible. As the former Chair of the HFEA, Suzie Leather noted, 'it is important that all of us in the fertility treatment and research sector keep a careful watch on what the future is bringing'.[219] However, it is not just those in the fertility sector that need keep a watchful eye; as Chapter 5 examines, uterus transplantation represents a new

---

[216] G. Hinsliff, 'MPs Back Artificial Sperm for Childless', *The Guardian*, 9 March 2008.

[217] See J. Harris, 'Goodbye Dolly? The Ethics of Human Cloning' (1997) 23 *Journal of Medical Ethics* 353–360.

[218] See also subsequent legal challenge brought by the Pro Life Alliance arguing that the Human Fertilisation and Embryology Authority did not have authority to licence research with regards to cloning – *R* v. *Secretary of State for Health, ex parte Bruno Quintavalle (on behalf of Pro-Life Alliance)* [2003] 2 WLR 692. The House of Lords adopted a 'purposive' interpretation of the HFE Act 1990 to enable it to encompass embryos created by cell nuclear transfer (CNR). For discussion, see further Brownsword, 'Regulating Human Genetics: New Dilemmas for a New Millennium'.

[219] S. Leather, 'Looking to the Future' – HFEA Conference Tackles Upcoming Issues in the Fertility Sector, 14 March 2005, www.hfea.gov.uk/en/1068.html.

collaboration between transplant medicine and fertility treatment. At present, uterus transplantation research trials have only been successful with the use of the implantation of IVF embryos into a donated uterus – if the procedure becomes possible in women with functioning ovaries, the procedure would fall completely outside the remit of the HFEA, since transplant procedures are governed under a completely separate statutory framework.[220]

As reproductive science continues apace and we charge towards a new era of human reproduction, it is clear that the concerns raised by IVF, which provided the impetus for regulation in this area, will only grow with the advent of new reproductive advances. The next chapter examines how the IVF, dubbed the second phase of reproductive technologies, in separating fertilisation from sexual reproduction created a plethora of legal and ethical questions regarding the status of in vitro embryos. It is important that consideration is given to the regulation and status of human embryos once they are no longer located in a woman's body and the dispositional power of each progenitor in relation to their gametes. This is an issue that grows in complexity when we consider third-wave reproductive technologies such as ectogenesis, which may raise the prospect that a fetus can be gestated completely in vitro.

This chapter has provided an account of how assisted reproductive technologies are regulated in the UK. Such an account was necessary before moving on, in subsequent chapters, to more dramatic possibilities on the horizon. Given the rate of scientific change and the complex ethical issues new advances raise, regulation of this controversial domain is no easy feat. I have argued that it is important the regulation remains connected to modern science and expressed my reservations that the present regulatory system in the UK has achieved the aim of being fit for purpose in the twenty-first century. The importance of the law being aware and alert to new possibilities is summed up well in the prudent words of the current President of the Supreme Court, Brenda Hale:

> The new balances between choice and regulation are all slowly emerging. The law cannot impose a dictatorship however benevolent, which insists that it knows best how people should conduct their private and family lives ... New possibilities are emerging all the time and the law will have to stay alert to develop in response to them.[221]

---

[220] The Human Tissue Act 2004.

[221] B. Hale, *From the Test Tube to the Coffin: Choice and Regulation in Private Life* (London: Stevens, Sweet and Maxwell, 1996) p. 125; Lee and Morgan, Human Fertilisation and Embryology: Regulating the Reproductive Revolution at p. 7.

Regulation of Gametes

Resolving Embryo Disputes between Gamete Progenitors

2.1   IVF and the 'De-Gendering of Reproduction'[1]

Wellin labelled in vitro fertilisation (IVF)[2] as merely 'the second era' of reproduction, whereby the fetus is fertilised outside the woman, but is later implanted into a female host where it is gestated until birth.[3] As we charge towards the 'third era' of human reproduction, science may go one step further and enable embryos/fetuses to be gestated outside a female host and in an artificial womb (ectogenesis). Jackson has noted how such technologies 'may in the future alter and perhaps eliminate gender differences in the reproductive process'.[4] The rights of the gamete progenitors when reproducing in these alternative methods necessitate careful consideration, for reliance on former case law to govern these novel scenarios – cases which were founded upon traditional methods of procreation whereby fertilisation and gestation took place in a female host – may serve to confine scientific advance to the very inequality it was designed to alleviate. Yet it is also crucial that new and evolving technologies that further remove reproduction from the female host do not erode the fundamental reproductive rights of women. As Daar observes:

---

[*] Some of the discussion and facts of the Evans v Amicus case have been reproduced by permission of Oxford University Press from A. Alghrani "Deciding the Fate of Frozen Embryos" (2005) 13(1) Medical Law Review 244–256.

[1] E. Jackson, 'Degendering Reproduction' (2008) 16(3) *Medical Law Review* 346–368.

[2] IVF refers to *In Vitro Fertilisation*, whereby a woman's ovaries are stimulated (usually as a consequence of fertility drugs). Several eggs are then retrieved and fertilised in the laboratory. One or two fertilised eggs are then transferred to a receptive uterus and, if all goes well, a normal pregnancy follows.

[3] S. Welin, 'Reproductive Ectogenesis: The Third Era of Human Reproduction and Some Moral Consequences' (2004) 10 *Science and Engineering Ethics* 615–626, at p. 617.

[4] Jackson, 'Degendering Reproduction' 348.

As the science of reproduction advances, we must take care that it does not outpace our slowly evolving, yet firmly established, fundamental rights.[5]

The in vitro fertilisation of embryos raises legal and ethical questions, which only grow in complexity when the prospect of in vitro gestation is considered. In light of the widespread use of IVF and the prospect of future advances that may further remove reproduction from the human body, it is imperative that consideration is given to whether women should retain the decisive say over their embryos, irrespective of whether they are *in vivo* or *in vitro*. Most of the case law relating to the status of the embryo has arisen in the context of *in vivo* embryos (those housed in the female body); it is questionable whether this provides appropriate guidance for governing the *in vitro* embryo. These questions are placed in context by considering two UK legal challenges regarding embryo disposition that have arisen between gamete progenitors. The first case of *Evans* v. *Amicus*[6] has been described as a 'tragedy of a kind which may well not have been in anyone's mind when the [1990] statute was framed'.[7] Whilst this case received significant media attention in the run up to the HFE Act 2008, it is questionable whether the later amendments to the consent provisions went far enough. Disputes surrounding the use of in vitro gametes have arisen again in subsequent challenges,[8] the most recent being that of *ARB* v. *Hammersmith Ltd* [2017], which is the second case examined.[9] In that case, a dispute arose when a man claimed that his former partner had used IVF embryos they had previously created together, without his consent.

---

[5] J. Daar, 'Assisted Reproductive Technologies and the Pregnancy Process: Developing an Equal Model to Protect Reproductive Liberties' (1999) 25(4) *American Journal of Medicine & Law* 455–477, at p. 477.

[6] *Natalie Evans* v. *Amicus Healthcare Ltd and Others; Lorraine Hadley* v. *Midland Fertility Services Ltd and Others* [2003] EWCH 2161, [2004] 1 F.L.R 67 (Fam) (HC); *Evans* v. *Amicus Health Care Ltd and Others* [2004] 2 WLR 713 (Fam.); [2004] WLR 681 (CA); *Evans* v. *United Kingdom* [2006] 1 FCR 585 (ECtHR); [2007] BHRC 190 (ECtHR).

[7] *Evans* v. *Amicus Healthcare Ltd* [2005] Fam 93 (CA), per Thorpe and Sedley LJJ.

[8] For instance, see *Jefferies* v. *BMI Healthcare & HFEA* [2016] EWHC 2493 – the High Court granted the applicant, Samantha Jeffries, a widow in her 40s, the right to keep the frozen embryos she had created with her late husband in storage for 10 years, after a dispute arose with the fertility clinic, which had wanted to destroy the embryos after two years, as NHS funding had expired to fund storage costs. Ms Jeffries had undergone two unsuccessful cycles of IVF funded by the NHS, and was about to embark on her third attempt, when her husband died of a brain haemorrhage. The couple had consented to storage of the frozen embryos for a period of ten years, and their use posthumously in the event that either were to predecease the other. The clinic then sought to alter the terms of the agreement by claiming it had the right to destroy the embryos after a two-year storage period when the NHS had stopped funding the storage costs. The court held the embryos should continue to be stored for the 10-year period as had originally been agreed, despite the lack of NHS funding.

[9] *ARB* v. *Hammersmith* Ltd [2017] EWCH 2438 (HC).

The child that was successfully born from that embryo implantation was, he claimed, 'unwanted and thus, he sought substantive damages from the clinic for the financial cost of her upbringing'. In this chapter and via examination of the *Evans* and *ARB* cases, I argue that, notwithstanding the failure of the government to substantively revisit the status of the in vitro embryo and the situation of the gamete progenitors in relation to it in 2008 when it amended the principal statute which governs both; disputes regarding disposition of embryos merit further legislative attention. As noted above, this is important as the controversial issue of the status of the in vitro embryo only grows in importance as we move into the third era of human reproduction.

This chapter is split into three parts. Part one (Section 2.2.1) provides a detailed critical analysis of both the *Evans* and *ARB* v. *Hammersmith* judgments and the legal provisions that govern embryo disposition. It is argued that the UK regulatory framework is ill equipped to adequately address the complex set of legal and moral questions these cases raised. How the courts responded to claims regarding the status of the in vitro embryo, and the claims of the gamete progenitors in relation to it, will be examined. Part two (Section 2.2.2) considers why the neutral location of the IVF embryo matters and how ARTs such as IVF are de-gendering reproduction and may now necessitate a new appraisal of gender roles when using novel methods of reproduction that no longer depend on a female host. The final part of this chapter (Section 2.3) examines alternate models Parliament could adopt to achieve a framework that is able to regulate such disputes, in an equitable and just manner, whilst also respecting the procreative liberties at stake.

2.2   Disputes over Frozen Embryos: The UK Regulatory Framework

> The whole scheme of the [Human Fertilisation and Embryology] 1990 Act lays great emphasis upon consent. The new scientific techniques which have developed since the birth of the first IVF baby in 1978 open up the possibility of creating human life in ways and circumstances quite different from anything experienced before then. These possibilities bring with them huge practical and ethical difficulties. These have to be balanced against the strength and depth of the feelings of people who desperately long for the children which only these techniques can give them, as well as the natural desire of clinicians and scientists to use their skills to fulfil those wishes. Parliament has devised a legislative scheme and a statutory authority for

regulating assisted reproduction in a way, which tries to strike a fair balance between the various interests and concerns.[10]

The comments above by Hale LJ, as she then was, in *Mrs U* v. *Centre for Reproductive Medicine* [2002], highlights the importance that the regulatory framework placed on consent and the fair balance it sought to achieve. In line with respect for autonomy and the importance of upholding consent in the UK, the HFE Act 1990 (as amended) holds that IVF embryos can only be used where there is an 'effective consent' from both gamete donors.[11] However, Miola noted:

> There are at times, in law, when a new case appears within which circumstances conspire to create a situation, which is both legally and morally complex.[12]

This observation above is certainly true in the context of disputes over the use of stored in vitro fertilisation embryos between gamete progenitors. Unlike in sexual reproduction, whereby conception takes place in a female host, when conception takes place in vitro, men's reproductive choices as regards their gametes may no longer entail a direct infringement of a woman's autonomy and bodily integrity.

2.2.1 Evans v. Amicus

The infamous *Evans* case arose following the fertility treatment Ms Natalie Evans had undergone with her (then) fiancé, Howard Johnston in July 2001 (and thus prior to the 2008 amendments).[13] During fertility treatment, the couple discovered Ms Evans had ovarian cancer. Prior to undergoing treatment for the cancer and the removal of her ovaries, the couple were able to undergo one cycle of IVF treatment, in which eleven

---

[10] *Mrs U* v. *Centre for Reproductive Medicine* [2002] EWCA Civ 565, paragraph 24.

[11] HFE Act 1990, Schedule 3, paragraph 6(3).

[12] J. Miola, 'Mix-Ups, Mistake and Moral Judgment; Recent Developments in U.K. Law on Assisted Conception' (2004) 12 *Feminist Legal Studies* 67–77, at p. 67.

[13] For commentaries on the case see A. Alghrani, 'Deciding the Fate of Frozen Embryos' (2005) 13(1) *Medical Law Review* 244–256. S. Sheldon, 'Evans v Amicus Healthcare, Hadley v Midland Fertility Services: Revealing Cracks in the "Twin Pillars"?' (2004) 16 (4) *Child and Family Law Quarterly* 437–452. K. Webster, 'Whose Embryo Is It Anyway? A Critique of Evans v Amicus Healthcare [2003] EWCH 2161' (2006) 7(3) *International Journal of Women's Studies* 71–86. A. Smajdor, 'Deciding the Fate of Disputed Embryos: Ethical Issues in the Case of Natallie Evans' (2007) 4(2) *Journal of Experimental Clinical Assisted Reproduction* 1–6. R. Thornton, 'European Court of Human Rights: consent to IVF treatment' (2008) 6(3) *International Journal of Constitutional Law* 17–30.

eggs were successfully harvested. When Ms Evans asked the clinic about the possibility of freezing her eggs, as opposed to fertilised embryos, she was informed that was not an option at the clinic. It was at this juncture that Mr Johnston assured Ms Evans that they were not going to split up and that he wanted to be the father of her children. Thereafter the couple entered into the necessary consents for the creation, storage and use of the embryos in accordance with the HFE Act 1990.

Ms Evans then underwent cancer treatment, which involved the removal of the tumours and was advised to wait a few years prior to having the embryos implanted. During this time, the relationship between the couple ended. As a result, Mr Johnston wrote to the clinic notifying them of the separation and his subsequent withdrawal of consent to the future use and storage of the embryos.[14] This was communicated to Ms Evans, who subsequently issued legal proceedings seeking an injunction that Mr Johnston's consent be restored. She argued that (i) the revocation of consent was unlawful under the provisions of the HFE Act 1990 and (ii) the relevant legislation was incompatible with her human rights and was in breach of Articles 2, 8, 12 and 14. Despite challenging the validity of this withdrawal of consent before the High Court,[15] Court of Appeal[16] and the European Court,[17] all upheld the initial finding of the High Court that the consent initially given by Mr Johnston to the use and storage of the embryos was no longer valid. His withdrawal of consent was lawful under the provisions of the HFE Act 1990 and effectively precluded Ms Evans from using the embryos. With regard to the complaint there had been a breach of human rights; it was held the statutory requirement of continuing consent under the HFE Act 1990 was compatible with Articles 8 and 14 of the Convention, since the

---

[14] Note that whilst in this instance the dispute concerned Mr Johnston's request that the embryos be allowed to perish as he no longer consented to storage and did not want a child genetically related him to exist, there is statutory provision for the donation of embryos where the embryos are no longer wanted for 'use', although it has been noted that the uptake of embryo donation is low – for an interesting paper on reasons for this see S. Goedeke, 'Embryo Donation or Embryo Adoption? Practice and Policy in the New Zealand Context' (2017) 31(1) *International Journal of Law, Policy and the Family* 1. See also R. Scott, C. Williams, K. Ehrich and B. Farsides, 'Donation of "Spare" Fresh or Frozen Embryos to Research: Who Decides that an Embryo Is "Spare" and How Can We Enhance the Quality and Protect the Validity of Consent? Donation of Embryos to Research' (2012) 20(3) *Medical Law Review* 255.

[15] *Evans* v. *Amicus Healthcare Ltd and Others; Hadley* v. *Midland Fertility Services Ltd and Others* [2003] EWCH 2161 (Fam), [2005] Fam 1 (HC).

[16] *Evans* v. *Amicus Healthcare Ltd and Others* [2004] 2 WLR; [2004] EWCA (civ) 727 (CA).

[17] *Evans* v. *United Kingdom* (Application No. 6339/05); [2006] 1 FCR 585 (ECtHR).

requirement of mutual consent to implantation is proportionate to the legislative aim of protecting the rights and freedoms of both parties. Moreover, a non-viable embryo does not have a qualified right to life under Article 2.

The Legal Issues

The central question raised by this dispute was essentially who should decide the fate of an embryo when disputed by its two progenitors. It was a case of 'denying maternity or forcing paternity'.[18] Notwithstanding the courts' finding that Mr Johnston's withdrawal of consent was permissible under the 1990 legislative framework, it is questionable how adequate that was in addressing such disputes. It was upon a construction of the provisions of the HFE Act 1990 and, significantly, an examination of the compatibility of these provisions with the European Convention on Human Rights (ECHR) that the decision was made to refuse the declarations sought by Ms Evans. The court in *Evans* stated that the 'twin pillars'[19] underlying the HFE Act 1990 were (i) the welfare of any child who may be born as a result of the treatment[20] and (ii) the requirements of consent to treatment.[21] Whilst concerns pertaining to the former had already received substantial attention in the literature,[22] *Evans* thrust the consent provisions into the limelight and presented the first opportunity for the

---

[18] J. Bomhoff and L. Zucca, 'Evans v UK European Court of Human Rights' (2006) 2 *European Constitutional Law Review* 424–442, at p. 427.

[19] *Evans* (HC), n11, paragraph 37, per Wall J.

[20] HFE Act 1990, s13(5).

[21] HFE Act 1990, Schedule 3.

[22] A. Alghrani and J. Harris, 'Should the Foundation of Families Be Regulated?' (2006) 18(2) *Child and Family Law Quarterly* 191–210. J. Harris, 'The Welfare of the Child' (2000) 8 *Health Care Analysis* 27–34. E. Jackson, 'Conception and the Irrelevance of the Welfare Principle' 65 *Modern Law Review* (2002) 176. S. Millns, 'Making Social Judgements that Go Beyond the Purely Medical: The Reproductive Revolution and Access to Fertility Treatment Services' in J. Bridgeman and S. Millns (eds.), *Law and Body Politics: Regulating the Female Body* (Aldershot: Dartmouth, 1995). E. Sutherland, 'Man Not Included – Single Women, Female Couples and Procreative Freedom in the UK' (2003) 15(2)*Child and Family Law Quarterly* 155. E. Blyth and C. Cameron, 'The Welfare of the Child: An Emerging Issue in the Regulation of Assisted Conception' (1998) 13 *Human Reproduction* 2339–2355. E. Blyth, V. Burr and A. Farrand, 'Welfare of the Child Assessments in Assisted Conception: A Social Constructionist Perspective' (2008) 26 *Journal of Reproductive Infant Psychology* 31–43. E. Lee, J. Macvarish and S. Sheldon, 'Assessing Child Welfare under the Human Fertilisation and Embryology Act 2008: A Case Study in Medicalisation' (2014) 36 *Sociology of Health and Illness* 500–515. H. Reece, 'The Paramountcy Principle: Consensus or Construct?' (1996) 49(1) *Current Legal Problems* 267–304.

courts to examine the compatibility of the consent provisions in the HFE Act within the context of the ECHR.

Consent to 'Treatment Together'

The issue of treatment together was central to the case. The HFE Act 1990 provides that IVF embryos can only be used for the purpose for which there is 'effective consent'.[23] When signing the necessary consent forms, Ms Evans and Mr Johnston specified that the embryos were to be used in providing treatment services for themselves and their partner 'together'. Paragraph 4 of Schedule 3 conferred on both parties the statutory right to withdraw or vary that consent up until the point the embryo has been 'used'.[24] The courts rejected Ms Evans's contention that Mr Johnston could not withdraw his consent to treatment, because the date of harvest and storage of the embryos constituted 'use' and the point from which consent cannot be revoked. The Court of Appeal upheld the construction of Wall J that an embryo is only 'used' once implanted into the uterus of the woman. As the couple were no longer together and the embryos had not been used, the consent to treatment given by Mr Johnston was no longer valid. Thus, the court held there was no continuing consent from which Mr Johnston could be estopped from withdrawing. Counsel on behalf of Ms Evans failed in their submission that since there could be no dispute that effective consent operated at the date of harvest and storage, continuing consent must be assumed. Otherwise the clinic would be subjected to an intolerable responsibility in having to investigate the state of the relationship between the couple, including whether and to what extent they remained together. It was held that 'together' is an adverb qualifying the provision of treatment services to a man and a woman. The condition is satisfied provided, and so long as, the couple remained united in their pursuit of the treatment, whatever may otherwise be the nature of the relationship between them. As Wall J rightly acknowledged in the High Court, 'there are elements of artificiality about

---

[23] HFE Act 1990, schedule 3, paragraph 6(3): 'An embryo the creation of which was brought about *in vitro* must not be used for any purpose unless there is an effective consent by each person whose gametes were used to bring about creation of the embryo to the use for that purpose and the embryo is used in accordance with those consents.'

[24] HFE Act 1990, schedule 3, paragraph 4: '(1) The terms of any consent under this Schedule may from time to time be varied, and the consent withdrawn, by notice given by the person who gave the consent to the person keeping the gametes or embryo to which the consent is relevant. (2) The terms of any consent to the use of an embryo cannot be varied, and such consent cannot be withdrawn, once the embryo has been used – (a) in providing treatment services, or (b) for the purposes of research.'

the argument because, in conventional terms, the only "treatment" undergone by Mr Johnston was the provision of his sperm'.[25]

Whilst the Court of Appeal noted that accessing treatment together does not presuppose any family arrangements, the very purpose of the requirement of 'treatment together'[26] stemmed from the clear hetero-centric policy under pinning the 1990 legislation; as noted by Morgan and Lee who stated 'the policy behind the [1990] legislation is actively to discourage treatment for infertile people who live outside the umbrella of the nuclear family'.[27] The view of the Warnock Committee on the provision of IVF for single women was made clear in section 2.9 of their report:

> To judge from the evidence, many believe that the interests of the child dictate that it should be borne in a home where there is a loving, stable heterosexual relationship and that, therefore the deliberate creation of a child for a woman who is not a partner in such a relationship is morally wrong.[28]

As noted by Arden LJ, 'the requirement for "treatment together" appears to reflect a presumption that, if two persons are jointly involved in the creation of an embryo and its transfer to the woman, both will be responsible for the upbringing of the child when born'.[29] However, that aim is not necessarily achieved by a requirement for two people to be involved at that stage. The genetic father can effectively withdraw his agreement to be involved in the child's upbringing after implantation.[30] Thus, the requirement for treatment together does little to guarantee that two loving parents will raise a child. The twin pillars in the 1990 legislation perpetuate an undeniable hetero-centric approach to parenthood and reflect, within the legislation, a preference to emulate as much as possible the traditional nuclear two parent family model. Scully-Hill[31] noted how the legal requirement of consent (which is in effect consent to the obligations of parenthood, for once the man consents he cannot then

---

[25] *Evans* (HC), paragraph 135.

[26] *Evans* (CA), Arden L. J.'s comments, paragraph 97.

[27] D. Morgan and R. Lee, 'Into the Future & Back to the Basics: Assisted Conception and Family Structures' in S. Cretney (eds.), *Family Law: Essays for the New Millennium* (Bristol: Jordan Publishing, 2000) 181–194, at p. 187.

[28] Report of the Committee of Inquiry into Human Fertilisation and Embryology, Cmnd. 9314 (1984), (Hereafter 'Warnock Report') paragraph 2.9.

[29] *Evans* (CA), paragraph 97.

[30] Although it should be noted the legal responsibilities would be different.

[31] A. Scully-Hill, 'Consent, Frozen Embryos, Procreative Choice and the Ideal Family' (2004) *Cambridge Law Journal* 47, at pp. 47–48.

contract out of his parental and financial obligations to the child[32]) served to create a strong disincentive to use IVF, unless the couple were dreaming of a traditional family together.[33] The courts' construction of treatment 'together' endorsed this hetero-centric approach and ensured that Ms Evans did not bear a child that would be without a father figure. Such a construction overlooks the vital fact that reproductive technologies are welcomed essentially because they enable diverse family forms to exist by offering the potential fragmentation of parenthood amongst more than two individuals. The amendments introduced to the 1990 legislation by the Human Fertilisation and Embryology Act 2008, appeared to reflect the government's belated acceptance of alternate family structures that can exist and that a father figure is no longer deemed essential to ensuring the welfare of the child.[34] In light of this, it is argued that the meaning of 'treatment together' also requires a more contemporary meaning to reflect this.

Estoppel in Reproductive Medicine?

What of the assurances Mr Johnston gave his ex-fiancée? Ms Evans claimed that when she had asked the nurse about the possibility of freezing unfertilised ova, Mr Johnston made the following assurances:

> At this point Howard told me not to be stupid and that there was no need for that. He told me that he loved me, that we would be getting married and having a family together. I said "But what if we split up?" Howard told me that we were not going to and that I should not be such a negative person.
>
> I suggested that we freeze some of the eggs and that if we were still together in a couple of years' time and wanted to use them we could always fertilise them then. He told me again that we would not be splitting up, that our future was together and that he loved me ... I told him that I loved him and trusted him.[35]

---

[32] *Evans* (HC), paragraph 253.

[33] Scully-Hill, 'Consent, Frozen Embryos, Procreative Choice and the Ideal Family', at p. 48.

[34] HFE Act 2008, s14 (2)(b). Although note paper by Professors Julie McCandless and Sally Sheldon who, upon examination of the 2008 amendments, observe how the provisions continue reflect 'deep rooted assumptions and highly conservative understandings about who should count as a family' – see J. McCandless and S. Sheldon, 'The Human Fertilisation and Embryology Act (2008) and the Tenacity of the Sexual Family Form' (2010) 73(2) *Modern Law Review* 175, at p. 182.

[35] *Evans* (HC), paragraph 47.

Despite these assurances, Ms Evans's argument that the equitable doctrine of estoppel applied to her situation[36] faced a number of insuperable difficulties. The evidence of Mr Johnston differed slightly as to the exact nature of the assurances he gave Ms Evans, claiming he 'couldn't recall providing her with any specific reassurances'.[37] The court accepted the evidence that upon Ms Evans being informed that egg freezing was not a possible procedure at that clinic, Mr Johnston had indeed reassured Ms Evans that they were not going to split up, that she did not need egg freezing and should not be so negative; that he wanted to be the father of her children. Whilst it is conceded that couples frequently make promises to each other about the future, which by mere making are not binding, it is thought that where, as in the present case, one of the parties has relied on those assurances to her detriment; the principle of promissory estoppel should apply. The essence of the legal doctrine, as commented by Robert Walker LJ in *Jennings* v. *Rice*[38] is to do what is necessary to avoid an unconscionable result. Wall J stated that the three critical elements which must be present for the doctrine to apply are namely: (1) a clear representation by Mr Johnston; (2) reliance on that representation by Ms Evans to her detriment, and (3) a finding it would be unconscionable to allow Mr Johnston to go back on that representation.

On the facts of the case before him Wall J held that estoppel undoubtedly failed on the first and third of the essential ingredients. The assurances given to Ms Evans did not amount to a clear and unequivocal representation as to the use of the embryos and a promise he would not withdraw his consent to their use. Furthermore, he found the question of Ms Evans's reliance on the assurances difficult. Had Ms Evans requested egg freezing or artificial donor insemination, this would have induced the clinic to question the durability of her relationship with Mr Johnston. In the High Court, Wall J held that irrespective of the assurances given, in undergoing IVF with Mr Johnston, Ms Evans was taking the only realistic course that was open to her.[39] Further, it was held that, even if on the facts of the case the three critical elements for an estoppel to succeed were present, the HFE Act 1990 would exclude the

---

[36] For more on the doctrine of estoppel see P. Feltham, T. Leech, P. Crampin and J. Winfield (eds.), *Spencer Bower: Reliance-Based Estoppel*, Fifth Edition (London: Bloomsbury Professional, 2017). B. McFarlene, 'Understanding Equitable Estoppel: From Metaphors to Better Laws' (2013) *Current Legal Problems* 267. E. Cooke, *The Modern Law of Estoppel* (Oxford: Oxford University Press, 2000).

[37] *Evans* (HC), paragraph 49.

[38] [2003] 1 F.C.R.518F.

[39] *Evans* (HC), paragraph 309.

operation of an estoppel which would prevent a gamete provider withdrawing his/her consent to the use of an embryo(s). Wall J. accepted the Secretary of State's arguments and held (i) that there were substantial reasons of social policy underpinning the provisions of Schedule 3, which militate strongly against the operation of an estoppel in the case; (ii) allowing people to opt out of the statutory scheme by resort to estoppel arguments would place 'licence holders in the invidious position of having to investigate and make findings of fact in relation to what was said between male and female partners, and whether it was equitable to allow consent to be withdrawn'[40]; and (iii) that the consent regime in Schedule 3 provided a 'bright line' rule that enabled clinicians to operate with a high degree of certainty. While the estoppel argument received limited attention in the Court of Appeal, all three judges agreed that it should not succeed. Arden LJ commented:

> A person may give up a right created by statute for his benefit only, but here the right of withdrawal is granted in recognition of the dignity to which each individual is entitled. Such must include an individual's right to control the use of their own genetic material. In my judgment, it would be contrary to public policy for courts to enforce agreements to allow use of genetic material.[41]

The courts endorsed the view that granting both gamete progenitors the statutory right to withdraw consent at any point prior to implantation was important in the general public interest because it promoted clarity and certainty.[42] Yet as the facts of *Evans* demonstrated, the provisions of the HFE Act 1990 do not always allow such disputes to be resolved equitably. Alternate models (considered in detail in Section 2.3 of this chapter) could be used which also provide clarity and certainty whilst respecting the procreative autonomy of both parties, although they could not be deployed to resolve such disputes without revision of the present statutory framework which grants that both gamete progenitors can revoke consent to the use of their gametes prior to implantation.

The Human Rights Act 1998

Both the UK courts and the ECtHR dismissed Ms Evans' allegation that the embryos were worthy of protection under Article 2, and that the consent requirements of the HFE Act 1990 breached her Article 8 and 14 rights.[43]

---

[40] *Evans* (HC), paragraph 289.
[41] *Evans* (CA), paragraph 120.
[42] *Evans* (HC), paragraph 287.
[43] *Evans* v. *United Kingdom* (ECtHR).

Article 2: The Right to Life

Article 2 Right to life: Everyone's right to life shall be protected by law.

While Ms Evans conceded that an embryo is not a human life, she contended that an embryo has a sufficiently special status to attract a 'qualified' right to life.[44] Citing *Re F (in utero)*[45] and *Paton v. UK*[46] Wall J. rejected submissions that Article 2 was engaged, holding that 'if a fetus has no right to life under Article 2, it is difficult to see how an embryo can have such a right'.[47] The Court of Appeal refused leave to appeal on the Article 2 ground, Thorpe and Sedley LJJ highlighting the fact that no Convention jurisprudence extends the right to an embryo, much less to one which at that material point of time is non-viable. Furthermore, the court held that Ms Evans's case was not about the right to life; it was about the right to bring life into being.[48] Relying on dicta from the earlier case of *Vo v. France*,[49] the ECtHR concurred that there had been no breach of Article 2, and held that the position in English law that an embryo does not have independent rights or interests had to be respected. Member States enjoy a wide 'margin of appreciation' in this area, stemming from the lack of European consensus on when human life begins.[50] Yet a closer analysis of the cases invoked to dismiss Ms Evans claim reveal a fundamental oversight. *Paton, Re F, Vo,* and most of the other cases where the courts have considered the status to be accorded to the embryo/fetus and whether it attracts Article 2 protection, have been in the context of embryos in vivo – embryos conceived, housed and protected through the female body. This is significantly different from the situation of in vitro embryos, which can be protected in their own right without violating the bodily integrity of another. Consequently, invoking cases in which the embryo/fetus *was in vivo* sheds little guidance on the *in vitro* embryo. In this latter context, the needs of the mother and the fetus are not mutually exclusive. *Evans* provided the ECtHR with an ideal opportunity to re-examine the status of the embryo when a woman's bodily autonomy is not invoked via pregnancy, yet the court failed to give this issue the legislative attention merited. The court dismissed summarily Ms Evans's claim that the HFE Act 1990 failed to give adequate protection to embryonic life. The ECtHR recoiled

---

[44] *Evans* (HC), paragraph 174.
[45] *Re F (in utero)* [1988] Fam. 122.
[46] *Paton v. UK* (1980) 3 E.H.R.R. 408.
[47] *Evans* (HC), paragraph 176.
[48] *Evans* (CA), paragraph 19.
[49] *Vo v. France* (Application no. 53924/00) [2004] FCR 577 (ECtHR).
[50] *Evans v. United Kingdom* (ECtHR).

from confronting the fact that reproductive science has created a novel situation in which embryos can be created and located outside the maternal host and thus, can be protected or destroyed without violating her bodily autonomy. It is regrettable that this opportunity was not seized to directly address the convoluted issue of what status the in vitro embryo has, and whether or not Article 2 protects it. It becomes apparent how important this issue is in subsequent chapters when discussing ectogenesis.

Article 8: The Right to Privacy

Article 8 Right to respect for private and family life:
1 Everyone has the right to respect for his private and family life, his home and his correspondence.
2 There shall be no interference by a public authority with the exercise of this right except such as is in accordance with the law and is necessary in a democratic society in the interests of national security, public safety or the economic well-being of the country, for the prevention of disorder or crime, for the protection of health or morals, or for the protection of the rights and freedoms of others.

The wishes of Ms Evans to continue with IVF treatment and to have the embryos released from storage and transferred into her, engaged her right to respect for private life under Article 8. The Court of Appeal held that the refusal of treatment was an interference with, and therefore a failure to respect, Ms Evans's private life. The Court then turned to the question as to whether that interference was proportionate. Adopting the synoptic test propounded by Hale LJ in *Re W and B*,[51] the Court asked the question 'whether the proposed interference with the right to respect for private life is proportionate to the need which makes it legitimate'. The judges were united in agreement that it was. The judges held that Parliament had perceived the need for continued bilateral consent up to the point of implantation, not simply to the taking and storage of genetic material. That need cannot be met if half of the consent is no longer effective. The interference contained in Schedule 3 was both proportionate and necessary so as to protect both gamete providers from becoming a genetic parent against his/her will. The Court held that to have diluted the requirement in Schedule 3 in order to meet Ms Evans's intractable biological handicap, by making the withdrawal of the man's consent relevant but

---

[51] *Re W and B* [2001] 2 FLR 582.

inconclusive, would create new and even more intractable difficulties of arbitrariness and inconsistency.[52]

When Article 8 was considered before the ECtHR, the Court held that this right entails the 'right to respect for both the decisions to become and not to become a parent',[53] yet failed to delineate the extent of that right in the context of assisted reproductive technologies. The ECtHR evaded answering exactly when one person's exercise of decisional privacy should justifiably override another's and instead the court deferred the matter to the British legislature by accepting, without question, the political solution embodied in the HFE Act 1990.

Despite the Court's finding that the interference was proportionate under Article 8, this 'solution' offered by the British legislature, that mutual consent be a requirement up to the point of implantation, accorded no recognition to the poignant fact that this was Ms Evans last chance at genetic motherhood. Thorpe and Sedley LJJ stated that it was not possible to construct an alternative system that would have that effect, would be Convention-complaint and would still be able to achieve the legitimate objectives of the legislation.[54] I respectfully disagree on this point and alternative models that I consider below, illustrate that other frameworks could be utilised to resolve such disputes. For now it suffices to say that Parliament could have made consent irrevocable at the moment of sperm donation. As Arden LJ highlighted in the Court of Appeal, Parliament could have taken the view that, as in sexual intercourse, a man's procreative liberty should end with the donation of sperm or upon the creation of an embryo, but that in light of the woman's unique role in making the embryo a child, she should have the right to determine the fate of the embryo.[55] However, Parliament failed to adopt such a view, and instead imposed an on-going requirement of bilateral consent. The consent provisions of the HFE Act 1990 confer upon sperm donors the right to withdraw consent for the use of embryos created from their gametes until such time as those embryos are 'used'.[56] As counsel for Ms Evans submitted, it is a very bad law which would permit a donor to deprive a young cancer victim from bearing a child from an embryo fertilised with his sperm, when he might do so for no good reason, or no reason at all and perhaps years after he had made the donation (for which he might have been paid).[57] It is interesting to note that should such a scenario present itself, it

---

[52] *Evans* (CA), paragraph 69.
[53] *Evans* (ECtHR), paragraph 71.
[54] *Evans* (ECtHR), paragraph 67.
[55] *Evans* (ECtHR), paragraph 109.
[56] HFE Act 1990, schedule 3, paragraph 6(3).
[57] *Evans* (HC), paragraph 208.

may tilt the balance as to whether such interference, effectively depriving a person of their last chance at genetic parenthood, remained proportionate to the objectives of the HFE Act 1990.

Article 14: The Prohibition of Discrimination

The enjoyment of the rights and freedoms set forth in this Convention shall be secured without discrimination on any ground such as sex, race, colour, language, religion, political or other opinion, national or social origin, association with a national minority, property, birth or other status.

Ms Evans's complaint that she suffered discrimination in violation of Article 14 in conjunction with Article 8, in that her position compared unfavourably with that of healthy women, was arguably the most compelling element of her case. In order to succeed under this head, Ms Evans would have to provide a comparator; that is, a person in an analogous situation with which Ms Evans could draw a comparison and demonstrate discrimination. The analogous situation would be a woman who had conceived as a result of sexual intercourse. Submissions made that the grounds for discrimination was Ms Evans's infertility as against that of fertile, or alternatively, pregnant women failed. There was no discrimination between women who conceive naturally, because the donation of sperm through sexual intercourse is equivalent to that of the transfer of the embryo into the woman, and the moment of conception is equivalent to that of implantation. No embryo had been transferred into Ms Evans. Arden LJ commented that the correct focus should be on the (biological) father and the position of the fertile woman and an infertile woman in relation to the father. Seen from that perspective, there is discrimination between the position of Ms Evans and that of a woman who conceives through natural sexual intercourse. The genetic father is allowed to withdraw his consent in IVF later than he could do in ordinary sexual intercourse. In this manner, the HFE Act 1990 discriminates between women who can, and women who cannot, conceive through sexual intercourse. However, Thorpe and Sedley LJJ stated that even if this alternative argument had been raised, they would have likewise held that discrimination is objectively justified for the reasons given under Article 8(2).

Arden LJ pointed out a legal anomaly, in that legislation drafted to regulate reproductive science that could reverse nature's discrimination and assist the infertile, in reality grants infertile women fewer reproductive rights than their fertile counterparts. In natural reproduction, whereby fertilisation of the embryos takes place inside the body of a woman the law is quite clear: the reproductive choices of women are paramount and conclusive. A man has no legal right to prevent his partner from, or coerce her into having an abortion.[58] This is the case even within marriage, or if the man was deceived into believing she was using birth control at the time of sexual intercourse.[59] While it is acknowledged that men also have reproductive choices and interests, respect for the pregnant woman's bodily integrity means that the decisions regarding the pregnancy must ultimately be hers alone. In the context of frozen IVF embryos we are dealing with a situation where the male gamete donor's reproductive choices no longer entail infringements of a woman's autonomy and bodily integrity. Once fertilisation and the reproductive process are removed from the woman's body the dispositional position of the gamete progenitors is no longer clear-cut.

The Human Fertilisation and Embryology Act 2008

> Mary Warnock, the philosopher responsible for developing its conceptual underpinning, has described the 1990 Act as 'ambiguous' in the light of *Evans*, and confessed that the committee she chaired 'did not pursue a case ... where there is disagreement between the parties'.[60]

The decision to update the HFE Act 1990 could have remedied this omission. Yet the amendments made by the Human Fertilisation and Embryology Act 2008 do not substantially amend the provisions relating to consent to storage or use of embryos or gametes to create an embryo in vitro. Section 12(1)(c) of the 1990 Act (as amended by secondary legislation and the 2008 Act), provides:

> The following shall be conditions of every licence granted under this Act:
> (c) except in relation to the use of gametes in the course of providing basic partner treatment services or non-medical fertility services, that the provisions of Schedule 3 to this Act shall be complied with.

---

[58] In both the UK and the USA, a man has no legal right to prevent his partner (even if they are married) from having an abortion, nor may he force her to have an abortion: *Paton* v. *Trustees of BPAS* [1979] QB 276 and *Planned Parenthood* v. *Danforth* 428 US 52, 69 (1976).

[59] See S. Sheldon, '"Sperm Bandits", Birth Control Fraud and the Battle of the Sexes' (2001) 21(3) *Legal Studies* 460–480.

[60] S. Sheldon, 'Gender Equality and Reproductive Decision-Making' (2004) 12 *Feminist Legal Studies* 303–316, citing Warnock's comments as reported in: BBC News, 'Fertility Laws Branded "Ambiguous"' 24 August 2002.

Section 13 of the HFE Act 2008 introduced Schedule 3 (which amended Schedule 3 to the HFE Act 1990 and relates to consent to the use or storage of gametes or embryos) and provides, in so far as is material:

> (5) A woman shall not be provided with treatment services unless account has been taken of the welfare of any child who may be born as a result of the treatment (including the need of that child for supportive parenting, and of any other child who may be affected by the birth).
>
> (6) A woman shall not be provided with treatment services of a kind specified in Part 1 of Schedule 3ZA unless she and any man or woman who is to be treated together with her have been given a suitable opportunity to receive proper counselling about the implications of her being provided with treatment services of that kind, and have been provided with such relevant information as is proper.

Paragraph 4 of Schedule 3 to the 1990 Act required that a person varying or withdrawing their consent to the storage and/or use of gametes or embryos must give notice of this to the establishment holding the gametes or embryos. Post the HFE Act 2008, the amended paragraph 1(1) of Schedule 3 requires that such notice now be provided in writing and signed by the person withdrawing consent. Section 3(1)(3) to the schedule provides 'in this Schedule 'effective consent' means a consent under this Schedule which has not been withdrawn'. The HFE Act 2008 introduced a twelve-month period in cases where one person in a couple seeking fertility treatment, withdraws their consent to the storage of an embryo or, where donated gametes are used, where the gamete donor withdraws consent.[61] This provision does not alter the requirement that the consent of both parties is required to store the embryos, but it is intended to provide a year-long 'cooling off' period during which the embryos will not be destroyed unless all interested persons consent.[62] This 'cooling off period' was said to offer the parties' time to resolve any differences between them, either privately or through the courts.[63] Whilst those amendments were welcomed by the BMA,[64] the Joint Scrutiny Committee[65] and the government, I argue that the changes did not go far enough. Had this provision been in force, it would not have altered the

---

[61] HFE Act 2008, Schedule 3, paragraph 7, inserted new paragraph 4A to Schedule 3 into the 1990 Act.

[62] Human Fertilisation and Embryology Act 2008, Explanatory Notes.

[63] Joint Committee on the Human Tissue and Embryos (Draft) Bill, *Human Tissue and Embryos (Draft) Bill* (Volume I, HL Paper 169-I, HC Paper 630-I), paragraph 215.

[64] Ibid.

[65] Ibid.

injustice to Ms Evans who had been advised to wait a few years after treatment for cancer before attempting implantation, and whose partner still requested (after a lengthy court battle which lasted over four years) that the embryos the couple created together be destroyed. It also does not allow for exceptional circumstances such as when it is the last chance at genetic parenthood for one of the gamete progenitors. Nor does it allow couples to come to their own private agreements as to what should happen to their embryos upon separation.

Although the court in *Evans* referred to the 'twin pillars' of consent *and* welfare as the two most important principles underlying the HFE Act 1990,[66] the HFE Act 2008 only updated one of these substantively. In line with amendments to welfare of the child,[67] the HFE Act 2008 could have clarified the definition of 'treatment together' and 'use'. As noted earlier, interpreting consent to 'treatment together' as necessitating the couple to be united in pursuit of treatment at the date the embryo is transferred to the uterus stemmed from an outdated hetero-centric policy that intended to deter single women seeking fertility treatment.[68] Yet changes made by the HFE Act 2008, give the impression of the government's belated acceptance that it is no longer deemed essential to a child's welfare that a mother and a father bring up a child. The HFE Act 2008 amended section 13(5) of the HFE Act 1990. This provision pre-2008 mandated a clinic to consider the welfare of any child that may be created by IVF, stating:

> A woman shall not be provided with treatment services unless account has been taken of the welfare of the child who may be born as a result of the treatment (including the need of that child for a father), and of any other child who may be affected by the birth.

Section 14(2) of the HFE Act 2008 amended the reference to a child's need 'for a father' to the child's need for 'supportive parenting'.[69] The HFE Act 2008 also contained provisions to recognise same sex couples as legal parents of children conceived through the use of assisted reproductive technologies.[70] In line with these amendments, the government could have also given the words 'treatment together' a contemporary meaning to

---

[66] *Evans* (HC), paragraph 37, per Wall J.
[67] HFE Act 1990, s13(5); HFE Act 2008, s14(2)(b).
[68] *Evans* (CA), paragraph 97, per Arden LJ.
[69] For a discussion on the changes to s13(5) and a suggestion that the amendments did not represent a major change in law or how the clause would be interpreted in practice see J. McCandless and S. Sheldon, '"No Father Required?" The Welfare Assessment in the Human Fertilisation and Embryology Act 2008' (2010) *Feminist Legal Studies* 201–225.
[70] HFE Act 2008, ss42–47.

reflect changes in social attitudes towards parenting. The HFE Act 2008 could have also seized the chance to amend, clarify and incorporate the provisions on consent into the main body of the Act, so as to place these provisions on a par with the other fundamental pillar underpinning the HFE Act 1990. It is disappointing that the opportunity to update the 'twin pillars' together was not utilised by the 2008 Act amendments and it is regrettable that the two remain disjunctive. The HFE Act 2008 increased the statutory maximum storage period for embryos from five years to ten years.[71] *Evans* exposed the fact that the provisions of the HFE Act 1990 were unable to justly resolve the complex issues presented by this case. The fact the HFE Act 2008 increased the storage period of embryos may mean such embryo disputes will only increase. Ten years is a long time, in which circumstances may change and the fate of IVF embryos created may be thrown into dispute.

It is clear that, notwithstanding the 2008 legislative amendments, regulation of disputes concerning use and disposition of embryos continue to create dilemmas.[72] Consider the recent 'extra ordinary case'[73] of *ARB* v. *Hammersmith Ltd* [2017].[74]

2.2.2   ARB v. Hammersmith Ltd *[2017]: Embryo Bandits*

The dispute arose when a man, identified only as ARB, brought a legal action against Hammersmith Fertility Clinic, claiming the clinic had permitted his former partner (identified only as 'R') to thaw and implant embryos the couple had created together, without his knowledge or consent. Whilst the clinic had a form purportedly signed by him, R had forged his signature. The embryos that the clinic was storing had been created in 2008, when unable to conceive naturally and having unsuccessfully undertaken IVF treatment at two other clinics, the former couple had IVF at the Defendant's Clinic (the clinic) as private patients. After just one cycle, the couple had a son, D, who was born in late 2008. The remaining five IVF embryos were frozen, with the parties' consent,

---

[71] HFE Act 2008, s15(3) amends the maximum statutory storage limit for embryos from 'five years' to 'ten years' (to bring it into line with the ten-year limit applicable to the storage of gametes).

[72] On consent see also the DoH Guidance, 'Reference Guide to Consent for Examination or Treatment', Second Edition, 2009, and GMC Guidance, 'Consent: Patients and Doctors Making Decisions Together', 2008 Edition.

[73] As described by the judge Mr Justice Jay in *ARB* v. *Hammersmith Ltd* [2017] EWCH 2438 (HC) at paragraph 323.

[74] *ARB* v. *Hammersmith Ltd* [2017] EWCH 2438 (HC).

both signing agreements on an annual basis for these to remain in storage. On 5 March 2010, the couple attended the clinic for advice and at various stages forms were signed. The couple split up a few months later and R subsequently moved out of ARB's home. R later returned to the clinic in April, May and October 2010. On the second visit, R handed the clinic a 'consent to thaw' form, signed by her and purportedly signed by ARB and, on the basis of this document, an embryo was thawed and successfully implanted. Almost a year after the couple split, on 14 February 2011, R sent a text message to ARB announcing she was pregnant.[75] R subsequently gave birth to a daughter, E, in the summer of 2011. On 25 November 2012, ARB signed a form withdrawing his consent to the use and storage of any embryos fertilised by his sperm. When ARB later complained to the Human Fertilisation and Embryology Authority (HFEA) that the clinic had permitted R to thaw and implant the embryo without his consent, the HFEA's CEO wrote to ARB stating:

> What happened in your case if highly unusual if not unique. We are not aware of such an event occurring in any other UK clinics, either before or since your experience. That may be of little comfort but I am sure you will appreciate that it is very difficult for regulations and procedures to cover every eventuality, particularly where an act of deception is involved.[76]

Yet the HFEA's assertion that ARB's experience was 'highly unusual if not unique' was not quite accurate – the HFEA was at the time aware of impending legal action concerning a case in 2008, where a husband was threatening legal action after his estranged wife twice gave birth without his consent by using frozen embryos created whilst they were still together.[77]

ARB brought legal action against the clinic in contract: he claimed that there were no circumstances in which he would, or could have signed the consent to thaw form, since their relationship had irretrievably broken down by that point; that R had forged his signature and it followed that the daughter, E, was an 'unwanted child', for which he sought substantive damages, in recoupment of past and future financial losses for the cost of

---

[75] *ARB*, paragraph 47.

[76] *ARB*, paragraph 55.

[77] Mr Justice Jay explicitly noted this point at paragraph 58. See also 'Husband Discovered He Was a Father of Two after Estranged Wife Forged His Signature in IVF Deception', *Evening Standard*, 3 March 2008. M. Wardrop, 'Woman Had Two Children after Secretly Taking Ex-Husband Frozen Sperm', *The Telegraph*, 29 May 2011.

raising E.[78] The judge, Mr Justice Jay accepted that ARB did not sign the consent to thaw form in October, or at all and R forged his signature. Thus he held the clinic was in breach of its strict contractual obligation to ensure ARB's consent had been obtained.[79] Despite the fact that ARB had succeeded on all issues, his case failed on the issue of legal policy: it was held that the court was bound by the two House of Lords decisions in *McFarlane* v. *Tayside Health Board* [2000] 2 AC 59 and *Rees* v. *Darlington Memorial Hospital NHS Trust* [2003] UKHL 52. Both ruled that a claim for the upkeep of a healthy child is irrecoverable in law.[80] Mr Justice Jay noted he was 'acting in obedience with clear authority and principle'[81] which compelled him to uphold the clinic's submission that legal policy precludes all of ARB's pleaded claims. The judge stated:

> Looking again at Rees, the legal policy objections may be characterised as follows: the inherent difficulty, if not impossibility, of measuring the loss; the unwillingness to regard the child as a financial liability; the refusal to offset the benefits which will accrue from parenthood from any additional financial liabilities; the feeling that it is morally unacceptable to attempt

---

[78] Discussing the damages sought, the court noted that the object of an award of damages in contract is to place the innocent party in the position they would have been in had the contract been performed and the principle underlying the tortious measure of damages is to place the injured party in the position they would have been in had the breach of duty not occurred (paragraph 306). Had the clinic performed the contract, it would not have proceeded without ARB's written consent. ARB would not have given it, and E would not have been born. In this case, ARB sought substantial damages including the cost of private education, a gap year, university abroad, a generous wedding, refurbishing a bedroom, the cost of litigating with R etc. (see paragraph 325).

[79] *ARB*, paragraph 288.

[80] In *McFarlane* v. *Tayside Health Board* [2000] 2 AC 59, the House of Lords held that a claim in tort brought by parents for the upkeep of a healthy child born after negligence in connection with a vasectomy procedure could not be sustained in law. Their Lordships gave different reasons for arriving at the same conclusion. In *Rees* v. *Darlington Memorial Hospital NHS Trust* [2004] 1 AC 309, another tort claim, the mother was disabled and underwent a sterilisation procedure because she feared that her blindness would prevent her from looking after any child. The procedure was negligently performed. The House of Lords, reversing the Court of Appeal, held that the mother could not recover damages for any of the costs of providing for the child, although there would be a conventional award of £15,000 to reflect the fact that she was the victim of a legal wrong. For discussion of these cases see N. Priaulx, 'That's One Heck of an "Unruly Horse"! Riding Roughshod over Autonomy in Wrongful Conception' (2004) 12 *Feminist Legal Studies* 317. L. Hoyano, 'Misconceptions about Wrongful Conception' (2002) 65 *Modern Law Review* 883. V. Chico, 'Wrongful Conception: Policy, Inconsistency and the Conventional Award' (2007) 8 *Medical Law International* 139. Also note that Mr Justice Jay conceded, 'strictly speaking, such authority applies only to claims in tort', *ARB*, paragraph 289.

[81] *ARB*, paragraph 323.

this exercise; and the notion that it is not fair, just and reasonable to allow this sort of claim. These objections overlap, and may be expressed in different ways, with different emphasis. Most of them are apt to apply where the contractual obligation is strict. The last of these objections is expressly tied to considerations which traditionally have only operated in the tortious sphere, and it is to be noted that Lord Bingham also expressly referred to burdens on the NHS. However, the secondary obligation to pay damages arises by implication of the common law, and in my view the result should be the same even if one were notionally to strip away the tort-specific objections. Furthermore, I have difficulty with the notion that a private patient could succeed whereas an NHS patient could not.[82]

Thus policy reasons barred the claim and judgment was given for the clinic, with permission granted to appeal. The fact this was an action in contract was deemed insufficient to distinguish this case from wrongful conception cases. Examination of those cases reveals that not all the policy reasons in *McFarlane* and *Rees* for not permitting recovery of pure economic loss apply. For instance in contract, unlike the tortious wrongful life claims, there was not the hurdle of claiming for pure economic loss – arguably if the clinic accepts the benefits of a contract (financial payment) they should pay when things go wrong. Yet it is understandable why it might be undesirable to permit claims in contract but not tort, as it would mean private patients who have a contract could claim, but NHS patients cannot. This could be countered by the reality that most people who undertake IVF are private patients[83] and thus, the problem of scarce NHS resources being used to pay for healthy children is not present. However, this still gives rise to the undesirable task Mr Justice Jay alluded to above, of measuring the loss/damages.

---

[82] *ARB*, paragraph 319.

[83] HFEA Innovation in Regulation 2017 Report provides that the majority of services (some 60 per cent) are provided by the private sector, with the NHS providing the remaining 40 per cent. Note that NHS funding comes through Clinical Commissioning Groups (CCGs). NHS England provides commissioning guidance to CCGs. Although The National Institute for Health Care and Excellence (NICE) provides best practice guidance, and recommends in the context of access to IVF that 'In women aged under 40 years who have not conceived after 2 years of regular unprotected intercourse or 12 cycles of artificial insemination (where 6 or more are by intrauterine insemination), offer 3 full cycles of IVF, with or without ICSI. If the woman reaches the age of 40 during treatment, complete the current full cycle but do not offer further full cycles'. However, NICE guidance is not mandatory and is not necessarily followed by clinics. Fertility Network UK, which monitors provision, reported in 2017 that many areas in England are cutting back on provision of IVF on the NHS to save money – see 'NHS Access to IVF Being Cut in England', *BBC News*, 7 August 2017.

The further distinction from those wrongful life cases, as Mr Justice Jay acknowledged,[84] is that they were failed vasectomy and sterilisation cases, in which the whole object was to prevent pregnancy. In the instant case, this was a deliberate act to bring a child into being, the clinic being the custodians of the embryos which the law acknowledges has a 'special status'[85] and the whole purpose of the policy requiring written consent, is to ensure that there can be no dispute that both gamete providers are agreeing to the creation of human life.

Counsel for ARB were unsuccessful in their attempts to distinguish the facts of the present case from the wrongful conception cases, arguing ARB has been deceived by R and let down by the clinic, and E is an unwanted child, born in extremely fraught, possibly unique, circumstances. Susanna Rickard, who represented ARB, stated that the case was the first wrongful birth claim founded on breach of contract, rather than clinical negligence and is a landmark case on the duties owed by IVF clinics.[86] She noted:

> The IVF clinic was in breach of an express contractual term not to create a child without the father's consent. The claimant won every single legal point germane to his primary case, but by the application of the 'policy' point borrowed from the House of Lords' decisions in *McFarlane* and *Rees* – that a healthy child is a blessing rather than a detriment – the decision has conferred upon the IVF clinic effective impunity from the normal consequences of their breach of contract. It is time for the controversial decisions in *McFarlane* and *Rees* to be reviewed.[87]

As in *Evans*, again, in this judgment, the judge used policy formulated in the context of case law on wrongful conception, which involved in vivo conception and pregnancy, to decide how this dispute dealing with IVF embryos should be resolved. However, ARB is a new type of wrongful pregnancy case; whilst it is not wrongful *conception* as the conception was not negligent – it is the implantation that is negligent, so is more apt to refer to it as a case of *wrongful implantation*. The revised legal framework in the HFE Act, failed to provide a just and equitable resolution to the

---

[84] *ARB*, paragraph 326.

[85] The Warnock Report, paragraph 11.17. HFEA, *Code of Practice* (2015) paragraph 15.13. For criticism of the special status the Warnock Committee accorded to the human embryo see D. Jones, 'The Special Status of Human Embryo in the United Kingdom: An Exploration of the Use of Language in Public Policy' (2011) 1 *Human Reproduction & Genetic Ethics* 66–83.

[86] J. Miller, 'Time for "Wrongful Birth" Decisions to Be Reviewed' (2017) 167 (7765) *New Law Journal* 5.

[87] Ibid.

dispute which arose and as Mr Justice Jay observed, 'The 1990 Act is silent as to whether any breaches of its provisions, or the HFEA Code of Practice (made under section 25) gives rise to civil liability'.[88] Section 25(6) provides that 'a failure on the part of any person to observe any provision of the Code shall not of itself be liable to any proceedings'. So even in the instant case, where it was held that ARB did not give his signature and did not in fact consent (noting if he had been asked, he would have declined to proceed), he was left without legal remedy.

There are other ways in which the control and storage of embryos could be regulated which would avoid such disputes whilst still respecting the procreative autonomy of both parties. The HFE Act 2008 missed an opportunity to revisit whether the policy governing control and storage of embryos (and the policy that gamete progenitors have the right to withdraw consent prior to implantation upon notification in writing to a clinic) remains the correct stance to adopt in resolving such disputes. Priaulx observed that 'whatever way one interprets the 1990 Act in the context of *Evans*, one party must *necessarily* have their reproductive desires thwarted. So, the question must be then, whether such a conflict could have been avoided so as to facilitate the reproductive desires of both parties?'[89] This statement could apply equally to ARB, where it was evident that one party R wanted to use the embryos post separation and the other gamete progenitor R, did not. In light of this conflict, this chapter now proceeds to consider what alternative methods of regulation could be used to govern embryo storage and disposition, so as to avoid such conflicts.

2.3 Alternative Models for Resolution of Such Disputes

2.3.1 The 'Natural Pregnancy' Model

Academics criticised the fact that infertile women lack the same control over their embryos as their fertile female counterparts, who upon natural conception, can decide whether to carry the embryo to term or not, in spite of the male progenitors' objections.[90] It was questioned why a man

---

[88] *ARB*, paragraph 33.

[89] N. Priaulx, 'Rethinking Progenitive Conflict: Why Reproductive Autonomy Matters' (2008) 16(2) *Medical Law Review* 169, at p. 195.

[90] Daar, 'Assisted Reproductive Technologies'; J. Harris, 'Head to Head – Frozen Embryos', *BBC News*, 7 March 2006; H. Draper, 'Gametes, Consent and Points of No Return' (2007) 10(2) *Human Fertility* 105.

should be granted more rights in assisted reproduction, which is a collaborative reproductive enterprise that he has entered into with the sole purpose of procreation, when in natural reproduction his view is subordinated to the woman's. Colker made the following observation:

> If a man and woman have intercourse, and the woman deceives the man into thinking she is using birth control, we don't allow the man to exercise a veto over her desire to carry a pregnancy to term. In fact, we even impose child support on him, despite the possible fraud. In the frozen embryo context, the initial decision to donate gametes is for a very clear purpose – to become parents – rather than, for example sexual satisfaction. Because that initial consent existed, there is no good reason, to give presumptive value to the person who has changed his or her mind.[91]

The argument has been promulgated that women should retain the presumptive say, as not to do so, is to treat infertile women disadvantageously in comparison to their fertile female counterparts. For instance, consider Daar's comments:

> in the context of ART, pregnancy commences with an action done with the intent to produce a child. A woman using ART should have the same right to control her unimplanted embryo as she would have to control her early fetus in a traditional pregnancy. Anything less would deny women undergoing ART equal protection of precious reproductive liberties.[92]

It has been suggested that equal treatment of infertile women could be achieved by the adoption of a natural model of pregnancy to regulate assisted conception. Regulating frozen embryos in a similar way to natural pregnancy could be achieved in a number of ways: one way would be to impose a time frame that tracks the natural course of pregnancy. The time frame could be limited to the forty-week gestation period, during which time consent to the use of the embryos is irrevocable. Daar states:

> Using a natural gestation period as a limit on implantation rights creates the notice and certainty that has previously attracted courts to procreation avoidance, while not depriving fertility patients of rights enjoyed by their fertile female counterparts.[93]

Both gamete progenitors will be notified that a pregnancy may ensue from provision of one's gametes within this reasonably defined period of

---

[91] R. Colker, 'Pregnant Men Revisited or Sperm Is Cheap, Eggs Are Not' (1995–1996) 47 *Hastings Law Journal* 1063, at p. 1069.
[92] Daar, 'Assisted Reproductive Technologies' at p. 457.
[93] Ibid., 468.

time. Once the gestational window has passed neither could be forced into parenthood. Daar claims this would be 'a more just framework that would create equity between fertile and infertile women in the procreational process'.[94] (Although it should be noted that such a 'solution' would have been of little use to Ms Evans, however, who had been advised not to implant for a few years, during which time the couple separated.)

The natural model of pregnancy is also supported by Harris, who, speaking of the *Evans* case, argued that:

> These two people made a decision to try and have children. Howard Johnston gave his considered, fully informed, consent to fertilization of the eggs, the creation of the embryos and the 'procreative enterprise'. I do not see why he should now be permitted to break this contract and withdraw unilaterally from the procreative enterprise with such disastrous consequences for Natalie. This is her last chance to have her own genetic children. Normal sexual intercourse is the appropriate model here. The man consents to sexual intercourse. If the couple are trying to have children, he consents to the attempt to have children. If his partner becomes pregnant, he has no further say in the continuation of that pregnancy and the birth of that child. [. . .] Natalie Evans has much more to lose than Howard Johnston.[95]

Similarly, Draper suggested that in place of the current point of no return, which is the implantation of these embryos into a female host, the legislation 'should be amended so that the point of no return for withdrawal of consent to the use of gametes is the creation of an embryo with those gametes (fertilization)'.[96] Like Harris and Daar, Draper argues that it is the agreement to the creation of the embryos that is crucial and should be binding; she claims it could be argued 'that the act of donation or provisions itself marks the genuine point of no return'[97] and that '[f]ixing the point of no return here underlines the seriousness of the venture upon which people have embarked, and – for men at any rate – harmonizes natural and assisted conception'.[98]

Leaving aside Harris's comment that 'Natalie Evans has much more to lose than Howard Johnston',[99] the resolutions offered by Harris, Daar and Draper all appear to be premised on a notion of natural pregnancy which would vest the decisive say in the female progenitor. A model akin to that suggested by Daar, which emulated the natural model of

---

[94] Ibid., 477.
[95] J. Harris, 'Head to Head – Frozen Embryos', *BBC News*, 7 March 2006.
[96] Draper, 'Gametes, Consent and Points of No Return'.
[97] Ibid., p. 107.
[98] Ibid.
[99] Harris, 'Head to Head – Frozen Embryos'.

pregnancy, could be implemented to resolve such disputes.[100] Does the 'natural model of pregnancy' provide an equitable and just solution to such dilemmas? Holding that consent should become irrevocable upon fertilisation as suggested by Draper would place women using IVF on a par with their fertile female counterparts. Nor is this an impracticable solution for it has been adopted in other countries in Europe. For instance, in Austria, Estonia and Italy, the male progenitor can revoke consent only up to the point of fertilisation, beyond which it is the woman alone who decides if and when to proceed.[101]

However, it is not clear that making consent after fertilisation irrevocable would grant an equal say to male and female gamete donors over the fate of their stored embryos, for, as Bennett notes,[102] it is more likely that a woman will take advantage of such a change in the law and implant an embryo against the wishes of her ex-partner. In most cases she will not need the use of another's body to gestate the embryo. The male gamete donor needs to find a willing host for the embryo, which will prove far more difficult. He will either have to convince a new partner to bring to birth a child conceived with his previous partner or will have to find a suitable surrogate willing to be part of such an enterprise.[103] While the female donor is able to control whether she brings this embryo to birth, the male donor is still reliant on the will of a woman to achieve this goal. It seems that proposals like Draper's, still give the female donor more control over reproduction.[104] Furthermore, this 'solution' overlooks a vital fact: in natural conception, fertilisation takes place inside the maternal body, invoking her bodily autonomy, which justifies giving her the paramount say regarding the embryo. In assisted conception, fertilisation is not synonymous with implantation, and the egg is fertilised in a neutral environment, engaging neither one's bodily integrity. Arguably, both progenitors are equally situated in regards to the embryo their gametes have created – so arguments that the natural pregnancy model should be used to resolve such disputes are unconvincing.

---

[100] Daar, 'Assisted Reproductive Technologies'.

[101] *Evans* v. *UK* (ECtHR), paragraph 32.

[102] R. Bennett 'Is Reproduction Women's Business? How Should We Regulate Regarding Stored Embryos, Posthumous Pregnancy, Ectogenesis and Male Pregnancy?' (2008) 2(3) *Studies in Ethics, Law and Technology* 3, at p. 10.

[103] While future technologies such as ectogenesis and male pregnancy (through womb transplants) may alter this, at the current time and in the immediate future, the male progenitor will be dependent on finding a female host to gestate his embryo.

[104] Bennett, 'Is Reproduction Women's Business?'

There are a number of possible justifications for the notion that women should retain the decisive say over their in vitro embryos.

Women Give More to IVF Process

Ms Evans' counsel argued that her greater emotional and physical investment in the IVF process meant her Article 8 rights should override Mr Johnston's.[105] This submission seeks to assert that women should maintain the decisive say in assisted conception to represent the gamete donation process, which is more invasive for women. Unlike the provision of a man's gametes, which usually requires little more than sperm ejaculation in a cup, consider the following passage which describes what gamete donation involves for a woman:

> The process of retrieving eggs from a woman's ovaries poses significant risks. In most instances, drugs are administered to stimulate egg production so that eggs can be retrieved. These drugs pose an increased risk of multiple births and ovarian hyper stimulation syndrome, a condition that may result in abdominal blood clotting, major organ damage, respiratory distress, or stroke. Additionally, some studies suggest a correlation between fertility drugs and ovarian cancer. The egg extraction process is also burdensome. Extraction is accomplished by inserting a needle through the vaginal wall and into the ovarian follicle. Follicle fluid and the eggs contained within are then suctioned out. Clinics generally provide some sedation, but most women report moderate or severe pain despite the provision of analgesic. Common side effects following the procedure include abdominal or vaginal discomfort and bleeding from the vaginal puncture sites.[106]

In addition to the invasiveness of egg retrieval, it has been claimed that, combined with women's limited supply of eggs and declining fertility over time, frozen embryos are more important to women, and thus justifies giving them the presumptive say regarding embryos. Colker even goes so far as to say that 'sperm may be cheap and plentiful, but eggs are not'[107] and that 'these reproductive differences between women and men should be relevant to the disposition of disputes but are usually ignored by the courts and by society'.[108] This is not completely true; in some jurisdictions recognition has been given to the fact that IVF represents a heavier burden for the woman. For instance, in Hungary, absent

---

[105] *Evans* (ECtHR), paragraph 62.
[106] E. Waldman, 'Disputing over Embryos: Of Contracts and Consents' (2000) 32 *Arizona State Law Journal* 897–940, at p. 903.
[107] Colker, 'Pregnant Men Revisited'.
[108] Ibid.

any prior written agreement to the contrary, the woman is entitled to proceed with the treatment notwithstanding the death of her partner or the divorce of the couple.[109]

Whilst it is conceded the egg retrieval process in IVF is more invasive for women than men, the differences in gamete provision stem from biological gender differences. It is not clear why men should be penalised because it is easier for them to provide gametes than for women. Whilst IVF may be less invasive for men, men are also innately biologically disadvantaged when it comes to procreation; 'since a man cannot sustain a pregnancy in his own body, he will always need the assistance of a woman'.[110] Should men desire to reproduce, they must first find a female host willing to gestate the embryo.[111] Thus it is not clear, in disputes regarding embryo disposition and absent bodily integrity invoked through a pregnancy, why a woman should be granted decisive say. The argument that she should do so because she has given more to the IVF process is unconvincing.

Reproduction Is Central to Being a Woman

It has been asserted that women should be given greater dispositional control over in vitro embryos because reproduction is central to a woman's role. Grayling, commenting on the *Evans* case, argued that:

> the clincher is that parenthood is a more crucial matter for women ... [their] experience of pregnancy, childbirth and the early nurture of an infant and the bonds that persist for a lifetime thereafter outweigh a 'father's role [which] is nowhere so central, however important.[112]

Such arguments imply that to deprive women of childbearing is to remove from them their central role and render them obsolete. This view reinforces the stereotype in society that woman's primary function is to gestate and rear children and it is precisely this stereotype women should be trying to fight rather than enforce. Maintaining such a stance that a woman should have a primary role in reproduction arguably reinforces deep-seated notions that regard women primarily as baby makers and the value of a woman is determined by her status as

---

[109] *Evans* v. *UK* (ECtHR), paragraph 32.

[110] Colker, 'Pregnant Men Revisited' 1074.

[111] Although this may change should ectogenesis or male pregnancy (third wave reproductive technologies which are both addressed later on in the thesis) become safe methods of reproduction.

[112] A. C. Grayling, 'Embryo Case', *Evening Standard*, 2 October 2003 as cited in Sheldon, 'Gender Equality and Reproductive Decision-Making', at p. 310.

a mother.[113] In order to dispel such stereotypes we need a radical trans-
formation of the social construction of artificial reproductive technologies and of the value placed on childrearing in society at large.[114] There
may well be sound reasons to grant women more of a decisive say in the
domain of artificial reproduction, but to advocate that this should be on
the basis that women play more of a central role in childrearing and
reproduction is not the way forward. Such a line of argument will only
perpetuate the stereotypes that reproduction should be the central role of
a woman, and serve to contribute to a reinforced patriarchal society,
which in the long term will be to the detriment of women. Thus, unless
good reason can be adduced to demonstrate why women should retain
a paramount say in reproduction, it follows that men should be allowed
an equal say, when to do so does not violate the autonomy and bodily
integrity of the woman concerned.

Gender Equality in All Domains

While many have commented on how the court's refusal to grant the
declarations sought by Ms Evans discriminated against women,[115] many
neglected to note, or welcome the case for introducing a notion of
enhanced gender equality in the domain of assisted reproduction. This
point was not lost on Arden LJ, who commented in the Court of Appeal
that the wider issue to have arisen from this case was 'whether in a world
in which many people have come to accept a woman's right of choice as
to whether she should have a child or not, the genetic father should have
the equivalent right – a right greater than that conferred by nature'.[116] All
those who believe in gender equality should arguably welcome men and
women having equivalent rights. In the context of family rights, men
continue to fight against their discrimination and over the last decade we
have witnessed the growing voice of men; consider the various high-
profile demonstrations that have been staged by activists campaigning for
increasing fathers' rights in order to improve access to their children.[117]

---

[113] See G. Corea, *The Mother Machine: Reproductive Technologies from Artificial Insemination to Artificial Wombs* (New York, NY: Harper and Row, 1985).

[114] B. Rothman, *Recreating Motherhood: Ideology and Technology in a Patriarchal Society* (New York, NY: W. W. Norton, 1989); E. Wright Clayton, 'A Ray of Light about Frozen Embryos' (1993) 2(4) *Kennedy Institute of Ethics Journal* 347–359, at p. 357.

[115] Draper, 'Gametes, Consent and Points of No Return'; J. Harris, 'Head to Head – Frozen Embryos', *BBC News*, 7 March 2006.

[116] *Evans* (CA), paragraph 89.

[117] J. Halliday, 'Men Stage Child Custody Protest on Jeremy Corbyn's Roof', *The Guardian*, 5 August 2016. M. Lawson, 'No Justice 4 Fathers', *The Guardian*, 20 January 2006;

In conjunction with the promotion of gender equality in other contexts[118] it could also be argued that assisted reproductive technologies that allow for procreation to be fragmented and conception to take place outside a female host makes this a ripe time to acknowledge greater equality in the domain of reproduction.[119] Procreative liberty encompasses the right *not to* reproduce as much as it does the right *to* reproduce.[120] Unlike conventional sexual reproduction, whereby sexual intercourse results in conception and the gestation of the fetus in the maternal womb, thereby engaging a woman's bodily autonomy, fertilisation outside the maternal womb does not invoke anyone's bodily autonomy. In the absence of this justification, it is not clear why a woman should have the decisive say regarding an embryo, or why her views should prevail over the man's.[121] Arguably in *Evans*, by declining to invest decisive say in the female progenitor, the court recognised that outside pregnancy that invokes a woman's bodily autonomy, women and men have equal rights in the arena of reproduction. But absent the policy enacted in the HFE Act 1990 (as amended) which states that prior to use/implantation either party can withdraw consent to treatment, or the natural pregnancy model advocated by some which invests the female progenitor with the paramount say, what alternative 'solutions' can be offered to resolve disputes over the fate of in vitro embryos?

2.3.2   The 'Contractual' Model

Instead of provisions which allow parties to vary or withdraw their consent at any time prior to implantation, an alternative framework that would provide certainty to both gamete progenitors would be to

R. Little, 'Fathers Still Need Justice', *The Sunday Times*, 22 January 2006; E. Mayne and M. Beckford, 'Fathers for Justice Force the National Lottery Off Air', *The Mail on Sunday*, 21 May 2006.

[118] See generally R. Collier, 'A Hard Time to Be a Father? Reassessing the Relationship between Law, Policy, and Family (Practices)' (2001) 28 *Journal of Law and Society* 520; R. Collier, 'Fathers 4 Justice, Law and the New Politics of Fatherhood' (2005) 17(4) *Child and Family Law Quarterly* 511. R. Collier and S. Sheldon, *Fragmenting Fatherhood: A Socio-Legal Study* (Oxford and Portland: Hart, 2008). R. Collier, *Men, Law and Gender: Essays on The 'Man' of Law* (London and New York, NY: Routledge, 2011).

[119] See Priaulx, 'Rethinking Progenitive Conflict: Why Reproductive Autonomy Matters' for an analysis of the concept of reproductive autonomy and how it is limited in cases of progenitive conflict.

[120] I. G. Cohen, 'The Constitution and the Rights Not to Procreate' (2008) 60 *Stanford Law Review* 1135–1196.

[121] Sheldon, 'Gender Equality and Reproductive Decision-Making'.

mandate that, before couples embark on creating embryos, they draw up an agreement specifying what is to happen upon separation or divorce. Sozou, Sheldon and Hartshorne have argued that offering couples only one type of consent agreement, as happens at present, is too restrictive and one 'gender neutral' solution is, alongside the current form of agreement, to offer an alternative form of agreement, in which one of the gamete progenitors agrees to forego the right to future withdrawal of consent.[122] They contend that (i) giving couples such a choice will better enable them to store embryos under a consent agreement that is appropriate for their circumstances and (ii) allowing such a choice, with robust procedures in place to ensure the validity of consent, is the best way to respect patient autonomy.[123] This would also prevent disputes such as those that arose in both *Evans* and *ARB*.

Chan and Quigley proposed that the difficult issue of resolving disputes over frozen embryos could be resolved by a solution which 'dissect[s] out the issues involving an isolated framework: the concept of embryos as property'.[124] Their analysis, which is based on 'the purely genetic component of parenthood',[125] suggests that upon the creation of an embryo, the two parties are 'joint-owners' which involves both parents giving up 'some rights over their genetic information in pursuit of the creation of the embryo'. Once this has happened, they argue that:

> [A]ny rights of the parents not to have those embryos created (as new genetic entities from their genetic information) is lost, and only the physical rights to the embryos persist ... Therefore, where there is a dispute over the fate of IVF embryos, the not wanting a genetically-related child argument from one of the parties cannot supply adequate grounds to prevent the implantation and bringing to birth of the embryos.[126]

Whilst Quigley and Chan also support fertilisation as the point of no return, their suggestion that embryos be treated as property may also lend support to arguments that such disputes could be avoided if they were treated as property and a contractual model governed their use, setting out terms of disposition. There are many scholars in favour of the creation and enforcement of pre-existing dispositional contracts in the context of such

---

[122] P. D. Sozou, S. Sheldon, G. M. Hartshorne, 'Consent Agreements for Cryopreserved Embryos: The Case for Choice' (2010) 36 *Journal of Medical Ethics* 230–233.

[123] Ibid.

[124] S. Chan and M. Quigley, 'Frozen Embryos, Genetic Information and Reproductive Rights' (2007) 21 *Bioethics* 439.

[125] Ibid., at 441.

[126] Ibid., at 447–448.

disputes.[127] For instance, Waldman advocates a contractual model to regulate such disputes, and outlines the benefits of this in the following passage:

> Contracts are useful precisely because they enable individuals to plan and order their lives. Contracts in the frozen embryo setting are also useful, because reproductive options are neither constant nor eternal. Because the ability to plan and preserve one's reproductive future is so important, dispositional agreements deserve more, not less judicial respect than agreements forged in business or other settings.[128]

The benefits of a contractual model have also been noted and utilised in similar disputes across the Atlantic. In *Davis* v. *Davis*[129] the Tennessee Supreme Court held 'prior agreements should be enforced unless there is a mutual modification. Only if there is prior disagreement should the burdens on the disagreeing gamete progenitors be considered'.[130] Similarly, in *Kass* v. *Kass*,[131] the New York Court of Appeal held embryo agreements governing embryo disposition should be presumed valid and enforced.

A contractual model may be rejected in the UK precisely because it treats embryos as property, or appears to do so.[132] The Warnock

---

[127] J. Robertson, 'Prior Agreements for Disposition of Frozen Embryos' (1999) 51 *Ohio State Law Journal* 407; J. A. Robertson, 'In The Beginning: The Legal Status of Early Embryos' (1990) 76 *Virginia Law Review* 437; M. Trespalacios, 'Frozen Embryos: Towards an Equitable Solution (1992) 46 *University of Miami Law Review* 803. But against the contractual model see G. Annas, 'The Shadowlands – Secrets, Lies, and Assisted Reproduction' (1998) 339(913) *New England Journal of Medicine* 935; T. Pachman, 'Disputes over Frozen Embryos and the Right Not to Be a Parent' (2003) 12 *Columbia Journal of Gender & Law* 128.

[128] Waldman, 'Disputing over Embryos', at p. 939.

[129] *Davis* v. *Davis* 842 S.W.2d 588 (Tenn.1992).

[130] C. Perry and L. Schneider, 'Cyropreserved Embryos: Who Shall Decide Their Fate?' (1992) *The Journal of Legal Medicine* 463–500 at 493.

[131] *Kass* v. *Kass* 673 N.Y.S 2d 350 (N.Y 1988).

[132] Although note *Yearworth and others* v. *North Bristol NHS Trust (Yearworth)* [2009] EWCA Civ 37 the Court of Appeal for England and Wales accepted that men who had deposited their semen for freezing before undertaking cancer treatment 'owned' the semen for the purposes of a claim in negligence because it was deposited solely for their benefit and that constituted a bailment. Many lawyers, philosophers and other commentators have discussed whether the law should recognise proprietary rights in bodily material. See, for example, *Self-Ownership, Property Rights & the Human Body: A Legal & Philosophical Analysis* (Cambridge: Cambridge University Press, 2017), I. Goold, *Flesh and Blood: Owning Our Bodies and Their Parts* (Oxford: Hart Publishing, 2016); L. Skene, 'Proprietary Interests in Human Bodily Material: Yearworth, Recent Australian Cases on Stored Semen and Their Implications' (2012) 20(2) *Medical Law Review* 227. S. Harmon and G. Laurie, 'Yearworth v. North Bristol NHS Trust: Property, Principles, Precedents and Paradigms' (2010) 69(3) *Cambridge Law Journal* 476–493; S. Harmon, 'Yearworth v. North Bristol NHS Trust: A Property Case of Uncertain

Committee took the view that granting 'rights' to in vitro embryos, or ownership of IVF embryos would not work in practice and thus a compromise position was reached in that in vitro embryos were accorded 'special status' and limited protection.[133] The Warnock Report adopted the position that 'there should be no ownership in a human embryo'.[134] In the UK, it is because of the special status accorded to the embryo, the law has chosen to limit the ability of gamete providers to have complete discretion with respect to disposition of their frozen embryos. In *Evans*, both the High Court and Court of Appeal held that any verbal assurances given that consent would not be revoked would not be enforced; they were deemed to be contrary to the public policy and the consent scheme enshrined in the legislation that both gamete providers should be entitled to vary or revoke consent prior to the 'use' of the embryo. Any legislative change to amend the law and allow the enforcement of agreements, or promises which have been relied upon in the context of frozen embryos, would have to be made by the legislature. Whether this is a change that Parliament would be inclined towards making is questionable. Parliament is uneasy about allowing individuals to contract on matters as personal as reproduction. Although writing on US law, Daar's statement applies equally to the UK when she states: 'In the past, even today, the law has resisted coupling a body of law that was deigned to address commercial disputes to something as personal and intimate as child birth'.[135] English law has rejected the use of contracts in the reproductive context of surrogacy; see for example the Surrogacy Arrangements Act 1985, s1A of which provides that 'no surrogacy arrangement is enforceable by or against any of the persons making it'. However, arguments that seek to distinguish surrogacy contracts from those pertaining to the disposition of frozen embryos could

---

Significance?' (2010) 13 *Medicine, Healthcare & Philosophy* 343–350; J. Herring and P.-L. Chau, 'My Body, Your Body, Our Bodies' (2007) 15 *Medical Law Review* 34; R. Hardcastle, *Law and the Human Body – Property Rights, Ownership and Control* (Oxford and Portland, OR: Hart, 2007); D. Nicol, 'Property in Human Tissue and the Right of Commercialisation: The Interface between Tangible and Intellectual Property' (2004) 30 *Monash University Law Review* 139. J. Wall, 'The Legal Status of Body Parts: A Framework' (2011) *Oxford Journal of Legal Studies* 1. L. Skene, 'Proprietary Rights in Human Bodies, Body Parts and Tissue' (2002) *Legal Studies* 102.

[133] As is demonstrated in Chapters 3 & 4 of this monograph, maintaining this compromise position as we enter into the third phase of human reproduction becomes increasingly difficult to sustain.

[134] Warnock Report, paragraph 10.11.

[135] Daar, 'Assisted Reproductive Technologies' at p. 474.

be made. To enforce the former may be to force a woman to become pregnant against her will, or to hand over a baby she has just gestated for nine months. Furthermore, one of the reasons surrogacy arrangements were made unenforceable by the Surrogacy Arrangements Act 1985, was to outlaw commercial surrogacy and, more generally, to discourage surrogacy arrangements. Yet the law recognises the reality that private, non-commercial surrogacy arrangements will occur and cannot easily be monitored or banned.[136] In such cases, the current law attempts to regulate these arrangements as far as is practically possible. Accordingly, Parliament could have considered the contractual model to regulate disputes over frozen embryos, for it could arguably achieve policy aims of providing a 'bright line rule' and granting gamete progenitors pro-creative control over their gametes.

The Warnock Committee also stated 'the couple who stored the embryo should have the use and disposal rights, although these rights ought to be subject to limitation'.[137] Arguably, if couples do have the right to use and dispose of their embryos, the law should allow couples to enter into agreements regarding the disposition of their gametes, providing of course these agreements do not contravene public policy. Such agreements that specify what is to happen upon incapacity, death, separation or divorce, would respect both gamete progenitors' reproductive autonomy and would provide a 'bright line rule' of certainty, to both the couples undergoing IVF and the clinic treating the couple. The law already mandates that provision be made for the first two of these eventualities,[138] so arguably this could also be extended to encompass what should happen upon separation or divorce.

In light of the objections against allowing contractual models to govern disposition, a model in between a contract and the present legal framework which allows only a single type of consent agreement for the future use of cryopreserved embryos, would be to allow people a choice of agreements in line with proposals suggested by Sozou, Sheldon and Hartshorne.[139] They argue that in addition to the option that consent

---

[136] HFE Act 2008, s59 amends the Surrogacy Arrangements Act 1985, and allows bodies that operate on a not-for-profit basis to receive payment for providing some surrogacy services. It does so by exempting them from the prohibition in the current law. For more on surrogacy see A. Alghrani, D. Griffiths and M. Brazier, 'Surrogacy Law: From Piecemeal Tweaks to Sustained Review and Reform' in A. Diduck, N. Peleg and H. Reece (eds.) *Law and Michael Freeman* (Brill Publishers, 2014).

[137] Ibid.

[138] HFE Act 1990, schedule 3, paragraph 2(2)(b).

[139] Sozou, Sheldon and Hartshorne, 'Consent Agreements for Cryopreserved Embryos'.

can be varied or withdrawn by either genetic parent at any time up to embryo transfer, a second, additional option, could be permitted in which one genetic parent can agree to cede control of the embryos to the other. Under this option, it would be up to the genetic parent who retained control to determine in future whether any of the embryos are transferred, subject to the prevailing regulations for treatment; the other genetic parent would not have a veto over their use. Couples would agree, before fertilisation, whether they choose to share control over the future use of embryos, or alternatively, one of them will have sole control. In the event of the genetic father having sole control, he would be able to seek a surrogate mother to carry the embryos to term. However, it is likely that in most agreements in which one parent has sole control this would be the genetic mother, as she would commonly have more limited future fertility options than her partner (with Ms Evans' situation representing an extreme example of this). The greater invasiveness of assisted conception methods for women, in comparison with men, may also have an influence. They argue that this proposal better recognises and protects individual autonomy than the current legal framework; which disadvantages women, whose biological investment in reproduction is more substantial than that of men, and who are more vulnerable to the possible loss of future genetic parenthood as a result of withdrawal of consent by another party. The case of *ARB* however demonstrates that, in such disputes, it may be the male gamete progenitor whose reproductive autonomy is violated, via non-consensual use of his gametes and such an agreement may also mitigate such reoccurrences of one party deceiving a clinic, without the other gamete progenitor's consent. Their proposal is intuitively appealing as both parties could choose an agreement that offered the decision about the use of the embryos to their partner, and the proposal itself is gender neutral. It also does not remove any options currently open to people wishing to store embryos for future use, but rather simply creates an extra option that they may choose should they both agree to it.

I argue that if the contractual model is to be rejected, then the least that can be done to improve the present situation is to consider amending consent forms so that provision is made for what is to happen upon separation, as well as incapacity or death. Clauses regarding disposition should not be buried in a consent form that discusses the benefits and risks of the proposed treatment, but rather in a separate consent form focused solely on disposition of one's gametes, for, as noted by Waldman:

the signing of consent documents and the creation of dispositional agreements treat different subjects, implicate different concerns, and deserve
separate contracting procedures.[140]

2.3.3   The 'Last Chance' Rule

Reproductive choices, as protected by a right to procreative liberty or
autonomy, have a claim to be taken seriously.[141] Harris notes that,
because creating genetically related individuals is part of sexual reproduction, it is natural to see the freedom to create closely genetically
related individuals as a plausible dimension of reproductive liberty; not
least because so many people and agencies have been attracted by the idea
of the special nature of genes and have linked the procreative imperative
to the genetic imperative.[142] Where procreative liberties, such as the right
to reproduce versus the right not to reproduce conflict, the burdens that
denying one person that right entail, must be considered in comparison
to the burdens unwanted reproduction would cause the objecting party.
In *Evans*, Ms Evans and Mr Johnston were not equally situated in regard
to decision-making concerning their embryos, because ovarian cancer
had rendered the disputed embryos Ms Evans's last chance at genetic
motherhood. It was for this reason that her plight evoked sympathy
from the public, press and judiciary. But the Court of Appeal held that
'the sympathy and concern which anyone must feel for Ms Evans is
not enough to render the legislative scheme of Schedule 3
disproportionate'.[143] The court was right to hold that, as a general rule,
we should not foist parenthood on those who do not wish to be a parent,
or have a genetically related child of theirs out there in the world.
The right not to reproduce should prevail when the other progenitor
has alternative means of genetic parenthood. However the situation alters
drastically when unfortunate circumstances have rendered it the last
chance at genetic parenthood. Robertson cogently argued that when

---

[140] Waldman, 'Disputing Over Embryos', at p. 925.

[141] Reproductive rights are protected in both the *Universal Declaration of Human Rights* and
the *European Convention for the Protection of Human Rights and Fundamental
Freedoms*. In the former Article 12 proves 'there will be no arbitrary interference
with ... privacy' and in Article 16 that 'men and women of marriageable age ... have
the right to marry and found a family'. In the latter, Article 8(1) provides 'everyone has
the right to respect for his private and family life, according to the national laws
governing the exercise of this right'.

[142] Alghrani and Harris, 'Should the Foundation of Families Be Regulated?'

[143] *Evans* (CA), paragraph 69.

embryos represent the last chance for the persons wishing to save them to have genetically related offspring to rear, a plausible case could be made for allowing them use of the gametes:

> In that case, the harm from losing the opportunity to reproduce seems greater than the harm to the other party of unwanted genetic reproduction without support obligations.[144]

Applied to Ms Evans, it was precisely because it was her last chance at genetic motherhood that allowing her use of the embryos outweighed the burdens of foisting unwanted fatherhood on her former partner, Mr Johnston. Allowing the right to produce to prevail where it is 'the last chance' would enable such disputes to be resolved fairly and equitably, without favouring one sex/gender over the other. For it is worth bearing in mind that, as Wall J. pointed out in the High Court, the scenario could easily have been reversed so that it was a man in an analogous situation to Ms Evans:

> It is not difficult to reverse the dilemma. If a man has testicular cancer and his sperm, preserved prior to radical surgery which renders him permanently infertile, is used to create embryos with his partner; and if the couple have separated before the embryos are transferred into the woman, nobody would suggest that she could not withdraw her consent to treatment and refuse to have the embryos transferred into her. The statutory provisions, like Convention Rights, apply to men and women equally.[145]

It is correct to state that no one would coerce a woman to have embryos implanted into her uterus against her will. Yet if the roles were reversed, and it was the man's last chance at genetic fatherhood, upon the same analysis of the burdens of unwanted parenthood versus the last chance of parenthood, the man would retain control of the embryos. He could then find a willing surrogate or female host to gestate them, or via ectogenesis or male pregnancy should these become safe methods of gestation. Therefore, it could be argued that the right not to reproduce should as a general rule prevail in such disputes, save where the stored embryo(s) represent the last chance at genetic parenthood for one of the progenitors. In this case, the balance is tilted in favour of permitting their use. This could be applied equally to either gender. Interestingly, the view that the right to reproduce should prevail when it is the last chance at genetic

---

[144] J. Robertson, 'Disposition of Frozen Embryos by Divorcing Couples without Prior Agreement' (1999) 71(6) *Fertility and Sterility* 996–997, at p. 997.

[145] *Evans* (HC), paragraph 320.

parenthood, was favoured by the courts in Israel.[146] It was also deemed to be the correct approach in the opinion of dissenting Judges Traja and Mijovic:

> the correct approach in our view would be as follows: the interests of the party who withdraws consent and wants to have the embryos destroyed should prevail (if domestic law so provides), unless the other party (a) has no other means to have a genetically-related child; and (b) has no children at all; and (c) does not intend to have recourse to a surrogate mother in the process of implantation. We think this approach would strike a fair balance between public and private interests, as well as between conflicting individual rights themselves. This test is neutral, because it can equally apply to female and male parties.[147]

This would result in a more equitable and just solution than currently offered in the HFE Act 1990 (as amended). It has similarly been adopted across the Atlantic. For instance, in *Davis* v. *Davis*,[148] the Tennessee Supreme Court set out a three-part test to be applied when a couple disagrees over the disposition of their embryos: the first was to pay due regard to the preferences of the progenitors, secondly if gamete donors disagree over disposition, the courts are directed to enforce any prior agreements between the parties, and thirdly, in the absence of prior agreement, courts are advised to balance the relative interests of the parties. When those interests are in equipoise, courts are advised to favour the party wishing to avoid procreation, as long as the other party 'has a reasonable possibility of achieving parenthood by other means than use of the pre-embryos in question'.[149] It is regrettable that in the 2008 amendments to the HFE Act, the government did not consider this as an alternative framework to regulate such disputes.

It is not only UK regulation of embryos that leaves a lot to be desired; disputes regarding disposition of embryos continue to unfold in the USA. Writing in 2016 on embryo disposition disputes in the USA, regulation of

---

[146] In *Nachmani* v. *Nachmani* 50(4) P.D. 661 (Isr.) the Israeli Supreme Court in 1996 awarded a couple's frozen pre-embryos to the wife, Ms Nachmani, who was childless, so that she could attempt to implant the frozen pre-embryos in a surrogate. Control over the pre-embryos was Ms Nachmani's sole means of fulfilling her desire to become a mother to a biologically related child, as she could no longer produce eggs. See C. Breen Portnoy, 'Frozen Embryo Disposition in Cases of Separation and Divorce: How Nachmani v Nachmani and Davis v Davis Form the Foundation for a Workable Expansion of Current International Family Planning' 28(1) *Maryland Journal of International Law* 275.

[147] *Evans* v. *UK* (ECtHR), paragraph 9.

[148] *Davis* v. *Davis* 842 S.W.2d 588 (Tenn.1992).

[149] Ibid.

which varies amongst states, Professors Glen Cohen and Eli Adashi observed, 'anyone looking at the case law on embryo disposition would find it a mess'.[150] To help untangle the mess, they suggest reform that involves aspects from the last two models considered, where embryos may represent a last chance of genetic parenthood and embryos being governed by a embryo disposition agreement. Cohen and Aldashi propose a set of uniform rules in regulation throughout the USA and federal legislation, which includes the following five elements: (i) clear differentiation between informed consent and agreements for embryo disposition through standardised forms; (ii) a requirement for an embryo disposition agreement prior to embryo cryopreservation and that no cryopreservation should take place in the USA without a fully executed disposition agreement; (iii) a rule that embryo disposition agreements should ordinarily be binding even if one party later changes his or her mind (the authors acknowledge this is their most controversial recommendation and one on which legal scholarship is divided, they support it for they claim it recognises 'the importance of treating these contracts as binding in order to allow for future planning, invite reliance and investment, and protect the interests of parties whose preferences have not changed, including individuals who have religious objections to the destruction of embryos'; (iv) recognition that embryo disposition agreements should not impose legal parenthood obligations on the objecting party: this is appealing for whilst one gamete progenitor can no longer veto use of the embryos, s/he will not be made a *legal* parent against his or her will – instead, they suggest in those cases they should be treated akin to sperm donors, absolving the objecting genetic parent of legal parentage obligations (and rights) if that person states in writing that he or she does not want to be the legal parent of the resulting child; and lastly (v) consideration of special rules for loss of fertility, for instance where one party who was fertile at the time of embryo fertilisation has now lost fertility in an unforeseen way and access to the embryos thus represents his or her last chance to reproduce. They give examples of infertility being unforeseeable, for instance, if one member of a couple that has cryopreserved embryos now requires medical treatment or suffers an accident that makes him or her infertile. These proposals are appealing, since they offer certainty to both gamete progenitors, respects both their procreative autonomy and also allows some flexibility to allow

---

[150] I. Glenn Cohen and E. Y. Adashi, 'Embryo Disposition Disputes: Controversies and Case Law' (2016) 46(4) *Hastings Centre Report* 13–19.

for disputes to be dealt with justly, should unforeseen circumstances later arise which render it one of the gamete progenitors last chance at genetic parenthood. Such proposals, if incorporated into the UK legislation, could improve on the UK regulatory system governing embryo disposition, which I have argued throughout this chapter could better regulate embryo disposition.

2.4   Conclusion

Both *Evans* and *ARB* concerned disputes that were not envisaged when the HFE Act 1990 was drafted. In the context of the former case, the decision to update and amend this statute in 2008 provided an opportunity for the UK government to reconsider the status of the in vitro embryo and the position of the gamete progenitors in relation to it. In this context, and absent pregnancy and bodily autonomy of the mother being invoked, the reasons for giving women the paramount say they possess in natural pregnancy no longer apply. It is no longer clear whose views should prevail in such disputes. The question of how disputes over frozen embryos should be resolved merited fresh consideration in light of this dispute. Yet the amendments introduced by the HFE Act 2008, as demonstrated by *ARB*, made the regulatory framework no better equipped to deal with embryo disposition dispute scenarios like that of *Evans* reoccurring, as evidenced by the facts of *ARB*. It is clear, however, that if the legislation is to be better equipped at resolving disputes concerning the fate of disputed embryos, Parliament must consider alternative regulatory models for governing such disputes.

This chapter considered three models that could have been considered by Parliament to resolve such disputes. The first advocated that a model which chartered the natural course of pregnancy. For instance, stating that consent cannot be withdrawn for a set period of time (perhaps nine months), as would be the case had fertilisation occurred in vivo and via sexual intercourse. Alternatively, the law could state that 'use' and the point of no return should be at fertilisation. Both would place infertile women on a par with their fertile female counterparts. This model was rejected, because absent bodily integrity arguments, it was argued that there is no reason why women should have this paramount say over their embryos. Secondly the 'contractual model' was also considered. Since the law already mandates couples to specify what should happen to their frozen embryo(s) upon death or separation,[151] Parliament could have decided to extend this and mandate that couples also specify what should happen to their embryos upon separation or divorce. Such an amendment may have minimised the chance of such disputes arising in the future. It is unclear whether such an amendment would have received much support in light of the comments made by the judiciary in *Evans* that one cannot promise to do what the law does not permit him/her to do. A written agreement/contract concerning the fate of embryos upon separation or divorce would at present be contrary to public policy and the statutory right of both gamete progenitors to withdraw or vary consent to the use of an embryo up until the moment of 'use'. Lastly the 'last chance' rule model was examined. Under this model the right not to reproduce would prevail when the other gamete progenitor has alternative means of genetic parenthood. However, when the frozen embryo-(s) represent the last chance for the person wishing to save them, to have genetically related offspring to rear, they should be allowed to use the gametes and override the other progenitor's wishes. It was argued that the last two models both provide alternate frameworks that could have been considered by Parliament to regulate such disputes.

The issues raised in *Evans* and *ARB* will only grow in complexity as we charge towards the third era of human reproduction. New reproductive technologies raise difficult legal and moral dilemmas, and the dispositional authority of gamete progenitors over their embryos becomes more complex when we consider not just embryos growing in vitro, but fetuses that can be gestated and maintained in an artificial womb (ectogenesis), which I discuss in the next chapters.

---

[151] HFE Act 1990 (as amended by the HFE Act 2008), Schedule 3.

PART II

Regulating New Reproductive Technologies

In Vitro Gestation I

The Road to Artificial Wombs (Ectogenesis) and Mechanical Reproduction

> Current medical advances in the area of infertility medicine and neonatology have made total ectogenesis (the gestation of a human being entirely outside the body of a human female) less a figment of the imagination of science fiction fantasy writers and more a realistic possibility for those living in the not so distant future. Partial ectogenesis is already a reality, as demonstrated by the creation and short-term gestation of embryos in vitro, and the gestation of premature babies in incubators.[1]

Ectogenesis is a term coined by geneticist and evolutionary biologist Haldane, who as far back as 1928 acclaimed that the technology was one of the most important biological discoveries mankind could ever make.[2] Complete ectogenesis, the gestation of a human fetus entirely outside the body of a human female,[3] represents 'the final severing of reproduction from the human body'[4] and will eliminate the need for a human host to gestate; consequently it will have repercussions far greater than other advances in the arena of assisted reproductive technologies.

Research into ectogenesis may develop in two ways: firstly by extending the length of time human embryos can be kept alive in vitro. When IVF was first achieved, Patrick Steptoe warned that 'this is not the end, it is only the beginning'.[5] Advances in embryology and fertility have enabled embryos to be conceived and kept alive prior to implantation in the mother for 13 days.[6] Beyond 14 days, any research into complete ectogenesis in the UK, which involves placing a fertilised embryo into an

---

[1] L. Cannold, 'Women, Ectogenesis and Ethical Theory' in S. Gelfand (ed.), *Ectogenesis: Artificial Womb Technology and the Future of Human Reproduction* (Amsterdam, New York: Rodopi, 2006) p. 47.

[2] J. B. S. Haldane, *Daedalus or Science and the Future* (London: Kegan Paul, 1924).

[3] Cannold, *Women, Ectogenesis and Ethical Theory*, n. 1, p. 47.

[4] C. Rosen, 'Why Not Artificial Wombs?' (2003) 3 *The New Atlantis* 67–76.

[5] P. R. Brisden, 'Thirty Years of IVF: The Legacy of Patrick Steptoe and Robert Edwards' (2009) 12(3) *Human Fertility* 137.

[6] S. Reardon, 'Human Embryos Grown in Lab for Longer than Ever Before' (2016) *Nature* 533.

ectogenic device designed to carry the resulting fetus to term, is prohibited by the law and renders such an act a criminal offence.[7] Recent advances in this domain have reignited a debate surrounding the current prohibition on research on human embryos beyond 14 days.[8] Discovery of new methods of keeping the human embryo or fetus alive at the beginning stages may contribute towards knowledge needed for ectogenesis. At the other end of the spectrum, advances in neonatal technology have reduced the amount of time that the fetus needs to spend in the mother's womb from 40 weeks down to 24 weeks or less.[9] An appropriate ectogenic incubator is needed to bridge the 22 weeks in-between.[10] Research has been conducted, both directly and indirectly, into bridging this gap. Both of these avenues would contribute knowledge towards what is needed for the creation of an ectogenic device and, as noted by Singer: 'The period in which it is necessary for the human fetus to be in the womb is shrinking from both sides.'[11]

Whilst ectogenesis has attracted much curiosity, little attention has been given to the practical realities of conducting such research and how this new reproductive technology may come about. The present chapter addresses this lacuna and examines what may be entailed in the road to ectogenesis. This chapter commences with a brief discussion on ectogenesis alongside the potential benefits and objections that have been advanced towards the technology. There then follow two major sections that re-examine the research underway into this advance and whether the view taken by the Warnock Committee in 1984,[12] that ectogenesis was far off on the horizon, remains a valid statement. Section 3.2 examines animal research into ectogenesis that has been conducted internationally before examining how such research would be governed in the UK. Section 3.3 then considers research into ectogenesis that has been

---

[7] HFE Act 1990 (as amended), s3(3).

[8] G. Cavaliere, 'A 14-Day Limit for Bioethics: The Debate over Human Embryo Research' (2017) 18(38) *BMC Medical Ethics* 1–12.

[9] Viability is currently at 24 weeks gestation: from this point onwards the fetus is capable of survival outside the maternal host with mechanical assistance; however, the mortality and morbidity of extremely low gestational age newborn babies is extremely high, with fewer than 50 per cent surviving without disability.

[10] F. Simonstein, 'Artificial Reproductive Technologies and Ectogenesis' (2005) 1 *Eubios Journal of Asian and International Bioethics* 13–15, at p. 13.

[11] P. Singer and D. Wells, *The Reproduction Revolution* (Oxford: Oxford University Press, 1984) p. 132.

[12] Report of the Committee of Inquiry into Human Fertilisation and Embryology, Cmnd. 9314 (1984) (Hereafter, 'Warnock Report').

conducted using human embryos and fetuses internationally before again considering how such research would be governed in the UK. Throughout this chapter, the concern is primarily with ectogenesis as a future development and how research into making this advance a safe method of gestation could be safely performed in this jurisdiction. Discussion of some of the regulatory questions that will arise, should ectogenesis become a safe method of gestation, is deserving of its own chapter and thus will appear in Chapter 4. Despite endeavours in 2008 to update the legislation so that it was fit for purpose in the twenty-first century, I argue the existing legislation fails to provide an adequate framework in which to regulate research into this novel technology.

3.1 Ectogenesis: A Prospect to Be Welcomed?

Ectogenesis holds many benefits. Technology that can mimic the functions of the maternal uterus can help save the lives of extremely premature babies born on the cusp of viability. At present the mortality and morbidity of extremely low gestational age newborn babies (defined as less than 28 weeks estimated gestational age) is extremely high, with fewer than 50 per cent surviving without disability.[13] Such technology can also help women who suffer from uterus factor infertility and thus are unable to gestate their own child, providing a way to achieve genetic motherhood. The only other way such women can achieve genetic parenthood without recourse to a third party is via the possibility of research into uterus transplantation, which, as documented in Chapter 5, is still in its clinical experimental stage.[14] Ectogenesis provides an alternative site for gestation that does not require surgical interventions to either donor or recipient and thus may be regarded as more optimal than a uterus transplant.[15]

---

[13] K. N. Ray and S. A. Lorch, 'Hospitalization of Early Preterm, Late Preterm, and Term Infants during the First Year of Life by Gestational Age' (2013) 3 *Hospital Paediatrics* 194–203. 3. E. M. Boyle, G. Poulsen, D. J. Field et al., 'Effects of Gestational Age at Birth on Health Outcomes at 3 and 5 Years of Age: Population Based Cohort Study' (2012) *British Medical Journal* 344.

[14] M. Brännström, 'Uterus Transplant and Beyond' (2017) 28(5) *Journal of Materials Science: Materials in Medicine* 70, at p. 75.

[15] Uterus transplant carries risks to the female recipient (there is a risk of tissue rejection and immunosuppressant-related side effects such as increased risks of hypertension, diabetes, nephrotoxicity and accelerated arteriosclerosis). There is also the issue of organ availability. See Brännström, *Uterus Transplant and Beyond*.

Ectogenesis may also appeal to healthy women for whom pregnancy is possible but undesirable.[16] Murphy sums up why some women may prefer mechanical gestation to traditional pregnancy:

> A woman may find ectogenesis desirable because she is a smoker, drug user or casual drinker and does not wish to alter her behaviour or place her foetus at risk. Pregnancy might make a woman ineligible for certain career opportunities (e.g. athletics, dancing, modelling, and acting). Her job may be hazardous for pregnant women, yet the temporary transfer to safer working conditions may be impossible or undesirable. A woman may be in good health and fertile but may not want the emotional and physical stress of pregnancy.[17]

The ability to remove gestation from a woman's body to an alternative independent site has led some to also argue that ectogenic technology has the potential to promote gender equality. Radical feminist Firestone brought the potential benefits of ectogenesis to centre stage in the 1970s when she exclaimed that the only way to achieve the ultimate feminist revolution was an androgynous society.[18] Smajdor also argued that ectogenesis will equal out the burdens of reproduction and alleviate the natural inequality bestowed upon women, who alone bear the physical, social and economic burdens of pregnancy and childbirth:

> pregnancy is a condition that causes pain and suffering, and that only affects women. The fact that men do not have to go through pregnancy to have a genetically related child, whereas women do, is a natural inequality.[19]

Kendal goes further and claims that the state has an obligation to ameliorate this inequality and gender injustice, by not only funding research into ectogenesis, but also, once it becomes feasible, funding access to the technology.[20] Both Smajdor and Kendal cite Firestone's

[16] G. Pence, 'What's So Good about Natural Motherhood? (In Praise of Unnatural Gestation)' in S. Gelfand and J. R. Shook (eds.), *Ectogenesis: Artificial Womb Technology and the Future of Human Reproduction* (Amsterdam: Rodopi, 2006) 77–88.

[17] J. Murphy, 'Is Pregnancy Necessary?' in P. Hopkins (ed.), *Sex Machine: Readings in Culture, Gender and Technology* (Bloomington: Indiana University Press, 1998) p. 187.

[18] V. Bryson, *Feminist Debates: Issue of Theory and Political Practise* (London: NYU Press, 1999), p. 159.

[19] A. Smajdor, 'In Defense of Ectogenesis' (2012) 21 *Cambridge Quarterly of Healthcare Ethics* 336–345.

[20] E. Kendal, *Equal Opportunity and the Case for State Sponsored Ectogenesis* (Basingstoke and New York, NY: Palgrave Macmillan, 2015). See also book review by C. Limon, 'From Surrogacy to Ectogenesis: Reproductive Justice and Equal Opportunity in Neoliberal Times' (2016) 31(88) *Australian Feminist Studies* 203–219.

quote that 'pregnancy is barbaric',[21] yet both their accounts overlook the fact that some women enjoy pregnancy and both their accounts attract the criticism that they overlook the diversity and complexity of women's experiences.[22]

Yet it is not only women who stand to benefit from such radical technology. Men, who have historically always been dependent on a female host to gestate their child, may also welcome ectogenesis as enhancing their reproductive choices. Single men, those in same-sex relationships and those in unions where the female partner is unable to gestate, must resort to surrogacy if they want a genetically related child. Surrogacy, as a method of founding a family in the UK, is complex due to the incoherent regulatory framework currently in place.[23] It is a criminal offence to be commercially involved in the initiation and negotiation of surrogacy arrangements, or to be involved in publicising or advertising surrogacy arrangements.[24] Surrogacy arrangements are also not legally binding and thus there is always the risk that the surrogate could renege on the agreement.[25]

Not all are so optimistic about what science may bring, and the prospect of ectogenic technology has also raised much foreboding. As with other novel technological innovations, the potential misuse of ectogenesis has unsurprisingly generated fear and distrust. In Aldous Huxley's *Brave New World*,[26] first published in 1932, he famously set out how a dystopian future may look in a world where sex and procreation have become separated and women no longer give birth. Huxley's bleakly satirical vision of a technocratic, totalitarian state made up of bottle-grown babies hatched to fulfil their predestined roles and stupefied contentment through eugenics, drugs, mindless hedonism and

---

[21] S. Firestone, *The Dialectic of Sex* (New York, NY: William Morrow and Company, 1979), p. 188.

[22] See C. Limon, 'From Surrogacy to Ectogenesis: Reproductive Justice and Equal Opportunity in Neoliberal Times' (2016) 31(88) *Australian Feminist Studies* 203–219, at p. 212.

[23] See A. Alghrani and D. Griffiths, 'Surrogacy Regulation in the UK: The Case for Reform" (2017) 29(2) *Child and Family Law Quarterly* 165–186 and K. Horsey and S. Sheldon, 'Still Hazy after All These Years: The Law Regulating Surrogacy' (2012) 20 *Medical Law Review* 67.

[24] Surrogacy Arrangements Act 1985, section 2.

[25] Surrogacy Arrangements Act 1985 s1A provides: 'no surrogacy arrangement is enforceable by or against any of the persons making it'. This remains unchanged by amendments the Human Fertilisation and Embryology Act 2008, s59 makes to this legislation. See also *Re TT (Surrogacy)* [2011] EWHC 33 (Fam).

[26] A. Huxley, *Brave New World*, 1932 (England: Longman Group Ltd, 1991).

consumerism, tainted any rosy view one might glean from the technology.[27] The book, whilst critiqued on the grounds that 'biology is itself too surprising to be really amusing material for fiction',[28] also evoked much concern. Two years before his death, Huxley himself expressed caution about such 'ectogenic desire',[29] warning how the inexorable human desire to update, improve and perfect can have unforeseen consequences.[30]

Concerns have been expressed that externalising the experience of pregnancy may result in the commodification of the child[31] and disrupt the unique mother–child bond gained through a pregnancy.[32] There are also fears that this technology, in separating procreation from sex, may curtail the procreative liberty of women, since the right to an abortion in Anglo-American law has been conceptualised around a woman's bodily autonomy[33] and both countries have long protected the viable fetus. If science perfects complete ectogenesis, viability will be from conception, and thus in theory a woman may be able to expel a fetus from the uterus and end her pregnancy without ending fetal life.[34] For women who drink, smoke or take drugs, complete ectogenesis may offer a healthier environment for a fetus to gestate, and thus there are concerns that such technology could be mandated by the state in certain conditions of 'fetal rescue'. Such ramifications of complete ectogenesis, such as the impact on abortion legislation, are discussed in Chapter 4.

Suffice it is to state here that the potential benefits and drawbacks of ectogenesis, should it ever become possible, are heavily dependent on the use of the technology. The interrelationship of society and technology, as

---

[27] For a review of the book see P. Ball, 'In Retrospect: Brave New World' (2015) (503) *Nature* 338–339.

[28] C. Haldane, 'Brave New World: A Novel' (1932) 129 *Nature* 597–598.

[29] I. Aristarkova, 'Ectogenesis and Mother as Machine' (2005) 11 *Body Society* 43.

[30] C. Rosen, 'Why Not Artificial Wombs?' (2003) 3 *The New Atlantis* 67–76, www.thenewatlantis.com/publications/why-not-artificial-wombs.

[31] M. Armstrong, 'Woman and Board: Medical Advances in Reproduction: At What Costs?' (1987) 4 *Med Tech. Tech. Q.* 465. J. S. Murphy, 'Is Pregnancy Necessary? Feminist Concerns and Ectogenesis' (1989) 4 *Hypatia* 66.

[32] N. J. Wikler, 'Society's Response to the New Reproductive Technologies: The Feminist Perspectives' (1986) 59 *S. CAL. L. REV.* 1043.

[33] C. Overall, Ethics and Human Reproduction: A Feminist Analysis (London: Routledge, 2012) 68–87. J. Thomson, 'A Defense of Abortion' (1971) 66(1) *PHIL. & PUB. AFF.* 47.

[34] For America – see *Roe v. Wade* 410 U.S. 113 (1973); see also, I.Glenn Cohen, 'The Constitution and the Rights Not to Procreate' (2008) 60 *STAN. L. REV.* 1135, 1155 (2008) (observing that the Supreme Court's abortion jurisprudence centres on notions of privacy and bodily integrity).

Kranzberg noted, can be of two kinds: one is the sociological situation that gives rise to invention and discovery and their use by society; the other represents the effects upon society of the uses of invention and discovery.[35] Kranzberg highlighted the value of the contextual approach in understanding technical developments:

> Technology is neither good nor bad; nor is it neutral. By that I mean that technology's interaction with the social ecology is such that technical developments frequently have environmental, social and human consequences that go far beyond the immediate purposes of the technical devices and practices themselves, and the same technology can have quite different results when introduced into different contexts or under different circumstances.[36]

Thus, if ectogenic technology comes to fruition, the benefits and drawbacks surrounding the technology will all depend on the specific context in which it is used and how this novel technology is governed.

Whilst it is clear that enthusiasm towards the technology varies, first science must discover how to create the technology needed for ectogenesis. The potential ramifications of ectogenesis have played out in science fiction literature,[37] academia[38] and recently the media,[39] and yet the possibility of this technology and research into this advance were notably absent from the UK government debates in 2008 to update the HFE Act 1990. Little attention has been given to the practicalities of how this novel reproductive technology will come about. Whilst the Warnock Committee

---

[35] M. Kranzberg, 'Technology and History: "Kranzberg's Laws"' (1995) 15(1) *Bulletin of Science, Technology & Society* 5–13.

[36] Kranzberg, 'Technology and History: "Kranzberg's Laws"', p. 6.

[37] J. B. S. Haldane, *Daedalus or Science and the Future* (London: Kegan Paul, 1924). Huxley, *Brave New World*.

[38] C. Bulletti, A. Palagiano et al., 'The Artificial Womb' (2011) 1221 *Annals of the New York Academy of Sciences* 124. J. H. Schultz, 'Development of Ectogenesis: How Will Artificial Wombs Affect the Legal Status of Fetus or Embryo?' (2010) 84 *Chicago-Kent Law Review* 877. S. Wellin, 'Reproductive Ectogenesis: The Third Era of Human Reproduction and Some Moral Consequences' (2004) 10 *Science and Engineering Ethics*, 615–626. P. Singer and D. Wells, *The Reproduction Revolution: New Ways of Making Babies* (Oxford, New York, NY and Melbourne: Oxford University Press, 1984). S. Coleman, *The Ethics of Artificial Uteruses* (United Kingdom: Ashgate, 2004). G. Corea, *The Mother Machine: Reproductive Technologies from Artificial Insemination to Artificial Wombs* (New York: Harper and Row, 1979).

[39] A. Prasad, 'How Artificial Wombs Will Change Our Ideas of Gender, Family and Equality' *The Guardian*, 1 May 2017. A. Newson, 'From Foetus to Full Term – Without a Mother's Touch' *The Times*, 30 August 2005. J. Rifkin, 'The End of Pregnancy' *The Guardian*, 17 January 2002; S. La Fee, 'Will Artificial Wombs Mean the End of Pregnancy?' *SigOnSanDiego.com*, 25 February 2004. Rosen, 'Why Not Artificial Wombs?'

recognised, as far back as 1984, that ectogenesis might one day become a possibility, it was dismissed as 'well in to the future, certainly beyond the time horizon within which this inquiry feels that it can predict'.[40] In any event, the Warnock Committee was of the view that the problem would be abated by the recommendation 'that the growing of a human embryo *in vitro* beyond fourteen days should be a criminal offence'.[41] This chapter now turns to the research that has been developed over the 30 years since the Warnock Committee considered the issue, highlighting how, in light of this research, it would be imprudent to continue to dismiss ectogenesis as a fanciful notion belonging to the realms of science fiction.

3.2 Ectogenic Research in Animals

Internationally, research endeavours are underway into discovering the various elements that would be needed to create ectogenesis. It is speculated that an ectogenic device would function by connection to an extra-corporeal supply of maternal blood or replacement fluids and would need to be able to supply nutrients and oxygen to an incubated fetus, as well as having the capacity to dispose of waste material.[42] Thus, an artificial placenta is necessary to mediate the necessary exchange between fetal circulation and the system that would replace the maternal flow.[43] Research into an artificial placenta began over 50 years ago using animal bodies.[44] It was hoped that the creation of an artificial placenta based on extracorporeal life support (ECLS) could advance knowledge into how to recreate the intrauterine environment and ameliorate many of the complications associated with extreme prematurity. Research into an artificial placenta waned as the treatment of prematurity improved, with the advent of prenatal maternal steroids, exogenous surfactant and advanced modes of ventilation.[45] As outcomes for the most

---

[40] Warnock Report, pp. 71–72.

[41] Warnock Report, pp. 71–72.

[42] C. Bulletti, A. Palagiano, C. Pace et al., 'The Artificial Womb' (2011) 1221 *Annals of The New York Academy of Sciences* 124–128.

[43] Bulletti, Palagiano, Pace et al., 'The Artificial Womb', p. 124.

[44] L. Lawn, R. A. McCance, 'Ventures with an Artificial Placenta. I. Principles and Preliminary Results' (1962) 155 *Proceedings of the Royal Society of London Series B Biological Sciences* 500–509. W. Zapol, T. Kolobow, G. Pierce Jevurek et al., 'Artificial Placenta: Two Days of Total Extrauterine Support of the Isolated Premature Lamb Fetus' (1969) 166 *Science* 617–618.

[45] B. Bryner, B. Gray, E. Perkins et al., 'An Extracorporeal Artificial Placenta Supports Extremely Premature Lambs for One Week' (2015) 50(1) *Journal of Pediatric Surgery* 44–49.

premature infants have remained disappointing, interest has once more returned to the development of an artificial placenta.[46] In 1997, Yoshinori Kuwabara undertook research on 17-week-old goat fetuses and reported that after they were removed from the natural uterus, they had survived in extrauterine incubation for three weeks – the equivalent of one human trimester.[47] Kuwabara had threaded catheters carrying nutrient-enriched blood into the umbilical arteries and veins of the fetuses, which were held in a tank of amniotic fluid.[48] The experiment was said to be complicated, as the goat fetuses tended to pull out the catheters as they twisted and kicked, and had to be paralysed with a muscle relaxant.[49] Two goats extracted from the uterus three weeks early survived until their normal term.[50] However the muscle relaxant prevented the fetuses from developing muscle tone, which meant they could not stand or breathe unassisted.[51] When the ventilator was removed after four weeks, the goats died within hours. Since then, research endeavours using lambs to create an artificial placenta have continued. In 2015, it was reported that a study had successfully kept premature lambs alive with an artificial placenta for one week.[52] Moving on from the limited success in the creation of an artificial placenta, in 2017 it was reported that a team had developed an extrauterine system to reproduce the environment of the uterus that consisted of three main components: a pumpless arteriovenous oxygenator circuit, a closed 'amniotic fluid' circuit with continuous fluid exchange and a new technique of umbilical vascular access.[53] They reported that the

---

[46] Y. Kuwabara, T. Okai, Y. Imanishi et al., 'Development of Extrauterine Fetal Incubation System Using Extracorporeal Membrane Oxygenator' (1987) 11 *Artificial Organs* 224–227. M. Yasufuku, K Hisano, M. Sakata et al., 'Arterio-Venousextracorporeal Membrane Oxygenation of Fetal Goat Incubated in Artificial Amniotic Fluid (Artificial Placenta): Influence on Lung Growth and Maturation' (1998) 33(3) *Journal of Pediatric Surgery* 442–8. J. A. Awad, R. Cloutier, L. Fournier et al., 'Pumpless Respiratory Assistance Using a Membrane Oxygenator as an Artificial Placenta: A Preliminary Study in Newborn and Preterm Lambs' (1995) 8(1)*Journal of Investigative Surgery* 21–30.

[47] F. Dolendo, 'Baby Machines: The Birth of the Artificial Womb' (2006) Spring *The Triple Helix*, p. 4, www.thetriplehelix.org/documents/issues/Berkeley_Spring_06.pdf.

[48] J. Knight, 'An Out-of-Body Experience' (2002) 419(12) *Nature* 106–107.

[49] Knight, 'An Out-of-Body Experience', p. 107.

[50] N. Unno et al., 'Development of an Artificial Placenta: Survival of Isolated Goat Fetuses for Three Weeks with Umbilical Arteriovenous Extracorporeal Membrane Oxygenation' (1993) 17(12) *Artificial Organ* 996–1000.

[51] Knight, 'An Out-of-Body Experience'.

[52] Bryner et al., 'An Extracorporeal Artificial Placenta'.

[53] E. A. Partridge, M. G. Davey, M. A. Hornick et al., 'An Extra-Uterine System to Physiologically Support the Extreme Premature Lamb' (2017) *Nature Communications* (published 25 April 2017 – pp. 1–16).

fetal lambs could be physiologically supported in this extrauterine device for up to four weeks. With appropriate nutritional support, the lambs on the system demonstrated normal somatic growth, lung maturation and brain growth and myelination.[54] After the four weeks, they were switched onto a regular ventilator like a premature baby in a NICU. The lambs' health on the ventilator appeared nearly as good as a lamb of the same age that had just been delivered by Caesarean section. Once removed from the ventilator, all lambs but one, which was developed enough to breathe on its own, were euthanised so the researchers could examine their organs. Their lungs and brains (the organ systems that are most vulnerable to damage in premature infants) appeared uninjured and developed, as they would have been if gestated to full term in utero.[55] The team reasserted that the aim behind the research was 'not to extend viability, but rather to offer the potential for improved outcomes for those infants who are already being routinely resuscitated and cared for in intensive care units'.[56]

The use of animals in ectogenic research remains deeply controversial. Anglo-American law has long attracted criticism for the way it characterises non-human animals and the failure to engage with the question of animal status.[57] Fox notes how law reflects dominant societal attitudes that there is a self-evident dividing line between human and non-human, according to which humans are designated as persons and animals their property.[58] The debate is often polarised between those who share the Aristotelian assumption of a fundamental difference between humans and other animals[59] and those who argue for animal 'liberation' on the basis of moral equivalence.[60] As the debates regarding the ethical legitimacy of animal research rages on,[61] animals continue to be used in a wide range of scientific research activities. As noted above, the most recent research on extrauterine environments used premature lambs that were

[54] Partridge, Davey, Hornick et al., 'An Extra-Uterine System to Physiologically Support the Extreme Premature Lamb'.

[55] R. Becker, 'An Artificial Womb Successfully Grew Baby Sheep – And Humans Could Be Next' *The Verge*, 25 April 2017.

[56] Becker, 'An Artificial Womb Successfully Grew Baby Sheep', p. 11.

[57] M. Fox, 'Rethinking Kinship: Law's Construction of the Animal Body' (2004) 57(1) *Current Legal Problems* 469–493.

[58] Fox, 'Rethinking Kinship' p. 469.

[59] P. A. B. Clarke and A. Linzey, *Political Theory and Animal Rights* (London: Pluto Press, 1990).

[60] P. Singer, *Animal Liberation: A New Ethics for Our Treatment of Animals* (New York: Avon Books, 1975).

[61] For more on the debate see The Nuffield Council on Bioethics, *The Ethics of Research Involving Animals* (May 2007).

subsequently euthanised to examine their organs. As Perry suggests, all too often the debate on animal research is portrayed in a polarised manner, differentiating only between those 'for' and those 'against' all animal research. The reality is far more complex, with people's views varying depending on particular kinds of research and factors such as the aims, type and location of research, the species of animal used and the degree of suffering experienced in the different contexts.[62]

The UK has been described as having 'the most detailed legislative framework regarding animal research in the world'.[63] A detailed exploration of how scientists undertaking ectogenic research using animals in the UK would be governed under such regulations is beyond the remit of this book, but at this juncture I wish merely to provide a brief outline.

The use of animals in experiments and testing in the UK is regulated by the Animals (Scientific Procedures) Act 1986 (ASPA), which was revised in 2012 to include the new regulations as specified by the European Directive 2010/63/EU on the protection of animals used for scientific purposes. The revised legislation came into force on 1 January 2013 and is now known as the Animals (Scientific Procedures) Act 1986 Amendment Regulations 2012 (ASPA 2012). The 2012 Act regulates the use of protected animals in scientific procedures, which may have the effect of causing the animal pain, suffering, distress or lasting harm. The law enshrines the famous three 'R' principles credited to British zoologist William Russell and the microbiologist Rex Burch. In 1959, they published *The Principles of Humane Experimental Technique*, a study of the ethical aspects of animal research commissioned by the Universities Federation for Animal Welfare.[64] They proposed that any experiments on animals should incorporate, so far as is possible, the following three principles: (i) replacement of animals with non-sentient alternatives wherever possible; (ii) reduction in the number of animals used for research; and (iii) refinement of any experiments to ensure that only minimum pain and distress is caused to the animals.[65] These guiding principles are now enshrined into domestic legislation under section 2A

---

[62] P. Perry, 'The Ethics of Animal Research: A UK Perspective' (2007) 48(1) *Institute for Animal Laboratory Research Journal* 42–46. See P. Singer, *Animal Liberation* (London: Pimlico, 1995). R. Burke and J. Tannenbaum, 'The Ethics of Animal Research: Two Views' (1986) 1(1) *The Scientist* 19.

[63] The Nuffield Council on Bioethics, paragraph 15.14.

[64] W. M. S. Russell and R. L. Burch, *The Principles of Humane Experimental Technique* (London: Methuen, 1959) at p. 238.

[65] P. Flecknell, 'Replacement, Reduction and Refinement' (2002) 19(2) *ALTEX* 73–78.

of the ASPA 2012. Before any animal experiments can take place, the ASPA regulations require that the appropriate licence must be applied for.[66] Without any one of these licences, no animal experimentation can legally take place. Applicants must be able to demonstrate that there is no scientifically satisfactory non-animal-based procedure that could be used instead of animal experimentation. This ensures that animals are used in scientific procedures only when there is no valid alternative and when the potential benefits outweigh the harms. A licence will be granted only once an explicit cost–benefit assessment has been undertaken to ascertain whether the likely benefits of the research (e.g. in terms of knowledge gained) outweigh the likely adverse costs to the animals concerned (possible pain, suffering or distress).[67] Any proposed ectogenic research in animals would be evaluated on its own merits on a case-by-case basis. Any potential harm and suffering to animals arising from the research or procedure should be assessed in advance and justified in terms of its possible benefit to society.

Whilst some promising animal research has been done internationally to discover the elements needed for ectogenesis, at present there are no reports of any ectogenic research using animals being done in the UK. In the absence of extensive animal experimentation, Raskin and Mazor argue that research should be limited to experiments with animals.[68] Ectogenesis, as with other new assisted reproductive technologies in their elementary stages, may well pose a high risk that the early fetuses entered into ectogenic incubators will not survive or will not emerge as healthy newborns. This is not to say, however, that such research is not justifiable, for that depends on whether the perceived benefits outweigh the risks. If scientific research were deemed unethical because of concerns around safety, scientific progress would never be made. Singer and Wells observe:

> if it is unethical to attempt ectogenesis in humans until we have reason-
> able assurance that it is safe, and we can have no reasonable assurance that

[66] Section 4 provides that there are three licences: (i) a personal licence, (ii) a project licence, (iii) an establishment licence.

[67] Section 5(1) provides: 'in determining whether and on what terms to grant a project licence the Secretary of State shall weigh the likely adverse effects on the animals concerned against the likely benefit to accrue as a result of the programme to be specified in the licence'.

[68] J. Raskin and N. Mazor, 'The Artificial Womb and Human Subject Research' in S. Gelfand (ed.), *Ectogenesis: Artificial Womb Technology and the Future of Human Reproduction* (Amsterdam and New York, NY: Rodopi, 2006) p. 172.

it is safe until it is carried out, we seem to be in a classic 'catch 22' situation. Work on ectogenesis will remain forever unjustifiable.[69]

Researching this advance is justifiable if the benefits outweigh the risks, and in the context of ectogenesis there are significant benefits: ectogenesis may present the only chance of survival a premature fetus has; it may provide information which can help sustain the lives of other premature babies; it will enable individuals to overcome uterus factor infertility and procreate without having to commission a surrogate; and lastly it will enhance the procreative choices of men, who will no longer be dependent on a female host. This chapter now proceeds to an exploration of the research into ectogenesis using human embryos and fetuses.

3.3   Ectogenic Research on the Human Fetus

3.3.1   International Human Research into Ectogenesis

Internationally, human research endeavours are underway into discovering the ingredients needed to support a device that could mimic the functions of the human uterus. Bulletti et al. reported that the first attempts to support the implantation of human embryos outside of the human body were conducted in 1982 in Italy, and continued in New York City in 1983, the results of which were first published in 1986.[70] The first human embryo implantation in an ex vivo, isolated, extra-corporeally perfused uterus occurred in 1989.[71] The study in Italy elicited ethical concerns and was stopped due to 'strong and vociferous opposition from the political community'.[72] They noted how other studies have been conducted using the ex vivo model; however, these studies were not performed to study embryo implantation, but rather the effects of various pharmacological effects on uterine psychology.[73] This work is helpful in

[69] Singer and Wells, *The Reproduction Revolution*, p. 145.
[70] C. Bulletti, V. M. Jasonni, S. Lubicz et al., 'Extracorporeal Perfusion of the Human Uterus' (1986) 154 *Am. J. Obstet. Gynecol.* 683–688. C. Bulletti, A. Palagiano, C. Pace et al., 'The Artificial Womb' (2011) 1221 *Annals of The New York Academy of Sciences* 124–128.
[71] C. Bulletti, V. M. Jasonni, S. Tabanelli et al., 'Early Human Pregnancy In Vitro Utilizing an Artificially Perfused Uterus' (1988) 49 *Fertility & Sterility* 991–996.
[72] Bulletti, Jasonni, Tabanelli et al., 'Early Human Pregnancy In Vitro', pp. 991–996; Bulletti, Palagiano, Pace, 'The Artificial Womb', at p. 124.
[73] C. Bulletti, R. A. Prefetto, G. Bazzochi et al., 'Electro-Mechanical Activities of Human Uteri during Extra Corporeal Perfusion with Ovarian Steroids' (1993) 8 *Human Reproduction* 1558–1563. C. Bulletti, D. De Ziegler and C. Flamingi, 'Targeted Drug Delivery in Gynecology: The First Uterine Pass Effect' (1997) 12 *Human Reproduction* 1073–1079.

detailing important characteristics of the uterus, which will facilitate research endeavours into imitating mechanisms governing human uterine receptivity and embryo implantation.[74]

Artificial Amniotic Fluid

In the early 1980s, physiologist Thomas Schaffer researched developing an artificial amniotic fluid, which would help extremely premature babies survive longer. Shaffer's hypothesis was that premature babies might fare better if they were able to breathe oxygen from liquid, as they do in the uterus. In a 1996 clinical trial, 13 infants born after 23–24 weeks' gestation with severe breathing difficulties were given oxygenated liquid for between four hours and three days. Although none had been expected to survive, seven were discharged from hospital and appeared to be healthy and normal several months later.[75] Despite such positive results, it was reported that Schaffer was unable to find a drug company willing to continue with the clinical experiments (it was suspected this was due to the small size of the neonatal market, which deterred firms from taking on the costs of clinical trials).[76]

Artificial Endometrium

In 2001, Hung-Ching Liu, a researcher at Cornell University, New York, performed research into how the embryo attaches itself to the lining of the womb, known as the endometrium, and, in particular, the creation of an artificial endometrium. Liu and her team claimed to have removed cells from a woman's uterus and, using hormones and growth factors, grew the cells on scaffolds of biodegradable material that had been modelled into shapes mirroring the interior of the uterus. As the model dissolved over time, the artificial womb continued to grow. Her team then placed 'surplus' human embryos obtained from fertility clinics into the artificial womb. In unpublished work,[77] Liu found that the fertilised eggs attached themselves to the plugs of the endometrial cells at six days

---

[74] Bulletti, Palagiano, Pace et al., 'The Artificial Womb' at pp. 124–125.

[75] C. L. Leach et al. (1996) 335 *New England Journal of Medicine* 761–767; Knight, 'An Out-of-Body Experience' at pp. 106–107.

[76] Knight, 'An Out-of-Body Experience' at p. 107.

[77] OBGYN.net Conference Coverage From the American Society of Reproductive Medicine, Orlando, Florida, October 22–24, 2001; 'Engineering Endometrial Tissue, Global Medical Director, Hans Van Der Slikke interviews Helen Liu, PhD'. www.obgyn.net/displaytranscript.asp?page=/avtranscripts/asrm2001-liu.

post fertilisation, just as they do in the human uterus. In an interview, Liu stated:

> That's my final goal; I call it an 'artificial uterus'. I want to see whether I can develop an actual external device with this endometrium cell and then probably with a computer system simulate the feed in medium, feed out medium, simulating the abrupt stream and also have a chip controlling the hormonal level. Because throughout the whole pregnancy the hormonal level is changing, protein is changing, and the growth factor is changing. So I want to use a computer to help me do this, and I believe if this can be achieved, we could possibly have an artificial uterus so then you could grow a baby to term.[78]

These experiments were not extended beyond six days due to legal limits on embryo research in the USA. Several studies have employed artificial endometrium models and reported their responses to steroid hormones in various contexts.[79]

Bioengineered Uterus

In 2017 in Sweden, it was announced that Brännström, who pioneered the world's first successful human uterus transplant trials in 2014, is now undertaking direct research into the creation of a bioengineered uterus.[80] Brännström stated the bioengineered uterus 'is based on the principle that the uterus is mostly created from the recipient's own stem cells that grow on a synthetic scaffold or a biologically derived scaffold'.[81] Buoyed on by the success of novel and promising concepts for functional organ and tissue replacement, which have emerged within the fields of regenerative medicine and tissue engineering,[82] Brännström argues that a bioengineered uterus using stem cells would be a superior treatment for women suffering from absolute uterine factor infertility, reducing or eliminating many of the risks associated with uterine transplant for both the donor and recipient. Using an artificially created uterus built from patients' own cells would also mean that fetuses would not be exposed to anti-rejection medications and women may feel as if they are experiencing a more genuine pregnancy, less alienated from

---

[78] Ibid.
[79] Bulletti, Palagiano, Pace et al., 'The Artificial Womb' at p. 125.
[80] Brännström, 'Uterus Transplant and Beyond' p. 70.
[81] Brännström, 'Uterus Transplant and Beyond' p. 75.
[82] For more on this, see *Exploring the State of the Science in the Field of Regenerative Medicine Challenges of and Opportunities for Cellular Therapies: Proceedings of a Workshop* (Washington, DC: National Academies Press, 2017). A. Mahalatchimy, 'Reimbursement of Cell-Based Regenerative Therapy in the UK and France' (2016) 24(2) *Medical Law Review* 234–258.

an organ built from 'self' tissue than one that was 'foreign'. Unlike Bulletti et al. and Liu, who were working towards an artificial/ectogenic womb that would act as a stand-alone external mechanic device and allow for the implantation and full development of fetuses in vitro, Brännström envisages a bioengineered uterus that could later be implanted into a female recipient who lacks a functioning uterus. Thus the embryo and fetus would be implanted and gestated *in vivo* in a female host, not *in vitro*. However it is speculated that this may advance knowledge into what may be needed for the creation of an ectogenic device. Thus it is clear that, internationally, there has been research into developing the elements needed for ectogenesis.

This chapter now turns to how human research into ectogenesis would be governed in the UK and whether the regulatory framework is equipped to deal with challenges raised by such research.

3.3.2 Human Research into Ectogenesis in the UK

Research into ectogenesis using live human fetuses may arise in three ways: (i) complete ectogenesis, whereby an embryo is placed directly in to an ectogenic incubator and gestated for the entire 40 weeks; (ii) partial ectogenesis, whereby a fetus is conceived in the mother's womb and gestated therein for some period of time before being transferred into an ectogenic incubator – for instance, as a consequence of premature labour; and (iii) ectogenic research on the live abortus.

3.3.2.1 Research into Complete Ectogenesis

Research into complete ectogenesis, whereby a 'live human embryo'[83] is placed into an ectogenic device designed to carry the resulting fetus to term, is governed by the HFE Act 1990 (as amended) and would under that statute be a criminal offence. English law clearly stipulates that embryonic research beyond 14 days is prohibited.[84] The legislation also makes it mandatory to obtain a licence before any research is carried out on a human embryo. Section 3(3)(a) provides that a licence cannot authorise the keeping or usage of embryos after the appearance of the primitive streak. Section 3(4) of the HFE Act designates the primitive streak to have appeared in an embryo no later than the end of the period of 14 days, beginning with the day on which the gametes are mixed, not counting any time during which the embryo is stored.[85] The reasoning

---

[83] HFE Act 1990 (as amended) s1(2)(a).
[84] HFE Act 1990 (as amended) s3(3).
[85] HFE Act 1990 (as amended) Schedule 2.

behind this was the view of the Warnock Committee that the embryo has a 'special status' and 'that the embryo of the human species should be afforded some protection in law'.[86] Consequently the Warnock Committee chose 14 days as the point from which a human embryo should not be maintained alive as this represented the appearance of the primitive streak and the formation of the central nervous system. As noted by Aach:

> The specific stipulations of 14 days and the primitive streak were adopted not because they were recognized as having intrinsic moral significance, but rather because they preceded the appearance of more morally sig-nificant features and provided unambiguous policy criteria for directing when to terminate experiments ... The 14-day rule has thus always been at best an uneasy compromise between divergent moral views, complex biology, and the needs of policy.[87]

The 14-day rule was a theoretical one, as up until recently, scientists had only been able to sustain embryos in vitro for seven days.[88] However, recent scientific advances have now reopened the debate. In August 2016, in a letter in *Nature*[89] and in an article published in *Nature Cell Biology*,[90] two groups based in different research centres in the UK (Cambridge and London) and in the USA (New York) presented the results of their experiments on in vitro human embryos. For the first time, the embryos were sustained in vitro for 12–13 days after fertilisation.[91] Consequently, there are now suggestions that the time limit should be increased in light of these scientific advances. Harris has argued that 'the time has come to consider redrawing the line',[92] adding that the overwhelming consensus of scientific opinion is that considerable scientific and therapeutic impor-tance can be gained by extending the 14-day limit.[93]

---

[86] Warnock Report, paragraph 11.17.
[87] J. Aach et al., 'Addressing the Ethical Issues Raised by Synthetic Human Entities with Embryo-Like Features' (2017) *elife* 21 March.
[88] I Hyun, A. Wilkerson, J. Johnston, 'Embryology Policy: Revisit the 14-Day Rule' (2016) 533 *Nature* 169–171.
[89] A. Deglincerti, G. F. Croft, L. N. Pietila et al., 'Self-Organization of the In Vitro Attached Human Embryo' (2016) 533 *Nature* 251–4.
[90] M. N. Shahbazi, A. Jedrusik, S. Vuoristo et al., 'Self-Organization of the Human Embryo in the Absence of Maternal Issues' (2016) 18 *Nature Cell Biology* 7.
[91] Deglincerti, Croft, Pietila et al., 'Self-Organization of the In Vitro Attached Human Embryo'.
[92] J. Harris, 'It's Time to Extend the 14-Day Limit for Embryo Research', *The Guardian*, 6 May 2016.
[93] Harris, 'It's Time to Extend the 14-Day Limit for Embryo Research'.

The arguments advanced in favour of extending the 14-day rule, namely (a) the beneficence of research and (b) technical feasibility, have been critiqued by Calaviere as problematic notwithstanding their popularity and widespread use.[94] Instead, she argues that the newly sparked debate on embryo research represents a valuable opportunity to begin a truly deliberative and democratic debate on this issue.[95] Whilst these debates may now be reopened, at present it is clear that the 14-day rule means that whilst no legal rights are bestowed upon the embryo,[96] it is afforded this limited protection by the law. Ectogenic research on human embryos beyond this time limit would constitute a breach of the current law.

But suppose for a moment that one concurs with the view espoused in the Warnock Committee, that the human embryo/fetus ought to have a 'special status' and thus should be respected; it is not clear, according to the Warnock Committee's reasoning, how an embryo is better protected by being destroyed at 14 days rather than being placed in an artificial/ectogenic womb. If, as the Warnock Committee believed, embryos should be respected, what is the justification for prohibiting ectogenic research, which, rather than destroying the embryo, could rescue it from its destruction and enable it to achieve its potential for life? Consider, for instance, surplus embryos, which have been donated for research by a couple; or 'orphan' embryos, generated in the course of fertility treatment and placed in storage, but where the gamete progenitors pass away or are abandoned, or contact with the clinic is lost. The only other option besides research is to allow the embryos to perish: that is, be destroyed. It could be argued that it would accord more respect to those embryos destined for death, to allow them to be placed into an ectogenic device, which may also allow them to develop and achieve their potential for life. Of course, this is not to suppose that such research should be permitted without the gamete progenitors' consent, but in circumstances where such consent is unobtainable (lost contact, for instance), or where consent for research has been given, it is not clear how mandating their destruction at 14 days respects the fetus. If, in these limited circumstances, ectogenic research were to be permitted, it is clear this could not take place without amendment to the HFE Act 1990 (as amended). Furthermore, when the Warnock Committee considered the issue of in

---

[94] Cavaliere, 'A 14-Day Limit for Bioethics'.
[95] Cavaliere, 'A 14-Day Limit for Bioethics'.
[96] *Paton v. British Pregnancy Advisory Service Trustees* [1979] QB 276.

vitro embryos in the early 1980s, the discussion centred on the development of IVF, which:

> for the first time gave rise to the possibility that human embryos might be brought into existence which might have no chance to implant because they were not transferred to a uterus and hence no chance to be born as human beings.[97]

Yet ectogenesis allows embryos that have already been created, that will otherwise only be discarded, or destroyed, a chance to achieve life by being placed into an ectogenic incubator. Thus, I argue that there is an important distinction to be drawn between embryonic research and ectogenic research. Consequently, the justifications for prohibiting embryo research, based as they are on the premise that such research is an affront to the fundamental respect that should be accorded to human embryos, does not apply. To the contrary, placing such doomed embryos that will not be implanted into a woman, into an ectogenic incubator, is actually more pro-life than prohibiting such action, since it is the only chance of life they have prior to destruction.

Concerns will no doubt be raised as to what should happen should the embryos progress and become in vitro fetuses: can they be gestated only to be destroyed at a later date or must they then be gestated to term if possible? What status will the law ascribe to the in vitro fetus? Complete ectogenesis, once it becomes a safe method of gestation, will raise a plethora of regulatory questions that I address in Chapter 4. For now, it suffices to state that it is clear that the government will have to consider the issue of research into complete ectogenesis afresh. In light of the many therapeutic benefits ectogenesis promises,[98] if direct research into complete ectogenesis is to be legally prohibited then it should at least be on a strong, justifiable basis. Just as the government acknowledged that legislation on embryonic research may thwart advances into stem cell research and amended the current legislation,[99] similarly the prospect of

---

[97] Warnock Report, paragraph 11.8.

[98] Singer and Wells, *Ectogenesis*, chapter 2.

[99] The Human Fertilisation and Embryology (Research Purposes) Regulations 2001: Section 2: (1) The Authority may issue a licence for research under paragraph 3 of Schedule 2 to the Act for any of the purposes specified in the following paragraph. (2) A licence may be issued for the purposes of – (a) increasing knowledge about the development of embryos; (b) increasing knowledge about serious disease, or (c) enabling any such knowledge to be applied in developing treatments for serious disease.

See also how the new regulations were challenged by CORE in *R (Quintavelle)* v. *Secretary of State for Health* [2003] 2 ALL ER 113.

ectogenesis may necessitate reconsideration of whether the present regulation unduly prohibits research into ectogenesis.

It is also necessary to address an argument made by Herring that there was a loophole in the 1990 legislation[100] that could have been seized upon to research complete ectogenesis, whereby an embryo created by cell nuclear replacement (CNR) could be placed directly into an ectogenic incubator from fertilisation and allowed to gestate. CNR is a method scientists have developed of creating an embryo that does not involve fertilisation, but instead involves introducing a nucleus taken from an adult human into an unfertilised egg. Herring noted that whilst the Human Reproductive Cloning Act 2001 (since repealed) had provided that a person who places in a woman a human embryo, which has been created otherwise than by fertilisation, is guilty of an offence:[101] 'the 2001 Act did not expressly prohibit the placing of a CNR embryo in an artificial uterus-like environment'.[102] However, the HFE Act 1990 was clear that the use of embryos is prohibited beyond the primitive streak.[103] Section 1(1)(a) of the 1990 legislation defined an embryo as 'a live human embryo where fertilisation is complete'. The courts clarified that an organism created by CNR falls within the definition of 'embryo' in section 1(1)(a) of the HFE Act 1990 and that 'the essential thrust of that subsection was directed to live human embryos created outside the human body, not to the manner of their creation'.[104] The HFE Act 2008 removed this lacuna and explicitly defined 'embryo' as a 'live human embryo'[105] and the previous reference to 'where fertilisation is complete' was removed. The definition of 'embryo' encompasses embryos created other than by fertilisation, e.g. by CNR. Consequently the legal lacuna mentioned by Herring is removed. The provisions of the HFE Act 1990 (as amended) which prohibit embryonic research beyond 14 days/ appearance of the primitive streak, thwart efforts to research complete ectogenesis in the UK.

I now turn to the research into partial ectogenesis, where fertilisation occurs in vivo and within a female, but at some point in the pregnancy the fetus is transferred into an ectogenic incubator.

---

[100] J. Herring, 'Cloning in the House of Lords' (2003) 33 *Fam Law* (663).

[101] Human Reproductive Cloning Act 2001, s1 provided a person guilty of the offence was liable on conviction to imprisonment for a term not exceeding 10 years, or a fine, or both.

[102] Herring, 'Cloning in the House of Lords'.

[103] HFE Act 1990, s3 (3).

[104] R. (Quintavelle) v. Secretary of State for Health [2003] 2 ALL ER 113.

[105] HFE Act 2008, s1(2)(a).

3.3.2.2   Partial Ectogenesis and Research Upon the Fetus

Research on human fetuses is controversial and, as Unterscheider and O'Donoghue note, the sanctity of the fetal environment provides a formidable barrier to research endeavour, and consequently fetal medicine lags behind other areas.[106] Unlike research and disposal of embryos created in vitro, which is governed under the HFE Act 1990 (as amended), for many years the regulation of fetal research in the UK was governed primarily by the quasi-official regulations found in a Code of Practice issued by the Polkinghorne Committee in 1989.[107] The Committee was formed in response to controversy surrounding the use of neural tissue derived from aborted fetuses as an experimental treatment for Parkinson's disease. The Polkinghorne guidelines were advisory, lacked sanctions and relied upon professional self-regulation rather than independent oversight.[108] No formal records were kept, so it was not possible to say how many aborted fetuses were annually collected, stored and used for research, nor for what purposes.[109] Similar to the Warnock Report, the Polkinghorne Report was also of the view that the live fetus merited profound respect based upon its potential for development into a fully-formed human being and thus should not be treated instrumentally, as a mere object available for investigation or use.[110] The Polkinghorne Report recommended that the live fetus be accorded a status 'broadly comparable to that of a living person'.[111] The Guidelines were criticised for insisting 'on a choreography' that was 'so complicated (and costly)' that it impeded research.[112]

The Human Tissue Act 2004 and the accompanying Codes of Practice, published by the Human Tissue Authority (HTA), now govern research on the dead fetus or fetal tissue. Although the disposal of pregnancy remains (which are considered to be the mother's tissue) are not within

---

[106] J. Unterscheider and K. O'Donoghue, 'Research in Fetal Medicine' in P. M. S. O'Brien and F. Broughton-Pipkin (eds.), *Introduction into Research Methodology for Trainees and Specialists* (Third Edition, Cambridge: Cambridge University Press, 2017) 208–226.

[107] DoH (1989) Review of the Guidance on the Research Use of Fetuses and Fetal Material, Cmnd. 762, 1989. Hereafter 'The Polkinghorne Report'.

[108] N. Pfeffer, 'How Work Reconfigures an "Unwanted" Pregnancy into "The Right Tool for the Job" in Stem Cell Research' (2009) 31(1) *Sociology of Health & Illness* 98–111.

[109] Pfeffer, 'How Work Reconfigures an "Unwanted" Pregnancy Into "The Right Tool for the Job" in Stem Cell Research'.

[110] Polkinghorne Report, paragraph 2.4.

[111] Polkinghorne Report, paragraph 3.1.

[112] N. Pfeffer, 'What Has Happened to the Review of the Polkinghorne Guidelines on Research Using Fetal Tissue?' *BioNews* 20 April 2009, www.bionews.org.uk/page_38275.asp.

the scope of the HTA regulatory remit, the HTA was asked by Professor Dame Sally Davies, the Chief Medical Officer, with responsibility for developing guidance in this area and working with other organisations to monitor compliance. In 2015, the HTA issued 'Guidance on the disposal of pregnancy remains following pregnancy loss or termination'.[113] The guidance applies to all pregnancy loss and terminations that have not exceeded the 24th week of pregnancy, where no signs of life have been detected following the loss. The guidance provides that disposal options are cremation, burial or, in certain circumstances only, incineration.[114] Stillbirths or terminations that exceed 24 weeks' gestation are subject to the Births and Deaths Registration Act 1953 and must be registered as stillbirths. Common law requires that stillbirths must be buried or cremated. A baby or fetus of any gestational age that is born showing signs of life and dies before the age of 28 days is regarded as a live birth and neonatal death: such births must be registered and they must be buried or cremated.[115] If a fetus is born prematurely but is alive, the fetus becomes a legal person and the general law applicable to children applies.[116]

Research on the Extremely Premature Fetus   A premature fetus that is born alive may spend some time in a neonatal intensive care unit. An estimated 15 million babies are born preterm.[117] The incubators that help to treat premature babies are in essence ectogenic incubators, mimicking the functions of the maternal womb in the later stages of pregnancy.[118] Advances in neonatal technology have meant that, whilst the normal gestation period that the fetus would spend in the mother's womb is 40 weeks, technology has managed to save the lives of fetuses born from 24

---

[113]   www.hta.gov.uk/sites/default/files/Guidance_on_the_disposal_of_pregnancy_remains .pdf. The guidance applies in England, Wales and Northern Ireland. The HTA website provides that this guidance is complementary to, and should be read alongside, the HTA's code of practice on disposal and guidance on the sensitive disposal of fetal remains published by the Royal College of Nursing.

[114]   Note that the incineration of fetal tissue is not banned in Scotland, but is considered unacceptable in any circumstance.

[115]   Ibid., paragraph 35.

[116]   Polkinghorne Report, paragraph 3.8. See also *Rance* v. *Mid-Downs Health Authority and Storr* (1990) 2 Medical Law Review 27.

[117]   J. E. Lawn, R. Davidage, V. K. Paul et al., 'Born Too Soon: Care for the Preterm Baby' (2013) 10 *Reproductive Health* S5.

[118]   This view is supported by Lupton: see M. Lupton, 'The Role of the Artificial Uterus in Embryo Adoption and Neonatal Intensive Care' (1999) 18 *Medical Law* 613–629 at p. 625.

weeks.[119] It has even been possible to salvage the lives of premature babies born earlier: the most premature baby to date is thought to have been a baby girl in Texas in 2014, born at just 21 weeks' and four days' gestation. In 2017 the unimpaired two-year outcome of the young female was reported, the authors noting, 'she may be the most premature known survivor to date'.[120] Despite this miracle story, it should be noted that for those born on the cusp of viability there is a 50 per cent or lesser chance of survival.[121] Whilst rates of survival – and survival without severe or moderate neuro, motor or sensory disabilities – have increased during the past two decades,[122] extremely premature babies remain at high risk of developmental delay.[123] One study showed that 'of babies born before 26 weeks of gestation, around one quarter grow up with serious disability. Mild disabilities are common amongst the remainder.'[124]

In the context of treatment of premature babies, arguably very few would dispute the use of such technology to rescue the lives of such babies born too early. The potential to treat such neonates provides an incentive for continued research into how the amount of time a fetus needs to spend in the maternal womb can be reduced further. The

[119] The Nuffield Council on Bioethics, *Critical Care Decisions in Foetal and Neonatal Medicine: Ethical Issues* (Hereafter: Nuffield Council, 'Critical Care Decisions'), November 2006, states that viability is said to be at 24 weeks. Prior to viability, for instance at 23 weeks, normal practice would be not to resuscitate (paragraph 9.18). Any attempts to resuscitate babies born before 22 weeks of gestation are to be regarded as experimental (paragraph 9.19).

[120] K. A. Ahmad, C. S. Frey, M. A. Fierro et al., 'Two-Year Neurodevelopmental Outcome of an Infant Born at 21 Weeks', 4 Days' Gestation' (2017) *Paediatrics* (in press).

[121] See V. Pierrat, L. Marchand-Martin, C. Arnaud et al., 'Neurodevelopmental Outcome at 2 Years for Preterm Children Born at 22 to 34 Weeks' Gestation in France in 2011: EPIPAGE-2 Cohort Study' (2017) 358 *BMJ*. See also Nuffield Council, 'Critical Care Decisions', paragraph 5.4.

[122] Pierrat, Marchand-Martin, Arnaud et al., 'Neurodevelopmental Outcome at 2 Years for Preterm Children Born at 22 to 34 Weeks' Gestation in France in 2011'.

[123] P. Y. Ancel, F. Goffinet, P. Kuhn et al., 'EPIPAGE-2 Writing Group. Survival and Morbidity of Preterm Children Born at 22 through 34 Weeks' Gestation in France in 2011: Results of the EPIPAGE-2 Cohort Study' (2015) 169 *JAMA Pediatrics* 230–238. K. L. Costeloe, E. M. Hennessy, S. Haider et al., 'Short Term Outcomes after Extreme Preterm Birth in England: Comparison of Two Birth Cohorts in 1995 and 2006 (The EPICure Studies)' (2012) 345 *BMJ* 7976. V. Fellman, L. Hellström-Westas, M. Norman et al., 'EXPRESS Group. One-Year Survival of Extremely Preterm Infants after Active Perinatal Care in Sweden' (2009) 301 *JAMA* 2225–2233. B. J. Stoll, N. I. Hansen, E. F. Bell et al., 'Eunice Kennedy Shriver National Institute of Child Health and Human Development Neonatal Research Network. Trends in Care Practices, Morbidity, and Mortality of Extremely Preterm Neonates 1993–2012' (2015) 314 *JAMA* 1039–1051.

[124] N. Marlow, 'Outcome Following Extremely Preterm Birth' (2006) 16 (3) *Current Obstetrics & Gynaecology* 141–146.

Nuffield Council in 2006 noted that the limits of viability have fallen by approximately one week every decade over the past 40 years, and that 'may be attributed at least in part to advances in technology and care'.[125] It is anticipated that as neonatal care continues to improve, viability will continue to be pushed back to earlier stages of gestation. Through sustained improvement in neonatal care, inadvertently we are discovering what ingredients are needed for an ectogenic incubator, which can gestate from fertilisation to term. As noted by Coleman, 'if premature new-borns are saved from earlier and earlier stages of gestation, then eventually the technique of ectogenesis may be discovered almost by default'.[126]

Treatment of premature babies and the continued development of sophisticated technology and treatment have indirectly contributed to research into what is needed for partial ectogenesis. But if advances in neonatal care are to improve, we must accede that some types of fetal research are essential to ensure the delivery of healthy babies. In order to examine how ectogenic research would be conducted on premature babies in the UK, imagine a situation whereby a pregnant woman was having complications in pregnancy, at a stage when her fetus was pre-viable – that is, below 24 weeks gestation. In such cases, the Royal College of Obstetricians and Gynaecologists issued the following recommendation:

> It is professionally acceptable not to attempt to support life in fetuses below the threshold of viability. It is extremely important to distinguish between physiological movements and signs of life, as well as being aware that observed movements may be of a reflex nature and not necessarily signs of life or viability.[127]

If attempts were to be made to save a fetus using ectogenic technology it should be in line with the Nuffield Council's recommendation that below 21 weeks and six days a baby should only be admitted to neonatal

---

[125] Nuffield Council, 'Critical Care Decisions', paragraph 5.1. See also S. E. Seaton, S. King, B. N. Manktelow et al., 'Babies Born at the Threshold of Viability: Changes in Survival and Workload over 20 Years' (2012) 98 *Archives of Disease in Childhood – Fetal and Neonatal Ed.* F15–F20.

[126] S. Coleman, *The Ethics of Artificial Uteruses: Implications for Reproduction and Abortion* (Aldershot: Ashgate, 2004) p. 45.

[127] Royal College of Obstetricians and Gynaecologists (2001) *Further Issues Relating to Late Abortion, Fetal Viability and Registration of Births and Deaths.* See also Royal College of Obstetricians and Gynaecologists (2010), *Termination of Pregnancy for Fetal Abnormality in England, Scotland and Wales.*

intensive care within an ethically approved research study.[128] This was also confirmed by the Polkinghorne Report, which stated that a local ethics committee must oversee fetal research and that research on the living fetus be treated on principles broadly comparable to those applicable to adults and children. The Polkinghorne Report provided that in the case of

> [t]he live whole fetus beyond 14 days after fertilisation, whether inside or outside the womb, research or other use should only take place if it carries only minimal risk of harm or, if a greater risk than that is involved, the action is, on balance, for the benefit of the fetus.[129]

Stringent ethical principles pertaining to research on children are considered to apply to the fetus.[130] Thus a clinic wishing to undertake ectogenic research on premature babies must do so only as part of a controlled research trial, which has obtained the necessary ethical approval.[131] Once this has been obtained, the necessary consents must be sought prior to entering the fetus into such a trial. But whose consent must be sought? The Polkinghorne Report had provided that written consent needed to be sought only from the mother:

> The written consent of the mother must be obtained before any research or therapy involving the fetus or fetal tissue takes place. Sufficient explanation should be offered to make the act of consent valid.[132]

Similar to its predecessor, the HTA considers fetal tissue as the mother's tissue, and only the mother must be required to give appropriate consent for research on the living fetus. If the mother consented to entering her fetus into an ectogenic trial, she would have to undergo surgery similar to a Caesarean section so that the fetus could be transferred intact. Fetal transfers shall be discussed in more detail in Chapter 4; suffice it to state that it is indisputable that a pregnant woman could not be forced to enter such a trial, even if this presents the only chance of survival for the fetus. The law is clear that a pregnant woman 'has an absolute right to choose whether to consent to medical treatment or refuse it or to choose one rather than another of the treatments offered'.[133]

---

[128] Nuffield Council, 'Critical Care Decisions', paragraph 9.19.
[129] Polkinghorne Report, paragraphs 2.4 and 3.2.
[130] Polkinghorne Report, paragraph 6.
[131] This must be applied for using the guidance provided by the National Research Ethics Service (NRES) and GMC.
[132] Polkinghorne Report, paragraph 4.1.
[133] *St George's Hospital NHS Trust* v. *S* [1998] 3 ALL ER 673.

But once the fetus is ex utero, it is no longer within her body and thus it is not clear why paternal consent is also not sought when considering what research the fetus ex utero may undergo. Neither the Polkinghorne Report nor the HTA Code of Practice requires that paternal consent be sought. The Polkinghorne Committee's view was that such consent was unnecessary, since the fathers relationship with the fetus is 'less intimate' than that of the mother[134] and because his consent is not needed for an abortion.[135] This is premised on the fact that, in natural pregnancy, the man has little say with regard to his fetus. Yet as Keown noted, it 'does not follow that because the father is denied a veto on abortion he should therefore be denied a veto on the use of the abortus'.[136] In the context of in vitro embryos,[137] the law has correctly held that gamete progenitors should be equally situated with regards to their in vitro embryos (save in exceptional circumstances, or where they agree otherwise). When fertilisation takes place in vitro, women no longer hold the privileged position and paramount say that they possess in natural pregnancy. It is argued that, in principle, this extends to the in vitro fetus, and once ex utero, and a woman's bodily integrity is no longer invoked, the male progenitor should have an equal say with regard to fetal research/treatment. Ectogenic research on his fetus will also have implications for him, and since he too will have parental responsibilities and obligations to the child born, his consent should also be sought. This would also be in alignment with the medical treatment of minors in other areas, where the courts have made it clear that in potentially contentious cases doctors should seek a dual consent.[138] Thus it is submitted that paternal consent should be sought as much as maternal consent; and once it becomes possible to remove a fetus into an ectogenic incubator and the fetus is ex utero, the father has just as much right to be consulted regarding his fetus as the mother. A woman's right to control her body does not grant her unfettered rights over the body of the fetus/neonate ex utero. However, it is acknowledged that in certain circumstances obtaining paternal consent may be difficult, for instance, where the parents are unmarried/separated

---

[134] Polkinghorne Report, paragraph 6.7.

[135] Abortion Act 1967 (as amended by The Human Fertilisation and Embryology Act 1990).

[136] J. Keown, 'The Polkinghorne Report on Fetal Research: Nice Recommendations, Shame about the Reasoning' (1993) 19 *Journal of Medical Ethics* 114–120, at p. 116.

[137] See Chapter 2 for discussion on how UK law governs regulation and disposition of IVF embryos.

[138] Cases such as immunisation and male circumcision require dual parental consent: *Re B (A Child) (Immunisation)* [2003] EWHC 1376, [2003] EWCA Civ 1148. *Re J (Child's Religious Upbringing and Circumcision)* [2000] 1 FCR 307.

and/or the mother does not wish to inform the father of the pregnancy, or he wishes to have no involvement.[139]

Benefit–Risk Ratio   Research into ectogenesis will require not only the creation of the artificial and mechanical ectogenic chamber which can mimic the functions of the womb, but also appropriate drugs and other pharmaceutical products, and thus the Medicines for Human Use (Clinical Trials) Regulations 2004 will apply.[140] The 2004 Regulations provide little guidance for governing an ectogenic research trial, but do state that such research should relate directly to a condition from which the minor suffers and cannot be done on any other group of subjects. There must also be some direct benefit to the group of patients to which the subject belongs, which ectogenic research will provide. Ectogenic research on premature babies should also seek to comply with the EC Regulation No 1901/2006, so as 'to provide assurance that the rights, safety and well being of trial subjects are protected and the results of any clinical trial are credible'.[141]

Brazier and I have argued elsewhere[142] that whether research into ectogenesis is in the best interests of those early fetuses entered into such trials is not incontestable. Those initial ectogenic research trials may benefit other babies born at an early gestational age in years to come, but not necessarily the first subjects entered into the trials. They may be

---

[139] There will clearly be issues regarding the privacy/confidentiality of a woman where a man does not even know she is pregnant. It is also worth noting that an unmarried father has no automatic right to be consulted about his child being put up for adoption because this would breach a woman's privacy. The Adoption and Children Act 2002 s52 (6) defines a 'parent' as a parent with parental responsibility, requiring the agreement of all such parents to be obtained (or their permission to be dispensed with by the court) before a child is placed for adoption. A father without parental responsibility has no absolute right to be involved in the proposed adoption of his child.

[140] SI 2004/1031. The Regulations implemented the EU Clinical Trials Directive (Clinical Trials Directive 2001/20) into UK law. Although note on 29 March 2017, the United Kingdom gave notice to the European Council under Article 50 of the Treaty on European Union of the United Kingdom's intention to leave the EU. The Government's Great Repeal Bill is intended to affirm the status of UK legislation passed pursuant to EU Directives, but much of this legislation will need to be amended to take into account the new relationship with the EU, such as the appointment and oversight of new UK regulators in place of the EU institutions.

[141] For more on these regulations see B. Lehmann, 'Regulation (EC) No 1901/2006 on Medicinal Products for Paediatric Use & Clinical Research in Vulnerable Populations' (2008) *Child and Adolescent Psychiatry and Mental Health* 2–37.

[142] A. Alghrani and M. Brazier, 'What Is It? Whose Is It? Re-positioning the Fetus in the Context of Research?' (2011) 70 *Cambridge Law Journal* 51–82.

subjected to a battery of tests and procedures likely to cause at least some degree of pain and distress if the fetus survives. If, as is likely, the fetus does not live to leave hospital, what benefit have they gained? If a baby survives with multiple disabilities, are his/her interests served? Further, in a series of judgments[143] raised in the context of interventions to prolong the life of severely disabled babies, the judges have emphasised that it in some cases it will be impossible to justify the degree of suffering occasioned to the baby for a slender chance of allowing the baby to survive a little longer. Yet without such research trials, technology, which has the potential to help those born on the thresholds of viability, will not come about. Elsewhere the Polkinghorne Report had recommend that:

> The live fetus, whether *in utero* or *ex utero* ... should be treated on principles broadly similar to those which apply to treatment and research conducted with children and adults.[144]

The Declaration of Helsinki,[145] the Royal College of Paediatrics and Child Health,[146] the Medical Research Council[147] and the British Medical Association[148] all accept that non-therapeutic research on children is justified when it is intended to benefit other children, although it should not be carried out if it can be done equally well using adults.[149] The prospects of survival for a pre-viable fetus are minimal, and the ectogenic research trial may offer the best hope of survival. Whilst such trials may not help the first premature babies entered into such trials, it may help those born at that stage in the future. This kind of research cannot be carried out other than on neonates.

Whether a fetus should be entered into an ectogenic research trial is a decision that should fall to the parent(s) and healthcare professionals to

---

[143] Wyatt v. *Portsmouth NHS Trust and another* [2004] EWHC 2247; [2005] EWHC 117; [2005] EWHC 693 (Fam) *Re L (Medical Treatment: Benefit)* [2004] EWHC 2713 (Fam) *Re C* [1998] 1 FCR 1.

[144] Polkinghorne Report, paragraph 1.1(a).

[145] World Medical Association, *Ethical Principles for Medical Research Involving Human Subjects* (Revised, 2000).

[146] Royal College of Paediatrics and Child Health: Ethics Advisory Committee, 'Guidelines for the Ethical Conduct of Medical Research Involving Children' (2000) 82 *Arch Dis Child* 1777.

[147] Medical Research Council, *Medical Research Involving Children*, 2004.

[148] British Medical Association, *Consent, Rights and Choice in Healthcare for Children and Young People*.

[149] J. K. Mason and G. T. Laurie, *Mason and McCall Smith's Law and Medical Ethics, Seventh Edition* (Oxford: Oxford University Press, 2006) p. 687.

make, and arguably it is, or should be, lawful for parents to consent to entering their child into an ectogenic research trial, which offers the best chance of survival and is 'intended directly to benefit the child'.[150] The potential to improve the care of premature babies provides a strong case for allowing fetal research into ectogenesis in those limited circumstances where the research may represent the last hope of survival for the fetus/baby. As with research in other areas, the question to be asked is whether the benefits outweigh the risks. As observed by Raskin and Mazor in the context of research on the early embryo:

> We do choose, as a society, to make sacrifices if the benefit is agreed to be large enough. Research with in vitro fetuses carries its own benefits to our society. A major benefit of such research would be to increase knowledge of fetal development, understanding genetic deformities and treating horrible diseases. Other significant benefits would be to allow women who cannot gestate the opportunity to do so without using a surrogate, to protect a developing embryo/fetus from conditions in the womb that may be harmful, and to permit accessibility for corrective surgery to a fetus.[151]

The potential to improve the care of premature babies provides a strong case for permitting ethically approved research to help those born early from the maternal womb. The issue of whether women should be permitted to opt for ectogenesis where it is not for the sole/immediate benefit of the fetus, but rather for non-medical reasons, is dealt with in Chapter 4, since it pertains to a regulatory issue once ectogenesis is possible, rather than the regulation of ectogenic research.

3.4 Research on Aborted Fetuses

Controversially, the question has been raised whether, in light of the medical benefits ectogenesis promises, aborted fetuses should be utilised for research into partial ectogenesis: for instance, a woman who chooses abortion because she does not wish to be a mother to that child in any sense, but who would, for the benefit of future children, be prepared to consent to using the unwanted fetus in ectogenic research. The argument poses that if the fetus is doomed to be destroyed, could entering the fetus

---

[150] See Royal College of Paediatrics, 'Child Health: Ethics Advisory Committee Guidelines for the Ethical Conduct of Medical Research Involving Children' (2000) 82 *Archives of Disease in Childhood* 177–182.

[151] J. Raskin and N. Mazor, 'The Artificial Womb and Human Subject Research' in S. Gelfand (ed.), *Ectogenesis: Artificial Womb Technology and the Future of Human Reproduction* (Amsterdam, New York: Rodopi, 2006) p. 177.

into such research 'ennoble' its death if it is utilised 'to serve its more fortunate fellows'?[152]

Any attempts to use live terminated fetuses obtained through abortion for ectogenic research are likely to face insurmountable hurdles. While the current legislation does in certain circumstances allow for late abortion,[153] which could produce a live fetus that would be more optimal for ectogenic research, these are highly unlikely to be born alive. The Abortion Act 1967 (as amended) permits termination of pregnancy beyond 24 weeks' gestation if two medical practitioners agree in good faith that either the fetus is at substantial risk of serious handicap or there is a risk of grave, permanent injury to the life, or the physical and mental health, of the woman.[154] In England and Wales in 2016, 92 per cent of terminations were carried out under 13 weeks' gestation. Terminations after 20 weeks' gestation accounted for only 1 per cent (out of a total of 190,406).[155] For terminations after 22 weeks, feticide is recommended by the Royal College of Obstetricians and Gynaecologists (RCOG) to ensure that the fetus is not born alive.[156] In 2016, of the 1,508 terminations performed at 22 weeks and over, 48 per cent were preceded by feticide. A further 45 per cent were performed by a method whereby the fetal heart is stopped as part of the procedure.[157] Only eleven (0.7 per cent) of abortions at 22 weeks and beyond were confirmed as having no feticide. For the remaining 89 cases the DoH was unable to confirm whether feticide was used.

Therefore, given that in most cases the fetus will be dead, the fetus may be of little use to those wishing to research ectogenesis. However, if in a

---

[152] P. Ramsey, *The Ethics of Fetal Research* (New Haven, London: Yale University Press, 1975) p. 44.

[153] Abortion Act 1967 (as amended by Human Fertilisation and Embryology Act 1990) s1. Note this statute does not apply to Northern Ireland. On abortion legislation see S. Sheldon, 'British Abortion Law: Speaking from the Past to Govern the Future' (2016) 79 *Modern Law Review* 283–316. S. Sheldon, 'The Decriminalisation of Abortion: An Argument for Modernisation' (2015) *Oxford Journal of Legal Studies* 1–32. R. Scott, 'Risks, Reasons and Rights: The European Convention on Human Rights and English Abortion Law' (2016) 24(1) *Medical Law Review* 1–33. S. McGuinness, M. Thomson, 'Medicine and Abortion Law: Complicating the Reforming Profession' (2015) 23(2) *Medical Law Review* 177–199. M. Taylor, 'Women's Right to Health and Ireland's Abortion Laws' (2015) 130(1) *International Journal of Gynecology and Obstetrics* 93.

[154] Taylor, 'Women's Right to Health and Ireland's Abortion Laws'.

[155] Department of Health (2016) Statistical Bulletin 2008/1, *Abortion Statistics, England and Wales: 2016.*

[156] Royal College of Obstetricians and Gynaecologists (RCOG), *Termination of Pregnancy for Fetal Abnormality in England, Scotland and Wales* (London: 2010).

[157] Taylor, 'Women's Right to Health and Ireland's Abortion Laws'.

late termination a fetus emerges alive and lives ex utero, even if only for a short time, the fetus then becomes a legal person and the general law applicable to children applies.[158] The fetus must be treated in accordance with its best interests and the birth must be registered.[159]

The 2015 HTA Guidance on the disposal of pregnancy remains following pregnancy loss or termination notes the paramount importance of the woman's wishes and understanding of the disposal options. The HTA provides that the 'particular sensitive nature of this tissue means that the wishes of the woman and her understanding of the disposal options open to her, are of paramount importance and should be respected and acted upon'.[160] The HTA's guidance on valid consent, which must be based on persons' understanding of what the activity entails, supersedes that in the Polkinghorne guidance, which recommended that women should not know the purpose for which the fetal tissues would be used (formerly known as the 'separation principle'). In light of ectogenic research, should current policy that recommends that feticide be carried out on a late fetus[161] be amended so as to permit ectogenic research on aborted fetuses? It seems perverse that a woman may be allowed to abort her fetus, but not to donate the fetus to specific fetal research. This point is not lost on Gaylin and Lappe,[162] who note that 'in abortion we more or less readily condone procedures which subject the fetus to dismemberment, salt induced osmotic shock, or surgical extirpation; certainly no conceivable experiment would do the same'.[163] Yet arguments that contend that because we allow late abortions, we should then also allow research on living abortuses, have been plausibly rejected by Ramsey, who argues that just because the law permits woman in certain circumstances to abort a fetus, does not in itself justify fetal research per se.[164] Ramsey states that to agree with the above position is to argue that:

> We have by law given ourselves the right to do these unimaginable acts of violence in abortion procedures; we then can legitimately claim the right

---

[158] Polkinghorne Report, paragraph 3.8. See also *Rance v. Mid-Downs Health Authority and Storr* (1990) 2 Med LR 27.

[159] Nuffield Council, 'Critical Care Decisions', paragraph 4.14.

[160] Ibid.

[161] RCOG, Termination of Pregnancy for Fetal Abnormality in England, Scotland and Wales.

[162] W. Gaylin and M. Lappe, 'Fetal Politics: The Debate on Experimenting with the Unborn', unpublished manuscript, as cited in P. Ramsey, *The Ethics of Fetal Research* (New Haven, London: Yale University Press, 1975) p. 41.

[163] Ramsey, *The Ethics of Fetal Research*, p. 42.

[164] Ibid., p. 43.

to do lesser possible harms for the sake of other wanted babies. If that contention has any force at all, the argument more than borders on saying: Since we have given ourselves the right to do wrong, we have given ourselves the right to do other, lesser wrongs.[165]

As Ramsey points out, 'two wrongs do not make a right, a greater wrong does not help to justify a lesser one'.[166] There may be valid arguments for the morality of experimentation on the fetuses, but this is not one. He states:

> But there can be no obligation – indeed, it would be positively wrong – to obtain those results by means of abortuses who are hovering between life and death precisely because for them no such rescue or remedies were wanted. Those beneficial results should rather be among the research aims of therapeutic investigations that have as a first purpose the promotion of the survival of fetal patients and premature infants.[167]

Thus there are a number of potential ways in which research into partial ectogenesis can be undertaken in the UK. Whilst there are strong arguments to be made for permitting research into ectogenesis, I concur with view espoused by Ramsey that such research should not be performed on aborted fetuses, but rather reserved for those fetuses which stand a chance of benefiting from the treatment: a fetus that is wanted by its progenitors, but whose extreme prematurity would otherwise mean that it had no hope of survival. Thus the most optimal candidates for such research would be premature babies who stand a chance to benefit from partaking in such research.

Examining how research into ectogenesis will be governed in UK, it is clear there is a legal lacuna that must be addressed. Research into complete ectogenesis that involves sustaining the in vitro embryo is governed (and prohibited) by the HFE Act 1990 (as amended) that prohibits research beyond 14 days. Guidance on storage of fetal tissue is to be found only in HTA Guidance. Similar to its predecessor, the recommendations drafted by the Polkinghorne Committee in 1989, both are of little use when addressing the controversial issue of the use of fetuses in ectogenic research. Research on the human fetus continues to raise a constellation of difficult questions and, as the Warnock Committee noted many years ago:

[165] Ibid., p. 43.
[166] Ibid., p. 48.
[167] Ibid., p. 35.

It [is] totally illogical to propose stringent legislative controls on the use of very early human embryos for research when, while there is a less formal mechanism governing the research of whole live embryos and fetuses of more advanced gestation. Although we understand that these mechanisms have worked well, we consider that there is a case for bringing any research that makes use of whole live aborted embryos or fetuses – whether obtained from in vitro fertilisation, uterine lavage, or termination of pregnancy – within the sort of legislative framework proposed in this report. We suggest that this be given urgent consideration.[168]

Similarly, in 1989 the Polkinghorne Committee stated:

In time, we can expect our report to need reconsideration ... It is desirable that subsequent revision should be undertaken as it becomes necessary and not have to wait until the arousal of considerable public concern before being taken in hand. Accordingly, we recommend that the Health Departments should be take steps to keep these issues under regular review perhaps in consultation with the MRC and the profession.[169]

As we enter into the third phase of human reproduction, it is time to address this – specific guidance on fetal research as opposed to merely that on storage, or disposal, is now needed.

3.5   Conclusion

As scientists continue in their endeavours to create a mechanical ectogenic device, undertaking both animal and human research, the question is whether the progress made into research at the beginning of pregnancy and the end of pregnancy will one day converge.[170] Gelfand is optimistic they will:

I've talked to researchers who are doing research on partial ectogenesis – interventions for premature births, mainly – and I've talked to *in vitro* fertilisation researchers who are trying to extend the period of time an embryo can live outside the womb [...] Put the two together and eventually we're going to be able to do this.[171]

Not all share his optimism. Morris warns of the practical difficulties with building a functional artificial/bioengineered womb/ectogenic incubator:

The uterus of a pregnant woman draws about twenty five per cent of the heart's output, every minute of the day. That's an enormous amount of

---

[168] Warnock Report, paragraph 11.18.
[169] The Polkinghorne Report, paragraph 3.
[170] Rosen, 'Why Not Artificial Wombs?', pp. 67–76.
[171] Ibid., pp. 67–76.

blood flow that an artificial womb would have to duplicate. Beyond that, you'd have to know exactly how much oxygen to infuse within that blood, how much nutrients and what kinds, what sorts of hormones and when. I truly doubt we know enough about how to gestate a natural pregnancy, let alone put all of that into action in a laboratory setting.[172]

Despite such scepticism, some of those working in the field predict they will in the future achieve the desired aim of creating an ectogenic incubator.[173] I argue it is imprudent to dismiss ectogenesis as being confined to the realms of science fiction. Both directly and indirectly, scientific endeavours continue to slowly make progress into what is needed for this advance. The perfection of technology, which could safely gestate a human embryo/fetus outside the womb, holds many advantages, not just for women who cannot carry a child of their own, but also for the many premature babies that die each year or are afflicted with disability because they were born too early. Given the advantages ectogenesis may bring, combined with the government stance that the human embryo/fetus is to be accorded some protection and should be respected, it is submitted that there is a moral imperative to conduct research into ectogenesis.

I have endeavoured in this chapter to outline how research into ectogenesis would be governed under the current regulatory framework. The discussion first focused on the law governing animal research, before examining the complex issue of using the human embryo/fetus in ectogenic research. Research into complete ectogenesis – gestating a human embryo to term – would incur many difficulties in the present legal climate. The policy behind the legislation, which imposes restrictions on the use of an embryo beyond 14 days, stemmed from the Warnock Committee's recommendation that that the embryo should be accorded a 'special status' and afforded some protection in law. This does not necessarily provide a justifiable reason to thwart research into complete ectogenesis – since, rather than destroying the embryo, ectogenesis is seeking to provide a way of allowing the fetus to continue to grow and achieve its potential to become a human being. It is not clear how mandating the embryo be destroyed affords it more protection than allowing its use in such research. In light of the benefits of ectogenesis, if such research is to be prohibited, legislators need to be clear on the justification for this.

---

[172] S. La Fee, 'Will Artificial Wombs Mean the End of Pregnancy?' *SigOnSanDiego.com*, 25 February 2004, www.signonsandiego.com/news/science/20040225–9999-mz1c25womb.html.

[173] Newson, 'From Foetus to Full Term – Without a Mother's Touch'.

The discussion then turned to partial ectogenesis – whereby a pregnancy begins in the maternal womb but the fetus is later transferred into an ectogenic device. This often occurs with premature babies. This is the most optimal way of researching ectogenesis by constantly reducing viability and improving the treatment of premature babies born on the cusp of viability. Such research, although experimental, could also be argued to be therapeutic. However, any attempts to use live abortuses would be likely to encounter grave legal, ethical and practical difficulties. Very few abortuses are born alive. To perform research on those that are would be to save the life of a fetus that its progenitors, or at least its mother, wanted dead. I rejected arguments that research is justified because a fetus, which its mother wanted aborted, is 'doomed' in any case, or that because we allow the fetuses to be terminated in abortion, we should also allow a fetus to be subjected to experimental research. Throughout the discussion it was apparent that there is a clear inconsistency between embryonic research, which is governed substantively by statute, and that of fetal research.

If research into ectogenesis advances and one day becomes a safe method of gestation, regulation of this technology will raise further complex questions. What status will the baby in the ectogenic incubator have? Can the machine be switched off mid-gestation? Will ectogenesis end the abortion debate as alleged by some? Given that scientists have predicted ectogenesis could become a reality in the future,[174] Chapter 4 addresses some of the many regulatory challenges posed by ectogenesis.

---

[174] Newson, 'From Foetus to Full Term – Without a Mother's Touch'.

In Vitro Gestation II

Ectogenesis: A Regulatory Minefield?

The invention of a method to gestate a baby outside the human womb has enormous implications for the way the courts, ethicists and society at large currently view the right of a fetus to be born. It also influences how society thinks about the relationship between the fetus and its parents. One issue that exemplifies the strain on social relationships is the right of a mother or father to end the life of a fetus prior to birth. In the case of in vitro fertilisation there is one moment in time, when the fetus can be given a chance at life, implanted, or discarded. At this point, the fetus is an independent living being, separate from the body of both mother and father. Ectogenesis stretches out this moment into a nine-month continuum.[1]

If ectogenesis becomes possible, it is clear that regulating this advance will revolutionise reproduction and generate a 'glittering constellation of legal and ethical questions'.[2] Technology will now make the hidden fetus visible. Although the courts have often stated that the fetus has no legal personality, the law so far has evaded answering conclusively what moral and legal status should be ascribed to the fetus, relying on the fact it is housed in a woman's body and thus engages her bodily autonomy and so her decisions regarding the fate of the fetus must prevail. What happens if instead the fetus is located in an independent ectogenic device, or can be safely transferred into one? Many of the cases that have generated legal rules and principles on the status of the fetus have developed in the context of the abortion debate[3], and cases of maternal–fetal conflict, where a fetus is being gestated in its mother's

---

[*] Part of the material in this chapter has been developed from an earlier paper titled 'Regulating the Reproductive Revolution: Ectogenesis – A Regulatory Minefield' published in "Law and Bioethics: Current Legal Issues Volume 11" edited by Michael Freeman (2005). It is reproduced with permission of Oxford University Press (www.oup.com).

[1] J. S. Bard, 'Immaculate Gestation? How Will Ectogenesis Change Current Paradigms of Social Relationships and Values?' in S. Gelfand (ed.), *Ectogenesis: Artificial Womb Technology and the Future of Human Reproduction* (Amsterdam and New York, NY: Rodopi, 2006) at p. 150.

[2] M. Brazier, 'Regulating the Reproduction Business?' (1999) 7 *Medical Law Review* 166–193, at p. 168.

[3] *Paton* v. *BPAS* [1979] Q.B 276, *C* v. *S* [1987] 1 ALL E.R 1230.

womb.[4] This is significantly different from the situation of fetuses that would have an independent physical existence and that would be gestated by a machine/ectogenic device.

In considering the complex myriad of legal and ethical questions that ectogenesis raises, this chapter will focus primarily on the legal and regulatory issues generated by this advance. It is split into two parts; the first part (Section 4.1) examines partial ectogenesis, whereby conception and gestation initially take place within the woman's body, but at some point during the pregnancy the fetus is transferred to an ectogenic device for the remaining period. This section will consider how partial ectogenesis has the potential to increase the reproductive choices of women who may want to end their pregnancy but not the life of the fetus. Having addressed this, the reverse scenario will then be considered; namely whether ectogenesis could be used to extend fetal protection and be mandated by the state in lieu of abortion. The bold assertion that ectogenesis could 'end the abortion debate'[5] will be examined.

The second part of this chapter (Section 4.2) focuses on complete ectogenesis, whereby a fetus is created outside a woman's body (via IVF) and immediately transferred into an artificial womb where it is gestated for the entire forty-week period. The mother's body is never used in the gestation process. This section focuses on questions legislators will have to address in developing a regulatory framework that accommodates this new technological advance. Here the following will be examined: (Section 4.2.1) whether current legislation could be extended to ectogenic fetuses; (Section 4.2.2) what status and legal protection should be conferred on the independent fetus gestating outside the maternal womb; (Section 4.2.3) disputes concerning the fate of the ectogenic fetus; and (Section 4.2.4) concerns regarding the welfare of the ectogenic baby.

4.1   Partial Ectogenesis

If partial ectogenesis and fetal transfer become medically safe, this will raise two important questions for regulators: firstly, can women who

---

[4] *Re MB* (1997) 38 BMLR 175, *St George's Health Care Trust v. S* [1998] 1 All ER 673, *Rochdale Healthcare (NHS) Trust* v. C [1997] 1 FCR 274, *Norfolk and Norwich Health Care (NHS) Trust* v. W [1996] 2 FLR 613, *Bolton Hospitals NHS Trust v. O* [2003] I FLR 824, *Vo v. France* ECHR Application Number 53924/00 [2004] 2 FCR 577.

[5] C. Kaczor, 'Could Artificial Wombs End the Abortion Debate?' (2005) 5(2) *National Catholic Bioethics Quarterly* 283–301.

wish to end their pregnancy but not the life of the fetus opt for ectogenesis? Secondly, if legislators are interested in protecting fetal life, particularly after viability (and the current stance adopted by the government is that both human embryo and fetus have a 'special status'[6] and thus should be afforded some protection in law), could ectogenesis signal an end to abortion?

4.1.1 Can Women Opt for Ectogenesis?

As the preceding chapter noted, partial ectogenesis already exists in the form of incubators in the neo-natal intensive care unit. However, this is reserved for cases of medical necessity, where a wanted pregnancy incurs complications that make early birth necessary in order to preserve the health of the mother or fetus. What if a pregnancy was not incurring any complications but the mother wanted to transfer her fetus into an ectogenic incubator? The motivations for such a request may vary. It could stem from the fact that a woman is having a horrible but not life-threatening pregnancy, to a change of circumstances, a break-up in her relationship, the death of a partner, or simply a change of mind. It could be that pregnancy may render her ineligible for certain careers (for instance, athletics, dancing, modelling and acting). Or alternatively, a woman who discovers she is pregnant and wishes to cease to be pregnant and avoid motherhood herself, but who is happy for the fetus to have a chance of life, perhaps with a view to its adoption. Such a course would end her pregnancy without ending fetal life. Whilst an abortion would also allow her to end the pregnancy it would also end the life of her fetus, which the mother does not want. Would this be lawful or ethical?

Terminating a pregnancy in such circumstances so as to transfer the fetus into an ectogenic incubator may give rise to criminal liability. Section 58 of the Offences Against the Persons Act 1861 provides:

---

[6] The Committee took the view that the embryo has a 'special status' and should thus be accorded protection; *Report of the Committee of Inquiry into Human Fertilisation and Embryology* (Cmnd. 9314), 1984, (hereafter 'Warnock Report') paragraphs 71–72. Similarly the Polkinghorne Report stated that the fetus merits 'profound respect based upon its potential for development into a fully-formed human being' (paragraph 2.4); consequently, a live fetus should be accorded a status 'broadly comparable to that of a living person' (paragraph 3.1): *Review of the Guidance on the Research Use of Fetuses and Fetal Material* (Cmnd 762, 1989) paragraph 3.1 (hereafter The Polkinghorne Report).

Every woman, being with child, who, with intent to procure her own miscarriage, shall administer to herself any poison or other noxious thing, or shall unlawfully use any instrument or other means whatsoever with the like intent, and whosoever, with intent to procure the miscarriage of any woman, whether she be or be not with child, shall unlawfully administer to her or cause to be taken by her any poison or other noxious thing, or shall unlawfully use any instrument or other means whatsoever with the like intent, shall be guilty of felony, and being convicted thereof shall be liable to be kept in penal servitude for life.

It is not clear whether transferral into an ectogenic incubator would be regarded as 'procuring a miscarriage' and thus fall foul of the 1861 Act. Yet it would be ludicrous to retain what can only be regarded as an archaic provision drafted at a time when ectogenesis was not even dreamt of, to regulate this revolutionary technology. Furthermore, a distinction can be drawn between procuring a miscarriage and a fetal transferral. The former envisaged a process inevitably designed to kill the fetus. This process offers a chance of life. However, if an attempt to transfer a fetus were made at a relatively young gestational age – say, for instance, nineteen weeks, when there is no record of a fetus having survived outside the maternal womb at this gestational age – it could be argued that fetal death was virtually certain, and thus was contrary to the 1861 statute. Furthermore, whilst a pregnant woman retains autonomy over her body, as Judge LJ noted in *St George's Health Care Trust* v. *S*,[7] 'it does not follow without any further analysis that this entitles her to put at risk the healthy viable fetus which she is carrying'.[8] If the pregnancy were terminated so that the fetus could be transferred into an ectogenic chamber, and the fetus subsequently dies, the criminal and the ancient (but still living) 'born alive' rule[9] may also apply. This rule states that if a person either deliberately or grossly negligently injures a child in the womb, and that child is born alive but later dies of his injuries, the perpetrator can be criminally liable for murder or manslaughter.[10] Lord Mustill also suggested that where injury does not cause death but lasting harm, a prosecution for causing grievous bodily harm could lie.[11]

Regard must also be given to the Abortion Act 1967, section 1 of which provides for circumstances in which 'termination of pregnancy' may be

---

[7] [1998] 3 All ER 673.
[8] Ibid., 686.
[9] *AG's Reference (No 3 of 1994)* [1997] 3 ALL ER 936 (HL).
[10] Above.
[11] Above, 942.

lawful.[12] Since termination of the pregnancy is just what fetal transfer entails, Section 1(1) (a) (the so-called 'social ground') could apply if two doctors were to certify that the risk of continuation of the pregnancy were greater than its termination. Such a conclusion may be problematic given that a fetal transfer at an early gestational age is likely to involve major surgery on the woman who, if the pregnancy continued to term, might well be able to give birth naturally at less risk to her.[13] So other grounds might be invoked perhaps 'grave injury to her mental health' and distasteful though it sounds, termination of a pregnancy on the ground of fetal disability may fall within the letter of the law, allowing women carrying disabled fetuses to opt for partial ectogenesis, since the presence of serious fetal handicap would render the termination of the pregnancy lawful.[14]

A woman, who was willing to donate her fetus to ectogenic research and subsequent adoption should the fetus survive, could be regarded as acting for the benefit of the fetus, if the alternative is death. The Polkinghorne Report had provided that research involving much more than minimal risk should 'on balance, for the benefit of the fetus',[15] and thus such research would appear to be in compliance with this

---

[12] Abortion Act 1967 (as amended by Human Fertilisation and Embryology Act 1990) s1(1) provides: 'Subject to the provisions of this section, a person shall not be guilty of an offence under the law relating to abortion when a pregnancy is terminated by a registered medical practitioner if two registered medical practitioners are of the opinion, formed in good faith (a) that the pregnancy has not exceeded its twenty-fourth week and that the continuance of the pregnancy would involve risk, greater than if the pregnancy were terminated, of injury to the physical or mental health of the pregnant woman or any existing children of her family; or (b) that the termination is necessary to prevent grave permanent injury to the physical or mental health of the pregnant woman; or (c) that the continuance of the pregnancy would involve risk to the life of the pregnant woman, greater than if the pregnancy were terminated; or (d) that there is a substantial risk that if the child were born it would suffer from such physical or mental abnormalities as to be seriously handicapped.'

[13] A fetal transfer may pose grave risks for the woman. Caesarean sections at pre-viability or borderline viability are more hazardous than near-term caesarean sections. As the Nuffield Council point out, at an early stage of pregnancy: 'a classical caesarean section would be required, which involves opening the abdomen at the upper part of the uterus, unlike the operation which is usually performed at or near term in which only the lower part of the uterus is opened (lower segment caesarean section). The uterus is more likely to rupture in a future labour if there is a scar from a previous classical caesarean section than from a lower segment caesarean section.' The Nuffield Council on Bioethics 'Critical Care Decisions in Foetal and Neonatal Medicine: Ethical Issues' November 2006, paragraph 5.5.

[14] Abortion Act 1967, s(1)(1)(d). For criticism of this controversial section see S. McGuinness, 'Law Reproduction and Disability: Fatally "Handicapped"' (2013) 21 (2) *Medical Law Review* 213–242.

[15] Polkinghorne Report, paragraphs 2.4 and 3.2.

requirement. Prior to the HTA 2015 Guidance, provisions in the Polkinghorne Report, most notably the 'separation principle' would have made it inherently difficult for such a procedure to take place. The Polkinghorne Report had provided that:

> Great care should be taken to separate decisions relating to abortion and to the subsequent use of fetal material. The prior decision to carry out an abortion should be reached without consideration of the benefits of subsequent use.[16]

The Polkinghorne Committee feared that knowledge of the potential use of fetal material might affect the timing when the woman requested an abortion and induce her to act contrary to what is in her best interests. For example, the Polkinghorne Committee believed that it is normally in the mother's interest that a termination should be carried out as early as possible.[17] They stated that 'the management of the pregnancy of any mother should be dictated by her health care needs alone and this will include the method and timing of abortion'.[18] Consequently, the Polkinghorne Committee took the view that 'arguments for separation are of such ethical importance that they outweigh those for allowing the mother to make any direction regarding the use of her fetus or fetal tissue'.[19] Thus, the 'separation principle' espoused in the Polkinghorne Report precluded the possibility that a woman should be able to terminate her pregnancy and have the fetus transferred into an ectogenic device. However a request to transfer a fetus into an ectogenic device or trial of ectogenesis acts to give some sort of chance to a fetus that will otherwise be destroyed. It is also unclear how prohibiting women from electing such a procedure if it were to become possible would advance the view held by both the Warnock Committee and the Polkinghorne Committee that the embryo/fetus should be accorded respect. Allowing women seeking to end their pregnancy the choice to opt for fetal transfer/ectogenic research both accords the fetus more respect than only permitting its destruction and at the same time enhances the woman's autonomy and her range of procreative choices. It would be perverse to allow women to destroy their fetus within the current laws on abortion and yet prohibit a woman the option to end her pregnancy but offer her fetus a chance of survival, whilst also providing prospective benefits to future babies born so early in the gestational stage that ectogenic technology provides their only hope of survival.

---

[16] Polkinghorne Report, paragraph 4.1.
[17] Ibid., paragraph 4.3.
[18] Ibid., paragraph 4.3.
[19] Ibid., paragraph 4.6.

The HTA 2015 guidance now provides that fetal tissue is regarded as the mother's tissue;[20] the mother must therefore give appropriate consent for research on the fetus.[21] The HTA guidance on consent now supersedes the Polkinghorne Report's stipulation that women should not know the purpose for which fetal tissue will be used: in order to give valid consent it must be based on the mothers understanding of what the research involves. Under this guidance, provided such research obtained the necessary ethical approval, a woman would now be able to consent to the fetus being used in such research.[22] However even this guidance is premised on the assumption that what was in issue was fetal tissue from a dead fetus and not an entity that might have even the slimmest hope of survival via ectogenic research. It is clear that specific guidance is needed to govern ectogenic research, specifying in what circumstances parents should be permitted to enter their fetus into such research.

What of the reverse scenario, whereby it is not the woman requesting transfer into an ectogenic incubator but rather the government seeking to protect all fetal life?

4.1.2   Can Ectogenesis Be Mandated in Lieu of Abortion on 'Social Grounds'?

4.1.2.1   The Fetus Is Protected

It is clear that while English law bestows no actionable rights on the fetus,[23] the fetus has long had the protection of the criminal law in England and Wales.[24] The first statutory prohibition of abortion arose in 1803, when The Ellenborough's Act made the act of procuring the miscarriage of a woman who was 'quick with child' a statutory offence

---

[20] Human Tissue Authority, 'Guidance on the Disposal of Pregnancy Remains Following Pregnancy Loss or Termination' 15 March 2015.

[21] Human Tissue Authority, Code of Practice A, Guiding Principles and the Fundamental Principle of Consent, 2017.

[22] Storage as opposed to research is licensed by the HTA and the Code of Practice makes it clear that the HTA's remit does not cover ethical approval for research, which must be sought in accordance with guidelines of the National Research Ethics Service (NRES) and the General Medical Council (GMC). The UK Medical Research Council also sets out the conduct expected when undertaking research that involves human tissue and biological samples.

[23] Any rights are contingent upon being born alive: Paton v. BPAS [1979] Q.B 276.

[24] For a discussion of the law see J. Fortin, 'Legal Protection of the Unborn Child' (1988) 51 Modern Law Review 54–83.

subject to capital punishment.[25] This latter act was succeeded by the Offences against the Person Act 1837 which abolished the death penalty for abortion but revoked the long-standing distinction between pre- and post-quickening abortion. This was then replaced by sections 58 and 59 of the Offences against the Person Act 1861 which removed pregnancy as a necessary element of the offence when committed by a third party, prohibited attempted self-abortion by a pregnant woman, and created a new offence of obtaining or supplying means knowing that they are intended to be used to procure an abortion. Contraventions of the above sections are punishable by a maximum of life imprisonment. It was clear that the fetus gestated in the maternal body was protected throughout a pregnancy with no distinction with regard to gestational age. It was not until 1929 that a specific statutory exclusion for therapeutic abortion was enacted with the Infant Life Preservation Act 1929. This Act made it an offence to destroy the life of a child 'capable of being born alive' unless done in good faith and in order to save the life of the mother. The 1929 Act held that there was a presumption that a fetus was 'capable of being born alive' at twenty-eight weeks. The defence of therapeutic abortion was first raised in *R* v. *Bourne*[26] when an eminent surgeon was charged with unlawfully pro-curing a miscarriage, contrary to section 58 of the 1861 Act. Dr Bourne had performed a termination on a fifteen-year-old girl, who had become pregnant after being violently raped by a number of men after she had gone to the Horse Guards Parade in London with a friend to watch the changing of the guard.[27] MacNaghten J stated that section 58 of the 1861 Act is, and always was, qualified by a proviso that a doctor would not be acting 'unlawfully' if a miscarriage were procured in good faith to preserve the life of the mother.[28] Dr Bourne was acquitted following MacNaghten J's direction to the jury that if:

> the probable consequence of the continuance of the pregnancy will be to make the woman a physical or mental wreck, the jury are quite entitled to take the view that the doctor, who, in those circumstances and in that

---

[25] See J. Keown, *Abortion, Doctors and the Law: Some Aspects of the Legal Regulation of Abortion in England from 1803–1983* (Cambridge: Cambridge University Press, 2009).

[26] *R* v. *Bourne* [1939] 1 KB 687 (CA).

[27] See L. S. Bibbings, 'R v. Bourne Commentary' in S. Smith, J. Coggon, C. Hobson, J. Miola and M. Neal (eds.), *Ethical Judgments: Re-Writing Medical Law* (Oxford: Hart Publishing, 2017).

[28] Ibid., p. 691.

honest belief, operates, is operating for the purpose of preserving the life of the mother.[29]

It is clear from both the 1861 Act and 1929 Act, that Parliament was concerned with protecting the fetus from the point at which it was viable and thus capable of surviving outside the womb of its mother. Statutory defences (save for the Infant Life Preservation Act 1929) were not enacted until almost thirty years after *Bourne*. The Abortion Act 1967 permitted a pregnancy to be terminated by a registered medical practitioner if two registered medical practitioners were of the opinion, formed in good faith, that the grounds specified in the 1967 Act were met.[30]

The Abortion Act 1967 initially set no time limit as to when an abortion could be lawfully performed, but this was amended by section 37(4) of the HFE Act 1990, which inserted a fixed time limit of twenty four weeks for abortions carried out in order to prevent risk to the health of the pregnant woman or her children (s1(1)(a)).[31] After 24 weeks, abortion is only permissible if continuance of the pregnancy would be a risk to the life of the pregnant woman,[32] or cause grave permanent injury to her physical or mental health,[33] or if there is a substantial risk that if the child were born it would suffer from some physical or mental abnormalities as to be seriously handicapped.[34] Thus, under present legislation, a fetus is accorded a degree of protection and its destruction is permitted only under clearly invoked exceptions.[35]

There have long been demands to reform the regulation of abortion, which remains governed by the archaic provisions of the OAPA 1861 and the 1967 Abortion Act. In the discussions to update the HFE Act 1990, amendments to abortion law could have been accepted during the passage of the Human Fertilisation and Embryology Bill.[36] Despite the publicity proposed amendments to abortion law received,[37] the government

---

[29] Ibid., p. 694.

[30] Abortion Act 1967, s1.

[31] Ibid., s1(1)(a).

[32] Ibid., s1 (1)(c).

[33] Ibid., s1 (1)(b).

[34] Ibid., s1 (1)(d).

[35] For a criticism of the decision-making power granted to the medical profession by the Abortion Act 1967, see S. Sheldon, *Beyond Control; Medical Power and Abortion Law* (London: Pluto Press, 1997).

[36] Human Fertilisation and Embryology Act 1990, s37.

[37] These included new clauses to: remove the legal requirement for two doctors' signatures to authorise abortions; allow trained nurses and other health care practitioners to carry out abortions; extend the locations where abortions can take place to primary care level; remove conscientious objection in respect to providing emergency contraception provision; and extend the Abortion Act 1967 to Northern Ireland.

managed to circumvent a discussion of the provisions pertaining to abortion. As the Report Stage of the Human Fertilisation and Embryology Bill was delayed until the return of the House after the Summer Recess, a long list of amendments had been tabled on to the Bill. Consequently, a programme motion that moved the debate on new clauses to the end of the proceedings effectively prevented any of the abortion law amendments from being heard. Primarolo explained why this was done:

> Today is the last opportunity for the House to debate the Bill before it returns to the other place for consideration of the amendments that we have made. We have amendments for debate today that cover embryo research, the definition of embryos, the parenthood of people who receive assisted reproduction treatment, and saviour siblings. These matters go to the very heart of the Bill and they need consideration before it finally leaves this Chamber.[38]

This motion was met with disfavour amongst other MPs such as Abbot, who commented:

> I speak against the programme motion because – and I say this with no pleasure – it and the order of discussion appear to be a shabby manoeuvre by Ministers to stop the full debate of some very important matters. I appreciate that Ministers did not intend this to be a Bill about abortion. I am open to the argument that we should have another piece of legislation that would enable a full debate on most of the matters in relation to abortion that have been raised as amendments and new clauses to the Bill, but there is a special case for debating and voting on the particular new clause that I tabled to extend the 1967 Act to Northern Ireland.[39]

The legislative provisions pertaining to abortion were to remain unchanged by the HFE Act 2008.[40] The reluctance of Parliament and politicians to even discuss legislation dealing with abortion was clear in

---

[38] House of Commons, Report Stage and Third Reading of the Human Fertilisation and Embryology Bill, Commons Hansard, HC Deb, 22 October 2008 c324.

[39] Ibid., HC Deb 22 October 2008 c327.

[40] See also S. Childs, E. Evans and P. Webb, 'Quicker Than a Consultation at the Hairdressers': Abortion and the Human Fertilisation and Embryology Act 2008' (2013) 32 *New Genetics and Society* 119–134. The authors analysed parliamentary debate contributions (participation and content) in addition to parliamentary votes, and in both Houses of the UK Parliament, and considered the role of the sex of the representatives and the role that played in the outcome. They claim their analysis suggests that women not only over-participate in the division lobbies and vote in a more liberal fashion than their male colleagues, but that women MPs' and Peers' debate contributions and interventions are substantively different from men's. They thus argue that that whilst women's absence from Parliament might not have affected the legislative outcome in 2008, their presence was critical to the way in which the issue of abortion was discussed.

the passage below taken from a 2012 parliamentary discussion when MP Nadine Morris sought to raise the issue:

> The last time I introduced a debate on the 20-week limit was during the parliamentary stages of the Human Fertilisation and Embryology Act 2008, but my amendment was defeated. At that time, it had been 18 years since the upper limit had been debated and voted on.
>
> Abortion law is made in Parliament, and there should be no taboo on discussing it in Parliament. Abortion law should be debated and reformed here, yet each and every time I have raised an abortion issue in the House, one MP after another has risen to comment that this is not really the place to discuss abortion and that the Bill I seek to amend should not be hijacked by discussing abortion. There are many MPs, and I think I may include the hon. Member for Hackney North and Stoke Newington (Ms Abbott), who would quite like the Abortion Act 1967 to be put into a dark cupboard and left there, never again to be brought out and discussed. If we are not to discuss abortion in this House, I am not sure who is supposed to make up the laws as they go along.
>
> As it stands, the 1967 Act is a joke. Everyone knows that in this country abortion is obtained on demand by whoever wants it, whenever they want it. I am pro-choice, and I believe that, up until 12 weeks, that should be the case. I am delighted that more than 90% of abortions in this country take place before 12 weeks. But Parliament's reluctance and nervousness about reforming abortion law, or even discussing it, creates an atmosphere of disrespect for Parliament among abortion providers.[41]

It was deeply regrettable that the first realistic opportunity in almost 20 years for MPs to discuss liberalising the Abortion Act was lost in 2008.[42]

Calls for reform to abortion law once more appeared to gain traction in 2017. Following calls in 2016 from the Royal College of Midwives calls for the decriminalisation of abortion, in June 2017 doctors at the British Medical Association Annual (BMA) Conference supported these calls and also asked the BMA to give further consideration to the significance of viability in relation to the role of the criminal law.[43] In March 2017, The Reproductive Health (Access to Terminations) Bill 2016–17 was

---

[41] Hansard, House of Commons Debates, Column 69WH, Westminster Hall, *Wednesday 31 October 2012* [Mr David Crausby *in the Chair*], 'Induced Abortion' at 9.31am.

[42] S. Sheldon, 'A Missed Opportunity to Reform an Outdated Law' (2009) 4(1) *Clinical Ethics* 3–5. See also the paper by M. Fox, 'The Human Fertilisation and Embryology Act 2008: Tinkering at the Margins' (2009) 17(3) *Feminist Legal Studies* 333–344 in which it was also argued that, viewed from a feminist perspective, the reforms contained in the Human Fertilisation and Embryology Act 2008 represent a missed opportunity to rethink the appropriate model of regulation to govern fertility treatment and embryology research in the UK.

[43] www.bma.org.uk/collective-voice/committees/arm-2017

introduced at the House of Commons by former shadow health minister Diana Johnson proposing abortion be permitted until the end of the 24th week of pregnancy without the need to satisfy any statutory grounds, or to obtain two doctors' authorisation. Campaigners regarded this bill as a first step towards the longer-term goal of fully decriminalising abortion.[44] Despite a vote by 172 to 142 in favour of a second reading, the Bill never reached the scheduled second reading, as Parliament was dissolved ahead of a snap General Election called in June 2017. No further action has yet been taken.[45]

4.1.2.2   How Will Ectogenesis Impact Abortion Legislation?

Ectogenesis will undoubtedly impact on the laws pertaining to abortion since it is clear the concept of viability has influenced the legislation and once complete ectogenesis becomes possible, viability will arguably be from fertilisation. Section 1(1)(a) of the Abortion Act 1967 which permits abortion in order to prevent risk to the health of the pregnant woman or her children (often referred to as the 'social ground' for the frequency it is invoked[46]) is the only ground which imposes a twenty-four week time limit. This time limit was imposed as it was thought that this represented viability, the point at which a fetus was 'capable of being born alive'. In *Rance* v. *Mid-Downs Health Authority*[47] Brooke J regarded this phrase as being interchangeable with viability and stated: 'The primary diction-ary meaning of the word "viable", which is derived from the French word "vie" is "capable of living"'.[48] But using viability as a point from which to extend protection to the fetus is problematic as viability is an

---

[44] For example, the 'We Trust Women' campaign, which supports this Bill, seeks full decriminalisation. For an excellent short blog on the Bill see M. Neal, 'Abortion Decriminalisation and Statutory Rights of Conscience', *BMJ Opinion*, 24 March 2017. For an academic article on the topic of decriminalisation see S. Sheldon, 'The Decriminalisation of Abortion: An Argument for Modernisation' (2016) 36(2) *Oxford Journal of Legal Studies* 334–365.

[45] See www.parliament.uk and Hansard debates on Bill at vol 623, 'Reproductive Health (Access to Terminations)' *Motion for Leave to Bring in a Bill (Standing Order No. 23)*, 13 March 2017.

[46] In 2016, the vast majority of abortions were undertaken under s1(1)(a), see DoH, Report on Abortion Statistics in England and Wales 2016 (published 13 June 2017).

[47] [1991] 1 QB 587. Mr and Mrs Rance brought an action in negligence after Mrs Rance gave birth to a boy with spina bifida. They argued that Mrs Rance should have been given the opportunity to terminate the pregnancy. Brooke J held that, since the diagnosis was only possible at 26 weeks, at which point the fetus would be capable of being born alive, abortion would have been unlawful under the 1929 Act.

[48] Ibid., p. 621.

ever-changing concept, often dependent on both the technology available and where in the world one lives. As Herring notes, a twenty six week old fetus may be viable in some parts of Britain, but would not be viable in a developing country with limited medical facilities.[49] Viability as a point to confer moral status/protection on the fetus has clear limitations;[50] as Mason noted in the passage below:

> both medically and morally, viability is an imprecise determinant of 'human' life in that it depends not only on maturity of the fetus but also on the technology that is available to support its extra uterine life. A premature fetus may survive in a hospital neonatal intensive care unit while one of similar or greater maturity and health will die if born under a hedgerow; it is clearly illogical to suggest that the former was technically and morally 'alive' the latter was not.[51]

Thus claims that legal protection and moral status can be grounded in viability are tenuous to say the least. It also means that as medical science becomes better able to provide for the separate existence of the fetus, the point of viability is moved further back toward conception.

The present law on abortion remains clearly influenced by viability. After viability, an abortion is possible only under the extreme circumstances that the life of the pregnant woman is at risk[52] or the pregnancy may cause grave permanent injury to her physical or mental health,[53] or if there is a substantial risk that if the child will be seriously handicapped.[54] Once complete ectogenesis is possible, and 'viability' is from fertilisation, it is unclear if the government will retain viability as being an important cut off point, after which a pregnancy can only be terminated in extreme circumstances. If it did, this might mean ectogenesis could be used to extend legal protection to the fetus and mandate that women seeking to end their pregnancies under s1(1)(a) of the Abortion Act (to prevent risk to the health of the pregnant women or her children[55]) can only opt for fetal transfer into an ectogenic incubator, which will end the pregnancy but not fetal life.

---

[49] J. Herring, *Medical Law and Ethics* (Oxford: Oxford University Press, 2006) at p. 253.

[50] Ibid., p. 253.

[51] J. K. Mason, *Medico-Legal Aspects of Reproduction and Parenthood* (Aldershot: Dartmouth Publishing Company, 1990) p. 108.

[52] Abortion Act 1967, s1(1)(c).

[53] Ibid., s1(1)(b).

[54] Ibid., s1(1)(d).

[55] Abortion Act 1967, s1(1)(a) (as amended by section 37(4) of the HFE Act 1990) removed the possibility, which existed between 1967 and 1990, of an offence being committed under the 1929 Act for the destruction of a viable fetus which was 'capable of being born alive' despite compliance with the 1967 Act.

4.1.2.3 Will Ectogenesis Signal 'End of the Abortion Debate'?[56]

It has been boldly and naively asserted by Kaczor that ectogenesis can 'end the abortion debate'[57] since it provides a middle ground, allowing women to end pregnancies without ending fetal life. The abortion debate has been polarised between differing views centred on the moral status of the fetus and the protection it should be accorded when in conflict with the rights of the mother. For the 'pro-life' camp, human life is sacred from conception and thus should be protected. This is often pitted against the 'pro-choice' supporters who advocate that the woman in whose body the fetus resides has the paramount say as to what happens to her body and consequently her pregnancy.[58] At present termination of a pre – viable pregnancy and the death of a fetus are inextricably linked. Kaczor argues that an ectogenic device, which can gestate a fetus from conception, will allow a woman to end her pregnancy but maintain fetal life by transferring the fetus into such a machine where it can continue to safely gestate and thus he claims, provide both sides of this highly polarised debate with 'what they desire'.[59] Singer and Wells are also optimistic that ectogenesis will enable both sides to overcome divisions and 'embrace in happy harmony' when women can 'terminate their pregnancies without thereby choosing the inevitable death of the fetus they are carrying'.[60]

In light of ectogenic technology it has been argued that a right to an abortion does not necessarily mean a right to the death of the fetus;[61] that even the most prominent defenders of abortion have understood it as a right of evacuation and not a right of feticide. This is certainly true of Thomson, who conjured up the famous violinist analogy: Thomson asked the innocent reader to consider that one morning they awaken to find the Society of Music Lovers has kidnapped them, after canvassing all the available medical records and discovering that you alone have the

---

[56] P. Singer and D. Wells, 'Ectogenesis' in S. Gelfand (ed.), *Ectogenesis: Artificial Womb Technology and the Future of Human Reproduction* (Amsterdam and New York, NY: Rodopi, 2006) chapter 2. Kaczor, 'Could Artificial Wombs End the Abortion Debate?' See also C. Kaczor, *The Ethics of Abortion* (New York, NY and Oxford: Routledge, 2015).

[57] Kaczor, 'Could Artificial Wombs End the Abortion Debate?'

[58] For more on the abortion debate see S. McLean, 'Abortion Law: Is Consensual Reform Possible?' (1990) 17 *Journal of Law and Society* 106.

[59] Kaczor, 'Could Artificial Wombs End the Abortion Debate?'

[60] Singer and Wells, 'Ectogenesis' 12.

[61] E. Mathison and J. Davis, 'Is There a Right to the Death of the Foetus?' (2017) 31(4) *Bioethics* 313–320.

right blood type to cure a famous unconscious violinist.[62] The violinist has a fatal kidney ailment, and so his circulatory system has been plugged in to yours so that your kidneys can be used to extract poisons from his blood as well as your own. It is only for nine months. To unplug him would be to kill him. Thomson assumed that the moral conclusion that most would draw is that you are entitled to unplug yourself; that no one should be morally required to make the sacrifice of freedom and bodily integrity that keeping the violinist alive would require. Despite the apparently liberal view espoused by Thomson, that abortion is justified because of the violation on a woman's bodily autonomy, she made it clear abortion was defended not because of any inherent right a woman has to end the life of a fetus; that is an incidental and unavoidable consequence:

> A woman may be utterly devastated by the thought of a child, a bit of herself, put out for adoption and never seen or heard of again. She may therefore want not merely that the child be detached from her, but more, that it die . . . [But] the desire for the child's death is not one which anyone may gratify, should it turn out to be possible to detach the child alive.[63]

Similarly, Warren also defended abortion as a right to evacuation, noting that 'if abortion could be performed without killing the fetus, she [the mother] would never possess the right to have the fetus destroyed, for the same reasons she has no right to have an infant destroyed'.[64] Thus it is clear that Thomson and Warren advocate abortion merely as a right of evacuation. Kaczor claims are premised on the argument that such prominent philosophers have defended abortion as a right of evacuation and consequently this could justify mandating the use of artificial wombs in lieu of abortion.[65]

4.1.3 Problematic Claims about the Use of Ectogenesis in Lieu of Abortion

I argue that this claim that ectogenesis can be used in lieu of abortion suffers from two weaknesses:

---

[62] J. Thomson, 'A Defense of Abortion' (1971) 1(1) *Philosophy and Public Affairs* 47–66.

[63] Ibid. at p. 66.

[64] M. Warren, 'On the Moral and Legal Status of Abortion' in R. Wasserstorm (ed.), *Today's Moral Problems*, Second Edition (Macmillan: New York, NY, 1979) at p. 136; ' C. Overall, New Reproductive Technology: Some Implications for the Abortion Issue' in P. Hopkins (ed.), *Sex Machine: Readings in Culture, Gender and Technology* (Bloomington, Indiana: Indiana University Press, 1998) at p. 204.

[65] Kaczor, 'Could Artificial Wombs End the Abortion Debate?'

4.1.3.1   The Right Not to Reproduce

Firstly, procreative autonomy encompasses the desire not to reproduce as much as the right to reproduce. Kaczor's argument assumes that the advent of ectogenesis will lead all women to want to transfer a fetus into an ectogenic should they wish to end their pregnancies. But what if the woman (and her partner if there is one) wish to end not only the pregnancy, but also fetal life? Singer and Wells argue that, post ectogenesis, a woman should not be allowed to end fetal life any more than she would be allowed to kill a newborn baby:

> We do not allow a mother to kill her newborn baby because she does not wish to keep it or to hand it over for adoption. Unless we were to change our mind about this, it is difficult to see why we should give this right to a woman in respect in respect of a fetus she is carrying if her desire to be rid of the fetus can be satisfied without threatening the life of the fetus.[66]

This, however, overlooks an important and crucial distinction between killing a newborn baby and killing a fetus. The former, which has a separate existence to its mother, can be protected independently and is granted full legal status. The latter does not, and as Sir George Baker P., then President of the Family Division declared: 'in England and Wales the fetus has no right of action, no right at all, until birth'.[67] Thus, when housed within the mother, it is her autonomy that is the decisive influence. The courts in the context of enforced caesarean section cases have confirmed this and have held that a competent woman's refusal to consent cannot be overridden in the interests of the fetus.[68] This is so even after viability, when a fetus can be safely maintained outside the maternal womb.[69]

A woman seeking an abortion may desire to end fetal life and exercise her procreative autonomy and right to a private family life in deciding to avoid procreation. Fetal transferral and subsequent adoption would mean she still has a genetically related child out there in the world being raised by different parents. Even if no rearing duties or even contact result, she may still suffer from the knowledge a child genetically related child to her exists.[70] This notion of saying no to genetic

---

[66] Singer and Wells, 'Ectogenesis' 12.
[67] *Paton* v. *BPAS* [1979] QB 276, p. 279.
[68] [1997] 2 FCR 541, pp. 558–561.
[69] *S* v. *McC; W* v. *W* [1972] AC 24, *Re T (Adult: Refusal of Medical Treatment)* [1992] 4 All ER 649, CA, *Re MB* (An Adult: Medical Treatment) [1997] 2 FCR 541, St *George's Healthcare NHS Trust* v. *S* [1999] Fam 26, (CA).
[70] J. Robertson, 'In The Beginning: The Legal Status of Early Embryos' (1990) 76 *Virginia Law Review* 437–517, at p. 479; L. Hemphill, 'American Abortion Law Applied to New Reproductive Technology' (1992) 32 *Jurimetrics Journal* 361–386, at p. 374.

parenthood and exercising one's right not to procreate was successfully argued as an aspect of an individual's Article 8 right to a private and family life before the European Convention of Human Rights in in the case of *Evans* v. *Amicus*.[71] In this case, discussed in depth in Chapter 2, you will recall that the courts upheld Howard Johnson's decision to refuse his former partner, Natalie Evans, the use of the embryos they had created together through IVF, even though the stored embryos were her last chance at genetic motherhood. Johnson successfully argued his right not to procreate, setting out how he did not want a child of his out there in the world that he was not actively raising with the child's mother,[72] that fatherhood was a life-long commitment and given that he and Ms Evans had separated, the child would be raised with an absent father, a position he did not wish to have foisted upon him.[73] The European Court of Human Rights upheld his position.[74] Abortion is about more than ending an unwanted pregnancy, it is about maintaining control over ones decision whether or not to procreate; an argument accepted by the courts in *Evans*. Mackenzie explains this in the following way:

> abortion is not a matter of wanting to kill *this particular being*, which is, after all, as yet indistinguishable from oneself. It is rather a matter of not wanting there to *be* a future child, so intimately related to oneself, for which one either has to take responsibility or give up to another.[75]

This argument is supported by Räsänen who cites Mackenzie and argues that post ectogenesis, gamete progenitors have a right to end fetal life because to mandate gestation of a fetus in an artificial womb against the genetic parents' wishes violates their rights not to become a biological parent, their rights to genetic privacy and their property rights,[76] asserting:

> if ectogenesis abortions become reality, some women (and men) will have genetic children out there who carry their genetic material without their consent. In this scenario, their right to genetic privacy has been violated,

---

[71] Evans v. *Amicus Healthcare Ltd and Others* [2004] EWCA Civ 727, [2004] 2 FLR 766.

[72] Ibid, paragraphs 32 and 89.

[73] C. Lind, 'Evans v. United Kingdom – Judgments of Solomon: Power, Gender and Procreation' (2006) 18(4)*Child and Family Law Quarterly* 576.

[74] Evans v. *The United Kingdom* (Application No. 6339/05); [2006] 1 FCR 585.

[75] C. Mackenzie, 'Abortion and Embodiment' (1992) 70 *Australasian Journal of Philosophy* 136–155, at p. 152. Emphasis original.

[76] J. Räsänen, 'Ectogenesis, Abortion and a Right to the Death of the Fetus' (2017) 31(9) *Bioethics* 697–702.

and the only way to avoid this is if they have a right to the death of the fetus ... [and] there is yet another way to claim that the genetic parents have a right to the death of the fetus: the genetic parents own the fetus, and because of that, their property rights are violated if the fetus is gestated in an artificial womb without their consent.[77]

Räsänen argues in this context that the right to the death of the fetus, however, is not a woman's right but genetic parents' collective right, which can only be used together. Thus, the first weakness in the argument that ectogenesis may end the abortion debate is that it overlooks the fact that gamete progenitors may want to end not just the pregnancy, but also fetal life. They may want an abortion to ensure that there is no being at all who is their genetic offspring.

4.1.3.2   The Female Host and Her Bodily Autonomy Are Still Engaged

The second problem with this argument is that if a pregnancy has occurred via sexual intercourse, or IVF later implanted into a female host, the woman's bodily autonomy is still invoked and mandating fetal transfer into an ectogenic incubator would violate that. Dworkin describes the unique relationship between a pregnant woman and her fetus in the following terms:

> Her fetus is not merely 'in her' as an inanimate object might be, or something alive but alien that has been transplanted into her body. It is 'of her and hers more than anyone's' because it is, more than anyone else's, her creation and her responsibility; it is alive because she has made it come alive.[78]

If a woman is pregnant and the fetus located in her body, she would have to consent to any procedure performed with the aim of transferring the fetus intact to an ectogenic device. James explains how such a procedure would most likely require invasive surgery akin to a caesarean section:

> A foetal transplant would be an elaborate surgical procedure aimed at the delicate removal of the foetus from the mother's placenta and its transfer and attachment to the external artificial womb ... foetal transplantation would thus require general anaesthesia as well as surgical incision through

---

[77] Ibid.

[78] R. Dworkin, *Life's Dominion: An Argument about Abortion, Euthanasia, and Individual Freedom* (New York, NY: Knopf, 1993) p. 55; E. Jackson, *Regulating Reproduction, Law Technology and Autonomy* (Oxford: Hart Publishing, 2001) at p. 114.

the abdominal wall and uterus, with all the risks and complications which accompany these more invasive procedures.[79]

Contrast this to an abortion in the early stages of pregnancy: up until fourteen weeks after conception, abortion is a relatively minor procedure, which does not require major surgery or hospital admission. In 2016, 92 per cent of abortions were carried out at less than 13 weeks' gestation and 81 per cent were carried out at less than 10 weeks'.[80] The Department of Health policy is that women who are legally entitled to an abortion should have access to the procedure as soon as possible.[81] The risk of complications increases the later the gestation. In 2016, the number of abortions that were performed at 24 weeks gestation or over accounted for 0.1 per cent of the total. There were 226 such abortions in 2016.[82] Thus most abortions occur early on in the pregnancy.

A fetal transfer would require a woman to endure the pain, inconvenience and risks of carrying a pregnancy for twenty-four weeks (or for the necessary period until ectogenic technology can safely mimic the functions of the maternal womb[83]), then to have to undergo invasive surgery to transfer the fetus. At present, a pregnant woman cannot be forced to consent to a caesarean section, even if it is necessary in order to save the life of the fetus.[84] English law is clear on the point; a competent pregnant woman 'has an absolute right to choose whether to consent to medical treatment or refuse it or to choose one rather than another of the treatments offered'.[85] In *St George's Healthcare NHS Trust* v. *S* the Court of Appeal also adopted the view that even if the fetus had interests, their protection could not justify an unwanted medical intervention in a competent pregnant woman, and Judge LJ unequivocally stated 'she is entitled not to be forced to submit to an invasion of her body against her

---

[79] D. James, 'Ectogenesis: A Reply to Singer and Wells' (1987) 1(1) *Bioethics* 87.

[80] DoH, National Statistics, Report on abortion statistics in England and Wales: 2016. Summary Information from the abortion notification forms returned to the Chief Medical Officers of England and Wales, June 2017 at p. 5.

[81] Ibid., at p. 17.

[82] Ibid.

[83] Although, of course, the length of time the woman must gestate prior to transfer could be regarded as irrelevant since, irrespective of this time period, the surgical procedure necessary for a fetal transfer will still constitute a gross violation of a woman's bodily integrity.

[84] *Re MB (An Adult: Medical Treatment)* [1997] 2 FCR 541; 38 BMLR 175. But note how the court found the patient in this particular case was not competent to refuse consent. See I. Kennedy, 'Commentary to *Re MB (Medical Treatment)*' (1997) 5 *Medical Law Review* 317.

[85] *St George's Healthcare NHS Trust* v. *S* [1998] 3 ALL ER 673.

will, whether her own life or that of her unborn child depends on it. Her right is not reduced not or diminished merely because her decision to exercise it may appear morally repugnant'.[86]

To mandate that women continue their pregnancies until fetal transfer into an ectogenic chamber is possible is nothing short of endorsing a gross violation of one's bodily autonomy. The justifications Thomson offered in her hypothetical violinist scenario for prioritising the woman's bodily integrity still apply.[87] What if Thomson's scenario was altered slightly: things have moved on since 1971 and the time the violinist would have to be attached to you, is now reduced to four weeks, he can then be unplugged from you and placed on a dialyses machine, can you still request he be unplugged? In the initial violinist scenario, Thomson assumed that the moral conclusion that most would draw is that you are entitled to unplug yourself. That no one should be morally required to make the sacrifice of freedom and bodily integrity that keeping the violinist alive would require. This argument applies to partial ectogenesis. No one should be forced to sacrifice her body for a period of time, and then undergo invasive surgery in order to save the life of a fetus. As Thomson notes, we are not morally required to be Good Samaritans to one another; although she does question whether 'we must accede to a situation in which somebody is being compelled – by nature, perhaps – to be a Good Samaritan'.[88] But in the UK we do not legally compel anyone even to be a Minimally Decent Samaritan. There is no duty to rescue;[89] you can see a person dying on the road and walk by on the other side should you choose to do so and you will not be liable. You may choose to act as a Good Samaritan and come to the aid of those in need, but you are not legally obligated to do so. In the context of terminating a pregnancy, a woman may elect not to act as a good Samaritan, and in ending her pregnancy also end the life of the fetus, but to mandate otherwise would be to violate a woman's autonomy and compel women by law 'to be not merely Minimally Decent Samaritans, but Good Samaritans to unborn persons inside them'.[90] Just as one cannot force a women to undergo an abortion against her will, the state should not

---

[86] Ibid., at p. 691.

[87] Thomson, 'A Defense of Abortion'.

[88] Ibid., at p. 64.

[89] There is no duty in English law to rescue a person in danger. In *Yuen Kun Yeu* v. *Attorney General of Hong Kong* [1988] AC 175, Lord Keith stated that there is no liability on the part of a person 'who sees another about to walk over a cliff … and forbears to shout a warning'.

[90] Thomson, 'A Defense of Abortion' 63.

mandate that a woman should transfer her unwanted fetus into an ecto-genic chamber.

This is further supported by comments in the European Court of Human Rights in *Vo* v. *France*[91] where it was acknowledged that even if a fetus was regarded as having a 'right to life', the mother's rights and interests implicitly limit it.[92] In *Vo*, the applicant had attended hospital for a sixth month ante-natal check, but as a consequence of being mistaken for another patient with the same surname, was negligently given erroneous medical treatment which necessitated a therapeutic abortion. She complained that the failure of French law to classify this as unintentional homicide amounted to a breach of Article 2. The court categorically ruled out that Article 2 could be interpreted as recognising an absolute 'right to life' of the fetus having regard to the need to protect the mother's life, which was in dissociable from that of the fetus:

> The 'life' of the foetus is intimately connected with, and it cannot be regarded in isolation of, the life of the pregnant woman. If Article 2 were held to cover the foetus and its protection under this Article were, in the absence of any express limitation, seen as absolute, an abortion would have to be considered as prohibited even where the continuance of the pregnancy would involve a serious risk to the life of the pregnant woman. This would mean that the 'unborn life' of the foetus would be regarded as being of a higher value than the life of the pregnant woman.[93]

Although *Vo* did not address the 'independent' in vivo fetus, arguably this statement could be applied to legislation which sought to mandate that ectogenesis be used as a replacement for abortion; this would lead to the illogical position that the life of the fetus was being placed above that of the autonomous woman in whose body it was housed.

Caution must be advocated when discussing any suggestion of utilising ectogenic technology to promote fetal rights and thereby curtail the procreative rights of the pregnant women. In *R* v. *Scrimaglia*[94], in which a backstreet abortion took place after enactment of the Abortion Act 1967, the then Lord Chief Justice commented that 'one of the objects, as everyone knows, of the new Act was to try to get rid of back-street unsanitary operations'.[95] Any attempts to curtail the procreative

---

[91] *Vo* v. *France* ECHR Application Number 53924/00 [2004]2 FCR 577.
[92] Ibid., paragraph 80.
[93] Ibid., paragraph 77, citing *X* v. *UK* [1979] Application Number 8416.
[94] (1971) 55 Cr App R 280.
[95] See E. Jackson, *Medical Law Text and Materials* (Oxford: Oxford University Press, 2016) at p. 709.

autonomy of women in light of ectogenesis, may create more harm than good. This is supported by evidence that indicates maternal mortality owing to unsafe abortion is generally higher in countries with major restrictions and lower in countries where abortion is available without restrictions.[96]

These arguments also apply to claims that ectogenesis could be used as a green light for fetal rescue in cases were pregnant women endanger the health of the fetus during the nine months gestation, for instance via alcohol or drug exposure.[97] Excessive drinking during pregnancy can cause Fetal Alcohol Syndrome (FASD), a recognised disorder that can causes intrauterine growth retardation and limited growth potential. It can cause central nervous dysfunction; a feature of the disorder is that the brain is smaller and particularly affected. Many children with the disorder have severe learning difficulties. FASD is the biggest cause of non-genetic mental handicap in the western world and the only one that is 100 per cent preventable.[98] Once ectogenesis is a viable method of gestation, the question may arise of whether pregnant women who are addicted to alcohol or drug and whose fetuses are at risk of harm as a result could be mandated to have their fetuses transferred into ectogenic chambers, where they can gestate in a safe environment.

As noted above, in English law, women do not owe a duty of care in tort to their fetus. A competent woman cannot be forced to have a caesarean section or other medical treatment to prevent potential risk to the fetus during childbirth.[99] Nor can they be liable for criminal injuries committed by the mother during pregnancy. The English courts recently confirmed that a child born with FASD due to the mothers excessive drinking whilst pregnant could not claim criminal compensation against her mother for criminal harms sustained in utero.[100] There is

---

[96] L. Finer and J. Fine, 'Abortion Law Around the World: Progress and Pushback' (2013) 103(4) *American Journal of Public Health* 585–589.

[97] E. Grossman, 'The Obsolescent Mother: A Scenario' (1971) 5 *The Atlantic* p. 48; S. Eaton, 'The Medical Model of Reproduction' (2005) 1 *New Antigone*, 28–37, at p. 32.

[98] FAS Aware UK, 'A Preventable Tragedy', www.fasaware.co.uk.

[99] Although note that the negligent acts of a third party tortfeasor, which inflict harm on a fetus child, are actionable by the child on birth if the child is born with disabilities under section 1(1) of the Congenital Disabilities (Civil Liability) Act 1976. But there is maternal immunity from suit under this statute and a claim cannot be brought under this Act against the child's mother unless (section 2) the harm is caused by her when she is driving a motor vehicle.

[100] *CP (A Child)* v. *First-Tier Tribunal (Criminal Injuries Compensation)* [2014] EWCA Civ 1554.

a compelling public interest in safeguarding pregnant women and their fetuses from the detrimental effects of criminalisation. Compelling women who may put their fetus at harm, to undergo fetal transfer into an ectogenic incubator would likely cause more harm than good. In the USA, Paltrow and Flavin reported 413 cases from 1973–2005 in which a woman's pregnancy was a necessary factor leading to both attempts and actual deprivations of a woman's physical liberty through arrests, detentions or forced medical interventions.[101] They noted how in many cases criminal charges rested on the claim that there was a risk of fetal harm or a positive drug test, but no actual evidence of harm. Similarly in numerous cases were court orders were sought to enforce medical interventions, a risk of harm was identified that did not materialise. Their findings supported the medical and public health consensus that such punitive approaches undermined maternal, fetal and child health, by deterring women from care and from communicating openly with people who might be able to help them.

Ectogenesis could not signal a green light to those hoping to set out on acts of fetal rescue since any attempt to mandate ectogenesis in these circumstances would still violate the bodily autonomy of the woman and would most likely undermine rather than further maternal, fetal and child health.

4.2   Complete Ectogenesis: From Embryo to Baby

4.2.1   Regulating Complete Ectogenesis

Chapter 3 noted that, at present, research into complete ectogenesis is likely to be discovered by default through the convergence of research in IVF and treatment of extremely premature babies. Women or couples who want a genetically related child may desire full ectogenesis where the woman is unable to gestate: for instance, women for whom pregnancy poses grave health risks, or women who suffer from uterus factor infertility. Ectogenesis may be preferable to surrogacy, since in the UK surrogacy agreements are legally unenforceable,[102] thus there is always the inherent risk the surrogate could change her mind and decide to keep or

---

[101] L. Paltrow and J. Flavin, 'The Policy and Politics of Reproductive Health. Arrests of and Forced Interventions on Pregnant Women in the United States 1973–2005: Implications for Women's Legal Status and Public Health', *Journal of Health Politics, Policy and Law* 299–343.

[102] Surrogacy Arrangements Act 1985, s1B (as inserted by the Human Fertilisation and Embryology Act 1990) provides: 'No surrogacy arrangement is enforceable by or against

abort the child (which she would be legally permitted to do). Ectogenesis may offer an alternative way in which the couple could have a genetically related child. The couple could opt for in vitro fertilisation and have their embryo placed in an ectogenic incubator for the forty-week gestation period. But once complete ectogenesis becomes possible, this will raise numerous regulatory questions. Could present abortion laws be extended to cover this situation? Consider how the current legislation would apply to the following hypothetical scenario:

> Jim and Jane desire a genetically related child. Their attempts to reproduce have been thwarted by the fact Jane suffers from uterus factor infertility. The couple have recently undergone IVF treatment and decide they wish to place one of their embryos into an ectogenic incubator to be gestated. Five months into the gestation the couple separate. They both agree that they no longer wish to have a child together and write to the hospital requesting that the machine be switched off.

Can the Couple Simply Request the Machine Be Switched Off?

Whether the couple can switch the machine off would depend on the legal status ascribed to the in vitro fetus. Once the fetus is outside the maternal womb, is it still to be regarded as fetus, or is it a baby? The issue of status and whether it is to be regarded as a 'baby' will be returned to later; for now, suppose it is still regarded as a fetus. Would switching off the machine amount to 'procuring a miscarriage' in contravention of the sections 58 and 59 of the Offences against the Person Act 1861? Section 58 of the Offences Against the Persons Act 1861 provides:

> Every woman, being with child, who, with intent to procure her own miscarriage, shall administer to herself any poison or other noxious thing, or shall unlawfully use any instrument or other means whatsoever with the like intent, and whosoever, with intent to procure the miscarriage of any woman, whether she be or be not with child, shall unlawfully administer to her or cause to be taken by her any poison or other noxious thing, or shall unlawfully use any instrument or other means whatsoever with the like intent, shall be guilty of felony, and being convicted thereof shall be liable to be kept in penal servitude for life.

Section 59 provides:

> Whosoever shall unlawfully supply or procure any poison or other noxious thing, or any instrument or thing whatsoever, knowing that the same

any of the persons making it.' This remains the case despite amendments made to the 1985 Act by s59 of the Human Fertilisation and Embryology Act 2008.

is intended to be unlawfully used or employed with intent to procure the miscarriage of any woman, whether she be or be not with child, shall be guilty of a misdemeanour, and being convicted thereof shall be liable to be kept in penal servitude.

Neither provision addresses what constitutes procurement of a miscarriage other than in a woman. This is hardly surprising since ectogenesis could not have been envisaged when the 1861 Act was drafted. There is little guidance that can be gleaned from case law on interpretation of the phrase 'procuring a miscarriage' since this has been considered by the courts only in the context of a natural pregnancy. In *R (On the Application of Smeaton)* v. *Secretary of State for Health*[103] the courts held that the prescription, supply, administration or use of the morning-after pill did not, and could not, involve the commission of any offence for it was not unlawfully 'procuring a miscarriage'. The court held that a miscarriage was the termination of post-implantation pregnancy. There could be no miscarriage if a fertilised egg was lost prior to implantation. An imaginative exercise which sought to apply this to ectogenesis could argue that, if the placing of the embryo into an ectogenic incubator is construed as being analogous to implantation in the maternal womb, then switching off the ectogenic incubator could be construed a procuring a miscarriage contrary to the Offences Against the Person Act 1861 (OAPA). Or the ectogenic embryo must be regarded as having no status at all. But sections 58 and 59 of the OAPA were enacted at time when ectogenesis was not even dreamt of, and envisaged a process inevitably designed to kill the fetus. This technology offers a chance of life. It is clear that present legislation fails to adequately address this novel technology or provide guidance on whether the ectogenic incubator could be switched off mid-gestation.

This is once again reaffirmed when we consider whether the Abortion Act 1967 could be stretched to cover this advance. The 1967 Act provides circumstances in which 'termination of pregnancy' may be lawful,[104] and termination of the pregnancy is just what fetal transfer entails. Under that legislation a termination is lawful if two medical professionals certify that the conditions set out in the 1967 Act (as amended) are satisfied. If the 1967 Act was extended to ectogenesis this would mean that couples could request that the ectogenic chamber be switched off if the time the fetus has been in the

[103] *R (On the Application of Smeaton)* v. *Secretary of State for Health* [2002] EWHC 610 (Admin) [2002] 2 FLR 146, [2002] 2 FCR 193, 66 BMLR 59.
[104] Abortion Act 1967 (as amended by Human Fertilisation and Embryology Act 1990) s1(1).

ectogenic chamber has not exceeded its twenty-fourth week, and continuance of the ectogenic gestation would involve risk of injury to the mental health of the mother or any existing child of their family, greater than if the ectogenic gestation were terminated.[105] Or at any point of the gestational period if there is a substantial risk that the child in the ectogenic incubator may suffer from some physical or mental abnormalities as to be seriously handicapped,[106] the woman/couple could be allowed to request the machine be switched off.

Once again, any attempt to use this legislation to regulate ectogenesis raises problems. It is difficult to see how sections 1(1)(b) and (c) of the Abortion Act 1967 (which permit abortion post twenty-four weeks if there is a substantial risk to the life or health of the mother) could extend to ectogenesis, since the woman will not be gestating the child. Arguably, the wishes of both progenitors should be equally considered in the context of complete ectogenesis since the mother's bodily autonomy is no longer directly engaged. Furthermore, if the current abortion legislation is maintained and extended to cover ectogenic babies, the question then arises as to why twenty-four weeks should remain as the cut-off point. As outlined earlier, that is used in the present legislation as it is perceived as the current point of viability. But with complete ectogenesis, viability (if taken to mean the ability to sustain the life of a fetus outside the body of its mother) is from conception. Thus, will Parliament protect all ectogenic babies already located in an ectogenic incubator and state that because they are viable, and can be gestated without violating the pregnant woman's bodily integrity, the life of the in vivo fetus cannot be ended prematurely? It is clear that present legislation will not accommodate this advance, and new legislation will have to be drafted. The Offences Against the Person Act 1861 and the Abortion Act 1967 were drafted with the pregnant woman and in vivo fetus in mind, and as noted by Fortin:

> Since it was inconceivable until recently that a fetus could ever exist outside its mother's womb, hitherto the criminal law has only been concerned with the protection of the unborn child *in vivo* rather than *in vitro*.[107]

---

[105] Abortion Act 1967 (as amended) s1(1)(a).
[106] Ibid., s1(1)(d).
[107] J. Fortin, 'Legal Protection of the Unborn Child' (1988) 51 *Modern Law Review* 54–83, at p. 61.

4.2.2   What Is the Legal Status of the In Vitro or Ectogenic Baby?

English law has made it clear that the in vivo fetus, gestating in the mother's uterus, is not a person until it is born and has a separate existence from her.[108] Consequently 'the fetus has no right of action, no right at all, until birth'.[109] However, the law is far from clear on the matter, and while a fetus may not enjoy legal status it would be wrong to presume the law regards the fetus is a 'nothing'.[110] As noted by Pattinson: 'While the fetus is not treated as having *full* status, neither is it treated as having *no status*'.[111] In *St George's Healthcare NHS Trust* v. *S*[112] Judge LJ stated that a 36-week-old fetus is 'not nothing; it is not lifeless and it is certainly human'.[113] In *AG Reference (No 3 of 1994)*[114] the House of Lords rejected an argument by the Court of Appeal that a fetus should be regarded as a part of the mother, but instead regarded it as a unique organism.[115] However, many of the cases in which fetal status has been considered it has been in the context of the in vivo fetus, the focus is predominantly on balancing protection of the fetus, against the rights that must be accorded to the mother in whose womb the fetus is located. This is drastically different from an in vitro fetus gestating in an artificial womb; extending protection to which would *not* be a direct physical violation of its mother's bodily autonomy. Thus what legal or moral status should be conferred on the in vitro fetus gestating in an ectogenic incubator? Should the law regard the ectogenic baby no differently to a neonate and grant the in vitro fetus full legal status?

English case law does not appear to envisage that it could one day be possible for a fetus to be gestated externally. Once ectogenesis becomes possible a fetus will have the separate existence that Sir George Baker spoke of in *Paton* v. *BPAS*[116] and arguably does have a 'right of its own'. Similarly in *Vo* v. *France*,[117] in declining to treat a fetus as a person under Article 2 of the Convention, the Court reasoned that the life of the fetus 'was intimately connected with that of the mother and could be protected through her'.[118]

---

[108]   *Paton* v. *BPAS* [1979] QB 276, *Re F (In Utero)* [1988] Fam. 122.

[109]   *Paton* v. *BPAS* [1979] QB 276, p. 279.

[110]   J. Herring, *Medical Law and Ethics*, Sixth Edition (Oxford: Oxford University Press, 2016) at p. 307.

[111]   S. Pattinson, *Medical Law and Ethics*, Fifth Edition (London: Sweet & Maxwell, 2017) at 7-021-7-026.

[112]   [1998] 3 All ER 673.

[113]   Ibid., p. 688.

[114]   [1998] A.C. 245.

[115]   Ibid., 255–256 (Lord Mustil).

[116]   [1979] QB 276.

[117]   (Application No. 53924/00) [2004] 2 FCR 577.

[118]   Ibid., paragraph 86.

Again, this statement no longer applies if a fetus is conceived via IVF and directly placed into an ectogenic incubator for gestation. The nearest we have on how the courts may treat an in vivo fetus is to look at the protection accorded to embryos in vitro. When it comes to the legal and moral status of the in vitro embryo, it appears the government was unsure what status to confer it. The Warnock Committee avoided providing a definitive answer on the status of such embryos:

> Although the questions of when life or personhood begin, appear to be questions of fact susceptible of straightforward answers, we hold that answers to such questions in fact are complex amalgams of factual and moral judgments. Instead of trying to answer these questions directly we have therefore gone straight to the question of how it is right to treat the human embryo. We have considered what status ought to be accorded to the human embryo, and the answer we give must necessarily be in terms of ethical or moral principles.[119]

Parliament accepted the recommendations of the Warnock Committee that the embryo has a 'special status' and should be protected by the law after development of the primitive streak, said to occur at fourteen days.[120] This was affirmed in the amendments made to the HFE Act 1990 (as amended by the Human Fertilisation and Embryology Act 2008).[121] Notwithstanding this special status, and limited protection, the courts have recently confirmed that an in vitro embryo of below fourteen days does not have a 'right to life' under Article 2. In *Evans* v. *Amicus*,[122] Natalie Evans unsuccessfully argued that an embryo had a qualified right to life, in a bid to preclude her partner from requesting embryos the couple had created together be destroyed as he was no longer consenting to their use. Wall LJ responded:

> In my judgment, an embryo has no qualified right to life. This court rejected the argument that a foetus had a right to life protected by art 2 in *Re F (In Utero)* [1988] 2 All ER 193, [1988] Fam 122. So far as an embryo created by IVF is concerned, the claim to a right to life must be weaker.[123]

The certitude of Wall LJ's reliance on these authorities to aver that the in vitro embryo's claim to a right to life is weaker than that of the in vivo

[119] The Warnock Report, paragraph 11.9.
[120] HFE Act 1990, s3(3) states: 'A licence cannot authorise – (a) keeping or using an embryo after the appearance of the primitive streak. This is said to occur after fourteen days – this is thought to represent the stage at which the primitive streak, the precursor of the development of a nervous system, begins to appear.'
[121] HFE Act 1990, s4(3).
[122] [2004] EWCA (Civ) 727.
[123] Ibid., paragraph 107.

fetus is troublesome. Most of the jurisprudence on the status of the fetus has been in the context of the in vivo fetus where the interests of the mother are in conflict with those of the fetus. Rather than applying old legal principles to a new dilemma, perhaps regulators should have the temerity to consider this question anew, for an embryo/fetus which has an independent existence and which can be gestated entirely in vitro is substantially different from the in vivo fetus, as it no longer has to be subjugated to the rights of the pregnant woman.

Some may claim that the law should be consistent on the status conferred on the fetus, irrespective of where it is located. Moral (and thus legal) status should not be based exclusively on 'biological geography'. Harris asks: 'What do people think has happened in the passage down the birth canal to make it okay to kill the fetus at one end of the birth canal but not at the other?'[124] This echoes Gillon comments: 'what morally relevant changes can there have been in the fetus in its intrinsic passage from inside to outside its mother's body to underpin such a momentous change in its intrinsic moral status?'[125]

However, the absence of independent legal personality bestowed on the fetus in utero, appears the right compromise since, when housed in the maternal womb, the law is rightfully limited in the protection it can extend to the fetus, for it is situated within the body of an autonomous being on which it is dependent for survival. When gestating externally in the neutral territory of an ectogenic device, an in vitro embryo/fetus can be protected independently without violating a woman's bodily autonomy. On this basis, arguably a strong case can be made out for extending legal protection to the in vitro fetus. It is clear that revolutionary technology such as ectogenesis will necessitate a re-examination of the moral and legal status of the fetus gestating in an ectogenic device. This can no longer be resolved by recourse to the paramount say of the mother's bodily autonomy over a fetus housed therein.

4.2.3 Disputes over the Fate of the Ectogenic Fetus/Baby

Returning to the hypothetical scenario above of Jim and Jane, let us suppose that four months in to the ectogenic gestation, the couple separate. Jim no longer wishes to procreate with Jane? What should be

---

[124] See his interview with Sarah-Kate Templeton, 'Doctors: Let Us Kill Disabled Babies' *The Sunday Times*, 5 November 2006.

[125] R. Gillon, 'Is There a "New Ethics of Abortion?"' (2001) *Journal of Medical Ethics* 115–119.

done with the ectogenic baby safely gestating? Had this been a traditional pregnancy, as the woman's bodily autonomy is engaged she has the paramount say over her body and thus indirectly the fate of her embryo/fetus. This is fundamentally altered with the use of an ectogenic incubator to gestate the fetus. In this context, both their gametes have been used to create the ecto baby and both are arguably equally situated in relation to it. Thus, whose wishes should prevail?

In this context, it has been argued that there is a right to the death of the fetus gestating in an artificial womb, permitted only when genetic parents refuse collectively, as part of their rights not to become biological parents, their rights to genetic privacy and their property rights.[126] Räsänen cites the following example: 'when only one person wants to use a collective right, he or she cannot use that right. When Bob wants to marry Jane, but Jane does not want to marry Bob, Bob cannot use his right to marriage, because a right to marriage is a collective right and therefore cannot be used alone'.[127] Similarly, Räsänen argues that when Bob wants the fetus to die, but Jane wants it to live, Bob cannot use his right to the death of the fetus because this right is not an individual but a collective right. In cases of disagreement Räsänen suggests the status quo approach is followed, whereby change needs a stronger justification than keeping things as they are. Thus, when one parent wants the death of the fetus and the other does not, the fetus should not be killed or left to die: an already developing fetus would continue its development in the artificial womb.

An alternative approach may be to resort to how such disputes are resolved when it comes to the disposition of frozen embryos. In the USA, the courts have looked to any prior agreements made between the parties. In *Davis* v. *Davis*[128] the Tennessee Supreme Court set out a three-part test to be applied when a couple disagree over the disposition of their embryos: (1) the preferences of the progenitors; (2) if gamete donors disagree over the disposition courts are directed to enforce any prior agreements between the parties; and (3) in the absence of prior agreement, courts are advised to balance the relative interests of the parties. When those interests are in equipoise, courts are advised to favour the party wishing to avoid procreation, as long as the other party has a reasonable possibility of achieving parenthood by other means than

---

[126] Räsänen, 'Ectogenesis, Abortion and a Right to the Death of the Fetus'.

[127] Above 701; Quoting for a defence of a right to marriage as a collective right, R. Williams, 'Same-Sex Marriage and Equality' (2011) 14 *Ethical Theory and Moral Practice* 589–595.

[128] 842 S.W.2d 588 (Tenn. 1992).

the use of the embryo in question. Similarly, in *Kass* v. *Kass*,[129] the New York Court of Appeal held that embryo agreements governing embryo disposition should be presumed valid and enforced.

In England and Wales, when couples have created embryos in vitro through IVF only later to separate, the courts have made it clear that prior agreements made between the parties will not be enforced and are not binding. The legislation which governs assisted reproduction, the HFE Act 1990 (as amended by the HFE Act 2008), provides both gamete progenitors with the statutory right to withdraw or vary consent to the use of an embryo created through IVF up until the moment of implantation into a woman.[130] Thus in *Evans* v. *Amicus*,[131] the courts upheld the wishes of the partner wishing to avoid genetic parenthood and have the embryos destroyed, even though the embryos represented his former partner's last chance at genetic motherhood.[132]

Following on from this, should the placing of the embryo into an ectogenic incubator be construed as similar to implantation, a point from which consent cannot be revoked? This would have the advantage of being in line with IVF and the point of implantation into the biological womb. However, this leads to the disparity that a couple embarking on ectogenesis together can request that the machine is turned off up until 24 weeks, in accordance with abortion laws. But for a couple who separate during the time it is in the incubator, neither party can request it be turned off; for the point of no going back is the point at which it was placed in the ectogenic incubator. Should the couple change their mind, it will continue to be gestated and put up for adoption. Or alternatively could the point of 'no return' upon which consent is irrevocable depend on the stage of gestation? But again this may be problematic since drawing the line at a stage of the gestation process may be arbitrary given that, once complete ectogenesis becomes possible, the embryo/fetus is viable (capable of survival outside the maternal womb) from conception. This is yet another illustration of the regulatory issues that will arise should ectogenesis become possible.

---

[129] 673 N.Y.S 2d 350 (N.Y 1988).
[130] See HFE Act (as amended) Schedule 3 and paragraph 4A.
[131] Evans v. *Amicus Healthcare* [2003] EWHC 2161.
[132] Ibid. See also A. Alghrani, 'Deciding The Fate of Frozen Embryos: Evans v Amicus Healthcare Ltd and Others' (2005) 13 *Medical Law Review* 244–256.

4.2.4   The Welfare of the Ectogenic Baby

In relation to wholly artificial gestation, there will be concerns around the welfare of the first ectogenic babies brought into existence. The speculative welfare of future children is a frequently levied objection against the development of artificial reproductive technologies. The objection frequently made is that, because the technology is still in its early stages, it is impossible to accurately predict the outcome it may have on the children involved in the process. Concerns have been raised as to how the ectogenic womb/device will affect the social/psychological development of the fetus/child and also the relationship between mother and child. Consider the following statement:

> The artificial womb will duplicate the technology of a natural womb so as to enable the child to gestate and develop physically to maturity. However, unless it duplicates a heartbeat, the commissioning mother's voice and her typical movements in a day, her sleep patterns and rhythms and the sounds of the household, we could indeed create an alien baby – a little stranger, the little reification of our ideology. The foetus, deprived of the socialising contact of the human uterus, will inevitably develop differently in the important psychological sense. Whether such a child will be able to adapt and fit into the usual social structures is an unknown quantity. Will they form a new sub-class in our societies?[133]

In order to allay such concerns, any research into the development of ectogenesis must have the welfare of the ectogenic child as a paramount concern. As noted in Chapter 1, clinicians are currently mandated under the HFE Act 1990 to consider the welfare of the child who may be born as a result of the treatment (including the need of that child *for supportive parenting*), and of any other child who may be affected by the birth.[134] This may encompass consideration to the psychological and physical implications that may ensue from being gestated in an external ectogenic mechanism instead of a mother's womb. Increasing knowledge has evolved on the maternal fetal bond during the nine months' gestation, and the effects of the maternal environment on the fetus, and how it responds to the mother's voice, moods etc. Concerns have been raised that the absence of the mother–fetal bond during pregnancy will be detrimental to the fetus:

---

[133] M. O'Brian, The Politics of Reproduction; M. L. Lupton, 'The Role of the Artificial Uterus in Embryo Adoption and Neonatal Intensive Care' (1999) 18 *Medical Law* 613–629, at p. 620.

[134] See the HFE Act 1990 (as amended), s13(5). Guidance on this provision is also provided by the HFEA Code of Practice.

We know that a foetus responds to the mother's heartbeat, as well as her emotions, moods and movements. A subtle and sophisticated choreographic bond exists between the two and plays a critical role in the development of the foetus. What kind of child will we produce from a liquid medium inside a plastic box? How will gestation in an incubator affect the child's motor functions and emotional and cognitive development? We know that young infants deprived of human touch and bodily contact often are unable to develop the full range of human emotions and sometimes die soon after birth or become violent, sociopathic or withdrawn later in life.[135]

It is interesting to note that Rifkin raised similar concerns in relation to IVF back in 1977, months before the first child of IVF Louise Brown was born. Condemning IVF, he raised concerns about the psychological damage to the fetus, and warned that such a baby might be psychologically 'monstrous':

What are the psychological implications of growing up as a specimen, sheltered not by a warm womb but by steel and glass, belonging to no one but the lab technician who joined together sperm and egg?[136]

He was not alone in his expressed concerns over the safety and morality of IVF, and many welcomed it with fear and distrust.[137] However, IVF has gone on to be very successful, and since Louise Brown was born forty years ago, experts have reported that fertility treatment has resulted in more than a quarter of a million UK babies that have been born as a result of IVF.[138]

Until successful research trials and long-term follow-up studies are performed on the children entered into those first trials, it is unclear whether being gestated in an ectogenic incubator will affect the welfare of the child emotionally, or adversely affect a child later on in life. However, if, as discussed in Chapter 3, ectogenesis is discovered indirectly through ethically approved research trials on extremely premature babies where ectogenesis represents the last hope of survival for the first fetus/baby, this may resolve concerns around the welfare of the in vitro fetus. If the

---

[135] J. Rifkin, 'The End of Pregnancy', *The Guardian*, 17 January 2002.

[136] J. Rifkin and T. Howard, *Who Shall Play God?* (New York, NY: Dellacorte Press, 1977) p. 115 as quoted by S. Coleman, *The Ethics of Artificial Uteruses: Implications for Reproduction and Abortion* (Aldershot: Ashgate Publishing, 2004), at p. 43.

[137] P. Singer and D. Wells, 'In Vitro Fertilisation: The Major Issues' (1983) 9(4) *Journal of Medical Ethics* 192–195. J. Harris, 'In Vitro Fertilization: The Ethical Issues' (1983) 33 *Philosophical Quarterly* 217–237. T. Iglesias, 'In Vitro Fertilisation: The Major Issues' (1984) 10(1) *Journal of Medical Ethics* 32–37.

[138] 'More than 250,000 UK babies born through IVF' *The Guardian*, 4 November 2016.

age of viability continues to be reduced, then ectogenesis could be discovered almost by default. The welfare of the first premature babies entered into ectogenic research trials can be assessed, allaying speculative welfare fears of the ectogenic fetus/baby, and the effects of placing an embryo into an ectogenic incubator for the entire gestational period.

What Happens if Ectogenesis Results in a Live But Extremely Damaged Baby?

While ectogenesis may preserve the life of a fetus, concerns may be raised as the possibility that ectogenesis may sustain the lives of extremely premature babies, which are afflicted with extreme disabilities. However, the law is clear that 'any requirement to preserve life must be balanced against the quality of that life and the burdens of proposed treatment to prolong life'.[139] Furthermore, as with treatment in children and adults, when a baby is suffering, doctors and parents can agree to give the baby pain relief drugs to alleviate distress even though a side-effect of those drugs could be to shorten life.[140] As the Nuffield Council notes:

> The duty to care for the baby is not a duty to prolong life at all costs. Case law clearly establishes that where further treatment is futile and burdensome, the best interests of the baby may be to be allowed to die in as much comfort and dignity as possible.[141]

In the context of novel reproductive technologies and providing that the necessary ethical approval has been obtained to undertake research trials, I concur with an argument made by Blyth, that reproductive technologies should be permitted save where there was evidence that the technology would cause the child to suffer 'significant harm'.[142] Applied to ectogenesis, if the situation arose that the early premature babies entered into an ectogenic research trial survived, but were afflicted with extreme disabilities and in so much pain that they would be forced to live a 'demonstrably awful' existence, this would provide evidence that the technology poses a substantial risk of significant harm, which would justify prohibiting entering further fetuses/

---

[139] Re J (A Minor) (Wardship: Medical Treatment) [1990] 3 ALL ER 930, at p. 942.
[140] R v. Adams [1957] Crim. L R 365.
[141] Nuffield Council, 'Critical Care Decisions', paragraph 3.43.
[142] E. Blyth, 'Conceptions of Welfare' in K. Horsey and H. Biggs (eds.) Human Fertilisation and Embryology: Reproducing Regulation (London and New York, NY: Routledge, Cavendish, 2007) 17–45.

premature babies into ectogenic incubators/research trials until the technology improves.

4.3 Conclusion

As scientists constantly strive to achieve ectogenesis and developments in neonatal care continue to reduce viability, the reality of ectogenesis may not be as far off as the Warnock committee imagined when it stated in 1984 that 'such developments are well into the future'.[143] As this chapter and the one that preceded it have demonstrated, the present UK legislation fails to provide an adequate regulatory framework to govern this revolutionary technology or research into ectogenesis. If the law is to be reconnected with modern science, governments need to be proactive and consider not just present technologies, but those looming on the horizon such as ectogenesis. The advent of this technology will compel regulators to revisit the intensely politicised debate surrounding abortion law. I have argued that the possibility of babies being gestated by a machine will not end the abortion debate and allow all to embrace in 'happy harmony'. It will however undoubtedly impact on the laws pertaining to abortion, since viability, which currently influences the present legislation, will become irrelevant once complete ectogenesis is possible. New regulatory issues will emerge: for instance, what status should be accorded to a fetus being gestated in a neutral location; when if ever can a machine be switched off, and how will disputes between the gamete progenitors as to the fate of the ectogenic baby be resolved? Whilst it is conceded that at present ectogenesis is not yet possible, research into this advance has long been underway. The imperative to continue to help those premature babies born on the cusp of viability may eventually mean ectogenesis is discovered by default. It may well be that complete ectogenesis does not happen in our lifetime; but given the rate of scientific advance in this domain, it is imprudent to continue to dismiss ectogenesis as confined to the realms of science fiction.

---

[143] Warnock Report, 71–72.

5

Regulation of Uterus Transplantation

When Assisted Reproduction and Transplant Medicine Collide

5.1   The Race Is Over!

Almost 40 years on from the birth of Louise Brown and the world's first 'test tube baby',[1] recent technological advancements in reproductive medicine continue to revolutionise reproduction and generate new regulatory dilemmas.[2] Following on from the success of the transplantation of other reproductive tissue (including ovaries[3] and testes[4]) success has (finally) been achieved in the transplantation of a reproductive organ, the uterus, to treat absolute uterine factor infertility (UFI), which for many years has been regarded as untreatable.[5] Uterine transplantation (UTx) is now established as the first treatment for UFI. The birth of Vincent, the first child born following a uterine transplant in Sweden in 2014, marked the end of a long and hard-fought global race to perform the first successful human uterine transplant. There have been eight more live

---

[1]   Time Magazine, 'The Test Tube Baby' 31 July 1978; P. R. Brinsden, 'Thirty Years of IVF: The Legacy of Patrick Steptoe and Robert Edwards' (2009) 12(3) *Human Fertility* 137–143.

[2]   For regulatory dilemmas thrown up by earlier advances in assisted reproductive technologies see R. Lee and D. Morgan, *Human Fertilisation and Embryology: Regulating the Reproductive Revolution* (London: Blackstone Press, 2001). M. Brazier, 'Regulating the Reproduction Business' (1999) *Medical Law Review* 166. R. Brownsword, 'Regulating Human Genetics: New Dilemmas for a New Millennium' (2004) 12(1) *Medical Law Review* 14–39.

[3]   Human ovarian tissue transplantation has resulted in the birth of over 70 children worldwide – see S. Silber, 'Ovarian Tissue Cryopreservation and Transplantation: Scientific Implications' (2016) 33(12) *Journal of Assisted Reproduction and Genetics* 1595–1603. See also V. K. Blake, 'Ovaries, Tissues and Uteruses Oh My! Regulating Reproductive Tissue Transplants' (2013) 19(2) *William and Mary Journal of Women and the Law* 353–393.

[4]   G. Vince, 'Man fathers child after testicular transplant' *New Scientist*, 28 February 2001.

[5]   M. Brännström, 'Human Uterus Transplantation in Focus' (2016) 117(1) *British Medical Bulletin* 69–78. M. Brännström, L. Johannesson, H. Bokstrom et al., 'Livebirth after Uterus Transplantation' (2015) 385(9968) *The Lancet* 607–616.

births since then by the Swedish team.[6] Teams around the world sought to emulate their success and research trials into uterine transplantation were embarked upon in the USA,[7] Europe,[8] Asia[9] and the UK.[10] In December 2017, it was reported that the first successful uterine transplant had been performed in the USA.[11]

Moving forward rapidly in the clinical research phase, it is imperative that we begin to consider and discuss how this novel procedure will be regulated in practice and whether the current UK regulatory framework can accommodate this advance, which combines assisted reproduction technology with a transplantation procedure, and as Arora and Black note, represents a 'new level of collaboration between the two'.[12] This alone may generate regulatory difficulties, since the two fields are regulated differently in many jurisdictions, such as the UK and the USA. In regard to the former, as outlined in Chapter 1, the UK was the first country in the world to regulate ART with a comprehensive statutory framework when it enacted the Human Fertilisation and Embryology Act 1990 with oversight by the Human Fertilisation and Embryology Authority (HFEA).[13] Yet human tissue and organ transplantation is governed by a separate specialist statutory regime found in the Human Tissue Act 2004, with oversight by the Human Tissue Authority (HTA).[14] Both statutes were born amidst controversy to regulate arenas of medicine that have posed considerable ethical and regulatory

---

[6] M. Brännström, 'Uterus Transplantation and Beyond' (2017) 28 *Journal of Materials Science: Materials in Medicine* 70, at p. 75.

[7] B. M. Kuehn, 'US Uterus Transplant Trials Under Way' (2017) 317(10) *The Journal of the Medical Association* 1005–1007.

[8] S. Huet, A. Tardieu, M. Filloux et al., 'Uterus Transplantation in France: For Which Patients?' (2016)205 *European Journal of Obstetrics & Gynecology and Reproductive Biology* 7–10.

[9] N. Suganuma, A. Hayashi, I. Kisu, et al., 'Uterus Transplantation: Toward Clinical Application in Japan' (2017) 16(4) *Reproductive Medicine and Biology* 305–313.

[10] B. P. Jones, S. Saso, J. Yazbek and J. R. Smitha, 'Uterine Transplantation: Past, Present and Future' (2016) 123(9) *British Journal of Obstetrics and Gynaecology: An International Journal of Obstetrics & Gynaecology* 1434–1438.

[11] D. Grady, 'Woman with Transplanted Uterus Gives Birth, the First in the U.S.' *The New York Times*, 2 December 2017.

[12] K. S. Arora and V. Blake, 'Uterus Transplantation: Ethical and Regulatory Challenges' (2014) 40 *J Med Ethics* 396–400, at p. 396.

[13] See www.hfea.gov.uk.

[14] The Human Tissue Authority (HTA) controls the use of organs and cadaver material from people in the UK by licensing and inspecting research, education and medical organisations.

challenges.[15] Similarly in the USA, organ transplantations are regulated by federal rules, mainly the Uniform Anatomical Gift Act (UAGA) and National Organ Transplant Act 1984 (NOTA).[16] ARTs are regulated at state level and thus rules vary widely in their scope, context and existence between states.[17] Since uterus transplantation has characteristics of both, it is unclear which rules should apply and neither body of regulations applies perfectly.[18] It is thus imperative that, given the global advances into uterus transplantation, attention is paid to the constellation of regulatory challenges this advance will raise.

Blacke and Shah rightly note that uterus transplantation 'raises larger societal questions about how we wish to allocate health resources, what the boundaries of medicine and transplant medicine in particular are, and how far we will go in terms of research and individual risk in the pursuit of having children'.[19] But this novel technology raises far more

---

[15] The HFE Act 1990 was a response to IVF and the birth of Louise Brown; for more on how regulation initially arose from the widespread fears expressed by politicians, the media, the public and the professions about embryo research, its morality and its direction, see R. Deech, 'The HFEA – 10 Years On' in J. Gunning and H. Szoke (eds.), *The Regulation of Assisted Reproductive Technology* (United Kingdom: Ashgate Publishing, 2003). The Human Tissue Act 2004 was drafted in response to revelations about practices relating to the retention and use of human tissue in the Bristol Royal Infirmary (see Bristol Inquiry Interim Report: Removal and Retention of Human Material, 2000) and Alder Hey Children's Hospital in Liverpool (see The Royal Liverpool Children's Inquiry Report, The Stationery Office 2001 H.C. [Session 2000–1]; 112-II). See also the Isaacs Report (HM Inspector of Anatomy, The Investigation of events that followed the death of Cyril Mark Isaacs, May 2003). For more on the 2004 Act see D. Price, 'The Human Tissue Act 2004' (2005) 68(5) *Modern Law Review* 798–821.

[16] The NOTA established the Organ Procurement and Transplantation Network (OPTN) to maintain a national registry for organ matching. The Act also called for the network to be operated by a private, non-profit organisation under federal contract. The United Network for Organ Sharing (UNOS) administers the OPTN under contract with the Health Resources and Services Administration (HRSA) of the US Department of Health and Human Services (HHS). Prior to 1968 and enactment of the Uniform Anatomical Gift Act 1968 there were no federal laws governing organ and tissue donation. Organ and tissue donations were governed at state level only. Variation in state level regulation resulted in confusion. For more on regulation of organ donation in the USA see E. Pluribus, 'UNOS: The National Organ Transplant Act and Its Postoperative Complications' (2008) 8 *Yale Journal of Health Policy, Law, and Ethics* 145.

[17] For a comparison of regulation of ART between the UK and the US, see A. Ouellettea, A. Caplan, K. Carrollc et al., 'Lessons across the Pond: Assisted Reproductive Technology in the United Kingdom and the United States' (2005) 31 *American Journal of Law & Medicine* 419–446.

[18] V. Blake and K. Shah, 'Reproductive Tissue Transplants Defy Legal and Ethical Categorization' (2012) 14(3) *American Medical Association Journal of Ethics* 232–236.

[19] Ibid., p. 236.

controversial questions. Unlike the transplantation of other vast organs, uterus transplantation is not intended to save life, but to create it. Whilst the primary purpose of a human uterus transplant is to restore fertility in female patients, it has raised the prospect/speculation that the procedure may also work in transgender women[20] and, even more controversially, cisgender men[21]. Thus it has been queried whether uterine transplantation has the potential not only to restore fertility in women, but to realign the reproductive capacity of transgender women and enhance the reproductive capacity of cisgender men.[22] Brännström, who led the Swedish trial, stated in 2016 that his email inbox was inundated by men seeking a uterus transplant: 'I get emails from all over the world on this, sometimes from gay males with one partner that would like to carry a child'.[23]

The focus of the present chapter is to critically examine the regulatory issues raised by this new reproductive technology in the context of the immediate purpose of research into uterus transplantation; namely to treat uterus factor infertility in cisgender women. The different problems that surface when consideration is given to whether transgender women and cisgender men should be granted access to this clinical milestone will be addressed in the next chapter.

The structure of this chapter is as follows. Firstly, the research into uterus transplant surgery is outlined and how this advance has gone from science fiction to fact. As the UK has received research approval to

---

[20] For a discussion of the reproductive options for trans women see S. McGuinness and A. Alghrani, 'Gender and Parenthood: The Case for Realignment?' (2008) 16(2) *Medical Law Review* 261–283. P. Sutter, 'Gender Reassignment and Assisted Reproduction: Present and Future Options for Transsexual People' (2001) 16 *Human Reproduction* 612–614. J. Thomson, 'Transsexualism and Access to a Child' (1982) 8 *Journal of Medical Ethics* 72. D. Brothers and W. C. Ford, 'Gender Reassignment and Assisted Reproduction: An Ethical Analysis' 15 *Human Reproduction* 737–738 (2000). For news headlines speculating the prospect of Uterus Transplantation in trans women see D. Fine Maron, 'How a Transgender Woman Could Get Pregnant', *Scientific American* 15 June 2016. L. Samuel, 'With Uterus Transplants a Reality, Transgender Women Dare to Dream of Pregnancies', STAT Reporting from the frontiers of health and medicine, 7 March 2017.

[21] For media articles on the prospect of uterus transplantation into men see M. Bilger, 'Scientists Are Now Attempting to Figure Out How to Get Men Pregnant', *LifeNews.com*, 20 June 2016. D. Grady, 'Will Uterine Transplants Make Male Pregnancy Possible?' New York Times, 16 November 2015. For academic articles on male pregnancy see D. Teresi and K. McAuliffe, 'Male Pregnancy' in P. D. Hopkins (ed.), *Sex /Machine: Readings in Culture, Gender and Technology* (Bloomington, IN: Indiana University Press, 1998). R. Sparrow, 'Is it "Every Man's Right to Have Babies if He Wants Them"? Male Pregnancy and the Limits of Procreative Liberty' (2008) 18(3) *Kennedy Institute of Ethics Journal* 275–299.

[22] This is discussed further in the next chapter.

[23] Fine Maron, 'How a Transgender Woman Could Get Pregnant'.

commence with human research trials,[24] this chapter then examines how this advance would be governed in the UK under the current regulatory framework and the implications this advance raises for all three parties involved: the donor, recipient and potential child. This chapter identifies the regulatory problems that begin to surface when consideration is given to how uterus transplant surgery would be governed and probes into whether such a procedure constitutes fertility treatment (and thus should be governed akin to other ARTs) or as other organ transplants; or, alternatively, whether this unique development will merit separate regulation of its own.

5.2   Uterus Transplant Surgery: From Sci-Fi to Sci-Fact

The main function of the uterus is to accept a fertilised ovum, which becomes implanted into the lining of the uterine cavity and to provide it with nourishment derived from blood vessels that develop exclusively for this purpose.[25] Should pregnancy occur, the uterus serves as an incubator for the embryo where it can safely develop until birth.[26] In the UK alone, it is estimated that approximately 1 in 500 women of fertile age who seek the help of fertility specialists are found to be incapable of becoming pregnant because of uterine factor infertility (UFI).[27] The major groups of women with this type of infertility are those that lack the uterus from birth or after hysterectomy, or women with intra-uterine adhesions (caused by surgical abortion or infection).[28] While women with UFI may not be able to carry/gestate a child, most have normal functioning ovaries and thus have a chance to become genetic mothers via surrogacy.[29] Uterus transplantation is now an experimental clinical procedure for treatment of UFI.[30] The hope this advance has given in women with

[24] Jones, Saso, Yazbek and Smitha, 'Uterine Transplantation: Past, Present and Future'.

[25] K. S. Saladin, *Anatomy & Physiology: The Unity of Form and Function* Fourth Edition (New York, NY: McGraw-Hill, 2007) 1052–1053.

[26] E. P. Soloman and G. A. Phillips, *Understanding Human Anatomy and Physiology* (Philadelphia, PA and London: WB Saunders Company, 1987) at p. 334.

[27] S. Bosley, 'Surgeons Hail World's First Uterus Transplant' The Guardian, 7 March 2002.

[28] M. Brännström and C. A Wranning, 'Uterus Transplantation; Where Do We Stand Today and Where Should We Go?' (2007) 7(4) *Expert Opinion on Biological Therapy* 427–429, at p. 427. Note that it has not been reported since whether Del Priore and his team performed the surgery.

[29] While some claim genetic relatedness is over hyped, in some contexts, such as the Islamic culture, it is the only way in which lineage and parental ties are acknowledged.

[30] Brännström, 'Uterus Transplantation and Beyond' 70.

UFI is reflected in the words of Malin Stenberg, the mother of the world's first live birth following a uterus transplant, who stated, 'I have always had this large sorrow because I never thought I would be a mother . . . and now the impossible has become real'.[31]

Uterus transplantation may have given hope to thousands of women across the world, but Schattman, former president of the Society for Assisted Reproductive Technologies (in the USA), cautioned that uterus transplants are likely to remain exceptional, stating that 'this would not be done unless there were no other options . . . It requires a very long surgery and is not without risk and complications'.[32] Transplantation of this vast organ is technically difficult due to the complex vascular anatomy of the pelvic region and the difficulty of reconnecting the vascular supply, as the blood vessels to the uterus are much smaller than those in other organs.[33] Previously, there was also concern that immunosuppressant drugs which must be taken to prevent the recipient's body rejecting the organ could have adverse effects on the fetus.[34] Such concerns have not materialised and statistics by Johannesson et al. indicated that whilst a fetus growing in a transplanted uterus will unconditionally be exposed to the immunosuppressive treatment 'as of 2006, more than 14,000 children born from immune suppressed organ transplanted women have been reported, and no increased incidence of congenital malformations has been detected'.[35]

Whilst uterus transplantation is the latest breakthrough in the arena of ARTs, animal research into uterus transplantation is well established and has demonstrated that transplantation of the uterus is possible in both smaller and larger animals.[36] However, human research into uterus

---

[31] 'Woman Gives Birth To First Child Born after Womb Transplant', *The Huffington Post UK*, 14 October 2014.

[32] Ibid.

[33] D. Grady, 'Medical First Transplant of a Uterus' New York Times, 7 March 2002.

[34] M. Ostensen, 'Disease Specific Problems Related to Drug Therapy in Pregnancy" (2004) 13(9) *Lupus* 746–750.

[35] L. Johannesson, N. Kvarnström, J. Mölne, et al. 'Uterus Transplantation Trial: 1-Year Outcome' (2015) 103 *Fertility & Sterility* 199–204.

[36] S. Eraslan, R. J. Hamernik and J. D. Hardy, 'Replantation of Uterus and Ovaries in Dogs with Successful Pregnancy' (1966) 92(1) *Archives of Surgery* 9–12; E. Confino et al., 'Nonvascular Transplantation of the Rabbit Uterus' (1986) 24(4) *International Journal of Gynaecology and Obstetrics* 321–325; R. H. Yonemoto et al., 'Homotransplantation of Uterus and Ovaries in Dogs. A Preliminary Report' (1964) 104(8) *Am J Obstet Gynecol* 1143–1151. J. A. O'Leary, M. Feldman and D. M. Gaensslen, 'Uterine and Tubal Transplantation' (1969) 20(5) *Fertility & Sterility* 757–760. R. F. Mattingly et al., 'Ovarian Function In-Utero Ovarian Homotransplantations' (1970) 108(5) *American*

transplantation is still in its infancy and at the very experimental stage. The successful Swedish attempt had come after other unsuccessful human attempts made elsewhere. The first human uterine transplant had occurred over a decade earlier in Saudi Arabia in 2000.[37] The live donor was 46 years old and the recipient a 26-year-old woman who had undergone a hysterectomy six years prior. After cessation of hormonal therapy the transplanted uterus produced two menstrual periods, considered to reflect good blood perfusion and viability of the transplanted uterus. However, on the 99th day, an ultrasound confirmed cessation of the blood flow as a result of blood clots that had formed in the arteries. A hysterectomy became necessary and the transplanted uterus was removed. The team stated that the main difficulty was the vascular anastomosis between the uterine and donor vessels.[38]

The second human attempt occurred in Turkey in 2011, this time with a uterus from a deceased 22-year-old donor.[39] The recipient was a 21-year-old recipient with MRKH syndrome.[40] The use of a cadaver donor enabled removal of a wider section of tissue surrounding the uterus, along with longer vessels to support the organ. Although the transplanted graft has remained in situ, despite multiple embryo transfer attempts, no pregnancy with a viable heart has occurred and the recipient has yet to bear a child.[41]

Journal of Obstetrics & Gynecology 773–794; J. R. Scott, R. M. Pitkin and M. E. Yannone, 'Transplantation of the Primate Uterus' (1971) 133(3) *Surgery, Gynecology & Obstetrics* 414–418, as cited in W. Fageeh and G. Lucchini, 'Uterus Transplantation' in M. Lanzetta, J. Dubernard and P. Petruzzo (eds.), *Hand Transplantation* (Milan: Springer, 2007) p. 412. C. Wranning et al., 'Transplantation of the Uterus in the Sheep – Oxidative Stress and Reperfusion Injury after Short Time Cold Storage' (2007) *Fertility and Sterility* 817–826. In the 2007–8 Report, the UK's Human Fertilisation and Embryology Authority (HFEA) Horizon Scanning Panel noted that the 'primate uterus can be perfused, preserved and circulated with blood post transplantation. Other large animal pregnancies following uterus transplantation have been achieved.' See Scientific Horizon Scanning at the HFEA, Annual Report 2007/8.

[37] W. Fageeh et al., 'Transplantation of the Human Uterus' (2002) 76 *International Journal of Gynecology and Obstetrics* 245–251. Note this was conducted in Saudi Arabia: in that country the Islamic Jurisprudence Council had in 1990 passed approval to the transplantation of reproductive organs that do not transfer genetic coding.

[38] Ibid., p. 256.

[39] O. Ozkan, M. Erman Akar, O. Ozkan et al. 'Preliminary Results of the First Human Uterus Transplantation from a Multiorgan Donor' (2013) 99(2) *Fertility and Sterility* 470–476.

[40] MRKH (Mayer Rokitansky Küster Hauser) syndrome is a congenital (born with) abnormality, characterised by the absence of the vagina, cervix and uterus, which in the UK is said to affect one in every 5,000 women. Their ovaries, however, are present, with normal function and ovulation.

[41] Ibid.

Both those attempts were criticised by Brännström for being conducted 'without any research preparations'[42] and their non-compliance with the IDEAL (Innovation, Development, Exploration, Assessment, Long-term follow-up) concept for introduction of surgical innovations[43] and the international ethics guidelines for uterine transplantation.[44] Building upon their animal-based uterine transplantation research in 1999, Brännström's team performed the first successful clinical research trial in nine live donor human transplant procedures in Sweden in 2013.[45] Prior to the surgery, the recipients went through IVF treatments to cryopreserve embryos. During the initial stage, a hysterectomy had to be performed in two patients. In the seven remaining women, embryo transfers were performed 12–14 months after the transplant procedure. Two women became pregnant at their first embryo transfer attempts.

One of those embryo transfers resulted in the world's first live birth via uterus transplantation on 4 September 2014. The recipient was a 35-year-old woman with MRKH syndrome, who had learned she had no uterus at 15. She and her male partner, both described as 'competitive athletes'[46] underwent the experimental procedure fully informed of the risks. The donor from whom she received her uterus was a 61-year-old postmenopausal family friend, who had previously had two sons. Brännström and his team claimed their demonstration of the first live birth after uterus transplantation finally opened up the possibility to treat the many young women with uterine factor infertility worldwide.[47] As Williams notes, the birth of baby Vincent and the Swedish success marked the end of a long and hard-fought race between teams of researchers across the world to perform the first 'successful' experimental human uterine transplant.[48] There have been eight live births in total by the Swedish team.[49] The success of the Swedish trials reflects the primary purpose of UTx, which is

[42] Brännström, 'Uterus Transplantation and Beyond'.
[43] P. McCulloch, D. G. Altman, W. B. Campbell et al., 'No Surgical Innovation without Evaluation: The IDEAL Recommendations' (2009) 374 *The Lancet* 1105–1112.
[44] J. Milliez, 'Uterine Transplantation FIGO Committee for the Ethical Aspects of Human Reproduction and Women's Health' (2009) 106 *International Journal of Gynaecology & Obstetrics* 270. Brännström, 'Uterus Transplantation and Beyond'.
[45] Brännström, 'Uterus Transplantation and Beyond'.
[46] 'Woman Gives Birth To First Child Born after Womb Transplant', *The Huffington Post UK*, 14 October 2014.
[47] Brännström, Johannesson, Bokstrom et al., 'Livebirth after Uterus Transplantation'.
[48] N. Williams, 'Should Deceased Donation Be Morally Preferred in Uterine Transplantation Trials?' (2016) 30(6) *Bioethics* 415–424.
[49] Grady 'Woman with Transplanted Uterus Gives Birth, the First in the U.S.'

to *restore* fertility in female patients with uterus factor infertility (UFI). The outcome of uterus transplantation in this early stage of clinical implementation has aptly been described as 'astonishing'.[50] The Swedish team research trials follow the IDEAL framework,[51] which provides a set of recommendations for introduction of any novel or major surgery procedure. The purpose of IDEAL is to improve the quality of research in surgery by emphasising appropriate methods, transparency of data and rigorous reporting of outcomes and thus minimising the risks for the patients and enabling accumulation of important scientific data during clinical introduction. The Swedish research team reported in 2017 that currently, UTx is in the D (Development) phase of the IDEAL concept with their observational study, including their nine patients.[52] An International Society for Uterus Transplantation (ISUTx) was also formed which initiated the formation of an international registry, to follow all patients (donors, recipients and children) to accumulate data to also explore the L (Long-term follow-up) phase of the IDEAL concept.[53]

Building on other fields of regenerative medicine and tissue engineering of other organs and tissues, Brännström has announced that his team is now working towards the creation of a bioengineered uterus for future uterus transplants that will see the uterus mostly created from the recipients' own stem cells.[54] The creation of a bioengineered uterus could potentially negate the need for immunosuppressive medications, circumvent organ shortage and avoid surgery in a live donor situation.[55] Bioengineered uteri using the recipient's stem cells are regarded as a superior treatment for UFI, since it will reduce or eliminate many of the risks associated with uterine transplant for both the donor and recipient.[56] This research remains in the initial phase and the team predict that this will take at least a decade from the laboratory to the clinical setting.[57]

Success has not been limited to Sweden. The most recent success with uterus transplantation occurred in the USA at the Baylor University

---

[50] L. Johannesson and S. Järvholm, 'Uterus Transplantation: Current Progress and Future Prospects' (2016) 8 *International Journal of Women's Health* 43–51.

[51] McCulloch, Altman, Campbell et al., 'No Surgical Innovation without Evaluation: The IDEAL Recommendations'.

[52] R. Akouria, G. Maaloufc, A. Waked et al., 'Uterus Transplantation: An Update and the Middle East Perspective' (2017) *Middle East Fertility Society Journal* (in press).

[53] Ibid.

[54] Brännström, 'Uterus Transplantation and Beyond' 75.

[55] Ibid.

[56] Ibid., p. 70.

[57] Ibid.

Medical Center in Dallas. As part of a clinical research trial at Baylor, eight women have had transplants, one of who gave birth to a baby boy in November 2017. At the time of writing, one of the recipients is pregnant, and two others (one of whom received her transplant from a deceased donor) are trying to conceive. Four other transplants failed after the surgery and thus the transplanted uteri had to be removed.

Internationally, clinical trials of uterine transplantation are underway in North America,[58] Europe[59] and Asia.[60] The UK is no exception. Ethical research approval was obtained in 2015 from The Health Research Authority to commence uterus transplant research trials in the UK in ten patients.[61] Unlike the Swedish trial which used live donors, the UK team will use brainstem dead, heart-beating cadaver donors.[62] The study will be conducted in London, at Hammersmith Hospital, with fertility treatment taking place at The Lister Hospital. Subject to success in the current trial, the UK team is optimistic and has expressed a hope to offer this procedure to the public from 2020 onwards: 'although we may be accused of bias, we believe that this procedure will become an established treatment option, as an alternative to adoption or surrogacy, in a relatively small group of suitable women with AUFI [absolute uterus factor infertility]'.[63] Notwithstanding this approval, the UK government and the regulators that oversee transplantation and assisted reproduction have remained silent on whether this procedure may soon be permitted as clinical treatment to restore fertility in women unable to gestate.

In light of the success of the Swedish team and as the UK prepares to embark upon its own research trials, it is important that discussion advances beyond abstract narratives regarding the possibility of uterus transplantation as a future advance. This chapter moves the debate on by exploring the regulatory issues that arise, considering pragmatically how this innovation could be regulated under the current UK legal framework, and now addresses the regulatory implications of uterine transplantation for all three parties involved: the donor, recipient and potential child.

[58] Kuehn, 'US Uterus Transplant Trials Under Way'.
[59] The UK is now embarking upon uterine transplant research: see Jones, Saso, Yazbek and Smitha, 'Uterine Transplantation: Past, Present and Future'.
[60] Y. Shimbun, 'Japanese Team Aims to Perform Uterine Transplants' *The Japan News*, 9 January 2017.
[61] 'Womb Transplants: First 10 British Women Given Go-Ahead' *The Guardian*, 30 September 2015.
[62] Jones, Saso, Yazbek and Smitha, 'Uterine Transplantation: Past, Present and Future' 1435.
[63] Ibid., 1437.

5.3   Regulation of ART/Organ and Tissue Transplantation in the UK

i.The Regulation of ART in the UK

Uterus transplantation poses novel challenges in the worlds of ART and transplant medicine. While the potential benefits are enormous, the risks are also unprecedented. It is imperative that the ethical and legal challenges are addressed and discussed prior to further clinical research and implementation, particularly with attention to risks to living or deceased donors, recipients and resulting children and regulatory implications.[64]

The above quote presses upon the magnitude of the legal and regulatory challenges that uterus transplantation presents. For example, as alluded to earlier, this procedure combines both ART and organ transplantation and in both the Swedish and American research trials, conception occurred via implantation of IVF embryos harvested and stored pre-transplant, which were later implanted once the transplanted uterus was in situ. Thus, if the procedure were to take place in the UK, as it will likely necessitate creation of embryos via IVF, it is anticipated that a woman will be subject to the regulatory frameworks of both the Human Fertilisation and Embryology Act 1990 (as amended) and the Human Tissue Act (HTA) 2004. If this procedure comes under dual regulation it is important that attention is given to how the procedure can be safeguarded so as to avoid anomalies of a woman with UFI seeking to procreate via a uterine transplant having IVF, only to be later refused access to the uterus transplant procedure, or vice versa. If it does one day become possible to perform a uterus transplant that allows for natural conception in a woman with functioning ovaries, presumably the transplant would fall entirely outside the ambit of the HFE Act and be governed only via the HTA 2004. Once the woman conceives via sexual reproduction, the pregnancy would fall outside the remit of the 2004 Act, and the Human Tissue Authority (HTA) would have no authority to intervene to regulate the pregnancy. Whilst reproduction via uterus transplantation currently necessitates both a uterus transplant and IVF, as the law governing the latter and access to IVF is well documented,[65] the remainder of this chapter will focus on the law that would govern a uterus transplant.

---

[64] Arora and Blake, 'Uterus Transplantation: Ethical and Regulatory Challenges', at p. 399.

[65] See Chapters 1 and 2 for a discussion of the laws which govern IVF and disposition of IVF embryos. For more on this see K. Horsey (ed.), *Revisiting the Regulation of Human Fertilisation and Embryology* (London: Routledge, 2015).

5.3.1   Regulation of Uterus Transplantation: The UK Model

If a uterus transplant is to be regulated in the same manner as other organ transplants, it would fall under the Human Tissue Act 2004.[66] The Human Tissue Authority (HTA) is the statutory authority that regulates the removal, storage, use and disposal of human bodies, organs and tissues for a number of scheduled purposes, including transplantation. The rules that would govern uterus transplantation (notably a procedure which was not envisaged by the legislators when the 2004 statute was drafted) will vary depending on whether the uterus is sourced from a living or cadaver donor. At present, clinical research teams around the world are proceeding using both. The next section provides an in-depth analysis of the regulatory issues that will arise in the context of live donors and will examine the competent donor, the risk of family coercion and lastly, incapacitated donors.

5.3.1.1   The Donor

At the outset it is noted that should a bioengineered uterus one day enter the clinical arena, it will negate the need for a donor. However for the next few decades classical UTx with transplantation from live or dead donors is expected to be the predominant infertility treatment for women with UFI. Thus it is important to consider how UTx would be governed under the current domestic regulatory framework and the implications for donors.

5.3.1.2   Living Donors

In the successful human uterus transplant research trials to date, live donors were used. As noted above, in the Saudi trial, the donor was 46 years old and pre-menopausal. The donor surgery lasted 10.5–13 hours with a hospital stay of six days. The Swedish donation surgeries took less time at 7–11 hours,[67] but both trials required a very lengthy process. For living donors, the risks can be more tangibly characterised and paralleled to women undergoing hysterectomies.[68] The risks and complications associated with a hysterectomy are pre-operative and post-operative; they can vary from haemorrhage, ureteral bladder injury, thromboembolic disease, infections, vault prolapse and vaginal cuff evisceration.[69] Are the

---

[66] The 2004 Act is now the primary legislation regulating transplantation in England, Wales and Northern Ireland, but it does not apply in Scotland.

[67] J. A. Robertson, 'Other Women's Wombs: Uterus Transplants and Gestational Surrogacy' (2016) 3(1) *Journal of Law and the Biosciences* 68–86 at p. 72.

[68] Arora and Blake, 'Uterus Transplantation: Ethical and Regulatory Challenges', at p. 397.

[69] I. A. Yakasi, 'Complications of Hysterectomy: A Review' (2013) 9(2) *British Journal of Science* 78.

risks to the donor outweighed by the benefits of the donation? The principle of reproductive autonomy[70] supports a competent woman's right to donate her uterus as a non-vital organ. The long-term consequences on donor health from a hysterectomy are low, but uterus donation is much more complicated than even a radical hysterectomy because long veins and arteries must also be removed to allow for the uterus to be transplanted into a recipient. The surgery is challenging because of the complex vascular structures supporting the uterus, which are described as being wrapped 'like worms' around veins and arteries and which must be carefully unwrapped to avoid injury.[71] This lengthens the duration of anaesthesia and risks injury to the ureters.

Consent Obtaining appropriate consent from the live donor would be the first mandatory step in the removal, storage and use of a uterus for transplantation.[72] The HTA 2004 establishes the concept of 'appropriate consent' but does not explicitly define it. The Human Tissue Authority (HTA)[73] provides guidance on this in the Codes of Practice.[74] The donor must give valid consent, rules on which are established in common law and mental capacity legislation. The Mental Capacity Act 2005[75] enshrined the principle that 'a person must be assumed to have capacity unless it is established that he lacks capacity'.[76] Section three provides that a person is unable to make a decision for her/himself if s/he is unable to: (a) understand the information relevant to the decision; (b) retain that information; and (c) use or weigh that information as part of the process of making the decision or to communicate his decision (whether by talking, using sign language or any other means).[77] Provided that a

---

[70] E. Jackson, *Regulating Reproduction: Law, Technology and Autonomy* (Oxford: Hart Publishing, 2001).

[71] Robertson, 'Other Women's Wombs' 72.

[72] HTA, Code of Practice, Code A, published 3 April 2017, paragraph 12 provides 'consent and the wishes of the donor, or where appropriate their nominated representatives or relatives have primacy when removing, storing and using human tissue'.

[73] Human Tissue Act 2004, s33 extends the powers of the new HTA to oversee all live donations.

[74] HTA, Code of Practice, Code A, published 3 April 2017, paragraphs 78–94 and 113–134.

[75] HTA, Code of Practice – Consent Code A, published 3 April 2017.

[76] Section 1(2). For more on the Mental Capacity Act 2005 see the following special issue and A. Alghrani, P. Case and J. Fanning, 'The Mental Capacity Act: Ten Years On' (2016) 24(3) *Medical Law Review* 311–317.

[77] This replaces the common law test laid down in *Re C (Adult: Refusal of Treatment)* [1994] 1 All ER 819 which set out a test of understanding similar to MCA 2005 s3, but included a further requirement that the patient believes the information given to him.

woman can fulfil those criteria and is sufficiently informed of the risks entailed in the procedure, she may give appropriate consent to donate her uterus.

What of young women who have not yet had children who wish to donate their uteri; should there be a requirement that live uterus donors have completed their own family, or some reassurance that they do not want to bear a child of their own prior to donation? Mc Queen has noted how sterilisation requests made by young, child-free adults are frequently denied by doctors, despite sterilisation being legally available to individuals over the age of 18.[78] In light of the fact that the only successful research trials to date have been with uteri that have proven the ability to sustain gestation, it may well be that donors must have had at least one child first. Informed consent within the context of a decision for hysterectomy for women of any age should include balanced information and supportive exploration of the woman's values, goals and life plan.[79] As with young women under thirty years of age, or those who do not have children who opt for sterilisation or a hysterectomy, guidance could state that additional care must be taken when counselling such women so as to avoid the risk of later regret.[80] Women, who wish to donate a uterus, as with other women who request a sterilisation, may be urged to consider such possible future regrets. Mertes has written on how sometimes women wishing to undergo sterilisation are sometimes refused treatment in anticipation of such regrets.[81] This is despite the fact that for all age ranges, the majority of women undergoing a sterilisation do not regret the decision. She writes about the clear discrepancy in the way those who request medical assistance in pursuit of their reproductive choices are treated:

> Women who are voluntarily childless are likely to have a happier and more gratifying life than parents. On the other hand, women who request fertility treatment are not urged to second guess their desire for parenthood. Although the fact that the probability of regret is expected to be

---

[78] P. McQueen, 'Autonomy, Age and Sterilisation Requests' (2016) 43 *Journal of Medical Ethics* 310–313.

[79] E. W. Bernal, 'Hysterectomy and Autonomy' (1988) 9(1) *Theoretical Medicine and Bioethics* 73–88.

[80] Similar guidance has been issued for those opting for sterilisation treatment; see the RCOG, *Setting Standards to Improve Women's Health. Male and Female Sterilisation Evidence-based Clinical Guideline Number 4*, January 2004.

[81] H. Mertes, 'The Role of Anticipated Decision Regret and the Patient's Best Interest in Sterilisation and Medically Assisted Reproduction' (2017) 43(5) *Journal of Medical Ethics* 314–318.

higher in the former case than in the latter justifies this difference in treatment to a certain extent, the gap between the two different approaches is wider than it ought to be if we also take future well-being into consideration, instead of focussing exclusively on anticipated decision regret.[82]

There may also be unique psychological factors at play with living donation of a uterus. Although the donation is not reproductive per se (no gametes are donated), it does allow reproduction by the recipient to occur. The donor is providing the organ so that the recipient may then gestate and give birth, so there may still be symbolic and psychological meaning for the donor because she is providing the actual organ of gestation. The law defines a 'mother' as the woman that has gestated and given birth to the child.[83] Counselling prior to donation will need to address this issue, so that the donor does not believe that she is the 'mother' of the child because she has contributed the organ essential for the recipient's reproduction. In some cases, donors may experience even further loss than many women feel when they undergo hysterectomy.[84]

Availability

> In the future it is not going to be a problem to get a donor, not like a kidney, heart or liver. It is a sisterhood thing.[85]

Brännström's quote above reflects rather optimistically that camaraderie amongst women will mean there will not be the shortage there is of other organs for donation. Family or friends might choose to donate a uterus, particularly if they have completed their own families. Thus, women undergoing hysterectomies may thus be a likely source for uterine transplant. Consequently, Brännström argues that the issue of organ availability is a 'minor problem':

> in the case of UTx, the pool of living donors is predicted to be large, considering that the uterus is without any important function after child bearing. Thus, altruistic living donation from related and non-related donors will most likely be common, in particular when the surgery has developed further to considerably reduced surgery times and after the introduction of minimal invasive laparoscopic techniques for organ harvesting.[86]

---

[82] Ibid.
[83] HFE 2008, section 33.
[84] Robertson, 'Other Women's Wombs'.
[85] M. Brännström comments in 'Woman Gives Birth to First Child Born after Uterus Transplant', Huffington Post, 4 October 2014.
[86] Brännström, 'Uterus Transplantation and Beyond' 75.

Brännström is very presumptive here – just because an individual does not need an organ anymore, does not necessarily mean they will want someone else to have it. For instance, the UK has long had a shortage of donors on the organ donor register, and each year individuals die awaiting a transplant. Despite the fact that you cannot get more permanent than death, many each year die without donating their organs.

If uterus transplantation using live donation becomes routine clinical treatment, only time will tell if Brännström's prediction is correct and the supply is a forthcoming as he has optimistically predicted. Care must be made that donors who consent have given truly informed and voluntary consent that is free from coercion.

The Risk of Coercion   There may be a greater chance of success with uterus transplantation if there is a tissue match between donor and recipient. In Sweden the donors were mothers in five cases, one sister, one maternal aunt, one mother-in-law and one close friend.[87] The first live birth was in the case of the non-related donor and recipient. However, where a uterus has been donated altruistically and there is no genetic match between the donor and recipient, there is a higher risk that the body of the recipient may reject the uterus. Whilst high doses of immunosuppressant drugs may help to minimise and suppress this reaction, such drugs can only be given in limited quantities to live donors due to concerns surrounding the potential harmful effects. Thus a uterus transplant from a close relative, such as sister to sister, or mother to daughter, may be an optimal choice. The 2004 Act requires the Human Tissue Authority to approve all transplants from living donors (whether or not the donor is related to the recipient).[88] Thus doctors embarking on uterus transplantation in England and Wales must first refer the case to the HTA, who will then scrutinise the donation to ensure the donor has genuinely given free consent. What about the risks of coercion? Should a mother be allowed to act as an organ donor for her daughter 'raising the prospect of a woman carrying her children in the same uterus that carried her'?[89]

Fears that donations from close relatives may increase the risk of coercion are neither novel nor unique to uterus transplantation and apply to the donation of other organs. It is conceded that where the donor and recipient are genetically related, extra care must be taken to

[87]   Ibid., 74.
[88]   Human Tissue Act 2004.
[89]   M. Hutchinson, 'Uterus Transplant Baby "Within Three Years"' *BBC News*, 1 July 2003.

ensure that psychological pressure has not been exerted on the donor and that a genuinely free and informed consent has been given. For instance, it has been reported that mothers of daughters with MRKH Syndrome often volunteer to serve as surrogates for their daughters.[90] It is difficult to assess whether a mother in such a situation would be donating because of guilt. Notwithstanding this risk, mothers and sisters can and do donate other organs to their loved ones. For years, mothers and sisters have acted as surrogates for closely related family members.[91] If women can act as surrogates and gestate a child for a close relative, then it would be inconsistent and illogical to claim that allowing the donation of a uterus for the same purpose would somehow be more objectionable. Arguably adequate safeguards are already in place within the 2004 Act to ensure that donations are informed, truly voluntary and not the result of coercion.

Donors Who Lack Capacity   In a patient who lacks capacity, donation will be lawful only if it is deemed to be in accordance with the patient's 'best interests'[92] and after consideration has been given to: (a) the person's past and present wishes and feelings (and, in particular, any relevant written statement made by her when she had capacity); (b) the beliefs and values that would be likely to influence her decision if she had capacity; and (c) the other factors that she would be likely to consider if she were able to do so.[93] The Human Tissue Act 2004 (Persons who Lack Capacity to Consent and Transplants) Regulations 2006 provides consent can be deemed to be in place 'if given by a person who is acting in what s/he reasonably believes to be in the best interests of the person lacking capacity from whose body the material is to be donated'[94] and

---

[90] A. Altchek, 'Uterus Transplantation' (2003) 70(3) *The Mount Sinai Journal of Medicine* 154–162, p. 157.

[91] Cases have been reported where women have acted as surrogates for closely related family members. For instance see *AB* v. *CD* [2015] EWFC 17 when B, a single man in his midtwenties, entered into a surrogacy arrangement, leading to the birth of A, with his mother C (who had acted as the surrogate) and her husband D. As section 54(2) of the Human fertilisation and Embryology 2008 Act requires that the applicants for a parental order are husband and wife, or same-sex civil partners or two people who are living as partners in an enduring family relationship, the single father could only obtain legal parenthood for the child via adoption.

[92] Mental Capacity Act 2005, s1(5) provides 'An act done, or decision made, under this Act for or on behalf of a person who lacks capacity must be done, or made, in his best interests'.

[93] Mental Capacity Act 2005, s4.

[94] Donation must be for scheduled purposes. The scheduled purposes provided for under the Regulations are obtaining scientific or medical information about a living or deceased person which may be relevant to another (including a future person) and transplantation.

'where it is consistent with sections 30–34 of the Mental Capacity Act 2005, allowing for the storage and use of relevant material from persons lacking capacity for research in circumstances provided for'.[95]

Thus, in order to donate a uterus it must be decided that this course of action is in the donor's 'best interests'. Consider the bizarre scenario that patient X lacks capacity and it is proposed she should be sterilised in her 'best interests' – could this be by hysterectomy to give a uterus to her sister Y? This would turn on the definition of 'best interests', which has been interpreted widely by the courts in the health domain to encompass 'medical, emotional and other welfare issues'.[96] The House of Lords in *F v. West Berkshire Health Authority*[97] granted a declaration that the sterilisation of a thirty-six-year-old mentally handicapped woman was lawful, adopting the *Bolam*[98] test to define best interests. In *Re Y (mental incapacity: bone marrow transplant)*[99] the court ruled that donation of bone marrow by an incompetent adult to her desperately ill sibling was in her 'best interests'. While there was no medical benefit from acting as a donor, the court ruled it would be to her 'emotional, psychological and social benefit' to act as a donor, since her sister might otherwise die and their mother would have to assume a greater role in caring for Y's nieces and have less time to spend with Y. It was in her 'best interests' to donate because in this way her positive relationship with her mother was most likely to be prolonged.[100]

This case has been rightly criticised for applying a 'test for negligence to a question of clinical practice'.[101] Further, it should be noted that Connell J explicitly noted in his judgment that *Re Y* would not be a useful precedent in cases where the surgery involved is more intrusive, such as

---

[95] The Mental Capacity Act 2005 does not extend to Northern Ireland and accordingly a Research Ethics Authority must always approve the research.

[96] *Re A (Medical Treatment: Male Sterilisation)* [2000] 1 FCR 193. Also for an examination of best interests in the context of organ donation see J. Coggon, M. Brazier, P. Murphy et al., 'Best Interests and Potential Organ Donors' (2008) 336 *British Medical Journal* 1346–1347.

[97] *Re Y (Mental Incapacity: Bone Marrow Transplant)* [1989] 2 All E.R. 545.

[98] *Bolam v. Friern Hospital Management Committee* [1957] WLR 582 McNair J in his direction to the jury stated that a 'doctor is not guilty of negligence if he has acted in accordance with a practice accepted as proper by a responsible body of medical men skilled in that particular art...'

[99] [1996] 2 FLR 787.

[100] Note that the *Re Y* case occurred prior to the enactment of the Mental Capacity Act 2005. Such a scenario would now be governed by that legislation.

[101] J. K. Mason and G. T. Laurie, *Mason and McCall Smith's Law and Medical Ethics*, Tenth Edition (Oxford: Oxford University Press, 2016) 17.21.

solid organ donation, which is what a uterus donation would be. Since a uterus donation will permanently remove a woman's ability to give birth, where the proposed live donor lacks capacity, the procedure should be approached in the same manner as sterilisation in patients who lack mental capacity and be referred to the courts for judgment.[102] Therefore, in the former scenario, removal of X's uterus would be lawful only if in all the contemporaneous circumstances it was regarded as in her 'best interests' and if the procedure was sanctioned by a court.

Payment   In the UK, commercial dealings in organs is expressly prohibited by the 2004 Act,[103] and the HTA must be satisfied that no money has changed hands and that other conditions prescribed by regulations are met.[104] Similarly in the USA, payment for organ donation is strictly prohibited.[105] A complete ban on commercialisation of organs or body material is supported by those who fear such payment may result in commodification, exploitation and degradation of the human body and those who believe that donation of organs and human material should be donated altruistically under a 'gift relationship'.[106] Altchek notes why some women may wish to altruistically donate a womb:

> There are various situations in which uterus donation would make sense.
> For women who do not wish to become pregnant again, a standard

---

[102] Sterilisation of a person who lacks capacity requires the prior sanction of a High Court judge – see Practice Note (Official Solicitor): Declaratory Proceedings: Medical and Welfare Decisions for Adults who Lack Capacity [2001] 2 FLR 158.

[103] Human Tissue Act 2004, s32(1) provides: 'A person commits an offence if s/he: (a) gives or receives a reward for the supply of, or for an offer to supply, any controlled material; (b) seeks to find a person willing to supply any controlled material for reward; (c) offers to supply any controlled material for reward; (d) initiates or negotiates any arrangement involving the giving of a reward for the supply of, or for an offer to supply, any controlled material; (e) takes part in the management or control of a body of persons corporate or unincorporate whose activities consist of or include the initiation or negotiation of such arrangements.' This prohibition covers both cadaveric and living donation; see Human Tissue Act 2004 section 32(8) and 32(10).

[104] See The Human Tissue Act 2004 (Persons Who Lack Capacity to Consent and Transplants) Regulations 2006 (S.I. 2006/1659).

[105] The National Organ Transplant Act 1984 makes it a federal crime to 'knowingly acquire, receive, or otherwise transfer any human organ for valuable consideration for use in human transplantation if the transfer affects interstate commerce'. The definition of 'valuable consideration' excludes 'reasonable payments associated with the removal, transportation, implantation, processing, preservation, quality control, and storage of a human organ or the expenses of travel, housing, and lost wages incurred by the donor of a human organ in connection with the donation of the organ'. Violations of NOTA carry a $50,000 maximum fine, a maximum five-year imprisonment term, or both.

[106] R. Titmuss, *The Gift Relationship* (London: Harper Collins, 1971).

treatment for prolapse of the uterus is vaginal hysterectomy. A uterus that is removed in this procedure is usually normal and typically discarded. If the uterus is donated for transplant rather than discarded, the donor is placed at no additional risk.[107]

While the 2004 Act would only allow uterus donations to be made altruistically, commentators such as Erin and Harris have made a powerful case for allowing a market in organs from live donors.[108] It should also be noted that payment is permitted for other reproductive material and services; 'compensation'[109] for donating eggs[110] and sperm[111] is permitted in the UK. Similarly payment for gametes is permitted in the USA and has been described as 'a burgeoning market'.[112] Similarly, surrogacy has long generated debate as to whether a woman should be able to command payment for her gestational service.[113] In the UK, the payment of 'reasonable expenses' to surrogates[114] was stated to do no more than compensate for the inconveniences of pregnancy,[115] and the main purpose of the Surrogacy Act 1985 was to prohibit the making of surrogacy arrangement on a commercial basis.[116] Notwithstanding this legislative

---

[107] Altchek, 'Uterus Transplantation', p. 156.

[108] C. Erin and J. Harris, 'A Monopsonistic Market – Or How to Buy and Sell Human Organs, Tissues and Cells Ethically' in I. Robinson (ed.), *Life and Death under High Technology Medicine* (Manchester: Manchester University Press in association with the Fulbright Commission, London, 1994) 134–153; J. Harris and C. A. Erin, 'An Ethically Defensible Market in Organs' (2002) 325 *British Medical Journal* 114–15; J. Radcliffe-Richards et al., 'The Case for Allowing Kidney Sales' (1998) 351 *The Lancet* 1950; M. Radin, 'Market – Inalienability' (1987) 100 *Harvard Law Review* 1849; N. Duxbury, 'Do Markets Degrade?' [1996] 59 *Modern Law Review* 331.

[109] Payment is prohibited and compensation is the term preferred by the HFEA.

[110] An egg donor can receive compensation of up to £750 per cycle of donation, to reasonably cover any financial losses incurred in connection with the donation, with the provision to claim an excess to cover higher expenses (such as for travel, accommodation or childcare).

[111] A sperm donor can receive compensation of £35 to reasonably cover any financial losses incurred in connection with the donation, with the provision to claim an excess to cover higher expenses (such as for travel, accommodation or childcare).

[112] Blake and Shah, 'Reproductive Tissue Transplants Defy Legal and Ethical Categorization'.

[113] See A. Alghrani and D. Griffiths, 'The Regulation of Surrogacy in the United Kingdom: The Case for Reform' (2017) 29(2) *Child and Family Quarterly* 165–186.

[114] While commercial surrogacy is in theory forbidden by the Surrogacy Arrangements Act 1985, ss1–3, in practice the courts have allowed payments to surrogates to cover 'reasonable expenses' incurred. In *Re MW (Adoption: Surrogacy)* [1995] 2 FLR 789, £7,500 was allowed as 'reasonable expenses'.

[115] *Re an adoption application (surrogacy)* [1987] 2 All ER 826, per Latey J.

[116] See Surrogacy Arrangements Act 1985 (as amended by the Human Fertilisation and Embryology Act 1990), s3.

stipulation, parental orders have still been granted where payment has been made to a surrogate that has exceeded reasonable expenses.[117] In some States in the USA,[118] commercial surrogacy is legal and has flourished. Payment and altruism need not be mutually exclusive and can be intertwined; for instance, Kim Cotton, famous for her role as a surrogate in one of the earliest reported surrogacy cases in the UK,[119] stated she acted as a surrogate both for the money and because she wanted to help someone in their desires to found a family: 'I've always said that it was a two-fold thing'.[120] Whether money should also be allowed for payment or compensation for donating ones uterus (as it is for gametes) is an issue that merits further consideration.

5.3.1.2   Cadaver (Deceased) Donation

From the outset it should be noted that human uterine transplant using a cadaver donor has not yet proven to be successful. Despite the limited success in Turkey using a deceased donor, UK and US research teams have stated they will use cadaver donors in their trials. The UK team has stated that it will proceed with a cadaver donor as that will enable removal of a wider section of tissue surrounding the uterus along with longer vessels to support the organ, which would be a risk to a living donor. The UK team has acknowledged the disadvantages of using a deceased donor, such as the unpredictable nature at which donors become available, the logistics of planning such major surgery at short notice and the limited time available to investigate the donor.[121] The use of brain stem-dead, heart-beating donors will allow for a 24–36-hour window for appropriate empathetic counselling of family members.

In context of deceased donations, Agich argues that traditional transplantation and retrieval or organs from a corpse was based on a rescue

---

[117] *Re X and Y (Foreign Surrogacy)* [2008] EWCH 3030 (Fam); *Re S (Parental Order)* [2009] EWHC 2977 (Fam); *Re L (Commercial Surrogacy)* [2010] EWHC 3146 (Fam); *Re IJ (Foreign Surrogacy Agreement Parental Order)* [2011] EWHC 921 (Fam); *A v. another v. and others* [2011] EWHC 1738 (Fam); *J v. G* [2013] EWHC 1432 (Fam).

[118] Regulation of surrogacy in the USA is regulated at State level and thus there is variation between States in the USA. A few states, like California and Oregon, allow commercial surrogacy where Surrogates are compensated $40,000 for their time, effort and costs incurred from living expenses.

[119] *Re C (A Minor)* [1985] FLR 846.

[120] K. Gander, 'UK's First Surrogate Mother on Carrying Someone Else's Baby and How the Law Must Change', *The Independent*, 23 March 2017.

[121] Pre-operative investigations will include a cervical smear with HPV testing, a GUM screen and a trans vaginal ultrasound scan.

ethics theory – only a strong valued goal like restoring basic physiological function necessary for life would justify 'the desecration of a corpse and the removal or organs'.[122] Whilst it may be argued that harvesting uteri does not meet this threshold, arguably it is restoring basic physiological function (fertility) necessary to give life. Whilst not life-saving, it is life-giving. Furthermore, other non-life-saving organs (hand, corneal and face transplants) and reproductive tissue (such as sperm)[123] have been harvested posthumously. Contrary to the rescue theory of ethics, some argue that using deceased donors is preferable to live donors. According to the World Health Organization Guiding Principle, organ donations from deceased donors should always be developed to their maximum potential, evading the innate risks to live donors.[124] However, because of the global shortage of suitable organs from deceased donors, donations from live donors are necessary in order to meet current patient needs.[125]

If deceased donation is permitted, what would/should constitute consent by the dead donor of a uterus? In the context of harvesting organs from a deceased donor, it must be considered whether the uterus should be treated differently than other organs, given its purpose to enable reproduction in the recipient. Johannesson and Järvholm rightly note how uteri or gamete donations raise more significant issues than livers or kidneys because of their ability to create genetic offspring, thus touching upon important legal rights to reproduce (or not).[126] They note how posthumous reproduction remains a complex and unsettled legal and ethical question that some states have tackled in posthumous conception cases (where family members have asked to use deceased individuals' gametes to reproduce).[127] The HFE Act 2008 only permits donation of

---

[122] G. J. Agich, 'Extension of Some Organ Transplantation: Some Ethical Considerations' (2003) 7 (3) *Mount Sinai Journal of Medicine* 141–147.

[123] See *R v. HFEA, ex parte Blood* [1997] 2 WLR 806 and *L v. Human Fertilisation & Embryology Authority & Secretary of State for Health* [2008] EWCH 2149 (Fam).

[124] Sixty-Third World Health Assembly, World Health Organization WHO guiding principles on human cell, tissue and organ transplantation. (2010) 11(4) *Cell Tissue Bank* 413–419. Johannesson and Järvholm, 'Uterus Transplantation: Current Progress and Future Prospects'.

[125] Johannesson and Järvholm, 'Uterus Transplantation: Current Progress and Future Prospects'.

[126] R. Zafran, 'Dying to Be a Father: Legal Paternity in Cases of Posthumous Conception' (2007) 8(1) *Houston Journal of Health Law & Policy* 47–102; Blake and Shah, 'Reproductive Tissue Transplants Defy Legal and Ethical Categorization'.

[127] See R. C. O. Brien. 'The Momentum of Posthumous Conception: A Model Act' (2009) *Journal of Contemporary Health Law & Policy* 332. D. D. Williams, 'Over My Dead Body: The Legal Nightmare and Medical Phenomenon of Posthumous Conception through Postmortem Sperm Retrieval' (2011) *Campbell Law Review* 181.

certain reproductive tissue (embryos and gametes) with the individuals consent.[128] However a uterus does not have genetic potential and thus is more likely to be regarded as akin to other organs in the context of donation.

How would the use of a cadaver donor in uterus transplantation alter the regulation of uterus donation in the UK? As with live donations, the 2004 Act requires explicit consent for cadaver organ donation (with the exception of Wales). If the proposed donor died over the age of 18, removal of the uterus for transplantation will be lawful only if:[129] (1) the deceased herself gave appropriate consent before she died, for instance by carrying a donor card or being registered on the organ donor register,[130] or if she gave no consent, but nor did she veto organ donation; (2) consent is given by the deceased's nominated representative – that is a person expressly nominated by the deceased to make decisions about the use of her body parts before her death,[131] or if the deceased neither made her own decision about donation, nor did she nominate a representative; and, (3) consent is given by a close family member or friend.[132] Removal of a cadaver uterus without appropriate consent will constitute a criminal offence unless there was a reasonable belief that appropriate consent had been given. False representation that such consent has been obtained is also unlawful and both carry the possibility of imprisonment of up to three years upon conviction.[133]

---

[128] The use of gametes for fertility treatment and research is regulated by the Human Fertilisation and Embryology Act 1990 (as amended). One of the HFEA responsibilities as independent regulator in this field is to issue licences to centres to provide fertility treatment. Section 12 of the HFE Act obliges the holder of a licence to provide fertility treatment issued by the HFEA to obtain consent in accordance with schedule 3, which then sets out the detailed requirements for that consent. They can provide services using a person's gametes only where that person consents. Consent means 'effective consent' and so the HFE Act provides that, before treatment, a person must be given 'such relevant information as is proper' and offered counselling. The HFEA issues a standard form (a 'WD form'), which a centre can provide to a person who wants to donate eggs either before or after death or loss of capacity. For cases concerning the posthumous use of a loved one's gametes see in R v. HFEA ex parte Blood [1999] Fam 151. For a recent case, see R (on application of Mr and Mrs M) v. HFEA [2016] EWCA Civ 611.

[129] Human Tissue Act 2004, s3 (6).

[130] An organ donor card will suffice for this purpose.

[131] Human Tissue Act 2004, s4 provides the conditions for any such nomination to be valid.

[132] In this absence of express authorisation by the deceased or a proxy chosen by him, the power to donate organs falls to the family. Section 27 (4) HTA 2004 sets out a hierarchy of relatives: (1) parent or child; (2) siblings; (3) grandparent or grandchild; (4) nephews or nieces; (5) step-parents; (6) half siblings; (7) friend of long standing.

[133] Human Tissue Act 2004, s5.

At present, the 2004 Act is silent on the point of the permissibility of cadaver uterus donations. Given that, upon death, one can donate bodily organs, tissue[134] and gametes,[135] in the absence of justification to the contrary, there is no reason why women should not also be allowed to specify that upon death they also wish to donate their uterus. Would carrying a donor card suffice as consent for removal of a uterus, or should such a procedure necessitate *explicit* consent? Caplin et al. contends that consent to uterus donation should be explicit:

> Few, if any ... women ever thought that the uterus might be one of the organs considered for donation when they signed a donor card. A woman might not prove as willing to donate her uterus as she would be to donate her heart or liver. The transplant team would be on firmer ground if they used a donated uterus from a woman who had explicitly consented to donate that organ prior to death, and who made it very clear that she and her family renounced any and all claims to a relationship with any child that might result.[136]

Similarly, Robertson argued that whilst normal organ and tissue donation forms typically consent to removal of 'all organs and tissues', in signing them, donors or their families may have certain body parts in mind, e.g. internal transplantable solid organs and perhaps skin, bone and other tissue.[137] He claims that most would be shocked to discover that 'donation' also included the uterus (or hands, face, penis, larynx, or other body parts used in non-life-saving transplants). Thus, Robertson was also of the view that 'procuring uteruses or organs or tissue beyond those normally procured in the transplant context should obtain explicit consent from the donor or donor family to procuring those other organs or tissue'.[138]

Since the prospect of uterus transplantation is relatively new, few women who have signed donor cards will have provided explicit consent to donate their uterus. At present, under the current UK 'opt-in' scheme, one can specify which organs one wishes to donate by simply ticking the appropriate boxes on the NHS Organ Donor Register form or on the donor card.[139] The registration form currently allows one to donate all

[134] The Human Tissue Act 2004.
[135] HFE Act 1990 (as amended), schedule 3 stipulates that prior to embarking on IVF couples are asked to sign consent forms and are a clearly asked to specify what is to happen upon incapacitation or death. Donation of gametes is also an option.
[136] A. Caplan, et al., 'Moving the Womb' (2007) 37(3) *Hastings Center Report* 18–20, p. 19.
[137] Robertson, 'Other Women's Wombs' 73.
[138] Ibid.
[139] UK Transplant website (2008) – Become a Donor.

one's organs and tissue, or the alternative option of selecting the organs they wish to donate from the following options: kidneys, heart, liver, corneas, lungs and pancreas.[140] If consent to donate one's uterus should be explicit, once possible it could be added to the list. Whilst England currently has an opt-in scheme for organ donation, in October 2017 the government announced a consultation on changing the law to a system of presumed consent.[141] An 'opt-out' system is currently in force in Wales, following enactment of the Human Transplantation (Wales) Act 2013: consent is deemed (i.e. presumed) as a matter of course in the absence of an explicit refusal (with certain exceptions).[142] Should this replace the current system, explicit consent would be unnecessary and unless a woman communicates that she does not wish to be a uterus donor, this organ can be removed for donation. Under the present opt-in scheme, however, the law imposes no special condition to a uterus transplant, so if women carried a donor card allowing for donation of all organs and tissue this could encompass uterus donation. Once uterus transplantation moves from the clinical research arena to treatment, the HTA should provide clear guidance on whether a woman carrying a donor card would be regarded as having consented to donation of her womb.

Consideration must also be given to what significance will be given to the fact the uterus used for reproduction has come from a donor and, for instance, whether a child gestated in a donated uterus should be allowed to trace the uterus donor. There has been a widening of access to information about one's genetic origins[143] and increasing significance given to genetic relations, which asserts that knowledge of genetic origins is fundamental to donor-conceived children.[144] Following on from this it has been questioned whether gestational links should also be acknowledged, that in response to advances in our knowledge about epigenetics, gestation is possibly not as distinct from genetics as once thought.[145]

---

[140] Ibid.

[141] This means adults who do not wish to donate their organs after their death would have to make their feelings known during their lifetime, i.e. consent would otherwise be presumed. Safeguards would be in place for people who do not wish to donate their organs or whose family would be seriously distressed if donation were to proceed.

[142] T. Hayes, 'Donation and Devolution: The Human Transplantation (Wales) Act 2013' (2015) 59 *International Library of Ethics, Law, and the New Medicine* 141–155.

[143] HFE Act 2008, section 24.

[144] C. Smart, 'Family Secrets: Law and Understandings of Openness in Everyday Relationships' (2009) 38 *Journal of Social Policy* 551.

[145] In *M.R & Anor* v. *An tArd Chlaraitheoir & Ors* [2013] IEHC 91 the question was raised as to what role gestation should take when ascribing motherhood. An expert in that case

Notwithstanding this in the context of surrogacy, once a parental order is granted to the commissioning parents,[146] there is no formal mechanism that acknowledges a child's gestational origins. Thus in a uterus transplant procedure, the donor and her family should be notified that they will have no right to be informed of the identity of the recipient of the uterus, nor of any children born as a result of gestation in the donated uterus.

5.3.1.3   The Recipient

Robertson sets out that 'transplant candidates should be healthy enough to withstand a major surgical procedure, able to produce viable embryos for transfer, and as with all major organ transplants have a supportive spouse, partner, or family'.[147] As noted above, unless using donated embryos, prior to the transplant procedure, they must also be able to undergo IVF, which entails hyper stimulation and egg retrieval, which can then produce several embryos, which will be frozen for transfer after the transplant surgery. In addition to the medical suitability of the recipient, it is clear there must also be adequate legal safeguards in place to protect any potential recipient of a transplanted uterus. Full disclosure of risks and informed consent to the procedure would need to be given.[148] The women willing to undergo a UTx will be women with UFI, seeking the procedure so that they can overcome an inability to gestate. Some have questioned whether infertile patients may have a diminished capacity for voluntary consent because of their desperate desire for children: Caplan et al. argue that 'multiple studies demonstrate the difficulty of achieving informed consent with desperate patients'.[149] However, in the context of assisted reproduction in the UK, it is accepted that a woman can provide informed consent for IVF and other fertility treatment notwithstanding the fact that the woman or couple may have a 'desperate' desire to parent. Just because an individual is passionate to parent or gestate their own child, does not render them incapable of consenting. This is no different to a person with liver failure desperate for a liver transplant and does not preclude any other procedure. It may be that appropriate counselling should be in place and care taken to ensure

outlined the role of epigenetics and the capacity of the gestational environment to influence a child's genetic make-up.
[146] HFE Act 1990 (as amended), section 54.
[147] Robertson, 'Other Women's Wombs' 74.
[148] *Montgomery* v. *Lanarkshire Health Board* [2015] UKSC 11.
[149] Caplan et al., 'Moving the Womb', p. 20.

that any potential uterus recipient is sufficiently informed of the risks inherent in the procedure.

There should also be full disclosure of any material known risks and possible unknown risks.[150] The former may include 'risks associated with anaesthesia, surgery, graft rejection and anti-rejection medication, susceptibility to infection, and increased long-term possibilities of diabetes, hypertension, and neoplasia, as well as the risks of in vitro fertilization, should that be necessary'.[151] The patient should be told whether the organ is likely to be sourced from a dead or living donor and the chances of it being immunologically matched. Furthermore, it has been noted that a transplanted uterus 'may be unable to withstand the forces involved in natural contractions and labour'[152] and to prevent stress on the graft, a caesarean birth will also be required. The only successful trials to date have involved delivery via a caesarean section. Thus the recipient should also be informed of the risks associated with this delivery method. Recipients should also understand that it is not a 'typical' pregnancy. Robertson explained that as the uterus will not be innervated, the woman would not feel the fetus move, nor will she feel contractions even though hormonally mediated effects like morning sickness and fatigue will be present.[153] He warned that the lack of innervation alongside the fact that the uterus gestated another's pregnancies, might exacerbate feelings of mental estrangement to the transplanted organ and interfere with the recipient's ability to accept it as her own.[154]

The recipients should also be informed that the transplant is intended to achieve the short-term result of gestation. After this has occurred, it will be removed so as to reduce the long-term side effects caused by the immunosuppressive drugs, thus involving a second surgical procedure.[155] In the Swedish trial, the patients had been informed that the clinical team recommended the surgical removal of the uterus before a

---

[150] *Montgomery v. Lanarkshire Health Board* [2015] UKSC 11 provides that doctors are now obliged to take 'reasonable care to ensure that the patient is aware of any material risks involved in any recommended treatment, and of any reasonable alternative or variant treatments'. For a discussion of law on informed consent in the UK see R. Heywood, 'R. I. P. Sidaway: Patient Orientated Disclosure – A Standard Worth Waiting For? Montgomery v. Lanarkshire Health Board [2015] UKSC 11' (2015) 23(3) *Medical Law Review* 455–466.

[151] Altchek, 'Uterus Transplantation', p. 157.

[152] A. Richards, 'Transsexual Women (for Male-to-Female Transsexuals)' Second Type Woman, http://transwoman.tripod.com/pregnant.htm.

[153] Robertson, 'Other Women's Wombs' 74.

[154] Ibid.

[155] Brännström, Johannesson, Bokstrom et al., 'Livebirth after Uterus Transplantation'.

second pregnancy attempt in the case of any major side effects of immunosuppression. Brännström stated 'the autonomy of the patients should be respected and any future decision to surgically remove the uterus needs to be made in consensus with the recipient and her partner'.[156]

5.3.1.4   Funding of UTx

[I]t is an unhappy but unavoidable feature of state funded healthcare that . . . [clinical commissioning groups] . . . have to establish certain priorities in funding different treatments from their finite resources. It is natural that each authority, in establishing its own priorities, will give greater priority to life threatening and other grave illnesses than to others obviously less demanding of medical attention.[157]

Perhaps one of the most obvious challenges surrounding uterus transplantation, as with other assisted reproductive technologies, will be the cost of the procedure and how it may exacerbate the global inequitable distribution of access to healthcare/fertility treatment. In the UK the majority of fertility services (some 60 per cent) are provided by the private sector, with the NHS providing the remaining 40 per cent. The National Institute for Health Care and Excellence (NICE) provides best practice guidance and recommends in the context of access to IVF, state provision of three cycles of IVF in women aged under 40 years who have not conceived after two years of regular unprotected intercourse or 12 cycles of artificial insemination. However NHS funding comes through Clinical Commissioning Groups (CCGs) and despite the NICE guidelines, provision is dependent on local NHS CCGs policies that make the final decision about who can have NHS-funded IVF in their local area.[158] CCGs may impose stricter criteria than those recommended by NICE as a prerequisite to being eligible for IVF funding: such as, the recipient must not have children already from both their current and any previous relationships, that they are a healthy weight, a non-smoker and further age restrictions may be imposed (for example, some CCGs only fund treatment for women under 35). In 2017, Fertility Network UK figures

---

[156] Ibid.

[157] Per Auld LJ in R v. *North West Lancashire Health Authority ex p A, D, G* [2000] 1 WLR 977.

[158] The Health and Social Care Act 2012 introduced major structural changes to commissioning and procurement of NHS services. Previous Primary Care Trusts responsible for commissioning ere dissolved and their functions devolved to GP commissioning groups called Clinical Commissioning Groups.

revealed many areas have stopped offering three cycles of IVF to couples trying to conceive, against those government guidelines.[159] The data revealed that 13 areas of England have restricted or completely halted IVF treatment since the start of 2017, with a further eight consulting on taking similar steps. The figures also revealed that the number of clinical commissioning groups (CCGs) in England offering three full cycles of IVF has fallen by 46 per cent, from 50 in 2013[160] to 27 in 2017. The cutbacks have been taken in a bid to save money and have resulted in a postcode lottery, with variance on provision based on geographical location. Unsurprisingly, many individuals/couples seeking fertility treatment resort to private fertility centres; with a reported six out of every 10 IVF cycles funded privately in 2014.[161] The cost of private treatment can vary, but each cycle typically costs between £6,000 and £10,000, with top London clinics charging £15,000 or more.[162] The lack of public funding of fertility treatment has attracted criticism; Susan Seenan, the chief executive of Fertility Network UK, argues infertility can have a serious and lasting impact and denying people help is 'a short-sighted and false economy'.[163]

Consequently, it is fair to assert that in the UK the patchy funding, which varies between different regions, has resulted in the preferential availability of such treatment to individuals/couples in a position of financial strength.[164] Whilst the cost of a uterus transplantation procedure will vary among countries, in the UK it is estimated the procedure will cost in excess of £50,000 per operation.[165] Given the substantial cost of the procedure, some commentators have tackled the thorny question of whether, in countries with a publicly funded system, such as the UK, a case can be made for the

[159] S. Marsh, 'IVF Cut Back in 13 Areas of England to Save Money, New Data Shows', *The Guardian*, 6 August 2017.

[160] K. McVeigh, 'NHS Denying Women Fertility Treatment to Save Money, Watchdog Warns', *The Guardian*, 23 October 2014.

[161] D. Ferguson, 'IVF and the NHS: The Parents Navigating Fertility's Postcode Lottery' *The Guardian*, 10 May 2014.

[162] Ibid.

[163] Marsh, 'IVF Cut Back in 13 Areas of England to Save Money'.

[164] T. Jain and M. D. Hornstein, 'Disparities in Access to Infertility Services in a State with Mandated Insurance Coverage' (2005) 84(1) *Fertility and Sterility* 221–223. See also P. R. Brezina and Y. Zhao, 'The Ethical, Legal, and Social Issues Impacted by Modern Assisted Reproductive Technologies' (2012) *Obstetrics and Gynecology International* 1–7.

[165] See http://wombtransplantuk.org/everything-you-need-to-know-about-uterine-transplantation.

public funding of UTx.[166] Some claim that, given how costly the procedure will be, the state and society should not bear the costs, given the alternative available of surrogacy.[167] Such claims which posit surrogacy as a viable alternative to justify claims against state funding are tenuous, since surrogacy does not give a woman the ability to experience gestation of her own child and for some women, surrogacy may be undesirable for religious, cultural or personal reasons.[168]

If it is accepted that there is, or should be, a public commitment to treating infertility, it could it be argued that, just as IVF assists couples having difficulty in *conceiving*, uterine transplantation once safe, will assist women having difficulty *gestating* and thus should also be funded on the NHS. Uterus transplantation could similarly be made available for women suffering from uterus factor infertility, just as other forms of medical treatment to treat infertility are made available. The Warnock Committee had stated:

> There are many other treatments not designed to satisfy absolute needs (in the sense the patient would die without them) which are readily available on the NHS. Medicine is no longer exclusively concerned with the preservation of life but with remedying the malfunctions of the human body. On this analysis, an inability to have children is a malfunction and should be considered in exactly the same way as any other ... In summary, we conclude that infertility is a condition meriting treatment.[169]

These arguments may apply equally to uterus transplantation, which will help to create life and treat uterus factor infertility. However, IVF costs approximately £6000 per cycle, whereas uterus transplantation will cost almost ten times that, at an estimated £50,000 per procedure. This may evoke strong sentiments and objections as to why public taxpayers should be burdened with funding such treatments,[170] especially in an era of austerity and a time where the NHS is in crisis.[171] But there ought to be some consistency/rationale behind which treatments will be funded and which will not. It is conceded that the NHS, as a publicly funded

---

[166] S. Wilkinson and N. J. Williams, 'Should Uterus Transplants Be Publicly Funded?' (2016) 42(9) *Journal of Medical Ethics* 559–565.

[167] Ibid.

[168] Robertson, 'Other Women's Wombs' 70.

[169] Report of the Committee of Inquiry into Human Fertilisation and Embryology, 1984, Cm 9314 ('The Warnock Report') paragraph 2.4.

[170] See Wilkinson and Williams, 'Should Uterus Transplants Be Publicly Funded?'

[171] M. Kamal, 'This Crisis Is the Worst in NHS History – Our Health Service Is at Risk of Irreparable Damage', *Huffington Post UK*, 12 January 2017.

health system, has a limited budget and therefore some form of rationing policy must operate. NICE provides one way in which treatments can be rationed is by examining the increase in health likely to accrue as a result of introducing a new treatment – the so-called incremental cost effectiveness ratio. This is measured by the cost per quality adjusted life year (QALY).[172] Thus, whether a uterus transplant will be offered on the NHS could depend on the QALY assessment. Arguments have been made that uterus transplantation should not be publicly funded as it is not needed to preserve life. However such objections can be rejected by reference to the fact that numerous treatments are allowed on the NHS that are not life-saving. Consider kidney transplantation, which will significantly improve a patient's quality of life, and yet dialysis is a life-preserving alternative. Cornea transplants to restore the sight of people with clouded vision, and orthodontic treatment such as braces to help align teeth, are but two examples of well-accepted therapies performed only to improve a patient's quality of life, not to preserve it.

However we cannot get away from the fact that the political scenery and state of the NHS is quite different in 2018 to how it was when Warnock deliberated in the late 1970s. A government recession followed by a programme of unprecedented cuts has seen the NHS wilfully starved of funds, and as Kamal notes 'the NHS is now in the worst crisis in its history and is rapidly approaching breaking point'.[173] Whether the NHS can continue to fund some fertility treatment such as IVF in the coming years is unclear. Whether it could sustain the cost of even more expensive fertility treatment such as uterus transplantation is even more uncertain. It may well be the case that, as with the majority of IVF provision, this will fall to the private sector and may further exacerbate health/social inequality, in that it may well be that this advance will only be available to those individuals/couples in a position of economic strength who can afford to fund such treatment privately.

5.3.1.5   The Potential Child

The purpose of a uterus transplantation is the creation of a child and thus it is important that due attention is given to this 'vital stakeholder'[174] in

---

[172] S. Whitehead and S. Ali, 'Health Outcomes in Economic Evaluation: The QALY and Utilities' (2010) 96(1) *British Medical Bulletin* 5–21.

[173] Kamal, 'This Crisis Is the Worst in NHS History'.

[174] J. Daar and S. Klipstein, 'Refocusing the Ethical Choices in Womb Transplant, Peer Commentary Reviewing John A. Robertson, Other Women's Wombs: Uterus Transplant and Gestational Surrogacy' (2016) 3 *Journal of Law & Biosciences* 383–388.

any regulation governing this advance. As research teams around the world race to emulate the success of the Swedish team, the European Society of Human Reproduction and Embryology have stated that fertility doctors 'have a double responsibility: to the patient and the child'.[175] The importance of children's rights is well documented in both national[176] and international legislation.[177] Daar and Klipstein argue that it is important to focus on the developing fetus into the first transplanted uteri, analysing the importance of fetal health under two rubrics: firstly, they note that the medical literature suggests that gestating a fetus in a transplanted uterus poses several risks to the developing child, and secondly, they interpret the fetal risks posed by uterine transplantation under the principle of procreative beneficence, which entreats parents to select reproductive options that maximise the well-being of their future children.[178] Since there is a greater risk of fetal or offspring harm with uterus transplant, they argue that the ethical duty of procreative beneficence imposes a duty on prospective parents to choose gestational surrogacy over uterus transplant.[179]

Whilst Daar and Klipstein are right to note the importance of the fetus in this reproductive scenario and the vascular and immunosuppression effects of transplant on the resulting child and mother, I am not convinced that risk to the fetus or resulting children is high enough to persuade me that uterus transplant is wrong, or surrogacy is preferable. Firstly, in the successful human uterus transplant research trials, all children have been born healthy (albeit with some prematurity and low births) and there have been no known malformations or disabilities. This must be

---

[175] ESHRE Task Force of Ethics and Law 13: The Welfare of the Child in Medically Assisted Reproduction (2007) 22 (10) *Human Reproduction* 2585–2588.

[176] See section 1 of the Children's Act 1989, which renders the child's welfare a 'paramount consideration', and the Adoption and Children's Act 2002 (ACA 2002), which looks at children's rights 'throughout the child's lifetime'.

[177] Children's rights are set out in the European Convention on Human Rights (ECHR) incorporated in to domestic legislation via The Human Rights Act 1998, and the United Nations Convention on the Rights of the Child (UNCRC). Whilst the UNCRC is not directly incorporated into domestic law and not directly justiciable in UK courts, the principles of the UNCRC guide domestic law and practice. In December 2010, the UK government gave a commitment that due consideration would be given to the UNCRC in the making of new policy and legislation – see Joint Committee on Human Rights, 'The UK's compliance with the UN Convention on the Rights of the Child Eighth Report of Session 2014–15'. For an excellent article suggesting the two treaties be used together to maximise children's rights see U. Kilkelly, 'The Best of Both Worlds for Children's Rights? Interpreting the European Convention on Human Rights in the Light of the UN Convention on the Rights of the Child' (2001) 23(2) *Human Rights Quarterly* 308–326.

[178] Daar & Klipstein, 'Refocusing the Ethical Choices in Womb Transplant' 384.

[179] Ibid., 388.

monitored and an international registry to follow donors, recipients and children has been formed as part of the International Society of Uterus Transplantation (ISUTx). Data from that registry is important to monitor the safety of the procedure, concerning long-term effects of the participants and children born after the uterus transplant procedure.[180] They mention two kinds of risk: vascular complications and teratogenic effects of immunosuppressive drugs. As Robertson noted in his response to Daar and Klipsteins paper; doctors and ethics committees at institutions considering uterus transplant will have no doubt evaluated such risks, as well as risks to the health and life of the mother (and living donor if one is used); furthermore they would have also been extensively counselled, and not have been accepted as patients unless they fully understood the risks and uncertainties, had a social support system in place, and physicians are satisfied that the risks of transplant, while real, are ethically acceptable.[181]

Secondly, Daar and Klipstein also assume that surrogacy is readily available as an alternative to uterus transplant, which is not the case. In 2013, a report (commissioned by the European Parliament) on surrogacy across the EU Member States noted that eight out of the 28 Member States have a total ban on surrogacy (including France, Spain, Germany, Italy, Malta, Bulgaria and Portugal[182]) and eight more ban commercial surrogacy (amongst them the UK).[183] In countries such as India[184] and American states such as California,[185] where it is permissible, it may go against one's ethical or religious beliefs.[186] In the UK, the law regulating surrogacy has rightly been described as a 'mess', the ban on commercial surrogacy means there is a shortage of surrogates and even where it is available, it is shrouded in legal uncertainty since it is not legal enforceable and the surrogate can renege at any time.[187] Thus as observed by

---

[180] Brännström, 'Uterus Transplantation and Beyond'.

[181] J. Robertson, 'Impact of Uterus Transplant on Fetuses and Resulting Children: A Response to Daar and Klipstein' (2016) 3(3) *Journal of Law and the Biosciences* 710–717.

[182] Austria prohibits egg donation; gestational surrogacy is thus prohibited.

[183] See Comparative Study on the Regime of Surrogacy in the EU Member States, www.lse.ac.uk/businessAndConsultancy/LSEConsulting/pdf/Comparative-Study-Surrogacy.pdf.

[184] S. Amin and A. Rehman, 'Surrogacy in India and Its Legal and Ethical Implications' (2014) 2(4) *Journal of International Academic Research for Multidisciplinary* 41.

[185] K. M. Perkins et al., 'Trends and Outcomes of Gestational Surrogacy in the United States' (2016) 105 *Fertility & Sterility* 435–442.

[186] For instance, for people of the Islamic faith surrogacy is not permissible – see A. Alghrani, 'Womb Transplantation and the Interplay of Islam and the West' (2013) 48 (3) *Zygon: Journal of Religion and Science* 618–634.

[187] See Alghrani and Griffiths, 'The Regulation of Surrogacy in the United Kingdom: The Case for Reform'.

Robertson, 'a woman might reasonably choose uterus transplant over surrogacy to avoid the ethical and social complications of hiring a surrogate to do her own gestational work'.[188] He further notes that, even if there are some higher risks to mother and child from transplant, no child will be harmed by that choice, nor have family ideals been violated if a woman chooses to internalise physical and lifestyle burdens rather than transfer them to another woman for money.[189]

Thirdly, whilst the notion that parents should select reproductive options that maximise the well-being of their children is intuitively appealing, this conundrum suffers from Parfit's famous 'Non-Identity problem'[190]: as Parfit explains, 'where a child could not have existed otherwise than in his sub-optimal state ... he has not been harmed by being born in his damaged state'.[191] This approach implies that provided a child would have a worth-while life, an impaired child is not harmed by being brought into existence in their impaired state because that is the only condition they could have existed in.[192] Thus children can be harmed by a uterus transplant if they would not otherwise have been born without that transplant? If the child born via uterus transplant would not otherwise exist, it cannot be said to be better off.

Notwithstanding the above objections to Daar and Klipstein's argument that surrogacy is a preferable alternative to uterus transplantation, they are right to remind us of the importance of the effects of transplantation on the resulting child and mother and that these effects should not be slighted by ethics committees, physicians or commentators. Thus attention is now given to how fetal interests can be central to any regulation for uterus transplantation in the UK. As the only successful research trials have used IVF embryos after transplantation to achieve conception, prior to gaining any access to licensed fertility treatment services there will also be the pre-conception welfare assessment of any future children as mandated under the Human Fertilisation and Embryology Act 1990 (as amended in 2008).[193] Despite the extensive

---

[188] Robertson, 'Impact of Uterus Transplant on Foetuses' 716.

[189] Ibid.

[190] D. Parfit, *Reasons and Persons* (Oxford: Oxford University Press, 1984). See also C. Gavaghan, 'Regulating after Parfit: Welfare, Identity and the UK Embryology Law' in M. Goodwin, B. J. Koops and R. Leenes (eds.), *Dimensions of Technology Regulation* (Oisterwijk: Wolf Legal Publishers, 2010).

[191] D. Davis, *Genetic Dilemmas: Reproductive Technology, Parental Choices and Children's Futures* (Oxford University Press: Oxford, 2010) p. 35.

[192] Parfit, *Reasons and Persons* 359.

[193] Section 13(5). See also The Human Fertilisation and Embryology Authority: Code of Practice, Eighth Edition, 2017).

scholarly criticism that this mandate that clinicians consider the future child's welfare has attracted[194] and notwithstanding debate as to what constitutes 'harm',[195] this remains a legal requirement prior to fertility treatment being offered. Leaving well-rehearsed moral objections surrounding the pre-conception welfare principle to one side, there is no escaping the fact that research trials in their early stages may present unknown risks and harms to the fetus. If research into early uterus transplant trials shows a high rate of mid- or late-term miscarriage or severe prematurity, that will be an important part of the pre-transplant counselling and informed consent process. If the first UTx trials in the UK resulted in fetal harm, it is important to consider what legal liability may arise for fetal injury under domestic legislation.

Consider the following hypothetical scenario:

> Leona has MKRH, which means she has a congenital absence of the uterus. Her ovaries and fallopian tubes, however, are present, with normal function and ovulation. Leona and her husband undergo IVF prior to uterus transplant surgery. For 12 months the uterus functions well and she has menstrual periods. The IVF embryos are later successfully implanted. During the pregnancy problems develop. At 20 weeks' gestation the doctors treating Leona inform her that her body has begun to reject the uterus and recommend its removal. Continuance of the pregnancy is a threat to her life and that of the fetus.

Presuming Leona is competent and has the necessary capacity,[196] she has a right to refuse the recommended treatment even if this will result in her

---

[194] S. Sheldon, E. Lee and J. Macvarish, "'Supportive Parenting", Responsibility and Regulation: The Welfare Assessment under the Reformed Human Fertilisation and Embryology Act (1990)' (2015) 78(3) *Modern Law Review* 461–492. E. Lee, J. Macvarish and S. Sheldon, 'Assessing Child Welfare under the Human Fertilisation and Embryology Act 2008: A Case Study in Medicalization?' (2014) 26(4) *Sociology of Health and Illness* 500–515. E. Jackson, 'Conception and the Irrelevance of the Welfare Principle' (2002) 65 *Modern Law Review* 176; G. Pennings, 'The Welfare of the Child' (1999) 14 *Human Reproduction* 1146; S. Millns, 'Making "Social Judgements that Go Beyond the Purely Medical": The Reproductive Revolution and Access to Fertility Treatment Services' in J. Bridgeman and S. Millns (eds.), *Law and Body Politics: Regulating the Female Body* (Aldershot: Dartmouth, 1995) 79.

[195] Parfit, Reasons and Persons. J. Harris, *The Value of Life: An Introduction to Medical Ethics* (London: Routledge & Kegan Paul, 1985) 146–149. J. Savulescu, 'Procreative Beneficence: Why We Should Select the Best Children' (2001) 15 *Bioethics* 413–426. R. Bennett, 'When Intuition Is Not Enough. When the Principle of Procreative Beneficence Must Work Much Harder to Justify Its Eugenic Vision' (2014) 28(9) *Bioethics* 447–455.

[196] Mental Capacity Act 2005, s1(2) states that 'a person must be assumed to have capacity unless it is established that he lacks capacity'. Section 1(4) provides that 'a person is not to be treated as unable to make a decision merely because he makes an unwise decision'.

death, or result in her child suffering severe abnormalities. Following a series of cases involving pregnant women[197] the law is now clear that providing a woman is competent, she can decline any treatment which may save the life of herself or her fetus. Since a fetus has no actionable legal interests until birth,[198] the mother's wishes must prevail. To act otherwise would be an affront to her bodily autonomy and give rise to legal action.[199] As Butler Sloss LJ stated:

> A competent woman who has the capacity to decide may, for religious reasons, other reasons, for rational or irrational reasons or for no reason at all, choose not to have medical intervention, even though the consequence may be the death or serious handicap of the child she bears, or her own death. In that event the courts do not have the jurisdiction to declare medical treatment lawful and the question of her own best interests objectively considered, does not arise.[200]

Would there be any liability for harm caused to the fetus if s/he was born with severe abnormalities that occurred because the uterus failed to function as it should? In England, a failed transplant does not of itself give rise to any legal claim by the recipient. However the Congenital Disabilities (Civil Liability) Act 1976 provides a cause of action to a child born disabled as a result of the negligence[201] of another prior to his/her

---

Section 2(1) stipulates 'For the purposes of this Act, a person lacks capacity in relation to a matter if at the material time he is unable to make a decision for himself in relation to the matter because of an impairment of, or a disturbance in the functioning of, the mind or brain.' According to s3, a person is unable to make a decision for himself if he is unable: (a) to understand the information relevant to the decision, (b) to retain that information, (c) to use or weigh that information as part of the process of making the decision, or (d) to communicate his decision (whether by talking, using sign language or any other means).

[197] S v. McC, W v. W [1972] AC 24; Re T (Adult: Refusal of Medical Treatment) [1992] 4 All ER 649, CA; Re MB (An Adult: Medical Treatment) [1997] 2 FCR 541; St George's Healthcare NHS Trust v. S [1999] Fam 26, CA.

[198] Paton v. British Pregnancy Advisory Service [1979] 1 QB 276, C v. S [1988] 1 QB 135.

[199] Any non-consensual touching is a battery under English law – it does not have to harm the patient. A doctor can commit a battery even though the doctor considers he is acting in the best interests of his patient by treating him/her. In Devi v. West Midlands RHA [1980] C.L.Y. 687 a woman underwent a hysterectomy to which she did not consent (she had given consent to repair her uterus). The Court found the surgeon liable in battery as there was total lack of consent to the nature of the operation.

[200] Re MB (An Adult: Medical Treatment) [1997] 2 FCR 54, per Butler Sloss LJ.

[201] In order to show negligence it must be shown that the doctor breached the duty of care owed to the patient: 'A doctor is not guilty of negligence if he has acted in accordance with a practice accepted as proper by a reasonable body of medical men skilled in that particular art.' Bolam v. Friern Hospital Management Committee [1957] 2 All ER 118.

birth. An action only arises if the healthcare professional/team would have been liable to one or both parents in respect of the events causing disability. Let us for a moment suppose that the healthcare team responsible for the uterus transplant was aware that the uterus was not functioning effectively and antenatal screening revealed that a number of fetal abnormalities were present, but the transplant team delayed notifying the recipient patient because they wanted to see how long the uterus could function and sustain fetal life. In such circumstances an action may be brought under the Congenital Disabilities (Civil Liability) Act 1976, section one of which provides:

> (1) If a child is born disabled as the result of such an occurrence before its birth as is mentioned in subsection (2) below, and a person (other than the child's own mother) is under this section answerable to the child in respect of the occurrence, the child's disabilities are to be regarded as damage resulting from the wrongful act of that person and actionable accordingly at the suit of the child.

If, however, the mother was informed that the uterus transplant could result in fetal abnormality and that this risk had materialised, but she nonetheless decided to continue with the pregnancy, this will absolve the healthcare team of liability and the mother would be regarded as being *volenti* to the risk under section 1(4) of the 1976 Act.[202] The child will also have no action against his/her mother for subjecting him to such risk, since under the 1976 Act the mother is granted immunity from suit.

If the scenario were altered slightly, so that the transplant was successful and there were no complications, the fetus was safely gestating and all appeared well, but the mother decided she was no longer ready for motherhood and wished to terminate the pregnancy, would this be permissible given the vast cost of UTx? Whether a woman has conceived through sexual intercourse, artificial reproductive technologies or with the use of a transplanted uterus, she is entitled to the same legal rights as any other woman. Providing she falls within the scope of the Abortion Act 1967 (as amended by the Human Fertilisation and Embryology Act 1990) she could seek an abortion within the specified time limits. This is the case even if she has been selected from many women to have a uterus

---

[202] Congenital Disabilities (Civil Liability) Act 1976, s1(4) provides that in the case of an occurrence preceding the time of conception, the defendant is not answerable to the child if at that time either or both of the parents knew the risk of their child being born disabled (that is to say, the particular risk created by the occurrence); but should it be the child's father who is the defendant, this subsection does not apply if he knew of the risk and the mother did not.

transplanted and notwithstanding the fact that the fetus is developing healthily and the transplanted uterus is functioning perfectly. Under the aforementioned legislation, an abortion can be carried out by a registered medical practitioner if two medical practitioners are of the opinion formed in good faith, that the continuation of the pregnancy would involve greater risk than if the pregnancy were terminated; the risk in question is to the physical or mental health of the pregnant woman or any existing children of her family, and the pregnancy must not have exceeded its twenty fourth week;[203] or after the 24th week if there is a grave risk to the life or health of the pregnant woman;[204] or a substantial risk that the child may suffer from some physical or mental abnormalities as to be seriously handicapped.[205]

5.3.1.6   Dual Regulation: Square Pegs into Round Holes?

Given that in this reproductive scenario a woman will also require fertility assistance in addition to a donated uterus, she will be subject to the dual regulatory frameworks of both the HTA 2004 and the HFE Act 1990 (as amended in 2008). The problem of dual regulation may give rise to anomalies – for instance, could a woman be denied a UTx after she has undergone the physical, emotional and financial expenditure of IVF without which she has no chance of gestating? How can such regulatory anomalies be avoided? The problem of dual regulation could have been resolved by the creation of a body such as the Regulatory Authority for Tissue and Embryos (RATE),[206] which would oversee both assisted reproduction and transplantation. This proposal was suggested in the debates leading up to the HFE Act 2008, but were met with much hostility and therefore abandoned. Yet uterus transplantation illustrates how the marriage of the two statutory authorities could have worked well in this context: a woman or couple seeking uterus transplant could have applied to RATE for both the uterus transplant and IVF, since both would have fallen under its remit. There appears little point in a woman with UFI

---

[203] Abortion Act 1961 (as amended by the Human Fertilisation and Embryology Act 1990) s1(1)(a) .

[204] Ibid., s1(1)(b) and 1(1)(c).

[205] Ibid., s1(1)(d).

[206] Amidst calls to update the legislation, there were initially proposals to abolish the HFEA and instead merge its functions with that of the Human Tissue Authority (HTA) and some functions of the Medicines and Healthcare Products Regulatory Agency (MHRA) to create a new statutory body; the Regulatory Authority for Tissue and Embryos (RATE). See also the Draft Human Tissue and Embryo Bill (Cm 7087) and the House of Lords and House of Commons Joint Committee on the Human Tissue and Embryos (Draft) Bill, Session 2006–07, HL Paper 169-I and HC Paper 630-I, paragraph 73.

undergoing IVF only to later be refused a uterus transplant (not to mention a waste of expense and resources). One way in which guidance could resolve this would be to recommend that uterus transplantation be performed only in those women who have a reasonable prospect of gestating in the donated uterus. It is clear that should UTx move into the clinical treatment arena some form of guidance/regulation would be needed to govern uterus transplantation. The best guidance would be from the statutory authorities set up by Parliament to oversee regulation of assisted reproduction and transplantation – the HFEA and HTA. If such guidance was not forthcoming, then guidance could be issued from the Royal College of Obstetricians and Gynaecologists, British Transplantation Society, Royal College of Surgeons or other specialist professional bodies. As this section has demonstrated, the regulatory challenges that uterus transplantation will raise are many and varied. If this procedure is to be appropriately regulated, and absent specific legislation drawn up by Parliament to govern this advance, guidance must be issued.

Regulating ARTs is no easy feat and UTx may be yet another example of where the law remains at the rear of science, marching but limping a little. The law governing ARTs in the UK has mostly been reactionary. Despite the significant strides made in making human uterus transplantation scientifically possible, the government and statutory authorities that regulate transplantation and ARTs (the HTA and HFEA) have remained silent on the advance. This is not because they have been caught 'off-guard' by UTx. Animal research into UTx has been underway since the 1950s[207] and human clinical trials in UTx were already underway in Saudi Arabia in 2000. In light of this, it is interesting to note how absent the topic was in the debates to update the 1990 legislation. In the 2007–8 Report, the HFEA's Horizon Scanning Panel noted that the 'primate uterus can be perfused, preserved and circulated with blood post transplantation. Other large animal pregnancies following uterus transplantation have been achieved'.[208] Yet the Panel accorded it 'low priority' and since the birth of the first live birth following an UTx in

---

[207] Eraslan, Hamernik and Hardy, 'Replantation of Uterus and Ovaries in Dogs with Successful Pregnancy'; Confino et al., 'Nonvascular Transplantation of the Rabbit Uterus'; Yonemoto et al. 'Homotransplantation of Uterus and Ovaries in Dogs'; O'Leary, Feldman and Gaensslen, 'Uterine and Tubal Transplantation'; Mattingly et al., 'Ovarian Function In-Utero Ovarian Homotransplantations'; Scott, Pitkin and Yannone, 'Transplantation of the Primate Uterus'.

[208] HFEA, Scientific Horizon Scanning at the HFEA, Annual Report 2007/08 p. 18.

Sweden, both the HTA and HFEA have remained quiet on the topic. Legislation that was drafted when UTx was not within legislators' contemplation has thus had to be considered to see how, if at all, its provisions could be stretched to govern/accommodate the challenges that UTx will give rise to.

5.4 Conclusion

In 2007, the UK government acknowledged, 'time, particularly in this field does not stand still'.[209] The former chair of the HFEA, Suzi Leather was overly optimistic in 2008 in stating following the 2008 revisions that 'Parliament has provided a clear framework for the future and a solid base on which to regulate 21st century practice within 21st century law'.[210] A mere decade later, weaknesses in the current dual regulatory frameworks that would govern a novel procedure, such as uterine transplantation, which is both a reproductive and transplant procedure are illustrated in this chapter. This stems partly from the fact that the regulatory framework remains one that was created in response to ethical and legal issues that IVF and embryo research generated and what Wellin labelled the second era of human reproduction.[211] After much debate and activity[212] the amendments introduced by the HFE Act 2008 did not significantly alter the regulatory framework and in essence it was an amending statute, the regulatory structure from the 1990 statute remains and is one that is not appropriate for the regulation of uterine

---

[209] See Human Tissue and Embryos (Draft) Bill, (Cm 7087) foreword by Caroline Flint, Minister of State for Public Health, May 2007.

[210] Human Fertilisation and Embryology Authority, Press Release, 'HFEA Chair Welcomes Royal Assent for HFE Act' 13 November 2008.

[211] S. Wellin, 'Reproductive Ectogenesis: The Third Era of Human Reproduction and Some Moral Consequences' (2004) 10 *Science and Engineering Ethics* 615–626, at p. 617.

[212] The government announced a review of the HFE Act 1990 in January 2004 citing developments in reproductive medicine since the enactment of the 1990 legislation, and conducted a public consultation in 2005. In December 2006 the government published the policy proposals in the White Paper: *Review of the Human Fertilisation and Embryology Act: Proposals for Revised Legislation (including establishment of the Regulatory Authority for Tissue and Embryos)* (Cm 6989). The Human Tissue and Embryos (Draft) Bill (Cm 7087) followed in May 2007. This was scrutinised by the Joint Committee of both Houses; see the House of Lords and the House of Commons, *Joint Committee on the Human Tissue and Embryos (Draft) Bill*, July 2007 (HL Paper 169-I, HC Paper 630-I). Policy proposals from the White Paper and pre-legislative scrutiny were then incorporated into the Human Fertilisation and Embryology Bill, which was introduced into Parliament on 8 November 2007.

transplantation. As this chapter demonstrates, this new era of human reproduction has moved away from issues surrounding fertilisation of an embryo in vitro and uterine transplantation ushers in a different set of regulatory and legal and issues to those that arose from IVF. In theory the dual regulatory frameworks found in the HFE Act 1990 (as amended) and HTA 2004 can be stretched to accommodate this advance and govern uterus transplantation in cis-gendered women; however, careful attention must be given to ensure that the frameworks can work together on such procedures when they move from the clinical research phase to that of treatment. Functionality of the dual framework becomes slightly more complex when uterus transplantation is considered beyond its immediate purpose of restoring fertility in cis-gendered women and in the context of transgender women and cis-gendered men.

6

Uterus Transplantation beyond Cisgender Women

'O Brave New World, That Hath Such People In It'[1]

Gender binaries entrenched in biological sex have long influenced how the UK government confers legal parenthood:

> The distinction between male and female exists throughout the animal world. It corresponds to the different roles played in the reproductive process. A male produces sperm which fertilise the female's eggs. In this country, as elsewhere, classification of a person as male or female has long conferred a legal status. It confers a legal status, in that legal as well as practical consequences follow from the recognition of a person as male or female. The legal consequences affect many areas of life, from marriage and family law to gender-specific crime and competitive sport. It is not surprising, therefore, that society through its laws decides what objective biological criteria should be applied when categorising a person as male or female.[2]

Whilst 'gender' is now understood as different to 'sex', by reference to a difference between the body, biology and being male or female ('sex') and social and cultural roles inscribed on bodies; masculinity and femininity ('gender'),[3] this opening statement made by Lord Nicholson in *Bellinger* v. *Bellinger*[4] reflected the legal conception that one's gender was synonymous with sex and fixed at birth.[5] This binary understanding offered

---

[1] W. Shakespeare, *The Tempest*, Act 5, Scene 1

[2] Lord Nicholson in *Bellinger* v. *Bellinger* [2003] All ER (D) 178 AC, Paragraph 28. In this case the English courts refused to permit a declaration that a two-year marriage celebrated between a man and a trans woman (who had undergone irreversible gender reassignment surgery) was valid and subsisting. For a commentary on the case, see S. Cowan, '"That Woman Is a Woman!": The Case of Bellinger v. Bellinger and the Mysterious (Dis) appearance of Sex: Bellinger v. Bellinger [2003] 2 All E.R. 593; [2003] F.C.R. 1; [2003] 2 W.L.R. 1174; [2003] UKHL 21' (2004) 12(1) *Feminist Legal Studies* 79–92.

[3] Much debate has ensued in feminist theory about the usefulness of the distinction between sex and gender. For more on this see T. Laquer, *Making Sex: Body and Gender from the Greeks to Freud* (Cambridge MA: Harvard University Press, 1990). J. Butler, *Bodies That Matter: On the Discursive Limits of 'Sex'* (New York, NY and London: Routledge, 1993).

[4] Ibid.

[5] See *Corbett* v. *Corbett* [1970] 2 All E.R. 33 in which the judge, Mr Justice Ormrod, stated that if chromosomes, gonads and genitals are congruent – that is, if they all line up to being

only two possible classifications: male and female.[6] These two sexes/ genders are conceived as ontologically opposite; therefore belonging to one of the sexes/genders, implies being excluded from the other.[7] Artificial reproductive technologies blur this heterosexual binary and the different roles each sex/gender plays in the reproductive process. This may be further confused by the advent of uterus transplant technology, which raises the speculative prospect that that new advance can be used to also transplant a uterus into trans women[8] to realign reproductive capacity. Once a fetus can be gestated in a trans woman, by default, science will be one step closer to having the knowledge of how to achieve pregnancy in *cis-gendered* men.[9] Regulatory difficulties emerge from the new reproductive advance which challenges heterosexual binary identities and legal parental labels entrenched in such distinctions, that conceive of only two possible classifications: father as man who provides the sperm and mother as woman that gestates.

male at birth, the individuals is to be regarded as a male, even after sex reassignment. For more on the sex/gender distinction see J. Butler, *Gender Trouble: Feminism and the Subversion of Identity* (New York, NY: Routledge, 1990); C. Smart, 'Law's Power, The Sexed Body and Feminist Discourse' (1990) *Journal of Law & Society* 194.

[6] For an article that focuses on existing challenges to this binary understanding of legally sexed/gendered bodies, see D. A. Gonzalez-Salzberg, 'The Accepted Transsexual and the Absent Transgender: A Queer Reading of the Regulation of Sex/ Gender by the European Court of Human Rights' (2014) 29(4) *American University International Law Review* 797–829.

[7] Gonzalez-Salzberg, 'The Accepted Transsexual and the Absent Transgender', at p. 799.

[8] See D. Fine Maron, 'How a Transgender Woman Could Get Pregnant', *Scientific American*, 15 June 2016. L. Samuel, 'With Uterus Transplants a Reality, Transgender Women Dare to Dream of Pregnancies' STAT Reporting from the frontiers of health and medicine, 7 March 2016. Uterus transplantation into trans women has been explored in the following papers: A. Alghrani, 'Assisted Reproductive Technologies and Family formation: Womb Transplant Technology and the Allocation of Family Responsibilities' in C. Lind, H. Keating and J. Bridgman (eds.), *Taking Responsibility: Law and the Changing Family* (Routledge: 2010). A. Alghrani, 'Uterus Transplantation: Does Procreative Liberty Encompass a Right to Gestate?' (2016) *Journal of Law and the Biosciences* 636–641.

[9] The term *cisgender* (from the Latin *cis-*, meaning 'on the same side as') can be used to describe individuals who possess, from birth and into adulthood, the male or female reproductive organs (sex) typical of the social category of man or woman (gender) to which that individual was assigned at birth. Hence a cisgender person's gender is on the same side as their birth-assigned sex, in contrast to which a transgender person's gender is on the other side (trans-) of their birth-assigned sex – see B. Aultman, 'Cisgender' (2014) *Transgender Quarterly Studies* 61–62. For prospect of pregnancy in men via uterus transplant see M. Bilger, 'Scientists are Now Attempting to Figure Out How to Get Men Pregnant' 20 June 2016, LifeNews.com. D. Grady, 'Will Uterine Transplants Make Male Pregnancy Possible?' *New York Times*, 16 November 2015.

This chapter is thus devoted to exploring these novel possibilities and regulatory challenges uterus transplantation raises, in the speculative context of trans[10], and gender non binary, and cis-gendered male individuals. The chapter is divided into four main parts: Part I (Section 6.1) explores uterus transplantation in trans woman who wish to experience gestation and pregnancy equal to their cis-gendered female counterparts. This necessitates firstly background discussion on trans rights in the domestic context in order to examine how this novel technology could assist in their fundamental rights to found a family and realign reproductive function. Part II (Section 6.2) examines uterus transplantation into *cis-gendered* men who may also wish to experience gestation and access this one role that historically only cis-gendered women could do. Part III (Section 6.3) demonstrates how, under the current regulatory framework, the advent of uterus transplantation in transgendered and gender non binary individuals and cis-gendered men will force reconsideration of legal parental labels such as motherhood and fatherhood that are entrenched in biological function. Finally, Part IV (Section 6.4) explores, in the context of feminist discourse, whether uterus transplantation will eliminate or exacerbate inequality in the division of labour.

6.1   Uterus Transplantation to Enable Trans Pregnancy

Following on from the news that a healthy child had been born in 2014 via uterine transplant, media headlines publicised that this raised the prospect that the procedure may also be possible in trans women, so that they too can experience pregnancy and the gestation of their own children.[11] Whilst founding a family is regarded as a fundamental aspect of individual and social life, and thus the right to marry and found a family is a universal right, protected in both the Universal Declaration and the European Convention,[12]

[10] *Trans* is an umbrella term used which refers to all individuals whose gender identity (one's internal sense of gender and self) and/or gender expression differs from the legal gender that was assigned at birth. S Whittle, *Respect and Equality: Transsexual and Transgender Rights* (Oxford: Routledge, 2002). For more on language see M. Walker, 'Gender and Language: Examining the Use of Diagnostic Language in the Discussion of Gender Variance' (2014) 5(2) *International Journal of Child, Youth and Family Studies* 332–345.

[11] Fine Maron. 'How a Transgender Woman Could Get Pregnant'. Samuel, 'With Uterus Transplants a Reality, Transgender Women Dare to Dream of Pregnancies'.

[12] Article 16(1) of the United Nations Universal Declaration of Human Rights 1948 (the UN Declaration) provides that 'Men and women of full age, without any limitation due to race, nationality or religion, have the right to marry and to found a family'. The European Convention for the Protection of Human Rights and Fundamental Freedoms 1950 declares in Article 12 that 'Men and women of marriageable age have the right to

trans individuals remain a cohort of individuals for whom the right to reproduce and parent remains more observed in breach, than in observance.[13] As emerging reproductive technologies, such as uterus transplantation, promise more avenues in which trans individuals can actualise their reproductive rights, it will raise regulatory challenges and may finally necessitate a move away from the hetero-centric binaries that currently prevail throughout both domestic and international legislation when bestowing parental legal status. Some trans women may assert a right to uterus transplantation as a way of expressing and consolidating a maternal identity, namely a parental identity that aligns with gender identity. The question here may be regarded as not necessarily one of having children (some trans women may already be parents or could in theory attain parenthood via other avenues) but rather one of securing an experience imagined as important to one's (gender) identity and hoped-for parental bonds and whether this is enough to impose a public duty correlative to an individual right to uterus transplantation.

Transsexualism is defined as an extreme form of gender dysphoria.[14] Psychologically, trans individuals regard themselves as being of the opposite gender to that which they belong to on purely physiological criteria.[15] Hale LJ explained it well in the following passage:

marry and to found a family'. Article 8 provides for a right to a 'private and family life, his home and his correspondence'. Whilst there are not unqualified rights, and one is not entitled to positive assistance in founding a family, what it does mean is that certain sorts of impediments to founding a family are illegitimate.

[13]   S. McGuinness and A. Alghrani, 'Gender and Parenthood: The Case for Realignment' (2008) 16(2) *Medical Law Review* 261–283. C. A. Jones, L. Reiter, E. Greenblatt, 'Fertility Preservation in Transgender Patients' (2016) 17(2) *Journal of Transgenderism* 76–82. J. Obedin Maliver and H. J. Makadon, 'Transgender Men and Pregnancy' (2016) 9(1) *Obstetric Medicine* 4–8. K. Wierckx, E. Van Caenegem, G. Pennings et al. 'Reproductive Wish in Transsexual Men' (2012) 27 *Human Reproduction* 483–487. A. Light, J. Obedin-Maliver, J. Sevelius et al., 'Transgender Men Who Experienced Pregnancy after Female-to-Male Gender Transitioning' (2014) 124 *Obstetrics & Gynecology* 1120–1127. S. Ellis, D. Wojnar and M. Pettinato, 'Conception, Pregnancy, and Birth Experiences of Male and Gender Variant Gestational Parents: It's How We Could Have a Family' (2014) 60(1) *Journal of Midwifery & Women's Health* 62–69. T. Stocks, 'To What Extent Have the Rights of Transgender People Been Under-Realized in Comparison to the Rights of Lesbian, Gay, Bisexual and Queer/Questioning People in the United Kingdom?' (2015) 16(1) *International Journal of Transgenderism* 1–35.

[14]   P. Sutter, 'Gender Reassignment and Assisted Reproduction: Present and Future Options for Transsexual People' (2001) 16 *Human Reproduction* 612–614, at p. 612. On trans-issues in general see J. Butler, *Undoing Gender* (New York, NY and London: Routledge, 2004).

[15]   J. Thomson, 'Transsexualism and Access to a Child' (1982) 8 *Journal of Medical Ethics* 72.

Gender dysphoria is something completely different – the overwhelming sense that one has been born into the wrong body, with the wrong anatomy and the wrong physiology. Those of us who, whatever our occasional frustrations with the expectations of society or our own biology, are nevertheless quite secure in the gender identities with which we were born, can scarcely begin to understand how it must be to grow up in the wrong body and then to go through the long and complex process of adapting that body to match the real self. But it does not take much imagination to understand that this is a deeply personal and private matter; that a person who has undergone gender reassignment will need the whole world to recognise and relate to her or to him in the reassigned gender; and will want to keep to an absolute minimum any unwanted disclosure of the history. This is not only because other people can be insensitive and even cruel; the evidence is that transphobic incidents are increasing and that transgender people experience high levels of anxiety about this. It is also because of their deep need to live successfully and peacefully in their reassigned gender, something which non-transgender people can take for granted.[16]

Gender dysphoria is recognised as a mental disorder by a range of existing classification systems, such as the *Diagnostic Manual of Mental Disorders (DSM)*[17] and the *International Classification of Diseases (ICD)*.[18] Whilst in mainstream pop culture, the trans community has gained increasing prominence,[19] despite this increasing visibility; trans studies remain a relatively new academic discipline.[20] Literature begun to emerge in the 1990s, which examined: the deconstruction of gender; how transgender

---

[16] Hale LJ in *R (on the application of C) (Appellant)* v. *Secretary of State for Work and Pensions (Respondent)* [2017] UKSC 72, paragraph 1.

[17] American Psychiatric Association, Diagnostic and Statistical Manual of Mental Disorders DSM-5, 2000. For more on transsexualism as a medical condition see P. Currah, R. M. Juang and S. P. Minter (eds.), *Transgender Rights* (University of Minnesota Press, 2006) and V. L. Bullough, 'Legitimizing Transsexualism' (2007) 10(1) *International Journal of Transgenderism* 3–13.

[18] World Health Organisation, the ICD-10 Classification of Mental and Behavioural Disorders Diagnostic criteria for research, Geneva 2007, F64.0.

[19] In 2015, the story of Caitlyn Jenner (formerly Bruce Jenner, Olympian winner and father of reality television actresses, the Kardashians), who underwent gender confirmation surgery, attracted global media coverage. Jenner subsequently featured on the cover of Vanity Fair and, from 2015 to 2016, starred in the reality television series 'I Am Cait', which focused on her gender transition.

[20] See J. Verlinden, 'Transgender Bodies and Male Pregnancy: The Ethics of Radical Self-Refashioning' in M. Michaela Hampf and MaryAnn Snyder-Körber (eds.), *Machine: Bodies, Genders, Technologies* (Winter, 2012) pp. 107–136, at p. 110. See also Butler, Gender Trouble. S. Stone, *The Empire Strikes Back; A Post Transsexual Manifesto* in K. Straub and J. Epstein (eds.) *Body Guards: The Cultural Politics of Sexual Ambiguity* (New York, NY: Routledge, 1996).

practices disrupt gender binaries and subvert hetero-normativity; and the radical disconnect between body and gender expression.[21]

The UK legal framework, in which many provisions are steeped in heterosexual normative binary identities began to be challenged in the 1970s.[22] The case of *Corbett* v. *Corbett* [1970][23] challenged the failure to acknowledge a trans individuals gender reassignment for the purposes of marriage.[24] This decision determined that the sex of a person is dependant only upon their gonadal, genital and chromosomal sex at birth. The European Court of Human Rights (ECHR) subsequently ruled in *Goodwin* v. *UK*[25] and *I* v. *UK*,[26] UK law to be discriminatory and in need of review.[27] Finally, in *Bellinger*[28] the House of Lords found unanimously that the law on marriage in the UK, that conferred legal status based upon the biological distinction between the sexes as assigned at birth, was incompatible with a trans individuals rights under Articles 8 (right to a private family life) and 12 (right to marry and found a family) of the ECHR.[29] However, the court in *Bellinger* held that as the recognition of gender reassignment for the purposes of marriage would represent a major change in the law 'having far reaching ramifications'[30] it was a matter for Parliament, not the courts. These cases signified a change in

---

[21] Verlinden, 'Transgender Bodies and Male Pregnancy', at p. 113. Butler, Gender Trouble. J. Prosser, *Second Skins: The Body Narratives of Transsexuals* (New York, NY: Columbia University Press, 1998). L. Feinberg, *Trans Liberation: Beyond Pink or Blue* (Boston, MA: Beacon, 1998). H. Dover, *FTM: Female-to-Male Transsexuals in Society* (Bloomington, IN: Indiana University Press, 1997).

[22] See, for instance, legislation governing marriage and birth certificates.

[23] [1970] 2 All ER 33. This case concerned the model, dancer and trans woman April Ashley. On the breakdown of her marriage her husband petitioned for nullity on the grounds that the respondent remained a male and hence the marriage was void and the marriage was never consummated due to the incapacity of the respondent. Despite the fact Ashey had undergone gender reassignment surgery, Justice Ormrod determined that Ashley was not a legal female for the purposes of English marriage law because she lacked the 'biological' attributes, which are 'essential' for the 'role of a woman in marriage'.

[24] The Matrimonial Causes Act 1973, Section 11(c) specified marriage was a union 'between a man and a woman'.

[25] *Goodwin* v. *UK* (2002) 35 E.H.R.R.

[26] *I* v. *UK* [2002] 2 F.L.R 518.

[27] Cowan, 'That Woman Is a Woman!', at p. 80.

[28] Bellinger.

[29] A declaration of incompatibility under section 4(6) of the Human Rights Act 1998 was granted. Section 3(1) HRA places an obligation on the court, so far as it is possible to do so, to read and give effect to legislation in an ECHR compliant way. The facts of *Bellinger* predated the coming into force of the HRA and thus prevented the section 3 interpretative obligation from being operative, *R* v. *Lambert* [2001] UKHL 37.

[30] Bellinger, paragraph 37.

the tide and that a test of congruent biological factors could no longer be decisive in denying legal recognition to a trans individuals gender. Lord Nicholson acknowledged in *Bellinger* v. *Bellinger:* 'recognition of gender reassignment will involve further blurring. It will mean that in law a person who ... had all the biological characteristics of one sex at birth may subsequently be treated as a member of the opposite sex'.[31] The Government had, prior to the *Bellinger* case, already announced that this legal recognition would be given and that it would introduce comprehensive primary legislation on this difficult and sensitive subject'.[32]

In 2004, this primary legislation was to become enshrined in the Gender Recognition Act.[33] Perceived to be a 'ground breaking'[34] statute, it allowed for the first time the ability for trans individuals to legally change their gender from that assigned at birth. The 2004 Act provides that in order to obtain a gender confirmation certificate applicants need be aged 18 or over and must demonstrate that they have suffered gender dysphoria,[35] have lived as their 'new gender' for at least two years[36] and have sworn a statutory declaration that they intend to live permanently in the acquired gender until death.[37] The application must be supported by two medical reports from registered medical practitioners, one of whom must be a psychologist practising in the field of gender dysphoria.[38] Once a gender recognition certificate is granted, section 9 of the 2004 Act provides:

---

[31] Bellinger, paragraph 31.

[32] In 1999 an Interdepartmental Working Group was established. The terms of reference were 'to consider, with particular reference to birth certificates, the need for appropriate legal measures to address the problems experienced by transsexual people, having particular regard to scientific and societal developments, and measures taken in other countries to deal with the issue'. See Home Office Report of The Interdepartmental Working Group on Transsexual People (April, 2000) paragraph 37.

[33] A. N. Sharpe, 'A Critique of the Gender Recognition Act 2004' (2007) 4 *Journal of Bioethical Enquiry* 33–42. A. Sharpe, 'Endless Sex: The Gender Recognition Act 2004 and the Persistence of a legal category' (2007) 15 *Feminist Legal Studies* 57–84. See also C. Gray's criticisms of the UK Government for adopting the medical model of transsexualism when enacting the legislation. Her thesis proposes an alternative model of legal regulation based on gender self-declaration. C. Gray, 'A Critique of the Legal Recognition of Transsexuals in UK Law', PhD thesis (University of Glasgow, 2016).

[34] S. Cowan, 'Looking Back (To)wards the Body: Medicalization and the GRA' (2009) 18(2) *Social and Legal Studies* 247–252, at p. 247.

[35] Gender Recognition Act 2004, s2(1)(a).

[36] Gender Recognition Act 2004, s2(1)(b).

[37] Gender Recognition Act 2004, s2(1)(c) .

[38] Gender Recognition Act 2004, sections 2 and 3.

> Where a full gender recognition certificate is issued to a person, the persons gender becomes for all purposes, the acquired gender (so that, if the acquired gender was the male gender, the persons sex becomes that of a man and, if it is the female gender, it becomes that of a woman).

The medical framing of trans identities in the 2004 Act has attracted academic criticism and come under significant scrutiny.[39] In 2016, the Women and Equalities Select Committee Report on Transgender Equality reported that whilst the Gender Recognition Act 2004 was pioneering, it is now dated and its medicalised approach, pathologises trans identities and runs contrary to the dignity and personal autonomy of applicants.[40] They called for a model of self-declaration of gender identity to be adopted replacing the onerous, and often humiliating, process of having one's gender assessed.[41]

In regard to trans individuals' reproductive rights, this was given consideration prior to the 2004 legislation by the Home Office Working Group, set up in 1999 'to consider with particular reference to birth certificates, the need for appropriate legal measures to address the problems experienced by transsexual people, having due regard to scientific and societal developments, and measures undertaken in other countries to deal with the issue'.[42] The Report acknowledged that amongst trans individuals there is variation in reproductive and parenting desires:

> [The] government and the medical profession have had, in their dealings with transsexual people, a long history of misunderstanding and ill-judged attempts at social policing. An area of misunderstanding has been the unexamined assumptions that gender dysphoria automatically rules out a desire for reproduction and family life. Many transsexual people are not interested in bringing up children, and many are; a normal human range of variation applies here.[43]

Four years later, the 2004 legislation appeared to offer protection to trans parental rights via section 12, which provided:

---

[39] M. C. Burke, 'Resisting Pathology: GID and the Contested Terrain of Diagnosis in the Transgender Rights Movement' in P. J. McGann and David J. Hutson (eds.), *Sociology of Diagnosis* (Advances in Medical Sociology, Volume 12) (Emerald Group Publishing Limited, 2011) pp. 183–210. J. Chung, 'Identity or Condition: The Theory and Practice of Applying State Disability Laws to Transgender Individuals' (2011–2012) 21 *Columbia Journal of Gender and Law* 1.

[40] House of Commons (2016) *Transgender Equality: First Report of Session 2015–16.* London: The Stationary Office Limited, p. 3.

[41] Ibid.

[42] Home Office, Report of The Interdepartmental Working Group on Transsexual People (April, 2000).

[43] Ibid, p. 47.

6.1.1 Parenthood

> The fact that a person's gender has become the acquired gender under this Act does not affect the status of the person as the father or mother of a child.

The explanatory notes which accompanies section 12 add the following:

> This provides that though a person is regarded as being of the acquired gender, the person will retain their original status as either father or mother of a child. The continuity of parental rights and responsibilities is thus ensured.[44]

Whilst in theory this appeared to offer protection, it is clear in the years since that this protection towards trans parental rights is more illusory than apparent.[45] Research clearly indicates that trans individuals also have 'reproductive needs',[46] and among trans individuals there may be strong desires to parent and gestate a genetically related child of their own.[47] Whist many transgender, transsexual and gender-nonbinary individuals may want to have children post transition,[48] feminising/masculinising hormone therapy that trans individuals go through as part of gender reassignment treatment can limit fertility.[49] If reproductive rights of trans individuals are to be

---

[44] The Gender Recognition Act 2004, Explanatory Notes, paragraph 43.

[45] See the controversial case of *J v. B (Ultra-orthodox Judaism: Transgender)* [2017] EWFC 4 where Peter Jackson J. refused a trans woman direct contact with her five children – it was deemed contact would be adverse to their welfare as it would result in the children being marginalised by their orthodox Jewish community. It is clear contact was not permitted due to trans-phobic attitudes of the community – it is hard to conceive of its being deemed not in a child's best interests to have contact with a non-resident parent because they were part of an ethnic minority group and the community the child lived in was racist towards non-white people. See also *Re F (Minors) (Denial of Contact)* [1993] 2 FLR 677.

[46] A. Lawrence, J. Shaffer, W. Snow et al., 'Health Care Needs of Transgendered Patients' (1996) 276 *Journal of the American Medical Association* 874.

[47] A transsexual can have a genetically related child if their gametes are stored prior to sex reassignment surgery. *In vitro* fertilisation can then be undertaken to fertilise the spermatozoa with donated ova to create an embryo, which can then be implanted into a transplanted womb (once this technology becomes possible) or into a surrogate. This is discussed in more detail later on in the chapter.

[48] E. Coleman, W. Bockting, M. Botzer et al., 'Standards of Care for the Health of Transsexual, Transgender, and Gender-Nonconforming People, Version 7' (2012) 13(4) *International Journal Of Transgenderism* 165–232. The *Standards of Care (SOC) for the Health of Transsexual, Transgender, and Gender Nonconforming People* is a publication of the World Professional Association for Transgender Health (WPATH). See also H. von Doussa, J. Power and D. Riggs, 'Imagining Parenthood: The Possibilities and Experiences of Parenthood Among Transgender People' (2015) 17(9) *Culture, Health and Sexuality* 1119–1131.

[49] P. D. Darney, 'Williams Textbook of Endocrinology' in H. M. Kronenberg, S. Melmer, K. S. Polonsky and P. R. Larsen (eds.), *Hormonal Contraception* (Philadelphia, PA: Saunders) 615–644.

respected, it is important that fertility preservation options are raised early on in the transition process. Sutter et al. claim that cases are known of people who received hormone therapy and genital surgery and later regretted their inability to parent genetically related children.[50]

Research reveals deep cultural suspicion amongst some about the parenting rights and capacities of trans people.[51] When Thomas Beatie,[52] a trans man in Oregon, USA, publicly discussed his pregnancy on the *Oprah Winfrey Show*,[53] fascination and horror in the notion of a pregnant man dominated headlines. Media commentators suggested Beatie had forfeited his 'right' to become pregnant with his decision to become a man. This negated Beatie's maleness and rendered his pregnancy illegitimate.[54] In a commentary about Beatie's pregnancy, Blaze demonstrated there were also pejorative responses within television:[55] David Letterman called Beatie an 'androgynous freak show', while other network presenters described the pregnancy as 'disgusting' and 'useless'.[56] Von Doussa, Power and Riggs[57] argue that the Beatie case reflects the fact that whilst attitudes toward gay and lesbian parenthood have become more accepting of same-sex families, there is less cultural acceptance for parents who have changed gender or whose gender is not clearly defined as either male or female.[58] Trans individuals who wish to parent have to overcome these difficulties in negotiating parenthood within a society in which they may still face hostility towards their decision. Haines, Ajayi and Boyd write about the complex interaction between parenting identity and transgender identity and the ways in which gender

---

[50] P. De Sutter, K. Kira, A. Verschoor and A. Hotimsky, 'The Desire to Have Children and the Preservation of Fertility in Transsexual Women: A Survey' (2002) 6(3) *International Journal of Transgenderism* 1–12.

[51] D. Dempsey, 'Same-Sex Parented Families in Australia' (2013) *Child Family Community Australia, Australian Institute of Family Studies* 18. A. Martin and D. Ryan, 'Lesbian, Gay, Bisexual, and Transgender Parents in the School Systems' (2000) 29(2) *School Psychology Review* 207–216. A. T. Norton and G. M. Herek. 'Heterosexuals' Attitudes Toward Transgender People: Findings from a National Probability Sample of U.S. Adults' (2013) 68(11–12) *Sex Roles* 738–753.

[52] Read an article written by him about his pregnancy, entitled 'Labor of Love' *The Advocate*, 26 March 2008.

[53] American talk show.

[54] D. W. Riggs, 'What Makes a Man? Thomas Beattie, Embodiment, and 'Mundane Transphobia'' (2014) *Feminism and Psychology* 1–15.

[55] A. Blaze, 2008. 'Hate Starts Rolling In for Thomas Beatie' 2004–2015. The Bilerico Project.

[56] Ibid.

[57] Von Doussa, Power and Riggs, 'Imagining Parenthood'.

[58] B. D. Spidsberg, 'Vulnerable and Strong – Lesbian Women Encountering Maternity Care' (2007) 60(5) *Journal of Advanced Nursing* 478–486.

transitioning affects the dynamics within a family, not only due to potential trans phobia within the family and the conflict this may bring, but because parenting is culturally constructed in highly gendered terms.[59]

Whilst prior to transitioning some trans individuals may already be parents, or maintain a desire to become a parent,[60] Beatie's trans pregnancy evoked expressions of 'disbelief', 'annoyance' and 'revulsion'.[61] The negative response to Beatie's pregnancy centred around the notion that a trans individual has forfeited their right to parenthood and thus should not be helped in their desires to parent and that this is the 'price to pay' for transitioning – that being a trans individual and being a parent are mutually exclusive.[62] Internationally, some States appear to endorse this position, mandating trans individuals are sterile or 'continuously non-reproductive'[63] as a precondition to gender recognition. In 2017, across the Council of Europe, 20 countries continue to enforce a sterilisation requirement.[64] In its landmark 2017 opinion, *AP, Garcon, and Nicot* v. *France*,[65] the court held that, by conditioning gender recognition on submission to 'a sterilisation operation or medical treatment creating a high probability of sterilisation' France had violated the applicants' right to private life under Article 8 of the ECHR. Dunne noted that whilst this judgment follows recent decisions reached by national courts in Germany,[66] Sweden[67] and Italy,[68] and is a welcome affirmation of transgender rights, statements from the ECtHR, as well as the highest courts in Germany and Sweden, reveal a general assumption that, irrespective of disproportionality, transgender sterilisation requirements do pursue

---

[59] B. A. Haines, A. Ajayi and H. Boyd, 'Making Trans Parents Visible: Intersectionality of Trans and Parenting Identities' (2014) 24(2) *Feminism & Psychology* 238–247. S. Hines, 'Intimate Transitions: Transgender Practices of Partnering and Parenting' (2006) 40(2) *Sociology* 353–371.

[60] R. L. Stotzer, J. Herman, A. Hasenbush, The Williams Institute, Transgender Parenting: A Review of Existing Research (2014). Hines, 'Intimate Transitions'.

[61] P. Currah, 'Expecting Bodies: The Pregnant Man and Transgender Exclusion from the Employment Non-Discrimination' (2008) 36(3–4) *Women's Studies Quarterly* 330; as cited by P. Dunne, 'Transgender Sterilisation Requirements in Europe' (2017) (24) (4) *Medical Law Review* 554–581.

[62] Sutter, 'Gender Reassignment and Assisted Reproduction', at p. 612.

[63] Term used in German legislation that previously required that the trans person is 'continuously non-reproductive'. (TSG (1980) Second Section, SS 8. 1 (iii)).

[64] Dunne, 'Transgender Sterilisation Requirements in Europe'.

[65] (ECtHR, 6 April 2017).

[66] Federal Constitutional Court of Germany, 1 B v. R 3295/07 (11 January 2011).

[67] Stockholm Administrative Court of Appeals, *Socialstyrelsen* v. *NN*, Mål nr 1968–12 (19 December 2012).

[68] Ibid.

valid aims.[69] Dunne notes that from the existing case law, policy debates and literature, three central justifications become apparent as justifying the conditioning gender recognition on sterilisation: legal certainty, child welfare and natural reproduction. Critiquing all three, Dunne persuasively sets out how none pursue valid aims. In regards to legal certainty, whilst he concedes certainty so as to promote and allow for identification of existing familial relationships in family law is a legitimate goal, this does not legitimise sterilisation requirements to the extent that they are exclusively directed towards applicants for legal gender recognition, especially when a number of European states accept increased uncertainty for cis-gender procreation. In regard to child welfare arguments, framed through the fear that, in addition to third-party discrimination, trans parents themselves may cause harm to any offspring, he sets out how existing medical and social scientific evidence does not support the notion that trans individuals are incapable or unstable parents. Lastly, he addresses arguments that centre around the third justification of trans sterilisation as necessary as a way to preserve promote 'natural' and normative arguments about how proper reproduction and the creation of new life *ought* to be. To the extent that individuals deviate from a binary 'woman/mother/conception – man/father/begetter' schema, their reproductive possibilities are circumscribed by traditional procreative conventions. In this manner, existing rules of 'repro-normativity' have a particularly detrimental impact on lesbian, gay, bisexual and trans (LGBT) persons. As these individuals necessarily engage in atypical procreation, they automatically destabilise the sexual family model and are more vulnerable to social censure. There is evidence that, while same-gender *relationships* are increasingly accepted across the European Union, same-gender *parents* continue to encounter substantial opposition. He thus concludes that sterilisation requirements rely upon a weak, discriminatory and logically inconsistent framework.[70]

Whilst 20 countries across the Council of Europe mandate that trans individuals must prove their infertility before obtaining gender recognition, the UK is not one of them. Sterilisation is not a mandatory requirement in the Gender Recognition Act 2004. Whilst any requirement that the individual was non-reproductive was omitted from the 2004 Act, leading up to the statute, the UK Working Group in 2000 did consider imposition of sterilisation as a prerequisite to transitioning; under the banner of public interest, the Group reported:

---

[69] Dunne, 'Transgender Sterilisation Requirements in Europe'.
[70] Ibid.

> The transsexual community's concern about discrimination has, however, to be set against the great concern that would be felt by the general public if someone who is legally a man gave birth to a child or someone who was the legally a woman, became the father of one.[71]

In other contexts, such as forced sterilisation of a person with learning disabilities, sterilisation imposed on a person without consent and for non-therapeutic reasons, UK courts had acknowledged this involves a deprivation of one's right to reproduce.[72] As noted above, the Gender Recognition Act provides that, in order to obtain a gender confirmation certificate, applicants need to demonstrate that they have suffered gender dysphoria,[73] have lived as their 'new gender' for at least two years[74] and have sworn a statutory declaration that they intend to live permanently in the acquired gender.[75] It does not require applicants to undergo gender confirmation surgery, although it should be noted that the Home Office Working group did note in its report:

> Any proposed restriction on fertility treatment will achieve little if anything. Without these restrictions, transsexual people are already generally infertile shortly after commencing gender reassignment treatment. Yet despite this infertility many of them already participate in the raising of children. Any such restriction will fail, as medically induced infertility already fails, to ensure that children do not have an experience of being raised by a transsexual person, and it is undoubtedly the case, anyway, that children who are cared for by transsexual people do not suffer from that care.[76]

Therefore, this objection and the notion trans individuals have in some way chosen to be infertile and that this negates their rights to uterus transplantation, fertility treatment, or other assisted reproductive technologies is legally inconsistent with the legislative stance adopted in the 2004 Act which, in theory, intended to protect the parental rights of trans individuals post transition. It is also worth noting that the Human Fertilisation and Embryology Act 2008 contains provisions that grant greater parental recognition to same sex couples.[77] Implicitly, the UK

---

[71] Home Office Report of The Interdepartmental Working Group on Transsexual People (April, 2000) p. 21.

[72] Re D (A Minor) (Wardship: Sterilisation) [1976] Fam 185.

[73] Gender Recognition Act 2004, s2(1)(a).

[74] Gender Recognition Act 2004, s2(1)(b).

[75] Gender Recognition Act 2004, s2(1)(c).

[76] Home Office Report of The Interdepartmental Working Group on Transsexual People (April, 2000), paragraph 2.5.7.

[77] See Human Fertilisation and Embryology Act 2008, ss42–45. See also B. Hale, 'New Families and The Welfare of the Children' (2014) 36(1) Journal of Social Welfare and Family Law 26–35.

Government does not accept that a same-sex couple has not somehow waived away any rights to parent by the mere fact they have elected to be in a relationship where unassisted sexual reproduction is not possible. Having thus set out why trans individuals' reproductive rights should be respected, I now turn to address how reproductive science may not only enable trans individuals to overcome infertility caused by the gender recognition treatment, but go further and enable them to reproduce in their acquired gender.

6.1.2   Realigning Reproductive Function

For a trans woman, surgical treatment combined with hormonal therapy has now advanced significantly so that such individuals can attain the appearance of cis-gendered women. In many instances, unless disclosed by the individual, very few would know that the individual had undergone such treatment.[78] Whilst advances in gender reassignment treatment has relieved the pressures of individuals suffering from gender dysphoria, 'this potentially relatively satisfactory situation is still marred by the inability of transsexual women to bear children due to their lack of internal female reproductive organs'.[79] Trans women may seek access to uterus transplant technology, so that they too can experience pregnancy and the gestation of their own children.[80] It would enable trans women to express and consolidate a maternal identity, namely a parental identity that aligns with gender identity. Whilst parenthood may have already been attained prior to transition, or can be founded in other ways such as through adoption or surrogacy, some trans women may wish to become pregnant to secure an experience (pregnancy) imagined as important to one's (gender) identity and hoped-for parental bonds which may ensue from this.

Brännström, who led the Swedish team's success with the world's first live birth in 2014, acknowledged that in theory uterus transplantation in trans women is possible, although he warned of anatomical barriers that would have to be overcome due to the differing shape of a pelvis in a cis

---

[78] See success of supermodel trans woman Ines Rau. See J. Okwodu, 'Ines Rau is Speaking Out, Breaking Boundaries, and Lifting the Veil on the Life of Trans Models' *Vogue*, 19 May 2016.

[79] Ibid.

[80] The focus in this section shall be on trans women – trans men will be dealt with in the same position as other men seeking to access this technology. This is dealt with separately in the next section.

man.[81] Assuming such technical difficulties do not prove insurmountable and safety concerns for the donor, recipient and fetus can be overcome, I examine whether the present UK regulatory framework is equipped to govern this novel advance and how it would respond to a claim from a trans women who has legally transitioned seeking access to uterus transplant technology, so that she too may gestate her own child.

6.1.2.1 Obtaining a Uterus for Transplantation

Assuming uterus transplantation will soon become clinical treatment in cis women, the first step in the process will be for a trans woman to obtain a uterus from a donor. Whilst it is accepted that resources are limited and the government is not legally obliged to provide positive assistance to those seeking to become a parent, it is only right that if it does elect to offer such assistance, it will be offered on an ethical and fair basis.[82] As Douglas states: 'where resources are scarce, society is entitled to set priorities to their allocation, but the criteria to be fulfilled for eligibility must be legally, socially and ethically justifiable'.[83]

Under the present opt-in organ procurement system governed by the Human Tissue Act 2004, there is a clear shortage of organs for transplantation.[84] As noted in the previous chapter, in England, a person who wishes to donate their organs after death will normally do this by

[81] M. Henderson, 'How Mother and Daughter Could Share the Same Womb', *The Times*, 2 July 2003.

[82] Note that there is no positive right to fertility treatment to enable one to procreate. In the UK the majority of fertility services (some 60 per cent) are provided by the private sector, with the NHS providing the remaining 40 per cent. NHS funding comes through Clinical Commissioning Groups (CCGs). NHS England provides commissioning guidance to CCGs. Although The National Institute for Health Care and Excellence (NICE) provides best practice guidance, and recommends in the context of access to IVF that 'In women aged under 40 years who have not conceived after 2 years of regular unprotected intercourse or 12 cycles of artificial insemination (where 6 or more are by intrauterine insemination), offer 3 full cycles of IVF, with or without ICSI. If the woman reaches the age of 40 during treatment, complete the current full cycle but do not offer further full cycles.' However NICE guidance is not mandatory and is not necessarily followed by clinics. Fertility Network UK, which monitors provision, reported in 2017 that many areas in England are cutting back on provision of IVF on the NHS to save money – see BBC News, 'NHS access to IVF being cut in England' 7 August 2017.

[83] Douglas, *Law, Fertility and Reproduction*, 119.

[84] In 2016–2017, 457 patients died while waiting for a transplant; see C. Johnston, 'Shortage of Organ Donations Led to 457 Deaths Last Year, says NHS', *The Guardian*, 4 September 2017. Note the British Medical Association has called for an opt-out system for England, stating it is backed by two-thirds of the public – see A. Rimmer, 'BMA Annual Meeting: BMA Calls for Opt-Out Organ Donation to Become UK-wide' (2016) 3504 *British Medical Journal* 353.

registering on the NHS Organ Donor Register, which is managed by UK Transplant (UKT). UKT maintains the national waiting list of patients awaiting transplantation and has overall responsibility for co-ordination of transplant activities and the allocation of organs. The UKT or Human Tissue Authority (HTA) could not prioritise cis women over trans women when allocating uteri for donation – if the trans woman has undergone the recognition process in the GRA 2004, legally she must be treated equally to her female counterparts. In the context of uterus transplantation, eligibility criteria may still be lawfully imposed so as to maximise success and efficacy of the transplant.

Assuming from the public reaction Beatie received in the USA, alongside hostility that appeared in national newspapers in the UK in 2017, when it was publicised that trans pregnancy may become available on the NHS,[85] could donors direct donation only to cis women recipients? Nothing in the Human Tissue Act 2004 makes directed donation illegal; however, policy provides that deceased organ donation in the UK must be non-directed.[86] Thus, after death, donated organ and tissue enters an anonymous pool database, and are allocated to the person on the UK Transplant waiting list who is most in need and who is the best match with the donor. The policy was originally intended to stop racially motivated conditions being attached to donation, and arose following a case in 1998 in which relatives of a deceased man consented to the use of his organs for transplant, only on the condition that the organs went to white recipients. The Department of Health, in their report, *An Investigation into Conditional Organ Donation*,[87] condemned conditional offers of donation,

---

[85] A. Devlin, 'Trans Womb Row – Calls for Transgender Women Born Male to Be Given Womb Transplants on the NHS So They Can Have Kids – But Some Critics Slam Idea' *The Sun*, 2 July 2017. A. Alghrani, 'Medical Law Expert on Womb Transplants, Unisex Pregnancy, and the "Right to Gestate"', *The Independent*, 10 July 2017. C. Smith, 'Transgender Women "Have a Right to Be Pregnant"' *The Times*, 3 July 2017. S. Manning and S. Adams, 'Wombs for Men: Astonishing Prospect as Fertility Doctors Back Operations on NHS So Transgender Women Born as Boys Can Have Babies' *The Mail on Sunday*, 1 July 2017.

[86] DoH, *An Investigation into Conditional Organ Donation* (DoH, London, 2000) condemned the acceptance not only of racist conditions but any conditional offers of donation. The Panel reported that 'to attach any condition to a donation is unacceptable, because it offends against the fundamental principle that organs are donated altruistically and should go to patients in the greatest need'. Their recommendations have become National Health Service (NHS) policy. For more on directed and donation directed donation see A. J. Cronin, 'Directed and Conditional Deceased Donor Organ Donations: Laws and Misconceptions' (2010) 18(3) *Medical Law Review* 275–301.

[87] Ibid.

stating that 'to attach any condition to a donation is unacceptable, because it offends against the fundamental principle that organs are donated altruistically and should go to patients in the greatest need'.[88] Their recommendations have been both welcomed and criticised.[89] Thus, in the UK, it is clear from this that donation of a cadaver uterus, subject to the condition it did not go to a trans woman or cis male recipient would not, or at least under the present policy, be accepted.

From living donors, directed non-vital organs, such as kidneys, lobes of the lung or liver segments, are permissible. The majority of the living organ transplants that take place in the UK are kidney donations towards recipients with whom the donors have a genetic, or pre-existing emotional relationship.[90] Thus, directed donation amongst live donors is acceptable practice. The rules governing live uterus transplants as discussed in the previous chapter apply, so the removal and use of an organ from a live donor will be unlawful if any reward has been received for it.[91] If uterus transplantation is permissible in cis women, trans women who have undergone the recognition process in the GRA 2004, are in theory legally entitled to be treated as equal to their female counterparts and also permitted access to uterus transplant technology. Thus if uterus transplantation became clinical treatment to help women gestate a child, there is nothing in the current regulation that would bar a friend or relative donating a uterus to a trans woman.

6.1.2.2   Obtaining Fertility Treatment

Trans women who wish to gestate via uterus transplantation will also be dependent on the assistance of a fertility clinic to provide in vitro fertilisation – so that an embryo can be created and implanted into the donated uterus. The provisions of the Human Fertilisation and Embryology Act 1990 (as amended)[92] will apply. However, there is nothing in the HFE Act that bars a fertility clinic from assisting trans women in their reproductive endeavours. Schedule 2 of the HFE Act 1990 specifies activities that may be licensed under the 1990 Act. By virtue of sections 2(1) and 11(1) and paragraph 1(1)(d)(3) of Schedule 2 to the 1990 Act, the Human Fertilisation and Embryology Authority (HFEA) can issue a licence for

---

[88] Ibid., paragraph 1: 25.

[89] T. M. Wilkinson, 'What's Not Wrong with Conditional Organ Donation?' (2003) 29 *Journal of Medical Ethics* 163–164.

[90] M. Quigley, 'Directed Deceased Organ Donation: The Problem with Algorithmic Ethics', *Centre for Ethics, Law, and Society*, May 2008.

[91] Human Tissue Act 2004, s33.

[92] Hereafter referred to as the HFE Act 1990.

'treatment services' involving the use of an embryo where it appears to be necessary or desirable for the purpose of 'assisting women to carry children'.[93] As a trans woman who has gone through the process outlined in the GRA 2004, is for all legal purposes to be regarded as a woman, an IVF clinic that declined a trans woman fertility treatment on the grounds of her trans sexuality, could face discrimination charges.

An IVF clinic, however, may refuse treatment on the grounds that there are concerns regarding the welfare of any resulting child, which all licensed clinics are mandated by law to consider.[94] Section 13(5) of the HFE Act 1990 (as amended) states that consideration be given to the welfare of any child who may be born as a result of treatment (or any other child who may be affected) and the child's need for 'supportive parenting'.[95] Thus, before a trans woman is offered access to fertility treatment, consideration will first be given to whether or not the welfare of any future children can be met. The deployment of vague notions of welfare of any resulting child, allows value judgements to play a part in the allocation of who may be granted assistance to procreate and has long attracted criticism.[96] Consequently, it is more often the case than not, that patients who do not fit the standard model of a heterosexual couple in a stable relationship will be regarded as being less justified and less well equipped to be parents and less entitled to take up scarce resources.[97] Alluding to concerns as to whether a trans parent can meet the needs of a future child, Banzet and Revol comment:

> One concern for the well-being of the unborn child would be the mental stability of a parent who is undergoing, or who has undergone, such a fundamental change, and whether the root cause lies in psychological disturbance.[98]

---

[93] This remains unchanged by the HFE Act 2008.

[94] For some academic criticisms of the welfare of the child clause see E. Jackson, 'Conception and the Irrelevance of the Welfare Principle' (2002) 65 *Modern Law Review* 176. S. Millns, 'Making Social Judgements that Go Beyond the Purely Medical: The Reproductive Revolution and Access to Fertility Treatment Services' in J. Bridgeman and S. Millns (eds.), *Law and Body Politics: Regulating the Female Body* (Aldershot: Dartmouth, 1995), E. Sutherland, 'Man Not Included – Single Women, Female Couples and Procreative Freedom in the UK' (2003) 15(2) *Child and Family Law Quarterly* 155.

[95] HFE Act 2008, s14(2)(b).

[96] A. Alghrani and J. Harris, 'Should the Foundation of Families Be Regulated?' (2006) 18(2) *Child and Family Law Quarterly* 191–210.

[97] G. Douglas, 'Assisted Reproduction' (1993) *Current Legal Problems* 53–74 at p. 64.

[98] P. Banzet and M. Revol, 'The Surgical Experience' (1996) 180 *Bulletin de l'Académie nationale de medicine* 1395–1402; D. Brothers and W. C. Ford, 'Gender Reassignment and Assisted Reproduction: An Ethical Analysis' (2000) 15 *Human Reproduction* 737–738.

If such concerns are to be acted upon to deny trans individuals' access to fertility treatment and what could be the only option available to them to experience genetic or gestational parenthood, they necessitate substantiation with evidence that a parent who has undergone gender realignment surgery may be impaired in their capacity to provide adequate parenting. At present, there are very few studies of children raised by trans parents, and those that have been conducted show that these children do not fare any less well than children reared in other family units.[99]

Thus, unless clear evidence can be provided to show that harm would result from being raised by a trans parent, this ground may not provide a defence/justify a decision to decline assistance to trans women seeking fertility treatment. Gender reassignment should not be allowed to mask prejudices, and as noted by Brothers and Ford:

> The issue of gender reassignment must not be allowed to mask any other factors relevant to ethical decision making and the couple should be assessed using the same criteria as heterosexual couples within the overall restraint that the welfare of future children must be the paramount consideration.[100]

If a trans woman were able to access fertility treatment, there would still be obstacles to be overcome. A trans woman who, prior to gender

---

[99] R. Green, 'Sexual Identity of 37 Children Raised by Homosexual or Transsexual Parents' (1978) 135(6) *American Journal of Psychiatry* 692–697; R. Green, 'Children of Transsexual Parents: Research and Clinical Overview' in D. Di Ceglie and D. Freedman (eds.), *A Stranger in My Own Body: Atypical Gender Identity Development and Mental Health* (London: Karnac Books, 1998) 260–265; D. Freedman, F. Tasker and D. Di Ceglie, 'Children and Adolescents with Transsexual Parents Referred to a Specialist Gender Identity Development Service: A Brief Report of Key Developmental Features' (2002) 7 *Clinical Child Psychology and Psychiatry* 423. M. Dierckx, J. Motmans, D. Mortelmans and G. T'sjoen, 'Families in Transition: A Literature Review' (2016) 28(1) *International Review of Psychiatry* 36–43. S. Hunger, 'Commentary: Transgender People Are Not That Different After All' (2012) 21 *Cambridge Quarterly of Healthcare Ethics* 287–289. H. W. Jones, 'Gender Reassignment and Assisted Reproduction: Evaluation of Multiple Aspects' (2000) 15 *Human Reproduction* 987. McGuinness and Alghrani, 'Gender and Parenthood: The Case for Realignment'. T. M. Murphy, 'The Ethics of Helping Transgender Men and Women Have Children' (2010) 53 *Perspectives in Biological Medicine* 46–60. G. Pennings, 'Evaluating the Welfare of the Child in Same-Sex Families' (2011) 26 *Human Reproduction* 1609–1615. J. Sales, 'Children of a Transsexual Father: A Successful Intervention' (1995) 4 *European Child and Adolescent Psychiatry* 136–139. T. White, R. Ettner, 'Disclosure, Risks and Protective Factors for Children Whose Parents Are Undergoing a Gender Transition' (2004) 8 *Journal of Gay & Lesbian Psychotherapy* 129–145. T. White and R. Ettner, 'Adaptation and Adjustment in Children of Transsexual Parents' (2007) 16 *European Child and Adolescent Psychiatry* 215–221.

[100] Brothers and Ford, 'Gender Reassignment and Assisted Reproduction', at p. 738.

reassignment surgery, had her sperm frozen would require an egg donor. There is a shortage of egg, sperm and embryo donation in the UK; this shortage has increased following legislative changes that removed donor anonymity.[101] There may be a substantial waiting time – the HFEA has reported, 'some women have been known to wait 3–5 years to receive donated eggs'.[102] If a trans woman who has stored sperm and is fortunate enough to have friends or family willing to donate eggs, they can become a 'known donor'. If not, she will most likely be in the queue, waiting for sufficient anonymous donors to volunteer their eggs. For those trans woman that have not stored sperm and thus would require a donated embryo in order to gestate in a transplanted uterus, there is an even greater shortage of embryos for donation and they will most likely be placed on an even lengthier waiting list for treatment.

6.1.2.3   Conclusions on Uterus Transplantation in Trans Women

Following a successful application to the Gender Recognition Panel, a trans woman, from the date of recognition, acquires all the rights and responsibilities that fall to cis-gendered women. A trans woman who has obtained legal recognition of her chosen gender under the Gender Recognition Act 2004 is, in a legal and social context, to be treated as equal to other cis-gendered women. Under the legislative frameworks that would govern uterus transplantation (the HFE Acts 1990 and 2008 and the Human Tissue Act 2004), trans women are legally entitled to be treated consistently with other women. In theory, this novel technology should raise no greater regulatory issues than those discussed in the previous chapter. In practice, there will be further complications regarding parenthood due to the fact that the HFE Act 1990 (as amended by the HFE Act 2008) fails to adequately accommodate trans individuals when ascribing parental status. I deal with this is Part III below. For present purposes, it is sufficient to state that if uterus transplantation was deemed clinical treatment to facilitate cis

---

[101]   Donor anonymity was removed from 2005 following the Human Fertilisation and Embryology Act (Disclosure of donor Information) Regulations 2004. The Human Fertilisation and Embryology (HFE) Act 2008 included new disclosure provisions for donor-conceived individuals and gamete and embryo donors, and section 24 of the 2008 HFE Act replaced section 31 of the 1990 HFE Act with new sections 31–31ZG. For an interesting paper on donor anonymity see J. C. Harper, D. Kennett and D. Reisel, 'The End of Donor Anonymity: How Genetic Testing Is Likely to Drive Anonymous Gamete Donation Out of Business' (2016) 31(6) *Human Reproduction* 1135–1140.

[102]   Human Fertilisation and Embryology 'Egg Sharing Schemes', Background Briefings, www.hfea.gov.uk.

women in their reproductive desires, but not trans women, absent safety and efficacy concerns, this would constitute discrimination and a failure to legally recognise their legal gender in contravention of both the GRA and possibly Articles 8 and 14 of the ECHR.

6.2 Uterus Transplantation in Men

'Is society ready for the pregnant husband?'[103]

The above question was the opening sentence of an article published on 15 March 2008 by trans man, Thomas Beatie in LGBT magazine *The Advocate*.[104] At the time, Beatie was legally recognised as a male and his marriage to his (then) partner, Nancy, was legally recognised. The couple wanted to parent and as Nancy could no longer conceive, they decided he would gestate their child instead. Verlinden claims his appearance on prominent American talk show, *The Oprah Winfrey Show*, 'was a critical turning point in the representation of male pregnancy'.[105] The controversial issue with uterus transplantation is that, once safely performed in a trans woman (and as noted above, they have a legal right to access the same ARTs as their cis women counterparts) we will be a step closer to male pregnancy. There are crucial distinctions between transgender women and cisgender men gestating via uterus transplantation to be factored in: for instance, the former will most likely be in receipt of estrogen and other 'female' hormones and thus their testosterone may be significantly lowered. Professor Brännström who led the world's first successful uterus transplant procedure in Sweden has asserted that it could one day be technically possible to transplant a uterus into a cisgender man, combined with the use of hormone therapy to enable a pregnancy to succeed. The baby would be delivered via cesarean section and the uterus removed shortly after successful delivery. Whilst uterus transplantation arguably has the potential to enhance male reproductive capacity, as men have other methods of procreating, this may be regarded more as choosing an experience not now available to men. In this section I endeavour to illustrate how the existing law under the current regulatory framework might apply to such a scenario.

Whilst uterus transplantation may have reignited the debate on this topic, the notion of male pregnancy is not new or novel.[106] Silver notes

---

[103] Article was a first-hand account by Thomas Beatie, a FTM trans man from Oregon, who was five months pregnant.

[104] Ibid.

[105] Verlinden, 'Transgender Bodies and Male Pregnancy' 109.

[106] The idea of male pregnancy was circulating in the early 1980s amidst sporadic reports on whether male pregnancy may be possible in the abdominal cavity. See D. Teresi and K. McAuliffe, 'Male Pregnancy' in P. D. Hopkins (ed.), *Sex/Machine: Readings in Culture, Gender and Technology* (Bloomington, IN: Indiana University Press, 1998).

how 'the fantasy of a man becoming pregnant is probably as old as story telling itself'.[107] Whilst the notion is not new, the science that may permit it to happen – uterus transplantation – is. Corea, writing in 1986, foresaw the possibility that uterus transplantation may one day enable male pregnancy:

> Transplant or replacement medicine foresees the day, after the automatic rejection of alien tissue is overcome, when a uterus can be implanted in a human male's body – and gestation started by artificial fertilization and egg transfer.[108]

Up until now, the prospect that men may one day get the chance to experience pregnancy and independent control of their reproductive destinies had been relegated to the realms of fiction.[109] Once men were separated from the provision of sperm in an act of sexual reproduction, their reproductive control was limited. If conception occurs during sexual intercourse, men have little or no say in whether they will become a genetic father. The decision usually rests with the woman carrying the fetus; she may decide whether to terminate or not, irrespective of the father's wishes.[110] This is the case even if the couple are married, or even if he was deceived in to believing she was using birth control at the time of intercourse.[111] Advances in artificial reproductive technologies have altered this slightly in the context of IVF, where highly publicised disputes over IVF embryos have indicated that men have greater control over their in vitro gametes; in this context a man can veto the use of his gametes up until the point of implantation.[112] There is also research currently being undertaken on the possibility of developing a male contraceptive pill that will allow men to control their fertility in much the same way that the female contraceptive pill allows women to.[113] Now

---

[107] L. Silver, *Remaking Eden* (New York, NY: Avon Books, 1997) 193, p. 192.

[108] G. Corea *The Mother Machine; Reproductive Technologies from Artificial Insemination to Artificial Wombs* (New York, NY: HarperCollins, 1985), at p. 289.

[109] See U. Le Guin, *The Left Hand of Darkness* (New York, NY: Ace Books, 1969). This award-winning science fiction novel takes place in a world in which the same person can be either male or female. It challenges our assumptions about the relationship between sex and gender.

[110] The Abortion Act 1967 (as amended by The Human Fertilisation and Embryology Act 1990). *Paton* v. *British Pregnancy Advisory Service Trustees* [1979] QB 276. *C* v. *S* [1988] QB 135.

[111] S. Sheldon, '"Sperm Bandits" Birth Control Fraud and the Battle of the Sexes' (2001) 21 *Legal Studies* 460.

[112] *Evans* v. *Amicus* [2004] EWCA Civ 727.

[113] The male contraceptive pill is likely to work by blocking sperm production, using a combination of the sex hormones progestogen and testosterone. It is likely to become available as either a single pill or a longer-acting implant. However, as it only takes a single sperm to create a new life, scientists face a considerable challenge in trying to develop a pill that is 100 per cent effective in every man, all of the time. See O. Plana, 'Male Contraception: Research, New Methods and Implications for Marginalized

scientists are promising the most radical breakthrough yet, uterine transplantation with IVF to enable men to experience pregnancy and gestate their own child.

Safety issues surrounding performing a uterine transplant in a man have raised concerns; consider the following comments made by Caplan et al.:

> While this idea may seem appealing to some, the physiological requirements for nourishing a uterus and maintaining a pregnancy make it exceedingly unlikely that a uterus transplant would work in a man. During a pregnancy, up to one-fifth of a woman's cardiac output goes to the pregnant uterus. Since the vascular connections for a uterus do not exist in males, they would have to be created. Hormonal supplementation would also be required, along with the immunosuppression. Obviously, the bodily incompatibilities are so daunting that to even try for a male pregnancy seems inappropriate. While it makes for some fascinating science fiction scenarios, the risks involved make the selection of a male subject for this experiment ethically dubious.[114]

Not all are as pessimistic; Brännström acknowledged once uterus womb transplants in women is possible, it will also be technically possible one day to transplant a uterus into a man, this combined with the use of hormone therapy will enable the pregnancy to succeed.[115] Uterus transplantation in men, particularly those involved in first clinical research trials, may pose serious health risks to the male recipient and the fetus. Whilst risk to the latter would justify not permitting the procedure, in context of risk to the former, patients have the right to choose different risk levels, based on their own, private circumstances and desires. As noted by Sparrow, 'although there may be risks to the man involved in this procedure, it seems probable that they could be reduced to a level comparable to those associated with other reproductive projects that normally would be held to be ethical'.[116] This would accord with the current approach where pregnant/expectant mothers

Populations' (2015) *American Journal of Men's Health* 1–8. J. Pappenheim, 'The Male Pill Is Coming and It Will Change the Way You Do Too' *BBC News*, 11 January 2017.

[114] A. Caplan, C. Perry, L. Plante et al., 'Moving the Womb' (2007) 37(3) *Hastings Center Report* 18–20, at p. 20.

[115] M. Hutchinson, 'Womb Transplant Baby "Within Three Years"' *BBC News*, 1 July 2003.

[116] Sparrow, 2008, p. 278.

are allowed to carry on a pregnancy, even when there is a significant risk to her health.[117]

Why would men want to gestate? 'Part of the beauty of being a guy, is not having to get pregnant'[118]

The above comment was made by a character in the movie *Junior*, which revolved around a story line of a pregnant man,[119] yet if the significant medical obstacles can one day be overcome so as to enable safe gestation in men, some men may welcome the ability to have the intimate bodily relationship and experience of gestation. When news that a successful pregnancy had occurred following a hysterectomy, and tabloids reported that 'the era of pregnant men had arrived', Teresi and McAuliffe noted the high level of response by men who wanted to experience pregnancy:

> The story struck a nerve in many men. Scientists doing work on the cutting edge of human reproduction were barraged with letters from men who wanted to be mothers. Some were transsexuals. But others were conventional men who simply wanted to experience the joys of pregnancy.[120]

Two decades on from speculation of male pregnancy in the abdominal cavity, uterus transplantation 'puts gestation by males in a new light'[121] and may bring us one step closer to achieving male pregnancy. Brännström, who led the first successful uterine transplant trial to result in a live birth, stated his inbox was inundated from men seeking a uterus transplant: 'I get emails from all over the world on this, sometimes from gay males with one partner that would like to carry a child'.[122]

At present, men who wish to parent a genetically related child are dependent on a female host to gestate a child. Men who may seek to utilise such technology could be heterosexual and wish to share the burdens and joys of pregnancy. Same-sex male couples may also wish to procreate in this fashion, one of them donating the sperm whilst the other gestates the baby, involving both in the reproductive process and

---

[117] Consider caesarean section cases.
[118] Statement made by the Danny De Vito character in the movie *Junior*; see Silver, *Remaking Eden* at p. 228.
[119] Statement made by the Danny De Vito character in the movie.
[120] Teresi and McAuliffe, 'Male Pregnancy', at p. 175.
[121] T. Murphy, 'Assisted Gestation and Transgender Women' (2015) 29 *Bioethics* 390.
[122] Fine Maron, 'How a Transgender Woman Could Get Pregnant'.

avoiding the need to commission a surrogate. Single men may also wish to opt for this procedure, avoiding the legally uncertain route of commissioning a surrogate.[123] At present the only way single men or those in same sex relationships can genetically parent are via commissioning of a female host to gestate the child for them. The use of a surrogate as a method to founding a family in the UK is complex and regulation of surrogacy[124] has developed in a haphazard fashion[125] and discriminates against single parents who wish to attain legal parenthood in this way.

Men may seek to exercise greater control over their reproductive destiny. In traditional reproductive roles, Corea argues that men have been somewhat excluded from the reproduction process; men's sperm is alienated (that is, separated) from him in the sex act, and this alienation negates him as a parent. She contends:

> When his seed is alienated, man is separated from the continuity of the human species, from a sense of unity with natural process. He does not actually experience a link between generations. While woman has a sense of her connection with the next generation in the labor through which she births that generation, man is isolated within the dimensions of his own lifespan. He has not labored to produce the child, except in the relatively trivial expenditure of energy in sexual intercourse.[126]

---

[123] Surrogacy Arrangements Act 1985 (as amended by s59 Human Fertilisation and Embryology Act 2008).

[124] The practice is regulated by the Surrogacy Arrangements Act 1985 and (in respect of the making of parental orders) the Human Fertilisation and Embryology Acts 1990 and 2008.

[125] See DoH, Brazier Report, *Surrogacy: Review for Health Ministers of Current Arrangements For Payments and Regulation* (Cm 4068, 1998). M. Freeman, 'Does Surrogacy Have a Future after Brazier?' (1999) 7 *Medical Law Review* 1. K. Horsey and S. Sheldon, 'Still Hazy after All These Years: The Law Regulating Surrogacy' (2012) 20 *Medical Law Review* 67. A. Alghrani, D. Griffiths and M Brazier, 'Surrogacy Law: From Piecemeal Tweaks to Sustained Review and Reform' in A. Diduck, N. Peleg and H Reece (eds.), *Law in Society: Reflections on Children, Family, Culture and Philosophy – Essays in Honour of Michael Freeman Law* (Brill Publishers, 2014) 425. K. Horsey, 'Fraying at the Edges – UK Surrogacy Law' (2015) 24(4) *Medical Law Review* 608. E. Jackson, J. Millbank, I. Karpin and A Stuhmcke, 'Learning from Cross-Border Reproduction' (2017) 25(1) *Medical Law Review* 23. M. Crawshaw, E. Blyth and O. Akker, 'The Changing Profile of Surrogacy in the UK – Implications for National and International Policy and Practice' (2012) 34(3) *Journal of Social Welfare and Family Law* 265–275.

[126] G. Corea, 'The Mother Machine' in K. D. Alpern (ed.), *The Ethics of Reproductive Technology* (New York, NY and Oxford: Oxford University Press, 1992) 220–232, at p. 223.

Beside the provision of his sperm, after sexual intercourse a man has little say in the decision of whether or not to reproduce. Male pregnancy will not only allow men experience to gestation, but also to be more in control of their reproductive destinies. Hypothetically, should he elect to have a uterus transplant and manage to have an IVF embryo implanted, his bodily autonomy is engaged and for the next nine months he will have the decisive say over the fate of the embryo he is carrying.

However this is supposing that, with a great imaginative leap, uterine transplantation and IVF would be allowed in men so as to permit male gestation. As with other advances in the third era, the prospect of male gestation was not within contemplation of the legislature when UK's regulatory regime that governs ARTs was drafted. I now turn to apply the current regulatory framework to the speculative prospect and examine whether it is equipped to deal with the challenges it may bring.

6.2.1   Would Male Pregnancy Be Legally Permissible in the UK?

Let us consider the current law in the context of the following hypothetical scenario:

> Jack and Jill, a married couple are in their early thirties and have been trying for a child for many years. Jill has high blood pressure and thus has been warned that she is more likely to have potentially serious problems during pregnancy, such as: preeclampsia, a fetus that does not grow as much as expected, premature detachment of the placenta from the uterus (placental abruption) and stillbirth. Jack's sister, Leanne (who already has two children) has offered to donate her uterus to Jack, to help the couple in their desire to have a genetically related child. Tests indicate Leanne is a tissue match. Jack understands that this advance is still very much experimental, however he wishes to do all he can to gestate his own genetically related child, without recourse to a surrogate.

6.2.2   Uterus Transplantation in Men

Since there is no legal precedent to shed guidance on how such a scenario would be governed, how the present legislation could apply to this novel advance will now be considered. The legal complexities that would stem from male pregnancy are vast; if uterus transplantation were to fall under the regulatory framework that oversees transplantation of other organs and tissue, the Human Tissue Act 2004, the first question would be whether uterus donation in men would be allowed under this regime.

There is no gender-specific provisions contained in the 2004 Act. However, uterus transplantation will be limited by the chronic lack of organs available. As uterus transplantation was not within contemplation when the Human Tissue Act 2004 was drafted, it is not surprising the statute is silent on the topic of uterus transplantation. The Human Tissue Act 2004, Revised Code of Practice F 'Donation of Solid Organs for Transplantation' (April 2017) outlines the types organ donation that may take place.[127] HTA approval is needed for living donation. The UK Organ Donor Register (ODR) allows donors to specify which organs they wish to donate (e.g. kidneys, corneas, heart, lung, liver etc.), although a uterus is not one of the listed organs. Registrants can however tick a box specifying they wish to donate 'any of my organs and tissue'. No information about uterus transplant is provided to those who sign the ODR and it is not clear how individual women might feel about their uteri being made available for transplantation in either cis-gendered women, trans women or cis-gendered men.

Returning to the hypothetical scenario outlined above, Leanne is a living donor, thus directed donation is permitted with HTA approval.[128] In her desire to donate to her brother, provided the HTA approve, as a living donor, Leanne can request that her organ be directed to a named individual, the intended recipient.[129] Section 33 of the HTA 2004 provides that directed donations between close family members, including spouses, are lawful, provided that the HTA is satisfied that no element of reward or coercion exists. Thus a living donor can donate her uterus with a condition it went to a named individual who was a man, or conversely that it went to a cis-gendered or trans woman. Thus, in theory, a man could obtain a uterus if he had a living donor willing to donate her uterus to him and provided of course the HTA approved.

In contrast to living organ donation, deceased directed donation is not permitted. Thus donors who specified donation of uterus upon death was permissible only on the condition it only went to a cis-gender woman would not be valid. Such conditions would be treated as 'sexist' and parallels could be drawn with racist conditions, which led to much controversy in 1998 when organs were donated on condition of being allocated to white

---

[127] www.hta.gov.uk/sites/default/files/Code%20F%20-%20Organs%20for%20tx%20Final_0.pdf

[128] For ethical discussion on conditional donation see M. L. Volk and P. A. Ubel, 'A Gift of Life: Ethical and Practical Problems with Conditional and Directed Donation' (2008) 85 (11) *Transplantation* 1542–1544.

[129] HTA Code of Practice, paragraph 33.

recipients only. Mr Frank Dobson, the then Secretary of State for Health, made a statement (together with the President of the British Transplantation Society) affirming 'organs must not be accepted if conditions about the recipient are attached'.[130] Following the 2010 report titled 'An Investigation into Conditional Organ Donation' in 2000', the 'central principle' of organ allocation from deceased donors is that they will go to the person who is most in need and who is the best match with the donor.[131]

However on the basis of best match, cis-gendered women are no doubt likely to be prioritised and first in line to receive a uterus transplant from a deceased donor. In this context it is restoring biological functioning and allowing them to overcome uterine factor infertility. A uterus transplant in a man would not be restoring ordinary function, but rather giving him extraordinary function. Prioritising women in such a manner may also be regarded as in line with HTA policy, which provides:

> UK Transplant, part of the NHS, matches and allocates donated organs for transplantation in accordance with the principles and legal frameworks set out by the Human Tissue Authority. The system for allocating these precious resources is designed to ensure that the process is as fair as possible and that those who are most sick, and therefore in most need, are most likely to benefit.[132]

6.2.3   Fertility Treatment to Enable Male Pregnancy

If a man were to overcome the difficulties in obtaining a uterus, the second element needed to gestate a fetus therein, involves obtaining an IVF embryo that can be implanted into the donated uterus. The HFE Acts 1990 and 2008 regulate IVF and the provisions therein make it unlawful for a clinic to provide fertility treatment to assist a man to become pregnant. Assisting a male to become pregnant does not fall within the specified activities for which a licence can be granted when 'bringing about the creation of embryos *in vitro*'.[133] 'Treatment services' are

---

[130] F. Dobson, 'No Health Apartheid' http://news.bbc.co.uk/1/hi/health/387817.stm.

[131] DoH, 2000, An Investigation into Conditional Organ Donation. See also DoH 'Requested allocation of a deceased donor organ, 2010.

[132] UK Transplant statement on directed donation of organs after death, 15 April 2008; see www.uktransplant.org.uk.

[133] HFEA 1990, Schedule 2 lists the activities for which licences may be granted provides: s1 (1) A licence under this paragraph may authorise any of the following in the course of providing treatment services: (a) bringing about the creation of embryos *in vitro*; (b) keeping embryos; (c) using gametes; (d) practices designed to secure that embryos are in a suitable condition to be placed in a woman or to determine whether embryos are

defined by the HFE Act 1990 as being a range of services provided for a woman. No provision is made in the HFE Act 1990 (as amended) regarding the placement of an embryo into a man. The HFE Act 1990 further provides that 'a licence ... cannot authorise any activity unless it appears to the Authority to be necessary or desirable for the purpose of providing treatment services'.[134] Treatment services are defined as meaning 'medical, surgical or obstetric services provided to the public or a section of the public for the purpose of assisting *women* to carry children'.[135] Thus, the use of an IVF embryo in order to assist a man to experience pregnancy in the absence of a licence, would be in contravention of the HFE Act and could result in criminal sanctions of up to ten years imprisonment.[136]

It is clear that the HFE Act 1990 only permits provision of fertility treatment services to assist women to become pregnant. This remains the case under the HFE Act 2008. Without new legislation to govern this advance, or Parliament amending the present legislation so that the definition of 'treatment services' encompasses fertility treatment for the purpose of 'assisting *men and women* to carry a child', the current regulatory framework bars the placing an IVF human embryo into a man so as to achieve pregnancy.

6.2.4   A Right to Gestate?

Could a cis-gendered man argue that notions of procreative liberty encompass a right to gestate? In the context of procreative liberty, Robertson argued:

suitable for that purpose; (e) placing any embryo in a woman; (f) mixing sperm with the egg of a hamster, or other animal specified in directions, for the purpose of testing the fertility or normality of the sperm, but only where anything which forms is destroyed when the test is complete and, in any event, not later than the two cell stage; and, (g) such other practices as may be specified in, or determined in accordance with, regulations. The HFE Act 2008, Schedule 2, paragraph 2 amends paragraph 1 of Schedule 2 to the 1990 Act to enable treatment licences to be granted for the use of embryos for training persons in embryo biopsy, embryo storage and other embryological techniques, but only where the HFEA is satisfied that such use is necessary for that purpose. Paragraph 1 is also amended to ensure that only 'permitted embryos' within the meaning of new section 3ZA can be placed in a woman.

[134] HFE Act 1990, Schedule 2 (3).

[135] HFE Act 1990, s2 (1). My emphasis. This remains unaltered by the HFE Act 2008.

[136] HFE Act 1990, s41 provides: A person who: (a) contravenes section 3(2) or 4(1) (c) of this Act; or (b) does anything which, by virtue of section 3(3) of this Act, cannot be authorised by a licence, is guilty of an offence and liable on conviction on indictment to imprisonment for a term not exceeding ten years or a fine or both.

> liberty is a deeply held moral and legal value that deserves a strong measure of respect in all reproductive activities. While this value is widely acknowledged when reproduction occurs *au naturel*, this book will show that it should be equally honoured when reproduction requires technological assistance. As a result individuals should be free to use these techniques or not as they choose, without governmental restriction, unless strong justification for limiting them can be established ... Thus decisions about reproductive technology should, in almost all cases, be left to the individuals directly involved.[137]

In the quote, Robertson seems to acknowledge that in unconventional situations there could be such justification. Procreative liberty includes the right to bear children in unconventional family circumstances and in the absence of demonstrable harm to resulting children, establishes an extremely strong presumption against laws regulating who may have children, or when, or with whom individuals may have children.[138]

In the context of considering whether the notion of procreative liberty may extend to defend the idea that it is every man's right to gestate, Sparrow accedes that given the role played by the right to procreative liberty in other debates about reproductive technologies, it will be extremely difficult to deny that this right extends to include male pregnancy to bear genetic offspring. However Sparrow argues it is a grave mistake to conclude reproductive liberty entitles a male to the 'right' to become pregnant, or to promote this technology with reference to the reproductive liberty of men:

> this conclusion constitutes a reductio ad absurdum of the idea of reproductive liberty as it is currently used in bioethics. Any notion of a right to reproductive liberty that extends as far as a man's right to gestate has lost contact with the facts about the biology of reproduction and its significance in a normal human life that made it plausible to defend the existence of such a right in the first place.[139]

Sparrow argues that notions of reproductive liberty have gone awry in this context for the following reasons: firstly, the argument for reproductive liberty relies for its force on facts about the normative role reproduction plays in the human life cycle. Given the role that reproduction plays in human flourishing, the harms of infringing and frustrating this right for those unable to reproduce, or who need assistance so as to do so, are clear. However, as pregnancy is simply not a normal part of men's lives, it is not a tragedy when a man cannot become pregnant – no matter how

---

[137] J. Robertson, *Children of Choice* (Princeton, NY and Chichester: Princeton University Press, 1994) at p. 4.

[138] Sparrow, 'Is It "Every Man's Right to Have Babies if He Wants Them"?' 280.

[139] Sparrow, 'Is It "Every Man's Right to Have Babies if He Wants Them"?' 276.

strongly he desires it. Thus Sparrow argues barriers to men becoming pregnant do not constitute restrictions of reproductive liberty in the same way, as do barriers to women becoming pregnant. Sparrow's argument relies upon repro normativity and what may be regarded as intuition or common sense. Whilst it is true that one may not regard a male not being able to get pregnant as a human tragedy, this may be because it is not yet possible and people do not have sympathy because someone cannot do the impossible. For instance, I may not sympathise with someone for being unable to teleport. But in a world were men can get pregnant/ people can teleport we may think differently and see it as a tragedy. Furthermore rights are not based on whether something is perceived as tragedy or not. I would not regard it a tragedy if Katie Hopkins[140] was banned from appearing on television, but it might interfere with her fundamental human right to free speech as protected under the European Convention of Human Rights.[141]

Sparrow's second argument is that rights cannot be summoned into existence *ex nihilio*, whether an activity falls within a right depends in part on a set of substantive judgments about what sorts of projects can contribute to a meaningful life and the interests that found rights must be capable of being described in ways that can communicate their importance to others. That the application of a right always involves these sorts of judgments about the merits of the claim that some particular project falls within it, otherwise one would have no way of adjudicating when rights conflict. Again this is not convincing. Just because the importance of a right can be explained does not result in adjudication between conflicts of rights being possible. For instance the right to privacy might conflict with the right to free speech. We can explain that both are important. But the fact that they are important does not help us adjudicate conflicts between those rights.

Sparrow goes on to argue that the problem with grounding a male right to pregnancy in a general right to self-determination, then, is that in the context of the normal reproductive life cycle for men, it is a frivolous claim. This he claims accounts for the primary source of the intuition that defending 'men's right to have babies' is just plain silly. Men seeking to become pregnant should not be granted the same moral weight as women's desires to become pregnant, because pregnancy is not a reasonable expectation in men. He thus argues no negative right to male

---

[140] Katie Hopkins is an English media personality famous for making offensive, defamatory and racist comments.
[141] Article 10.

pregnancy exists and laws prohibiting men from becoming pregnant would not interfere with a project that is entitled to the same level of respect granted ordinary reproduction.

The rights rhetoric Sparrow deployed here clouds the issue. Whether men have the right to get pregnant depends upon what theory of rights one adopts. If one adopted a choice theory of rights or broad interpretation of procreative liberty, then one could say thwarting a man's decision to get pregnant, when this represents the only way he can genetically reproduce (someone in position of Jack and Jill in the above hypothetical scenario) would interfere with his rights. Sparrow has not provided a theory of rights or explained how we decide what rights people have and his argument against male gestation, is hidden behind rights rhetoric, repro normativity discourse and intuition.

Sparrow's analysis and can be summed up as follows: without some naturalistic and gendered account of parenthood, bioethics has opened the door to entirely degendered accounts of rights and duties in parenthood. He seems to favour a view that parental sex implies moral limits to the ways in which people should have children, at least as far as state subsidy is concerned. Acknowledging that that fertility clinicians help same-sex couples bypass their situational infertility; Sparrow's line of argumentation remains that individuals may still only have children in male-typical or female-typical ways, even if the parental roles of same-sex couples vary from the norm. Sparrow also argues against the use of public funds to support research into uterus transplantation for men (since he sees no right, there is no public duty to support research).

Robertson, the late great and influential writer on procreative liberty[142] offers a more convincing view on whether procreative liberty would extend to male pregnancy. Similar to Sparrow, Robertson, argues there is a strong argument against men having a right to gestate under the auspices of reproductive liberty:

> a right to gestate as part of procreative liberty is coherent only when it is integrally related to the gestator's own genetic reproduction. In many cases a phenotypical male who can produce sperm would not need a UTX to do so, since partners or gestational surrogates would be available. In that situation, the desire alone to experience what women feel in carrying and delivering a child would not be a strong enough reason to undergo the burdens and costs, not to mention the use of a scarce organ, simply to have a gestational experience unnecessary for his reproduction. Just because

---

[142] See J. A. Robertson, 'Procreative Liberty in the Era of Genomics' (2003) 29 *American Journal of Law & Medicine* 439.

women reproduce through pregnancy does not mean that men should be able to do so as well. Not all whims or even strong desires about passing on genes merit protection as part of procreative liberty.[143]

However, Roberson's view was based on the view that procreative liberty should include a right to gestate when gestation is essential to, or part of a person's way to have genetic offspring for rearing. He conceded that a man might have a stronger claim to gestate if there were no partner or surrogate available:

> if a high priority is given to enabling persons to have and rear their own genetic offspring; safety and efficacy have been established; and there is no other alternative for having genetic offspring, a rare case of male pregnancy as an aspect of procreative liberty might arise.[144]

However, he argues that even then it would not be 'strong enough to justify the gender conflation that might then occur'.[145] It is clear there is no consensus on whether procreative liberty would or should extend or trans or male pregnancy and answering this question is beyond the remit of this book. My intention here being merely to highlight some of the regulatory issues new technologies in the third era will raise and how capable the current regulatory framework is of accommodating them. I now turn the 'gender conflation' Professor Robertson alluded to as a justification not to permit trans and male pregnancy.

6.3 'Parenthood' Blurred Lines

> it is clear that new technological developments are capable of redefining some of the basic *facts* of reproduction.[146]

The above quote from Jackson's paper, 'Degendering Reproduction'[147] explores the 'implications of technologies which have already separated sex from reproduction and enabled fertilisation to take place in a laboratory, and which may, in the future further, alter and perhaps even eliminate gender differences in the reproductive process'.[148] As Jackson

---

[143] J. A. Robertson, 'Is There a Right to Gestate?' (2017) *Journal of Law and the Biosciences* 1–7.

[144] Ibid., p. 7.

[145] Ibid.

[146] *Frette* v. *France* (2004) 38 EHRR 438.

[147] E. Jackson, 'Degendering Reproduction' (2014) *Medical Law Review* 346–368. This argument is presented in the context of artificial gametes and ectogenesis.

[148] Ibid., p. 347.

acknowledges, such shifts in reproductive roles cannot be attributed solely to medical progress, as the meanings of motherhood and fatherhood has always been culturally, geographically and temporally specific: 'Whilst social change is significant in examining the meaning of parenthood, it is clear that new technological developments are capable of redefining some of the basic *facts* of reproduction'.[149] One way in which reproduction can be 'degendered' is via uterus transplantation in cis men. The prospect of gestation in trans and gender non binary individuals and cis-gendered men forces reconsideration of the heterosexist and biological framework that entrenches parental labels, such as motherhood and fatherhood, in biological sex/ function.[150]

When concerns first arose following IVF and the possibility that assisted reproductive technologies could fragment parenthood and the nuclear family model, the Warnock Committee was established in 1982 to consider recent and potential developments in medicine and science related to human fertilisation and embryology; to consider what policies and safeguards should be applied, including consideration of the social, ethical and legal implications of these developments; and to make recommendations.[151] The Committee's report published in 1984, was explicitly hetero-centric, stating 'we believe that as a general rule it is better for children to be born into a two-parent family, with both father and mother'.[152] The HFE Act 1990 was based upon the Warnock Committee's recommendations, thus the provisions which conferred legal parenthood in cases of assisted reproduction, were also hetero-centric and concerned with promoting the nuclear family model. In drafting its provisions, Sheldon noted that '[p]arliament attempted to foresee every possible reproductive scenario and to provide for the resulting family arrangement to conform as closely as possible to a nuclear family model'.[153] McCandless and Sheldon examined the reforms of the 2008 Act that determine the parenthood of

---

[149] Ibid.

[150] See J. L. Hill, 'What Does It Mean to Be a "Parent"? The Claims of Biology as the Basis for Parental Rights' (1991) 66 *New York University Law Review* 353. M. M. Shultz, 'Reproductive Technology and Intent Based Parenthood: An Opportunity for Gender Neutrality' (1990) 2 *Wisconsin Law Review* 297.

[151] Department of Health and Social Security, *Report of the Committee of Inquiry into Human Fertilisation and Embryology* (1984). For more on the Warnock Committee read N. Hammond Brown, 'Ethics, Embryos and Evidence: A Look Back at Warnock' (2015) 23(4) *Medical Law Review* 588–619.

[152] Warnock Report, paragraph 2.11.

[153] S. Sheldon, 'Fragmenting Fatherhood: The Regulation of Reproductive Technologies' (2005) 68(4) *Modern Law Review* 523 at p. 541.

children conceived by technologies regulated by the legislation.[154] They observe how the provisions reflect 'deep rooted assumptions and highly conservative understandings about who should count as a family'.[155] Adopting the conceptual tool of the 'sexual family' model (a term coined by Fineman to describe the ideal family type of a heterosexual couple, joined through a formally celebrated union with genetically related offspring[156]), they note how the 2008 amendments reflect a tenacious hold of this model on English law in the face of developments that might at first sight appear to herald its decline.[157] While the reforms of the 2008 Act have widened the scope of legal parenthood in cases of assisted reproduction, to allow for the possibility of two legal parents of the same sex, the family model continues to reflect that which consciously underpinned the 1990 Act,[158] which is the binary, two-parent model based upon the traditional, heterosexual, nuclear family. With the greatest respect to those responsible for updating the legislation, retaining the underpinning policy of the 1990 Act and merely amending the statute, was a missed opportunity to consider in depth the reproductive scientific advances that had already occurred since Warnock deliberated and those advances on the foreseeable horizon, such as uterus transplantation.

6.3.1   Blurred Lines: 'Parenthood'

Regulating and ascribing legal parenthood in the novel context of uterus transplantation into trans individuals and cis-gendered men necessitates stretching current legislative provisions which are entrenched in the binary, two-parent nuclear family model to see how (if at all) they may accommodate new advances such as uterus transplantation. It is clear in this context that retaining current legal definitions ascribed to 'mother' as female who

---

[154] J. McCandless and S. Sheldon, 'The Human Fertilisation and Embryology Act (2008) and the Tenacity of the Sexual Family Form' (2010) 73(2) *Modern Law Review* 175, at p. 182.

[155] Above, p. 176.

[156] M. Fineman, *The Neutered Mother, the Sexual Family and Other Twentieth Century Tragedies* (New York, NY and London: Routledge, 1995).

[157] McCandless and Sheldon, 'The Human Fertilisation and Embryology Act (2008)' 176. This is also evident from the exclusion single individuals face in the context of becoming a legal parent via surrogacy, where s54 of the 2008 Act provides that applicants for a parental order must be two individuals in an enduring relationship.

[158] HFE Act 1990 (as amended) ss42–48, which creates the possibility of legal parenthood for both members of a female same-sex couple in cases of assisted reproduction and s54, under which same-sex couples can apply for 'parental orders' in cases of surrogacy, once more retaining the two-parent family model.

gestates and 'father' as male sperm provider, predicated as they are in biological function,[159] will result in legal anomalies.

In the context of a uterus transplant to achieve male pregnancy, if we return to our former pregnant male hypothetical scenario of Jack and Jill, who would be deemed the legal mother and father of any child gestated by a male? Section 33 of the HFE Act 2008 provides 'the *woman* who is carrying or has carried a child as a result of the placing in her of an embryo or of sperm and eggs, and no other woman, is to be treated as the mother of the child'.[160] There is specific reference to the woman. Thus there are two possible options; the first is that a child gestated in a man would be regarded as being legally motherless since the child was not gestated in a woman. Secondly, if the HFE Act were (with a great imaginative leap) interpreted to embrace men, the man who is carrying or has carried a child as a result of a uterus transplant and the implantation of an IVF embryo, could be regarded as the 'mother' of the child.

This is already the case in the context of trans individuals who have legally been acknowledged in their preferred gender, but who procreate using their reproductive capacities, so for instance a trans man who has not undergone a hysterectomy and uses his uterus to gestate and beget a child. Even if he conceives and gives birth to a child, whilst legally recognised as a male, he is the regarded as the legal 'mother' of the child. The fear here is, as Dunne observes, 'that any resulting children will be confused about their genetic origins or denied important family relationships'.[161] Indeed this is the situation that transpired in 2017 when Hayden Cross, who had undergone gender reassignment treatment and for three years had been legally recognised as male, was registered as his child's 'mother'.[162] Cross was refused NHS assistance to preserve his fertility and, fearful his transition may limit his fertility, he placed his transition on hold and resorted to an informal sperm donor, which resulted in a successful conception and birth of his daughter. He stated 'having a biological child has always meant a lot to me'.[163] When he registered his daughter's birth, he was named as his daughters 'mother' and the child was deemed legally fatherless.

---

[159] As defined in Human Fertilisation and Embryology Act 1990 (as amended by the Human Fertilisation and Embryology Act 2008).

[160] My emphasis. This remains the same as the former definition of mother in section 27 of the Human Fertilisation and Embryology Act 1990.

[161] Dunne, 'Transgender Sterilisation Requirements in Europe' 565.

[162] C. Baynes, 'Britain's First Pregnant Man Gives Birth to Girl' *The Independent*, 8 July 2017.

[163] Ibid.

The child is deemed legally fatherless as the HFE Act defines 'father' with explicit reference to a child who is being or has been carried by a woman:

> 35 Meaning of 'father'
> (1) If— (a) at the time of the placing in her of the embryo or the sperm and eggs or of her insemination, W [the woman] was a party to a marriage [with a man], and (b) the creation of the embryo carried by her was not brought about with the sperm of the other party to the marriage, then, subject to section 38(2) to (4), the other party to the marriage is to be treated as the father of the child unless it is shown that he did not consent to the placing in her of the embryo, or the sperm and eggs, or to her artificial insemination (as the case may be).

The provision clearly applies to female pregnancy, rather than male pregnancy. This is but one illustration of the legal incongruity that will arise should uterus transplantation in cis men become possible.

The Government's retention of parental labels defined by biological characteristics at birth will mean that uterus transplantation in trans women will also pose novel challenges in regulation when ascribing parental status. If a trans woman, using pre-stored sperm, has a uterus transplant and, following IVF with donor eggs, successfully conceives and gestates a child. legal parenthood which remains defined by ones biological characteristics at birth may result in anomalies.[164] The trans woman who gestates is the legal mother, as it is the woman who gives birth to the child who is regarded as the 'mother'.[165] However, in this scenario, she would also be the *genetic* 'father', since the child was conceived using preoperatively stored spermatozoa, but would not be the *legal* father. A woman who has gender reassigned under the GRA is legally female and thus falls within the provision, unless interpreted as applying only to cis women. If the trans woman was married, or in a civil partnership at the time of treatment (when the embryo was implanted into her transplanted uterus), her husband or partner would be treated as the other parent of the child (unless it was shown that the partner did not consent to the placing of an embryo into her transplanted uterus). If she were single, then is she the legal mother and the child would be regarded as legally fatherless?[166] Section 41 of the HFE Act 2008 deals with the situations in which a child may be legally fatherless. It states:

---

[164] It is worth noting that gender-specific definitions of parents are problematic in other areas. See the remarks of Baroness Hale as reported in J. Rozenberg, 'Lesbians, Should Both Be Called Mother', *The Telegraph*, 21 June 2007.

[165] HFE Act 2008, s33 (formerly s27 of the HFE Act 1990).

[166] HFE Act 1990, Schedule 3, paragraph 5 (see also HFE Act 2008, s41).

(1) Where the sperm of a man who had given such consent as is required by paragraph 5 of Schedule 3 to the 1990 Act (consent to use of gametes for purposes of treatment services or non-medical fertility services) was used for a purpose for which such consent was required, he is not to be treated as the father of the child.

It is apparent from paragraph 5 of Schedule 3 of the HFE Act 1990 that the option of 'legally fatherless' is not applicable to this situation:

5.(1) A person's gametes must not be used for the purposes of treatment services unless there is an effective consent by that person to their being so used and they are used in accordance with the terms of the consent. (2) A person's gametes must not be received for use for those purposes unless there is an effective consent by that person to their being so used. (3) This paragraph does not apply to the use of a person's gametes for the purpose of that person, or that person and another together, receiving treatment services.[167]

Subsection 3 states that the gametes used in situations which give rise to legally fatherless children cannot be the gametes of the individual(s) seeking treatment. In this example, the child could not be legally father-less, as the sperm used belongs to the trans woman. There is no reason that the sperm would not be considered to belong to her. Section 9(1) of the Gender Recognition Act 2004 supports this:

9. (1) Where a full gender recognition certificate is issued to a person, the person's gender becomes for all purposes the acquired gender (so that, if the acquired gender is the male gender, the person's sex becomes that of a man and, if it is the female gender, the person's sex becomes that of a woman).

(2) Subsection (1) does not affect things done, or events occurring, before the certificate is issued; but it does operate for the interpretation of enactments passed, and instruments and other documents made, before the certificate is issued (as well as those passed or made afterwards).

If the above section is taken to mean that the (legal) 'person' remains the same, before and after transition, then the stored sperm is the product of the person wishing to use it. Further support for this view can be gained from later sections of the Gender Recognition Act 2004. The sperm was stored for the purposes of using it later in her procreative desires. If in this case she had wished for the sperm to be used for anonymous donation, then this decision would also still hold, although this may pose a problem to any future children wishing to gain access to information about their

[167] Ibid.

genetic parents,[168] as anonymity is no longer guaranteed to those who donate sperm for use in assisted reproduction.[169]

This must also be considered in light of section 12 of the Gender Recognition Act 2004. This section deals with parentage and states that parental status will not be altered by the Act:

> The fact that a person's gender has become the acquired gender under this Act does not affect the status of the person as the father or mother of a child.[170]

If this section is interpreted as being directed at children born prior to transitioning, it seems to accept that children are entitled to keep the parents they are born with and, more importantly, that novel accounts of parenthood can be acceptable. If this section relates to children born to a trans individual post transition, then this is problematic, for it will mean we have a definition that gives rise to theoretical order, but is not in line with the common usage of the term.[171] By forcing definitions to stretch to mean that there are males acting as 'mothers' and females as 'fathers' we are tacitly accepting that enforced definitions of gender roles are more important than an acknowledgement of the reality of these situations. Defining parental roles according to gender, rather than sex, will not be a perfect solution to all novel-parenting situations.

It is clear then that uterus transplantation in both trans individuals and cis men will confuse current legal definitions of parenthood. The fact the HFE Act is worded to permit only fertility treatment to assist *women* become pregnant, combined with the statutory provisions pertaining to parenthood and the underpinning outdated policy that favours a two-parent model, suggests that separate legislation would be needed to govern this novel method of procreation should it one day become scientifically feasible.

Uterus transplantation once more demonstrates how reproductive technologies are increasingly allowing us to separate genetic, gestational and social parenthood.[172] This reproductive advance also forces us to reconsider the primacy placed upon gestation in the current law and policy when ascribing 'motherhood'.[173] A genetic mother who

---

[168] Gender Recognition Act 2004, s22: Prohibition of disclosure information.
[169] Human Fertilisation and Embryology Act (Disclosure of Donor Information) Regulations 2004.
[170] Gender Recognition Act 2004, s22.
[171] Hill, 'What Does It Mean to Be a "Parent"?'
[172] Corea, 'The Mother Machine', at p. 226.
[173] In the Irish case of *M.R & Anor v. An tArd Chlaraitheoir & Ors* [2013] IEHC 91 the question of what role gestation should take when ascribing motherhood was once more

genetically contributes to the creation of an embryo, which is later transplanted into a surrogate, is not deemed to be the legal mother of the child. Rather it is the surrogate who gestates and carries the pregnancy to term. As noted above, a trans man who gestates is also deemed the 'mother' of the child he has gestated. Future artificial reproductive technologies such as uterus transplantation and ectogenesis, frustrate current definitions of 'motherhood' as the female host who gestates and gives birth to the child. A male who gestates his child may not wish to be regarded as a 'mother'. A mechanical or ectogenic device is not the 'mother'.[174] The possible relocation of the fetus from a female host forces us to reconsider how we think of reproduction and necessitates a rethink of parental labels as currently defined.

In *Re R (Children) (Residence: Same-Sex Partner)*, Hale LJ's tripartite definition of the term 'parent' acknowledged that it could denote the genetic, gestational, social and psychological.[175] A substantial body of literature has emerged on how assisted reproduction has fragmented parenthood and exploration of the idea of recognising multiple parents through law.[176] The time is ripe to revisit the concept of parenthood and ask the crucial question what makes someone a 'parent' and how should the law confer this status. One possible solution would be to revise 'mother' and 'father' to parent and parent; this would avoid the problems of ascribing parental status using labels which are predicated on one's biological sex, as 'mother' and 'father' are. Parenthood could be bestowed on those who specifically intend to create, nurture, rear and parent the

---

raised. An expert in that case outlined the role of epigenetics and the capacity of the gestational environment to influence a child's genetic make-up.

[174] For feminist arguments on embodied labour see R. Fletcher, M. Fox and J. McCandless, 'Legal Embodiment: Analysing the Body of Healthcare Law' (2008) 16(3) *Medical Law Review* 321.

[175] *Re R (Children) (Residence: Same-Sex Partner)* [2006] UKHL 43, paragraphs 33–35.

[176] See L. Smith, 'Tangling the Web of Legal Parenthood: Legal Responses to the Use of Known Donors in Lesbian Parenting Arrangements' (2013) 33 *Legal Studies* 355; R. Leckey, 'Two Mothers in Law and Fact' (2013) 21 *Feminist Legal Studies* 1; R. Leckey, 'Law Reform, Lesbian Parenting, and the Reflective Claim' (2011) 20 *Social & Legal Studies* 331; N. Bala, 'The Evolving Canadian Definition of the Family: Towards a Pluralistic and Functional Approach' (1994) 8 *International Journal of Law, Policy, and the Family* 293; J. Bridgeman, H. Keating and C. Lind (eds.), *Responsibility, Law and the Family* (Aldershot: Ashgate, 2008). R. Collier and S. Sheldon, *Fragmenting Fatherhood: A Socio-Legal Study* (Oxford: Hart, 2008); A. Diduck, '"If Only We Can Find the Appropriate Terms to Use the Issue Will Be Solved": Law, Identity and Parenthood' (2007) 19 *Child and Family Law Quarterly* 458. G. Douglas, 'Parenthood: Commitment, Status and Rights' in J. Eekelaar (ed.), *Family Law in Britain and America in the New Century* (Brill Nijhoff, 2016).

child.[177] A pluralist account of parenthood as advocated by Bayne and Kolers[178] is broad enough to grant parenthood to genetic, gestational, custodial and intentional parents.[179] Fletcher's argument that parenthood will have to be understood morally rather than biologically is intuitively appealing: arguing that parental relationships need to be reconceptualised, he states 'they cannot be based on blood, or womb or even genes ... the mere fact of conceiving a child or donating the elements of its conception or gestating it does not establish anyone as father or mother'.[180] The important factor of parenthood is how much that individual is willing to love and take responsibility for that child and secure its welfare.

6.4 Fostering Equality between the Sexes: Will Uterus Transplants Eliminate or Exacerbate Inequality in the Division of Labour?

[m]others are women who give birth and fathers are those who are the male genetic progenitors of children.[181]

Traditionally, fathers are the men who impregnate. Mothers are the women who gestate and beget children. Uterus transplantation and the prospect of pregnancy into cis men allows for a complete reversal of these traditional reproductive roles. Professor Jackson notes, 'feminists have long been interested in how men and women's uneven reproductive roles have influenced their relative status in society'.[182] How will uterus transplantation in cis men affect these 'roles'? Lam, writing on material feminist implications of new reproductive technologies, has observed how new reproductive technologies, such as IVF and the prospect of ectogenesis, facilitate the gradual disembodiment of reproduction and highlights the paradox of women's reproductive experience in patriarchal cultures in response to this as being both, and often simultaneously, empowering and disempowering.[183] This section explores uterus

---

[177] T. Bayne and A. Kolers, 'Toward a Pluralist Account of Parenthood' (2003) 17(9) *Bioethics* 221–242, at p. 221.

[178] Ibid.

[179] Ibid., p. 241.

[180] Corea, 'The Mother Machine', at p. 226.

[181] C. Lind and T. Hewitt, 'Law and the Complexities of Parenting: Parental Status and Parental Function' (2009) 31(4) *Journal of Social Welfare and Family Law* 391–406, at p. 392.

[182] Jackson, 'Degendering Reproduction' 346.

[183] C. Lam, *New Reproductive Technologies and Disembodiment: Feminist and Material Resolutions* (Routledge, 2015).

transplantation in the context of feminist discourse and considers whether this advance could finally free women from 'the tyranny of their biology'[184] or represents yet another attempt at patriarchal control over the reproductive process.

If uterus transplantation to enable male pregnancy soon becomes possible, it is clear that the paramount say in reproduction women have thus far held (by virtue of the fact her body is engaged in the gestational process) would be reversed. The fetus is not being housed on neutral territory (like in the ectogenic incubator) but in the body of an autonomous being. It seems clear that if we take respecting autonomy seriously, when the fetus is within a man's body the only ethically acceptable stance is that his choices about what happens to that fetus must be held as paramount and conclusive. This is further endorsed by the law, which is very clear on the matter; during female pregnancy a man has no legal right to prevent his partner from, or coerce her into, having an abortion.[185] The fact that her bodily autonomy is engaged means that the decision whether or not to carry her pregnancy to term is hers alone. Similarly, when a man is pregnant, the decision whether to continue with that pregnancy or terminate should legally and morally be his alone to make.

Feminist discourse is diverse in its response to artificial reproductive technologies such as male pregnancy that allow for a reversal of traditional sexual roles. Some would clearly welcome the prospect: in *The Dialectic of Sex*,[186] Firestone boldly argued that women are oppressed by the patriarchy through their biology – the physiological, psychological, social and economic disadvantages caused by pregnancy, childbirth and caring for children:

> Nature produced the fundamental inequality – half the human race must bear and rear the children of all of them – which was later consolidated, institutionalized in the interest of men. Reproduction of the species cost women dearly, not only emotionally, psychologically, culturally but even in strictly material (physical) terms: before methods of contraception, continuous childbirth led to "female trouble" early aging, and death ... .[187]

---

[184] S. Firestone, *The Dialectic of Sex: The Case for Feminist Revolution* (New York, NY: William Morrow and Company, 1979).

[185] See The Abortion Act 1967 (as amended by The Human Fertilisation and Embryology Act 1990).

[186] Firestone, *The Dialectic of Sex*.

[187] Ibid., 205–206.

Firestone argued that women have been defined and oppressed due to their unique childbearing capacity. She argued for an alternative system and:

> The freeing of women from the tyranny of their reproductive biology by every means available, and the diffusion of the childbearing and child raising role to the society as a whole, men as well as women.[188]

Thus if we accept Firestone's argument, male pregnancy via uterus transplant should be welcomed as a step closer towards sexual equality. Male pregnancy will not only liberate women from the burden of pregnancy and childbirth, but also children from the burden of possessive mothering:

> We must be aware that as long as we use natural childbirth methods, the "household" could never be a totally liberating social form. A mother who undergoes a nine-month pregnancy is likely to feel that the product of all that pain and discomfort "belongs" to her ("To think of what I went through to have you!") But we want to destroy this possessiveness along with its cultural reinforcements so that … children will be loved for their own sake.[189]

Not all share Firestone's support and for others, women should resist such reproductive advances and seek to retain the 'last bastion of female control'.[190] Rowland advocates caution when it comes to the use of artificial reproductive technologies that removes the childbearing function from women, stating:

> What may be happening is the last battle in the long war of men against women. Women's position is most precarious … we may find ourselves without a product of any kind with which to bargain. For the history of "mankind" women have been seen in terms of their value as child-bearers. We have to ask, if that last power is taken and controlled by men, what role is envisaged for women in the new world? Will women become obsolete? Will we be fighting to retain or reclaim the right to bear children – has patriarchy conned us once again? I urge you sisters to be vigilant.[191]

---

[188] Ibid.

[189] Ibid.

[190] Ibid.

[191] R. Rowland, 'Motherhood, Patriarchal Power, Alienation and the Issue of Choice' in G. Corea et al., *Man-Made Women: How New Reproductive Technologies Affect Women* (London: Hutchinson, 1985; Bloomington, IN: Indiana Press, 1987) pp. 74–87 as quoted by P. Singer and D. Wells, 'Ectogenesis' in S. Gelfand and J. Shook (eds.), *Ectogenesis: Artificial Womb Technology and the Future of Human Reproduction* (Amsterdam and New York, NY: Rodopi, 2006), p. 17.

This ties into the elimination of women argument and the notion espoused by Steinem 'if women lose our cartel on giving birth, we could be even more dispensable than we are'.[192] Murphy argues once reproduction can be supplied in another way to female gestation and women's unique contribution is gone, there is nothing to prevent 'men from making women extinct'.[193] The argument made by Rowland and others that women should retain hold of this was last thing only women can do, is a dangerous one and goes against the volume of work that has been done to separate women from their reproductive potential.[194] This presents a very dystopian view and counter to this runs the argument that a woman's ability/decision whether to reproduce or not, does and should not define her. Singer and Wells point out the following weakness in this argument:

> Can it seriously be claimed in our present society that the status of women rests entirely on their role as nurtures of embryos from conception to birth? If we argue that to break the link between women and childbearing would be to undermine the status of women in our society what are we saying about the ability of women to obtain true equality in other spheres of life? We, at least, are not nearly so pessimistic about the abilities of women to achieve equality with men across the broad range of human endeavour. For that reason, we think women would be helped rather than harmed by the development of a technology that makes it possible for them to have children without being pregnant.[195]

Supporting this, Takala notes that artificial reproductive technologies that break the link between being a woman and mother should be welcomed and benefit everyone:

---

[192] Teresi and McAuliffe, 'Male Pregnancy', at p. 182.

[193] Hopkins, Sex/Machine: Readings in Culture, Gender and Technology, p. 192. Whilst at present women would still be needed to provide eggs, this would not be the case if artificial gametes were to become reality – on artificial gametes see also A. Smajdor and D. Cutas, 'Will Artificial Gametes End Infertility?' (2015) 23(2) *Healthcare Analysis* 134–147.

[194] E. Anderson, 'Is Women's Labor a Commodity?' (1993) 19(1) *Philosophy and Public Affairs* 71–92. B. Bergmann, *The Economic Emergence of Women* (New York, NY: Basic Books, 1986). N. Chodorow, *The Reproduction of Mothering* (Berkeley, CA: University of California Press, 1978). S. Correll, 'Constraints into Preferences: Gender, Status and Emerging Career Aspirations' (2004) 69 *American Sociological Review* 93–113. R. Dworkin, *Life's Dominion* (New York, NY: Vintage, 1993). Fineman, The Neutered Mother, the Sexual Family and Other Twentieth Century Tragedies. Firestone, The Dialectic of Sex.

[195] Singer and Wells, 'Ectogenesis', at p. 21.

> Those females who cannot reproduce will no longer have to feel incomplete. Those who wish to take on motherhood can be praised and thanked for their contribution, as motherhood is no longer what was expected of them anyway. Women would have a choice as to whether they would like to take on the risks associated with natural pregnancy and put themselves through all the discomforts and pains.[196]

Despite the divergence of views on how technologies that remove reproduction from women's bodies should be received, it is clear that if male gestation via uterus transplants becomes possible, rightly or wrongly, women will no longer retain the paramount say they currently have in reproduction. Reproduction, gestation and childbirth can no longer be regarded as primarily a woman's domain, for the paramount say women have thus far held over their fetus/pregnancy stems from the fact that traditional sexual conception and reproduction occurs inside a woman's body, consequently respect for autonomy and bodily integrity requires the pregnant woman to have the conclusive say over the fate of the embryo/fetus growing within her. Thus traditionally the ethics and law of reproduction is dominated by the importance of respecting women's reproductive choices. As Bennett argues, emerging reproductive technologies that allow for creation and storing of embryos outside of a woman's body and the prospect of future possibilities, such as ectogenesis and male pregnancy raise important issues that cannot simply be answered by appealing to the rights of women in the reproductive process and demand a radical rethink of ethics and law in the area of reproduction.[197]

6.5   Conclusion

In light of rising speculation that uterus transplantation may one day be possible in trans individuals and cis men, this chapter has considered how current domestic regulation could apply in this context. Whilst the transplantation of a uterus into trans women does not appear to face any current prohibition, uterus transplant into a cis male to enable male pregnancy does. Whilst the HFE Act 2008 amends the 1990 legislation so as to

---

[196] T. Takala, 'Human before Sex' in F. Simonstein (ed.), *Reprogen – Ethics and the Future of Gender* (Dordrecht, Heidelberg, London and New York, NY: Springer, 2009) 187, at p. 190.

[197] R. Bennett, 'Is Reproduction Women's Business? How Should We Regulate Regarding Stored Embryos, Posthumous Pregnancy, Ectogenesis and Male Pregnancy?' (2008) 2(3) *Studies in Ethics, Law and Technology* 3.

accommodate same-sex parenting, the provisions are ill equipped to cover the prospect of uterus transplant technology that could allow trans women and cismen to gestate their child. Should this technology become possible, the legislation on parental status will necessitate revision. Any guidance issued by the HTA or HFEA to govern uterus transplantation in women, should address the controversial application of this technology in trans women and cismen.

This chapter has highlighted some of the many regulatory questions that will arise once this advance becomes possible, but thorough resolution of the challenges raised by uterus transplantation in trans individuals and cismen is beyond the scope and remit of this book. This chapter has highlighted that as we enter into the third era of human reproduction, there are reproductive advances on the foreseeable horizon, such as uterus transplant technology, which will raise a plethora of regulatory and ethical issues. Such a possibility will continue to blur the lines between parental labels such as mother and father, that ascribe legal parenthood on the basis of biological characteristics. As scientists around the world continue in their endeavours to emulate the success of Sweden, the many regulatory issues raised by the prospect of uterus transplant not only to restore fertility in women, but also to realign reproductive capacity in trans women and enhance reproductive capacity in cismen, merits careful attention.

The difficulties of framing legislation that could accommodate trans or male pregnancy are formidable. It is further conceded that contemplating how we should regulate an advance which is still speculative, and only possible in theory, is difficult and complicated since precise levels of risk and benefit are unknown. However, emerging technologies are marked by the rapidity with which they develop/emerge. The ability to develop sensible policy on how best to regulate a novel breakthrough in reproductive science necessitates systematic assessment of the new technologies at the development stage so as to better inform the process of policy formation. If the government is to monitor and maintain the pace of reproductive technologies, then it needs to be brave enough to tackle revolutionary advances looming on the horizon so that, when they are possible, considered and responsive legislation is drafted as opposed to reactive measures.

~

Conclusion

> In fifty years' time we may look back on this time as an age of discovery. But it is also possible that we may look back and see a time of tragic and social wrongs and inadequate legal safeguards. The task for lawyers and others is to ensure that the processes of legal reform are informed by social as well as scientific versions of the future.[1]

Whilst the above observation by Bennett was made in the context of the law's response to genetic research and cloning of people and parts, it remains apt also of assisted reproductive technologies. Reproductive science also holds the promise of a bold new future in which humanity has not only identified and conquered the roots of many causes of infertility, but also revolutionised how we reproduce. Yet whilst those desperate to procreate welcome these advances, novel assisted reproductive technologies are also depicted as a terrifying prospect.[2]

The government's pledge to reform the law in in relation to assisted reproduction in 2008 'to ensure it remains at the forefront of medical research' and is 'fit for purpose in the 21st Century'[3] was always an ambitious task. Throughout this book, the contention has been that if the law is to effectively sustain the pace of science it needs to be equipped not only to respond to challenges raised by IVF and embryonic research, but also the challenges raised by the third wave reproductive technologies

[1] B. Bennett, 'Written in Code: Diversity and the New Genetics' in M. Freeman and A. Lewis (eds.), *Law and Medicine, Current Legal Issues*, Volume 3 (Oxford: Oxford University Press, 2000) p. 203.

[2] Belinda Bennett, in her paper referenced in the previous footnote, argues that whilst genetic science promises to shed light on who we are, what it is that makes us tick and what it is that makes us the way we are – in short, what it is that makes us human and is a potential saviour (saving us from disease) – it also appears as a threat that, at the extreme, appears to be the stuff of our worst nightmares, such as the prospect, probably more imagined than real, of rows of cloned individuals.

[3] DoH, *Review of the Human Fertilisation and Embryology Act: Proposals for Revised Legislation (Including Establishment of the Regulatory Authority for Tissue and Embryos)*, Cm 6989 (DoH, London, 14 December 2006).

looming on the horizon. As noted in the beginning chapters, assisted reproduction is a politically charged area, and regulation is difficult precisely because it is an ethically divisive branch of medicine. Despite acknowledgements that 'the area of science and medicine regulated by the HFEA is fast-paced and can be controversial',[4] how effective the operation of the present framework will be in regulating novel reproductive advances remains uncertain. It is crucial that the HFEA, as the statutory authority overseeing regulation of assisted reproductive technologies, has the apparatus in place to effectively respond to reproductive advances looming ahead. Some developments suggest it has, for instance the Horizon Scanning Panel (HSP) stated to act 'as an early warning system that identifies new scientific and clinical developments that may impact on the field of assisted reproduction or embryo research',[5] which can later be considered in depth by the HFEA's Scientific and Clinical Advances Advisory Committee (SCAAC). These initiatives were designed to raise awareness of future reproductive advances and to give HFEA the 'time to consider the legal, ethical and scientific implications of the use of these techniques, prior to an application being received by a licence committee for their use in research or treatment'.[6] Whilst in theory HFEA has the apparatus is in place to prepare for emerging reproductive technologies, it is clear from the HSP's dismissive response to uterus transplantation that this apparatus will be of little use unless the panel has the tenacity to address advances looming on the horizon, despite the controversy they may provoke.

The government was perhaps overly optimistic in what it had achieved with the enactment of the Human Fertilisation and Embryology Act 2008. The Minister for Public Health at the time in 2008, Primarolo commented:

> Since the original HFE Act [1990] was conceived a generation ago, technology and society have changed beyond measure. This hugely important Act now reflects the new scientific order, will allow medical research and treatment to thrive, and maintain public confidence.[7]

---

[4] Human Fertilisation & Embryology Authority, Scientific Horizon Scanning at the HFEA, Annual Report 2006, para 2.2.

[5] http://hfeaarchive.uksouth.cloudapp.azure.com/www.hfea.gov.uk/Horizon-Scanning-Panel.html.

[6] www.hfea.gov.uk/en/1632.html.

[7] 'Royal Assent for Human Fertilisation and Embryology Act', *Medical News Today*, 14 November 2008.

Yet there is a question concerning whether this optimism is well founded. Chapter 2 illustrated how disputes over the fate of frozen embryos raised a number of issues regarding the status of the in vitro embryo and the position of the gamete progenitors in relation to it. In this context, and absent pregnancy and bodily autonomy of the mother being invoked, the reasons for giving women the paramount say they possess in natural pregnancy no longer apply. It is no longer clear whose views should prevail in a dispute. The question of how disputes over frozen embryos should be resolved, merited fresh consideration in light of this dispute, and the decision to update the legislation rendered this an opportune time to do so. Yet the amendments introduced by the HFE Act 2008 made the HFE Act 1990 no better equipped to deal with such disputes reoccurring. It is clear that if the legislation is to be better equipped at resolving disputes concerning the fate of disputed embryos, Parliament must consider alternative regulatory models for governing such disputes.

It was also noted that the HFE Act 1990 was drafted to deal with issues concerning the second wave of reproduction, namely IVF and human embryonic research. As Biggs observes:

> since Louise Brown was born, IVF and some other forms of assisted reproductive technologies have moved from experimental and audacious to commonplace, almost mundane.[8]

Third wave reproductive technologies raise controversies far greater than those envisaged when the second wave of reproduction came about in the early 1980s. The legal, ethical and regulatory issues raised by novel reproductive technologies, such as ectogenesis and uterus transplantation, clearly differ from the issues raised by IVF. If such advances are to be effectively monitored, then it is imperative that the government considers the regulatory challenges these advances will give rise to. In addressing the challenge of regulating this third phase of human reproduction, an outline of the salient legal issues raised by two of the 'third wave' reproductive technologies (ectogenesis and uterus transplant technology) was offered. Neither of these advances received consideration in the government scrutiny of the Human Fertilisation and Embryology Bill.[9]

---

[8] H. Biggs, 'The Quest for a Perfect Child: How Far Should the Law Intervene?' in K. Horsey and H. Biggs (eds.), *Human Fertilisation and Embryology: Reproducing Regulation* (London and New York, NY: Routledge, Cavendish, 2007) at p. 3.

[9] Joint Committee on the Human Tissue and Embryos (Draft) Bill, *Human Tissue and Embryos (Draft) Bill* (Volume I, HL Paper 169-I, HC Paper 630-I).

The 2008 updates which retained the regulatory architecture of the HFE Act 1990 and its under pinning policy, did little to make the present framework better equipped to deal with the regulatory challenges these technologies raise. The problem with the present regulatory framework, which will continue resurface with new technologies, is that, as noted by Brazier 'there is little conceptual depth underpinning British law'.[10] As Brazier comments:

> The result is that again and again, as new medical debates emerge we debate the same issues in different guises ... No single coherent policy philosophy underpins the laws response to reproductive medicine.[11]

With the decision to update the law in the field, a prudent approach would have been to re-examine the legal and ethical issues raised by the current and prospective reproductive technologies, since the present legislation was founded on the recommendations of the Warnock Committee, and public concerns have moved on greatly from those in 1984. The fact the HFE Act 2008 'lacks the equivalent of a Warnock Report establishing the ethical values and evidence-based pointers that should guide Parliament and the regulator in these novel areas of deci-sion-making' has evoked concerns.[12] For instance consider the following reservations articulated by the Joint Scrutiny Committee:

> We are concerned that the draft Bill lacks the explicit underpinning ethical framework which in 1990 was provided by the Warnock Report. Whilst we accept that the Warnock Report still provides a partial ethical framework, we agree with those who argue that scientific developments have made ethical decisions more difficult. Public consultation on indi-vidual issues is not a substitute. As a result, the draft Bill gives the impression of tinkering with existing legislative provisions rather than going back to first principles and seeking to take an overall view of where to go in the next 15 years or so.[13]

Thus one remains sceptical of the ethical framework, or lack of it, under-pinning the amendments in the HFE Act 2008. If a reformulated frame-work is to be put in place which can adequately address the third wave reproductive technologies, what is needed is a Committee of Inquiry to

---

[10] M. Brazier, 'Regulating the Reproduction Business' (1999) *Medical Law Review* 166, at p. 167.
[11] Ibid.
[12] As commented by the Opposition spokesperson for health, Earl Howe. www.epolitix.com /EN/Legislation/200611/d9d654c2-4a37-43e0-a355-a95ce7c72212.htm.
[13] Joint Committee on the Human Tissue and Embryos (Draft) Bill, *Human Tissue and Embryos (Draft) Bill* (Volume I, HL Paper 169-I, HC Paper 630-I) para 44.

present scientific developments in assisted reproductive technologies, similar to the Warnock Committee. A Committee which examines both assisted reproductive technologies which are presently possible and those looming on the foreseeable horizon. Hammond Brown makes the following observation:

> Advances in human fertilisation and embryology treatment and research have progressed far beyond what was envisaged by the Warnock Committee in the early 1980s. The recent womb transplant success in Sweden, the use of mitochondrial donation for reproductive purposes, and research with *in vitro*-derived gametes are all examples of treatment and research that were unheard of when the Warnock Committee was sitting and hearing evidence from interested parties.[141] A new committee that had as its remit the ethical, legal, and social consideration of these new and future uses of reproductive technologies and research would undoubtedly be of much value in regulating this next era of human fertilisation and embryology, in much the same way that Warnock has for the past 30 years.[14]

In suggesting that the time is ripe for a new committee, she notes that whilst bodies such as the Nuffield Council on Bioethics have produced excellent reports in this field, these reports are limited to specific areas of concern, such as the recent debate about mitochondrial donation. Noting the influence the Warnock Committee Report still has, over thirty years later, within the UK legislation on human fertilisation and embryology, she argues an 'overarching review of this contentious field would be worthwhile and could have a significant impact upon future regulation'.[15]

Reproductive technologies on the horizon raise issues that may well be the stuff of politicians' nightmares. Consider ectogenesis as discussed in Chapters 3 and 4. Despite the House of Commons Science and Technology Committee Inquiry in 2007 into scientific developments relating to the

---

[14] N. Hammond-Brown, 'Ethics, Embryos, and Evidence: A Look Back at Warnock' (2015) 23(4) *Med Law Rev* 588 at p. 617. In her paper, Brown notes that whilst much has been written about the recommendations made by the Committee and how they divided Parliament, the public and the scientific and religious communities, and how ultimately the recommendations were subsequently enacted; little had been written about the evidence on which the Warnock Committee reached its recommendations regarding the status of the human embryo and the protection that was to be accorded to it. Her article sought to address this lacuna, exploring the evidence upon which the Warnock Committee reached their recommendations with regard to human embryo research.

[15] Ibid., p. 617.

Abortion Act 1967,[16] the Committee concluded that they had 'seen no good evidence to suggest that fetal viability has improved significantly since the abortion time limit was last set'[17] and that 'while survival rates at 24 weeks and over have improved they have not done so below that gestational point'.[18] Yet, as Chapter 3 illustrated, research is currently being undertaken into making ectogenesis possible. Once ectogenesis becomes possible, viability will be a 'nonsense', since an artificial womb which could gestate from embryo to 'birth'[19] would render a fetus viable from fertilisation. Chapter 4 demonstrated how ectogenesis would have a direct impact on the abortion debate. In the discussions to update the HFE Act 1990, amendments to abortion law could have been accepted during the passage of the Human Fertilisation and Embryology Bill, as the Abortion Act 1967 was amended by the HFE Act 1990.[20] Despite the publicity proposed amendments to abortion law received,[21] the government managed to circumvent a discussion of these. The legislative provisions pertaining to abortion were to remain unchanged by the HFE Act 2008[22] and, as noted by Sheldon, the first realistic opportunity in almost 20 years for MPs to discuss liberalising the Abortion Act was lost in 2008.[23] This book has shown that

[16] House of Commons Science and Technology Committee, *Scientific Developments Relating to the Abortion Act 1967*, Volume 1 (Twelfth Report of Session 2006–07), HC 1045-I.

[17] Ibid., para 46.

[18] Ibid., para 35.

[19] In the context of ectogenesis, 'birth' would be the point at which the fetus was capable of breathing independently without mechanical support.

[20] Human Fertilisation and Embryology Act 1990, s37.

[21] These included new clauses to: remove the legal requirement for two doctors' signatures to authorise abortions; allow trained nurses and other health care practitioners to carry out abortions; extend the locations where abortions can take place to primary care level; remove conscientious objection in respect to providing emergency contraception provision; and extend the Abortion Act 1967 to Northern Ireland.

[22] See also S. Childs, E. Evans and P. Webb, 'Quicker Than a Consultation at the Hairdressers': Abortion and the Human Fertilisation and Embryology Act 2008' (2013) 32 *New Genetics and Society* 119–134. The authors analysed parliamentary debate contributions (participation and content) in addition to parliamentary votes in both Houses of the UK Parliament, and considered the role of the sex of the representatives and the role that played in the outcome. They claim their analysis suggests that women not only over-participate in the division lobbies and vote in a more liberal fashion than their male colleagues, but that women MPs' and Peers' debate contributions and interventions are substantively different from men's. They thus argue that, whilst women's absence from Parliament might not have affected the legislative outcome in 2008, their presence was critical to the way in which the issue of abortion was discussed.

[23] S. Sheldon, 'A Missed Opportunity to Reform an Outdated Law' (2009) 4(1) *Clinical Ethics* 3–5. See also the paper by M. Fox, 'The Human Fertilisation and Embryology Act 2008: Tinkering at the Margins' (2009) 17(3) *Feminist Legal Studies* 333–344 in which it is

the existing legislation that governs abortion and embryo and fetal research, fails to provide an adequate framework in which to regulate ectogenesis or research into this dramatic advance.

Similarly, the amendments the HFE Act 2008 introduced to the 1990 legislation allowed for recognition of same-sex couples who wish to use reproductive technologies to parent, and went some way to reflecting the changes in social attitudes since the second wave of reproduction and IVF. However, again the changes failed to go far enough. Despite recognition by the HFEA's Horizon Scanning Panel that the world's second attempt at a human uterus transplant was currently underway, and despite reports in the headlines that Beatie, an American trans man, was pregnant, and the prospect uterus transplant could be sought by trans women and may one day be possible in cis-gendered men, the Panel and government failed to address this controversial prospect. It is regrettable that this technology was not considered when the legislation was being updated, for as noted in Chapter 5, uterus transplant technology could fall under the remit of both the HFE Act 1990 (as amended by the HFE Act 2008) and also the Human Tissue Act 2004. Consequently it demonstrates how the marriage of the two statutory authorities regulating these controversial branches of medicine (the HFEA and the HTA) in the proposed joint regulatory authority, RATE could have worked well.

It is acknowledged that the regulation of novel assisted reproductive technologies raises many difficult and controversial issues. It may be the case that in vitro gestation (which will invoke the abortion debate) and the prospect of uterus transplant technology (which may enable either sex/gender to gestate) may not become possible in our lifetime. Yet waiting until these technologies are possible is an inadequate method of regulation, for new technologies are marked by the rapidity at which they develop. As cogently noted by Schroeder:

> Today science does not remain isolated in laboratories; it becomes involved with human life almost instantaneously. The protective time barrier between creating knowledge through science and applying knowledge through technology has disappeared. As the gap between scientific creation and technological development disappears and as the rate of technological innovation increases, the law loses its time for reflection.

also argued that, viewed from a feminist perspective, the reforms contained in the Human Fertilisation and Embryology Act 2008 represent a missed opportunity to rethink the appropriate model of regulation to govern fertility treatment and embryology research in the UK.

> The profusion of new legal problems removes the period of contemplation that lay behind the law's taking a decisive, calculated direction.[24]

Reproductive advances on the horizon promise exciting possibilities, but if the UK is to maximise its benefit from these advances and be adequately equipped to respond to the challenges raised by them, it needs to be prepared. The rapid rate at which reproductive technologies unfold means that they often leave in their trail a complex web of legal, ethical, social and regulatory questions which the government has no option but to address. It is inevitable that there is going to be some lack of synchronicity between the development of technology and the laws ability to address it, because of science's emphasis upon progress and the laws emphasis on process.[25] If the law is to sustain the march of science it needs to go 'beyond the mere problems faced today and decide fundamental issues which will provide the basis to solve tomorrow's problems. By doing this a more stable and predictable body of law will develop, enabling the legal profession to meet the dilemmas new technology proposes'.[26]

Despite the recent enactment of the HFE Act 2008, the law may still not be able to sustain the pace of reproductive technologies as we charge towards the new phases of human reproduction. Amending the statutory regime in the 1990 legislation, but retaining its outdated policy was a missed opportunity and did little to ensure the law is 'fit for purpose in the 21st Century'.[27] What is needed are mechanisms that allow for prospective consideration of reproductive advances whilst they are still on the horizon, as opposed to the reactive approach that all too often in this context epitomises the UK response. This complex task of trying to future-proof legislation to deal with speculative prospective technologies is not missed – this may well be one area where the law will be condemned to play the role of the Red Queen, forever rushing to stay in one place:

---

[24] O. Schroeder, *The Dynamics of Technology: From Medicine and Law To Health and Justice* (Cleveland, Law-Medicine Center, 1972); L. P. Wilkins, 'The Ability of the Current Legal Framework to Address Advances in Technology' (1999) 33(1) *Indiana Law Review* 1–15, at p. 12.

[25] S. Goldberg, 'Culture Clash: Law and Science in America' as cited in Wilkins, 'The Ability of the Current Legal Framework to Address Advances in Technology' at p. 13.

[26] M. Sublett, 'Frozen Embryos: What Are They and How Should We Treat Them' (1990) 38 (4) *Cleveland State Law Review* 585–616, at p. 616.

[27] DoH, *Review of the Human Fertilisation and Embryology Act: Proposals for revised legislation (including establishment of the Regulatory Authority for Tissue and Embryos)*, Cm 6989 (DoH, London, 14 December 2006).

'in our country' said Alice, still panting a little, 'you'd generally get to somewhere – if you ran very fast for a long time as we've been doing.' 'A slow sort of country!' said the Queen. 'Now, *here*, you see, it takes all the running you can do, to keep in the same place. If you want to go somewhere else, you must run at least twice as fast as that.'[28]

---

[28] 'Alice through the Looking Glass' in M. Gardner (ed.), *The Annotated Alice* (Harmondsworth: Penguin Books, 1960), p. 210; M. Ridley, *The Red Queen: Sex and the Evolution of Human Nature* (Harmondsworth: Penguin Books, 1994); R. Lee and D. Morgan, *Human Fertilisation & Embryology: Regulating the Reproductive Revolution* (London: Blackstone Press Limited, 2001) at p. 10.

INDEX

Stephen Smith
End-of-Life Decisions in Medical Care: Principles and Policies for Regulating the Dying Process

Michael Parker
Ethical Problems and Genetics Practice

William W. Lowrance
Privacy, Confidentiality, and Health Research

Kerry Lynn Macintosh
Human Cloning: Four Fallacies and Their Legal Consequence

Heather Widdows
The Connected Self: The Ethics and Governance of the Genetic Individual

Amel Alghrani, Rebecca Bennett and Suzanne Ost
Bioethics, Medicine and the Criminal Law Volume I: The Criminal Law and Bioethical Conflict: Walking the Tightrope

Danielle Griffiths and Andrew Sanders
Bioethics, Medicine and the Criminal Law Volume II: Medicine, Crime and Society

Margaret Brazier and Suzanne Ost
Bioethics, Medicine and the Criminal Law Volume III: Medicine and Bioethics in the Theatre of the Criminal Process

Sigrid Sterckx, Kasper Raus and Freddy Mortier
Continuous Sedation at the End of Life: Ethical, Clinical and Legal Perspectives

A. M. Viens, John Coggon and Anthony S. Kessel
Criminal Law, Philosophy and Public Health Practice

Ruth Chadwick, Mairi Levitt and Darren Shickle
The Right to Know and the Right Not to Know: Genetic Privacy and Responsibility

Eleanor D. Kinney
The Affordable Care Act and Medicare in Comparative Context

Katri Lõhmus
Caring Autonomy: European Human Rights Law and the Challenge of Individualism

Catherine Stanton and Hannah Quirk
Criminalising Contagion: Legal and Ethical Challenges of Disease Transmission and the Criminal Law

Sharona Hoffman
Electronic Health Records and Medical Big Data: Law and Policy

Barbara Prainsack and Alena Buyx
Solidarity in Biomedicine and Beyond

Camillia Kong
Mental Capacity in Relationship: Decision-Making, Dialogue, and Autonomy